As the various love stories move toward resolution, the story nears its end. What is everyone thinking, and how are they feeling? Get ready for volume 23!

Naoshi Komi

NAOSHI KOMI was born in Kochi Prefecture, Japan, on March 28, 1986. His first serialized work in *Weekly Shonen Jump* was the series *Double Arts*. His best-selling shonen manga series *Nisekoi* is available in North America from VIZ Media.

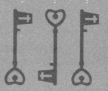

NISEKOI:
False Love
VOLUME 23
SHONEN JUMP Manga Edition

Story and Art by
NAOSHI KOMI

Translation ✦ Camellia Nieh
Touch-Up Art & Lettering ✦ Stephen Dutro
Design ✦ Izumi Evers
Shonen Jump Series Editor ✦ John Bae
Graphic Novel Editor ✦ Amy Yu

NISEKOI © 2011 by Naoshi Komi
All rights reserved.
First published in Japan in 2011
by SHUEISHA Inc., Tokyo.
English translation rights arranged
by SHUEISHA Inc.

The stories, characters and incidents mentioned
in this publication are entirely fictional.

Printed in the U.S.A.

Published by VIZ Media, LLC
P.O. Box 77010
San Francisco, CA 94107

10 9 8 7 6 5 4 3 2 1
First printing, September 2017

www.shonenjump.com   www.viz.com

NISEKOI

False Love

vol. 23: One Day

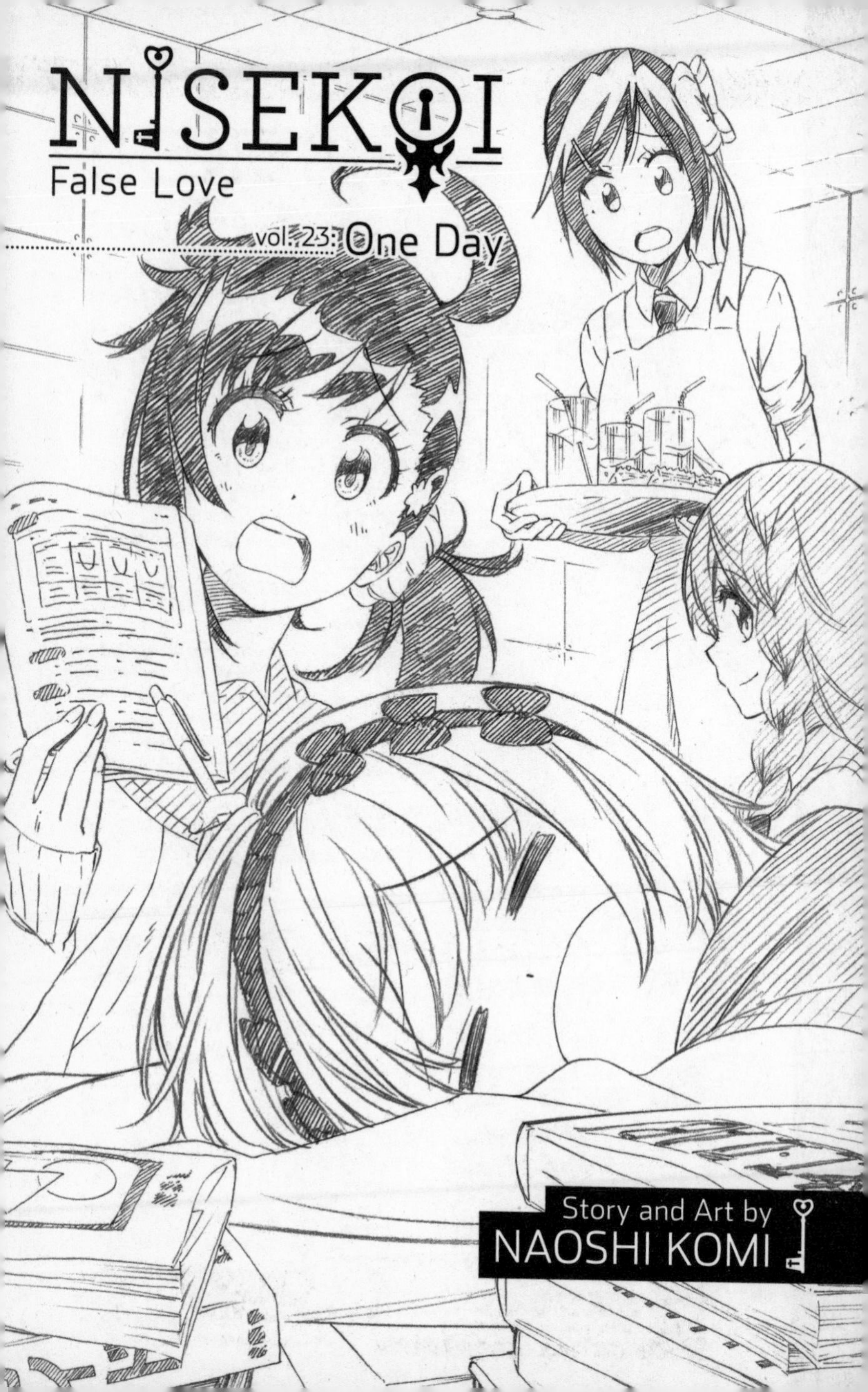

Story and Art by
NAOSHI KOMI

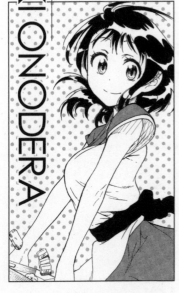

CHITOGE KIRISAKI

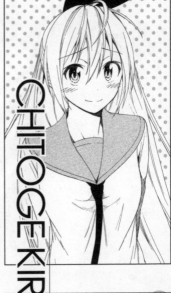

A half-Japanese bombshell with stellar athletic abilities. Short-tempered and violent. Comes from a family of gangsters.

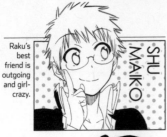

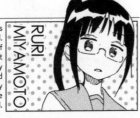

RAKU ICHIJO

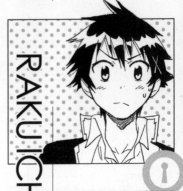

A normal teen whose family happens to be yakuza. Cherishes a pendant given to him by a girl he met ten years ago.

KOSAKI ONODERA

A girl Raku has a crush on. Beautiful and sweet, Kosaki has no shortage of admirers. She's a terrible cook but makes food that *looks* amazing.

SHU MAIKO

Raku's best friend is outgoing and girl-crazy.

RURI MIYAMOTO

Kosaki's best gal pal. Comes off as aloof, but is actually a devoted and highly intuitive friend.

MARIKA TACHIBANA

Daughter of the chief of police, Marika is Raku's fiancée, according to an agreement made by their fathers—an agreement Marika takes very seriously! Also has a key and remembers making a promise with Raku ten years ago. Due to a physical condition, she has to leave Japan for treatment in an American hospital.

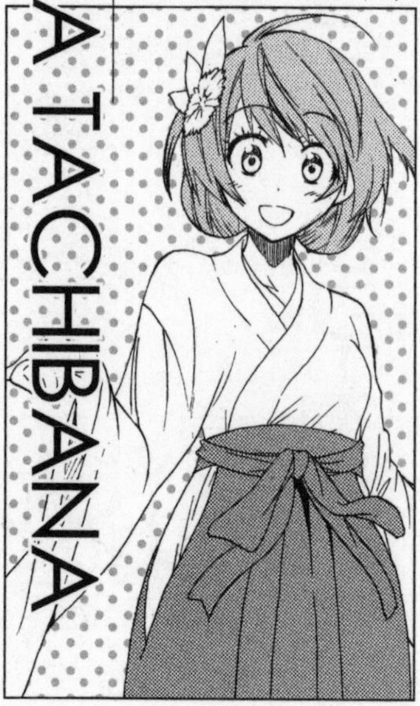

YUI KANAKURA

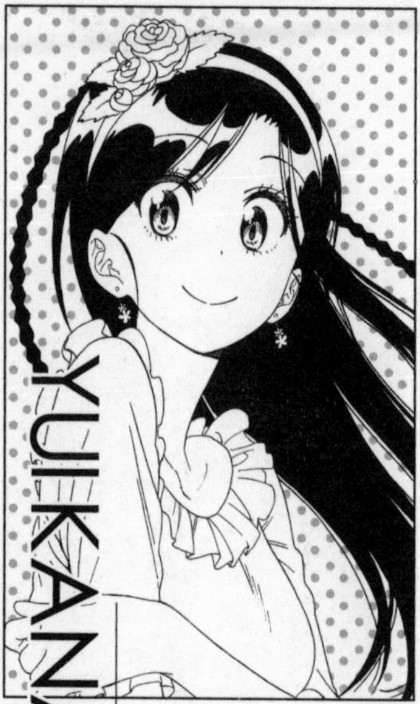

A childhood friend of Raku's, Yui is the head of a Chinese mafia gang and the homeroom teacher of Raku's class at his school. She was staying at Raku's house and professed her love to him. She also has a key that's linked to some kind of promise.

CHARACTERS & STORY

Ten years ago, Raku Ichijo made a promise with a girl he loved that they would get married when they met again...and he still treasures the pendant she gave him to seal their pledge.

Thanks to his family's circumstances, Raku has to pretend he's dating Chitoge Kirisaki, the daughter of a rival gangster. Despite their constant spats, Raku and Chitoge manage to fool everyone. Chitoge also has a token from her first love ten years ago—an old key. Meanwhile, Raku's crush, Kosaki, also has a key, as do Marika, the girl Raku's father has arranged for him to marry, and Yui, a childhood friend who's their homeroom teacher. Raku still doesn't know who his promise girl is when Marika confesses her love to him. He tells Marika he can't reciprocate her feelings, and he gets confused when she observes that he's drawn to both Kosaki and Chitoge. During Raku's next date with Chitoge, Chitoge's concern for Raku backfires...

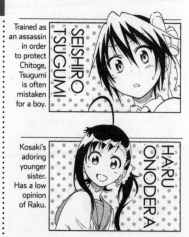

SEISHIRO TSUGUMI

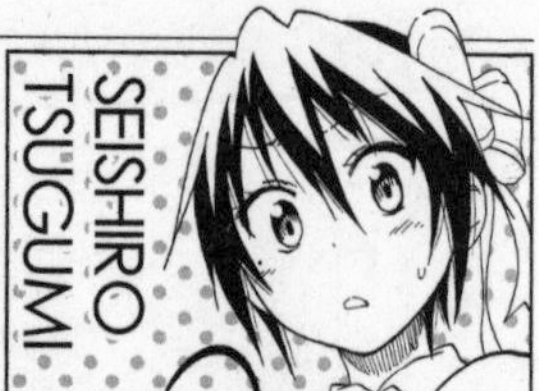

Trained as an assassin in order to protect Chitoge, Tsugumi is often mistaken for a boy.

HARU ONODERA

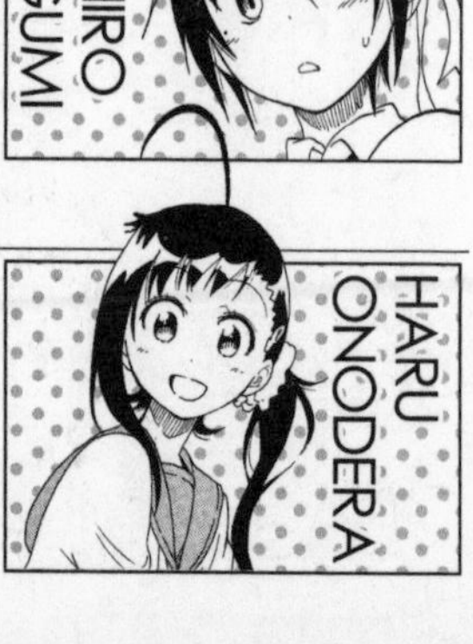

Kosaki's adoring younger sister. Has a low opinion of Raku.

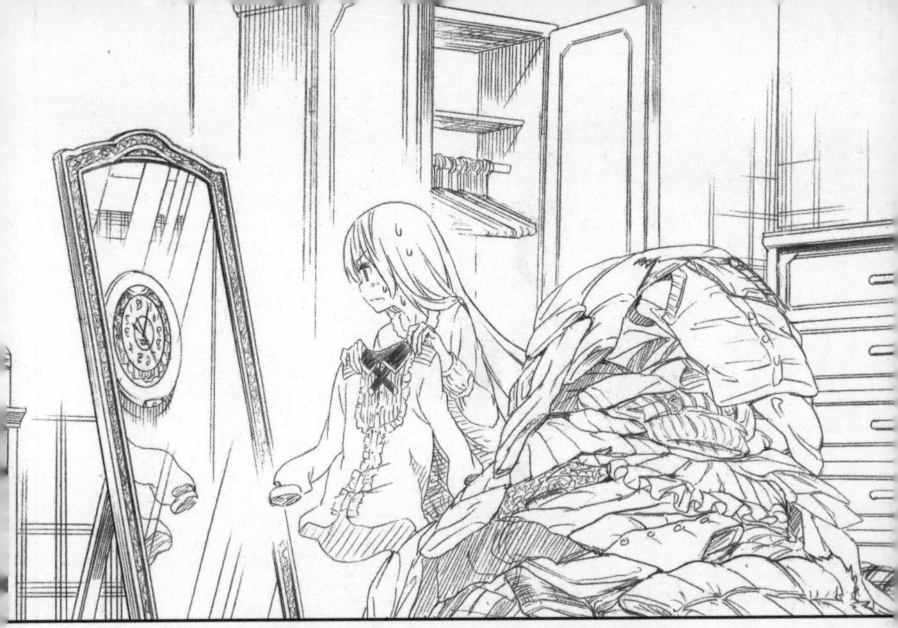

NISEKOI

False Love

vol. 23: One Day

TABLE OF CONTENTS

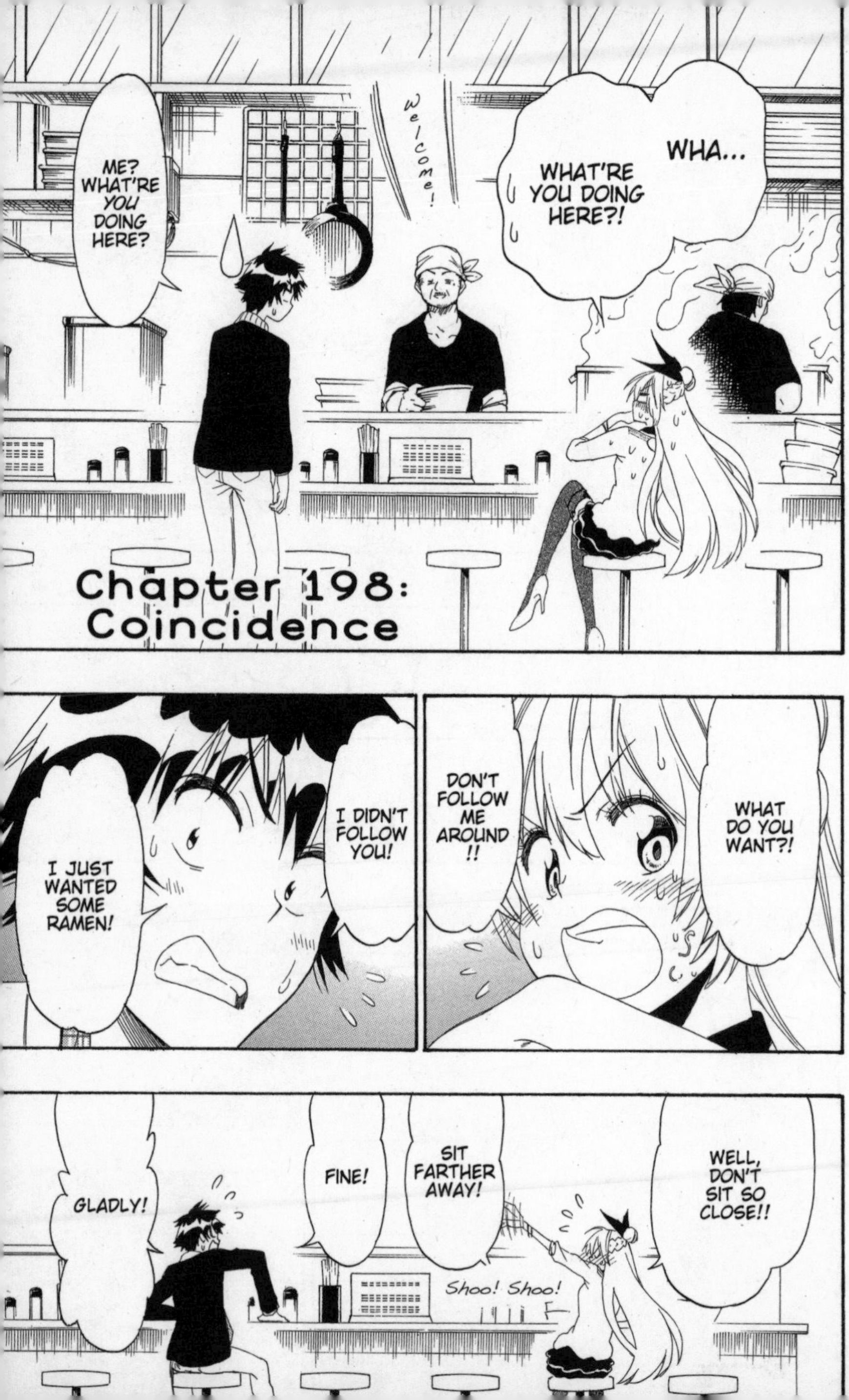
WHA...
WHAT'RE YOU DOING HERE?!
Welcome!
ME? WHAT'RE YOU DOING HERE?
Chapter 198: Coincidence
WHAT DO YOU WANT?!
DON'T FOLLOW ME AROUND!!
I DIDN'T FOLLOW YOU!
I JUST WANTED SOME RAMEN!
WELL, DON'T SIT SO CLOSE!!
Shoo! Shoo!
SIT FARTHER AWAY!
FINE!
GLADLY!

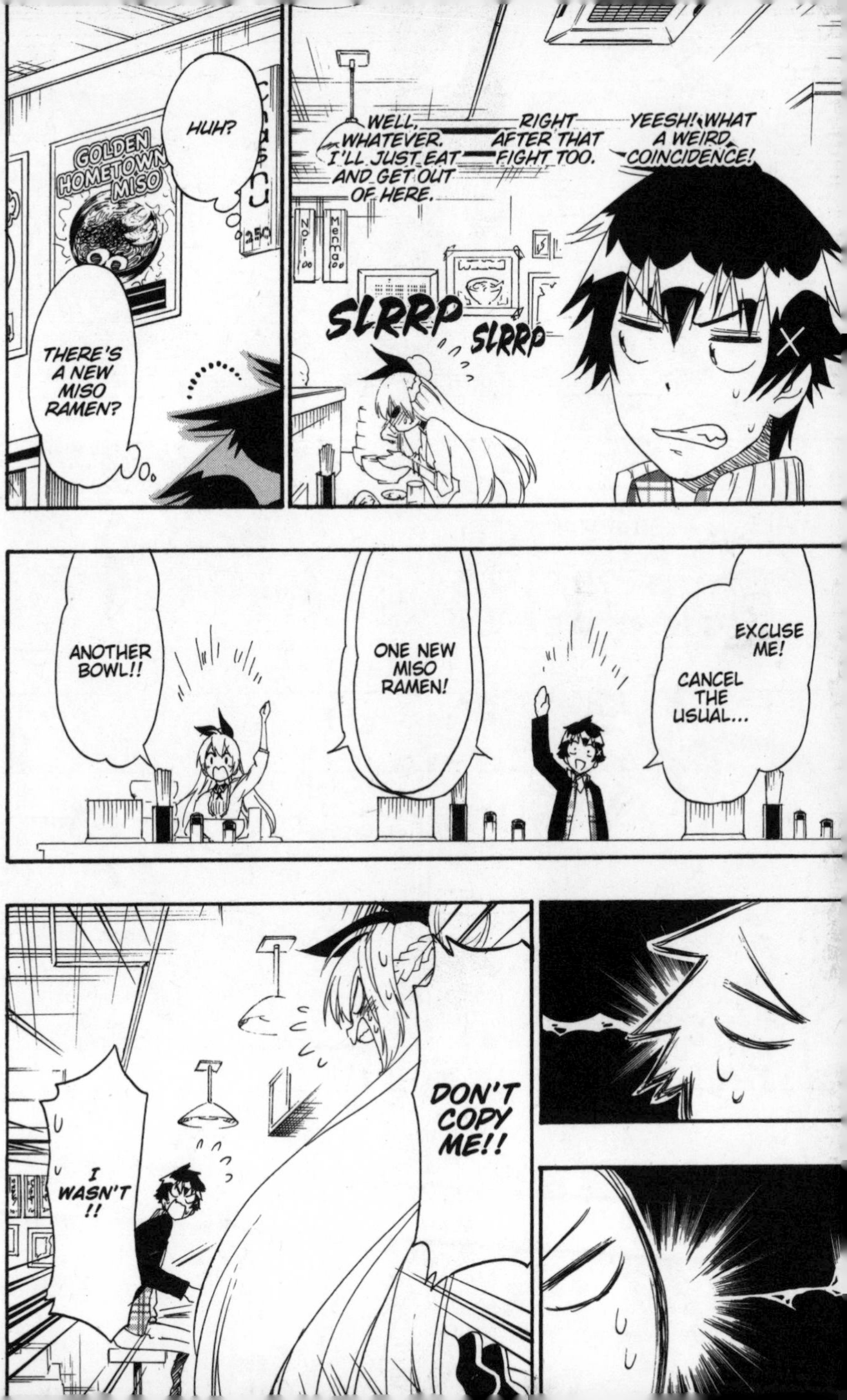
YEESH! WHAT A WEIRD COINCIDENCE!
RIGHT AFTER THAT FIGHT TOO.
WELL, WHATEVER. I'LL JUST EAT AND GET OUT OF HERE.
SLRRP
SLRRP
HUH?
GOLDEN HOMETOWN MISO
250
THERE'S A NEW MISO RAMEN?
EXCUSE ME!
CANCEL THE USUAL...
ONE NEW MISO RAMEN!
ANOTHER BOWL!!
DON'T COPY ME!!
I WASN'T!!

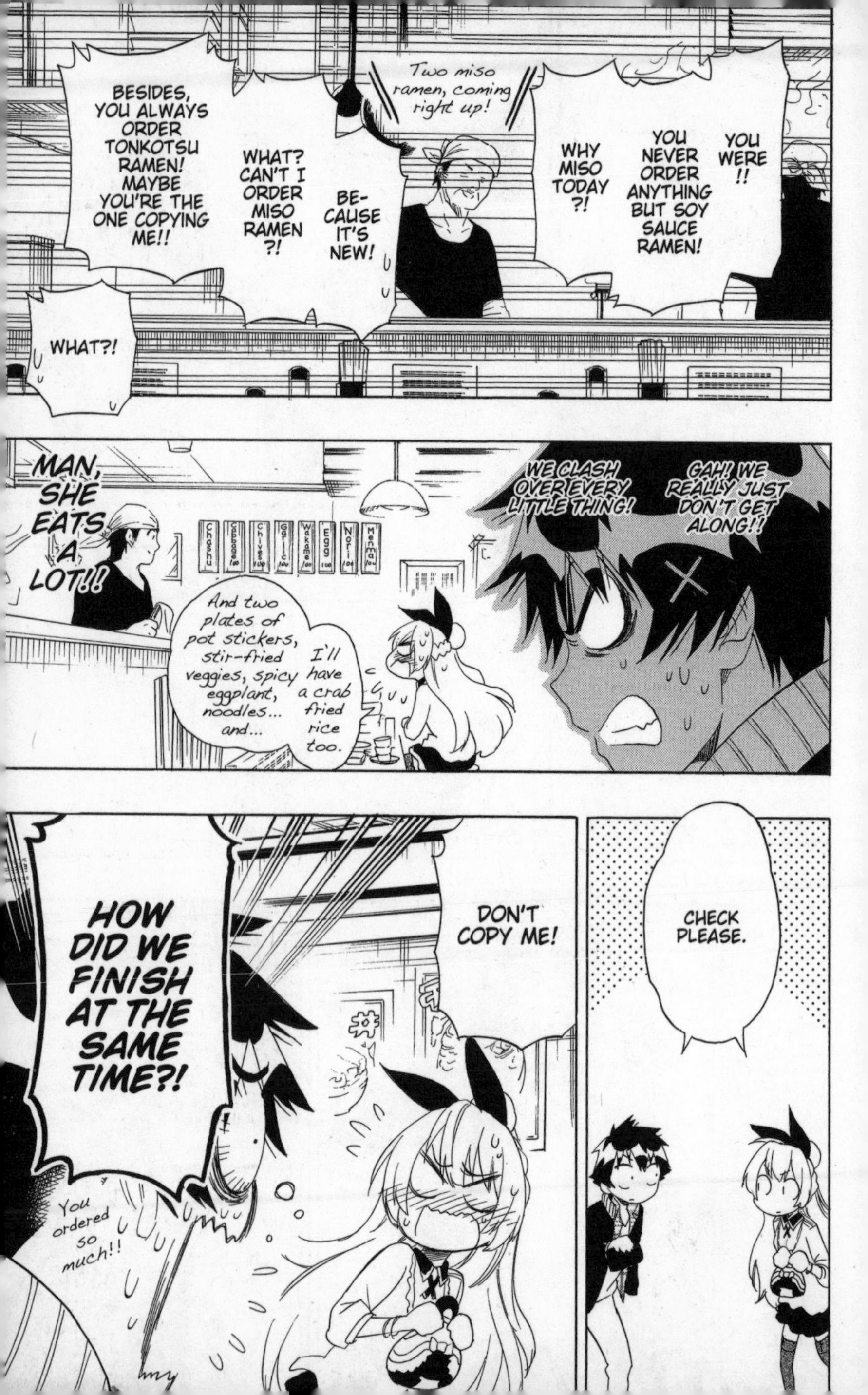
YOU WERE!!
YOU NEVER ORDER ANYTHING BUT SOY SAUCE RAMEN!
WHY MISO TODAY?!
Two miso ramen, coming right up!
BECAUSE IT'S NEW!
WHAT? CAN'T I ORDER MISO RAMEN?!
BESIDES, YOU ALWAYS ORDER TONKOTSU RAMEN! MAYBE YOU'RE THE ONE COPYING ME!!
WHAT?!
GAH! WE REALLY JUST DON'T GET ALONG!!
WE CLASH OVER EVERY LITTLE THING!
I'll have a crab fried rice too.
And two plates of pot stickers, stir-fried veggies, spicy eggplant, noodles... and...
Menma
Nori
Egg
Wakame
Garlic
Chives
Cabbage
Chashu
MAN, SHE EATS A LOT!!
CHECK PLEASE.
DON'T COPY ME!
HOW DID WE FINISH AT THE SAME TIME?!
You ordered so much!!

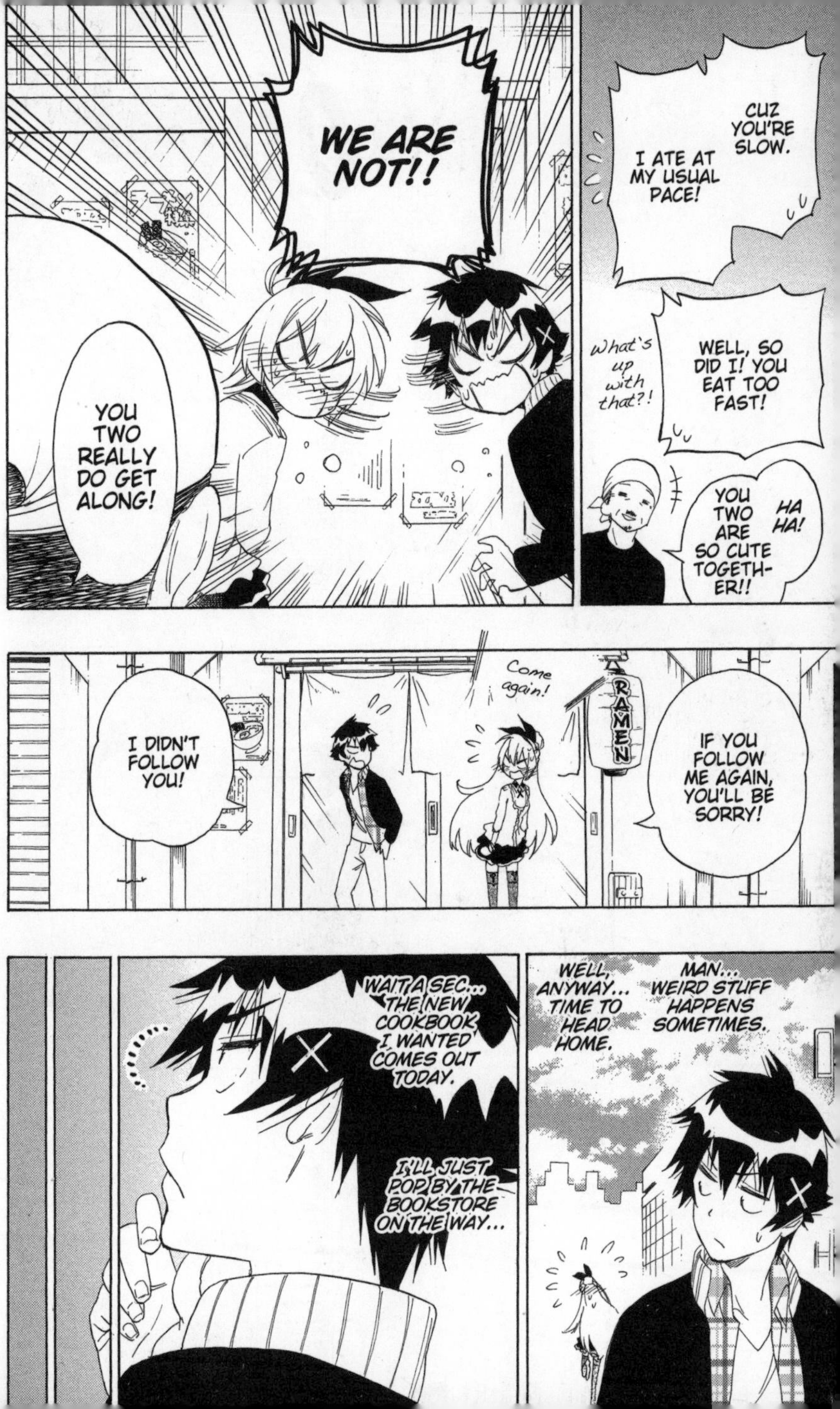
CUZ YOU'RE SLOW.
I ATE AT MY USUAL PACE!
WELL, SO DID I! YOU EAT TOO FAST!
What's up with that?!
YOU TWO ARE SO CUTE TOGETHER!!
HA HA!
WE ARE NOT!!
YOU TWO REALLY DO GET ALONG!
IF YOU FOLLOW ME AGAIN, YOU'LL BE SORRY!
RAMEN
Come again!
I DIDN'T FOLLOW YOU!
MAN... WEIRD STUFF HAPPENS SOMETIMES.
WELL, ANYWAY... TIME TO HEAD HOME.
WAIT A SEC... THE NEW COOKBOOK I WANTED COMES OUT TODAY.
I'LL JUST POP BY THE BOOKSTORE ON THE WAY...

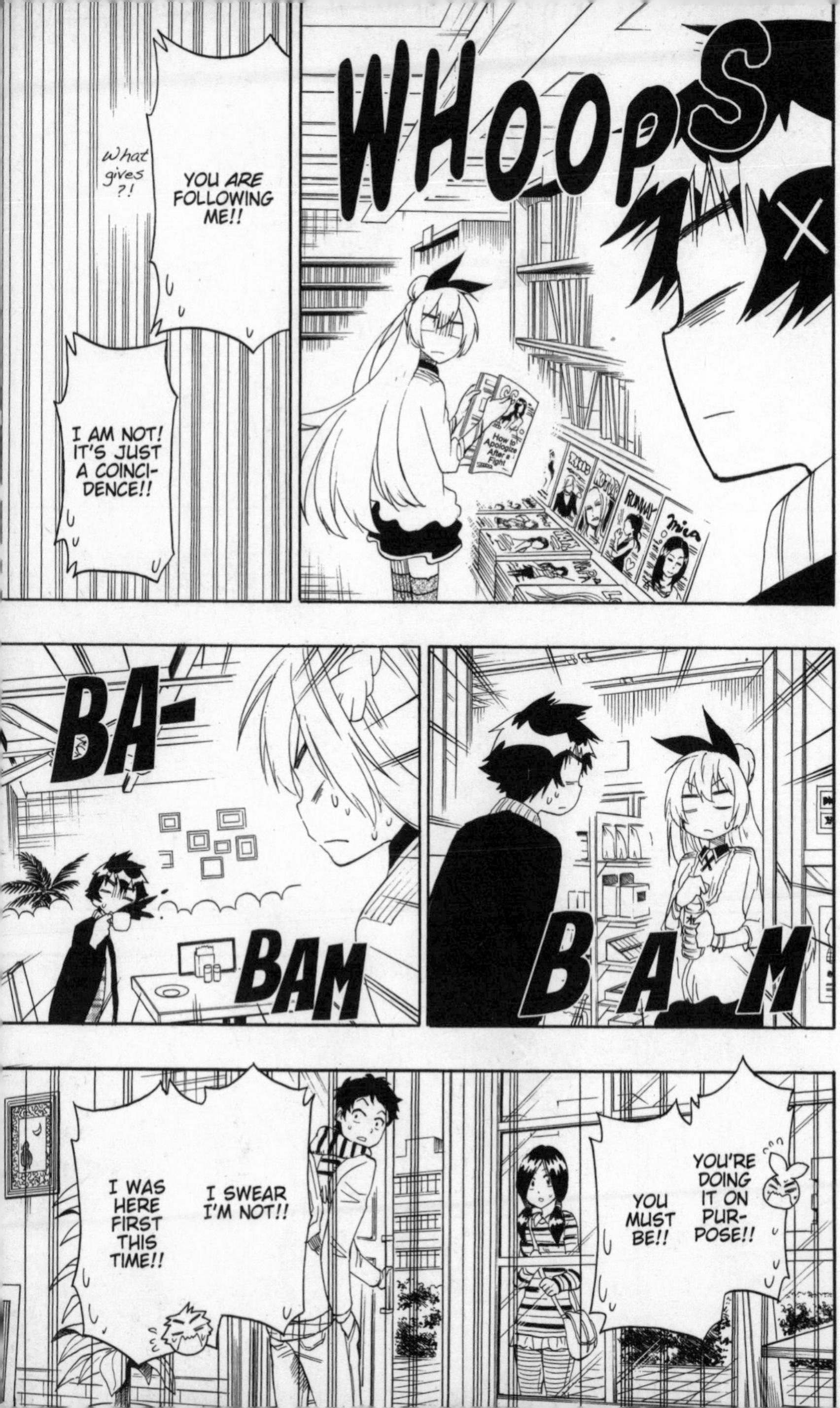
WHOOPS
How to Apologize After a Fight
RUNWAY
mira
YOU ARE FOLLOWING ME!!
What gives?!
I AM NOT! IT'S JUST A COINCIDENCE!!
BAM
BA-BAM
YOU'RE DOING IT ON PURPOSE!!
YOU MUST BE!!
I SWEAR I'M NOT!!
I WAS HERE FIRST THIS TIME!!

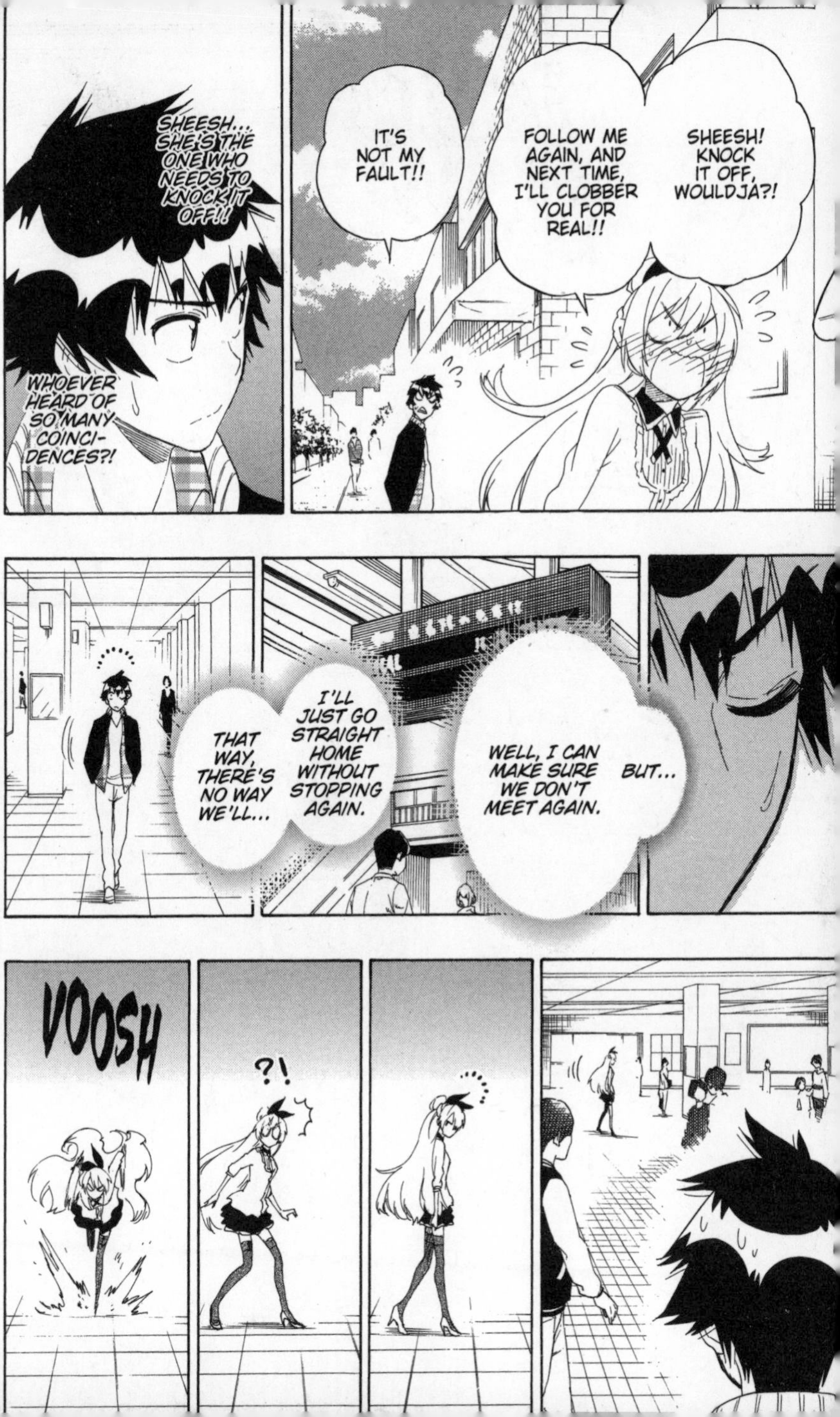
SHEESH! KNOCK IT OFF, WOULDJA?!
FOLLOW ME AGAIN, AND NEXT TIME, I'LL CLOBBER YOU FOR REAL!!
IT'S NOT MY FAULT!!
SHEESH... SHE'S THE ONE WHO NEEDS TO KNOCK IT OFF!!
WHOEVER HEARD OF SO MANY COINCI-DENCES?!
BUT...
WELL, I CAN MAKE SURE WE DON'T MEET AGAIN.
I'LL JUST GO STRAIGHT HOME WITHOUT STOPPING AGAIN.
THAT WAY, THERE'S NO WAY WE'LL...
?!
VOOSH

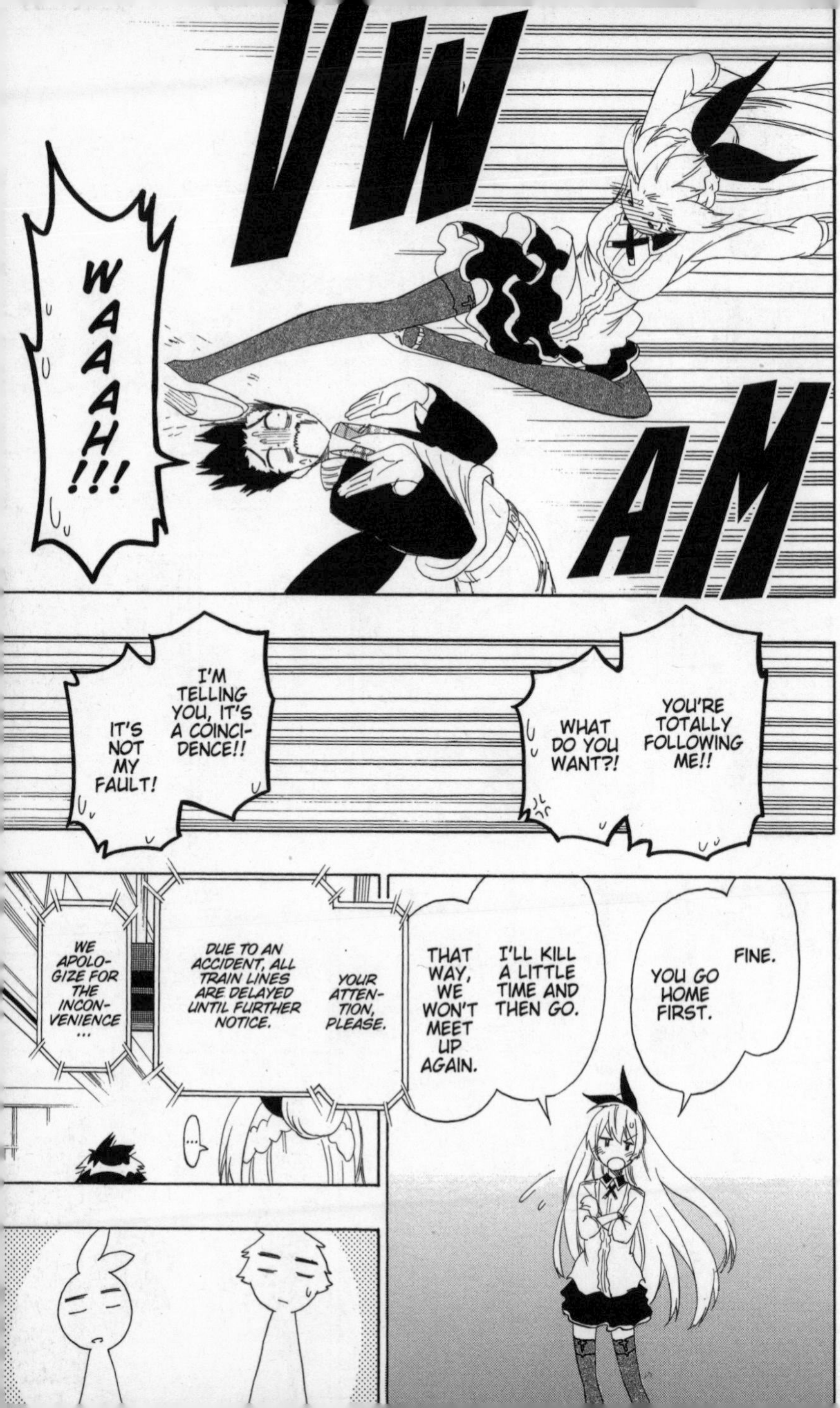
VWAM
WAAAAH!!!
YOU'RE TOTALLY FOLLOWING ME!!
WHAT DO YOU WANT?!
I'M TELLING YOU, IT'S A COINCI- DENCE!!
IT'S NOT MY FAULT!
FINE.
YOU GO HOME FIRST.
I'LL KILL A LITTLE TIME AND THEN GO.
THAT WAY, WE WON'T MEET UP AGAIN.
YOUR ATTEN- TION, PLEASE.
DUE TO AN ACCIDENT, ALL TRAIN LINES ARE DELAYED UNTIL FURTHER NOTICE.
WE APOLO- GIZE FOR THE INCON- VENIENCE ...
...

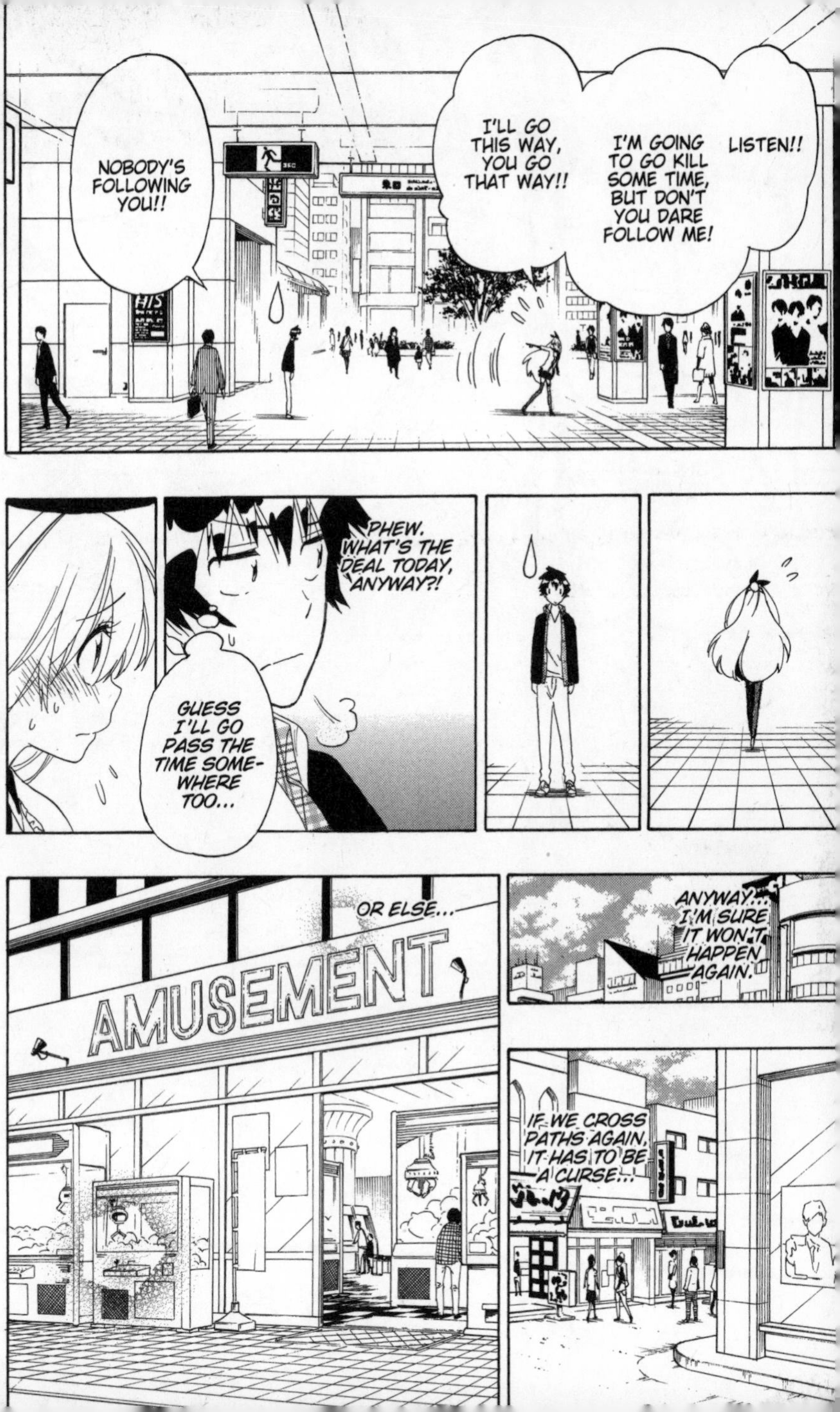
LISTEN!!
I'M GOING TO GO KILL SOME TIME, BUT DON'T YOU DARE FOLLOW ME!
I'LL GO THIS WAY, YOU GO THAT WAY!!
NOBODY'S FOLLOWING YOU!!
HIS
PHEW. WHAT'S THE DEAL TODAY, ANYWAY?!
GUESS I'LL GO PASS THE TIME SOME-WHERE TOO...
ANYWAY... I'M SURE IT WON'T HAPPEN AGAIN.
IF WE CROSS PATHS AGAIN, IT HAS TO BE A CURSE...!
OR ELSE...
AMUSEMENT

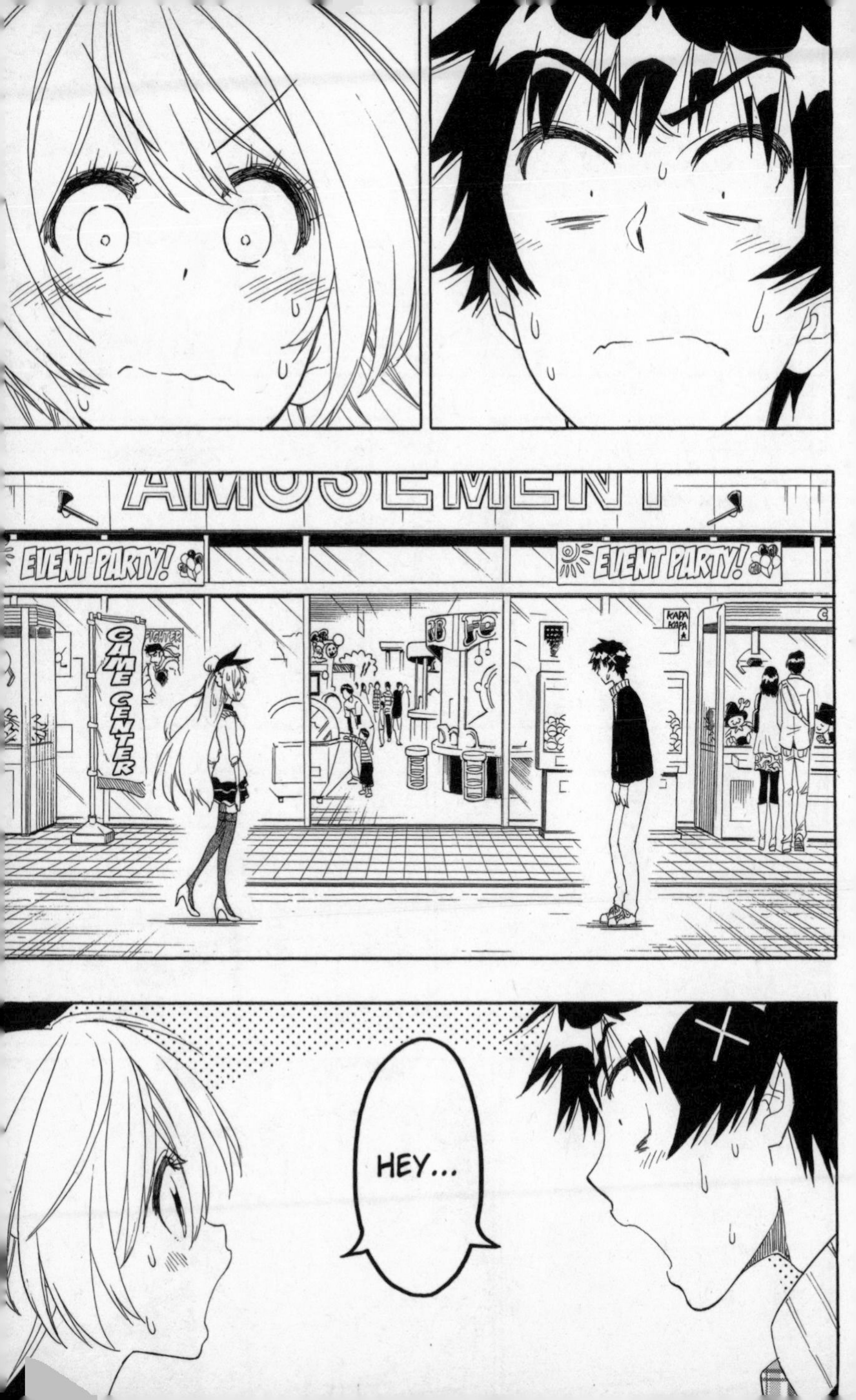
AMUSEMENT
EVENT PARTY!
KAPA KAPA
FIGHTER
GAME CENTER
EVENT PARTY!
HEY...

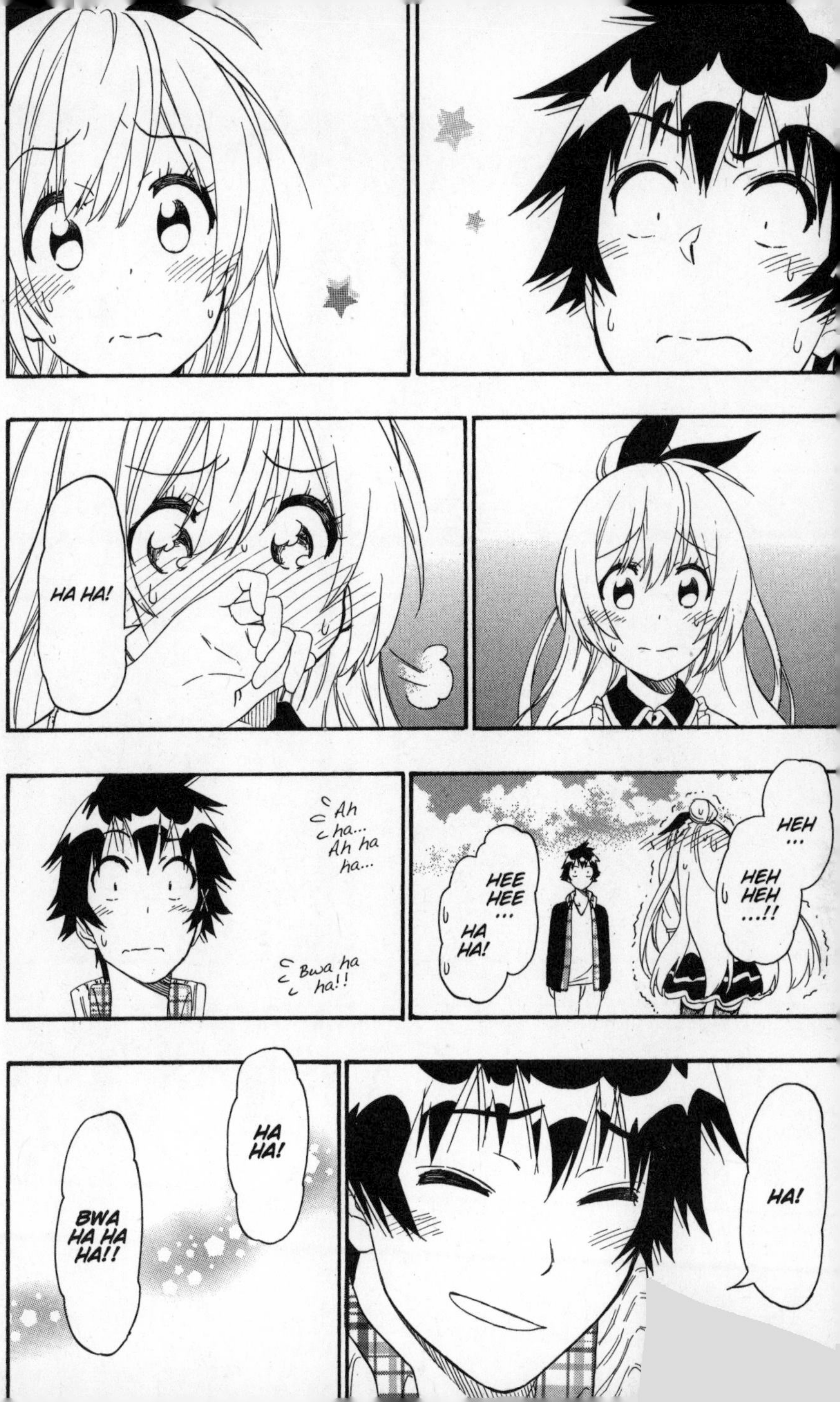
HA HA!
HEH... HEH HEH...!!
HEE HEE... HA HA!
Ah ha... Ah ha ha...
Bwa ha ha!!
HA!
HA HA!
BWA HA HA HA!!

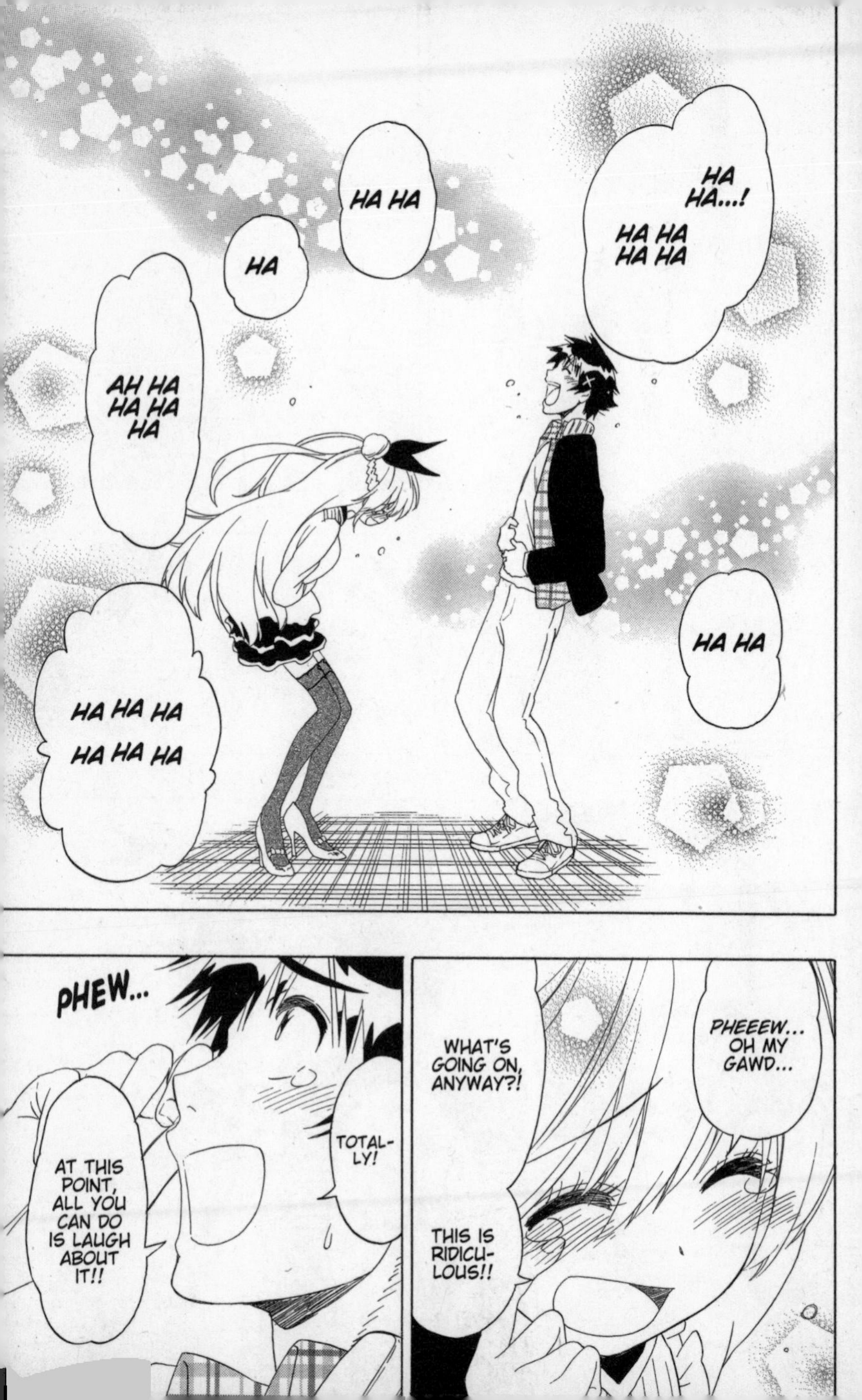
HA HA...! HA HA HA HA
HA HA
HA HA
HA
AH HA HA HA HA
HA HA HA HA HA HA
PHEEEW... OH MY GAWD...
WHAT'S GOING ON, ANYWAY?!
THIS IS RIDICU-LOUS!!
PHEW...
TOTAL-LY!
AT THIS POINT, ALL YOU CAN DO IS LAUGH ABOUT IT!!

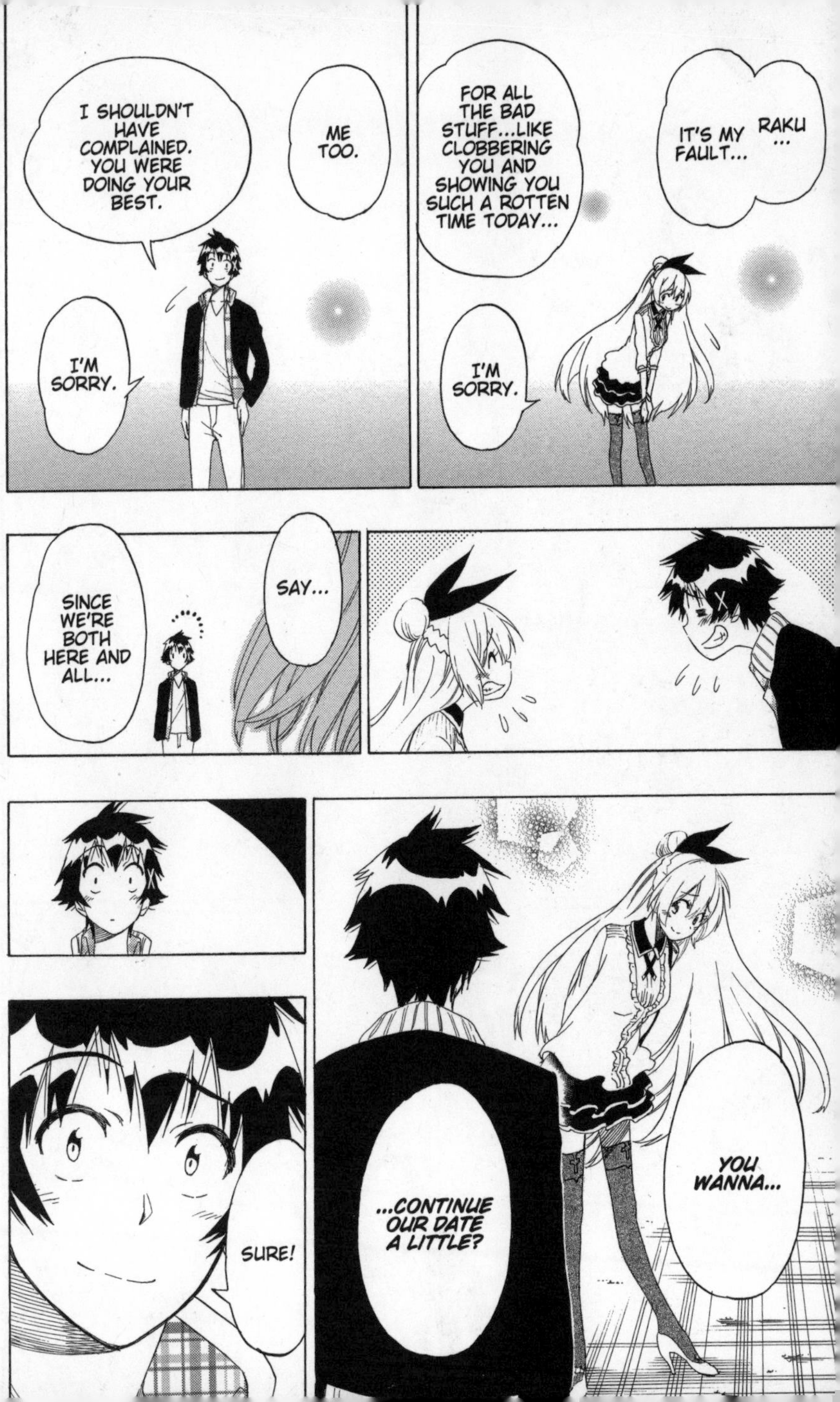
RAKU...
IT'S MY FAULT...
FOR ALL THE BAD STUFF...LIKE CLOBBERING YOU AND SHOWING YOU SUCH A ROTTEN TIME TODAY...
I'M SORRY.
ME TOO.
I SHOULDN'T HAVE COMPLAINED. YOU WERE DOING YOUR BEST.
I'M SORRY.
SAY...
SINCE WE'RE BOTH HERE AND ALL...
YOU WANNA...
...CONTINUE OUR DATE A LITTLE?
SURE!

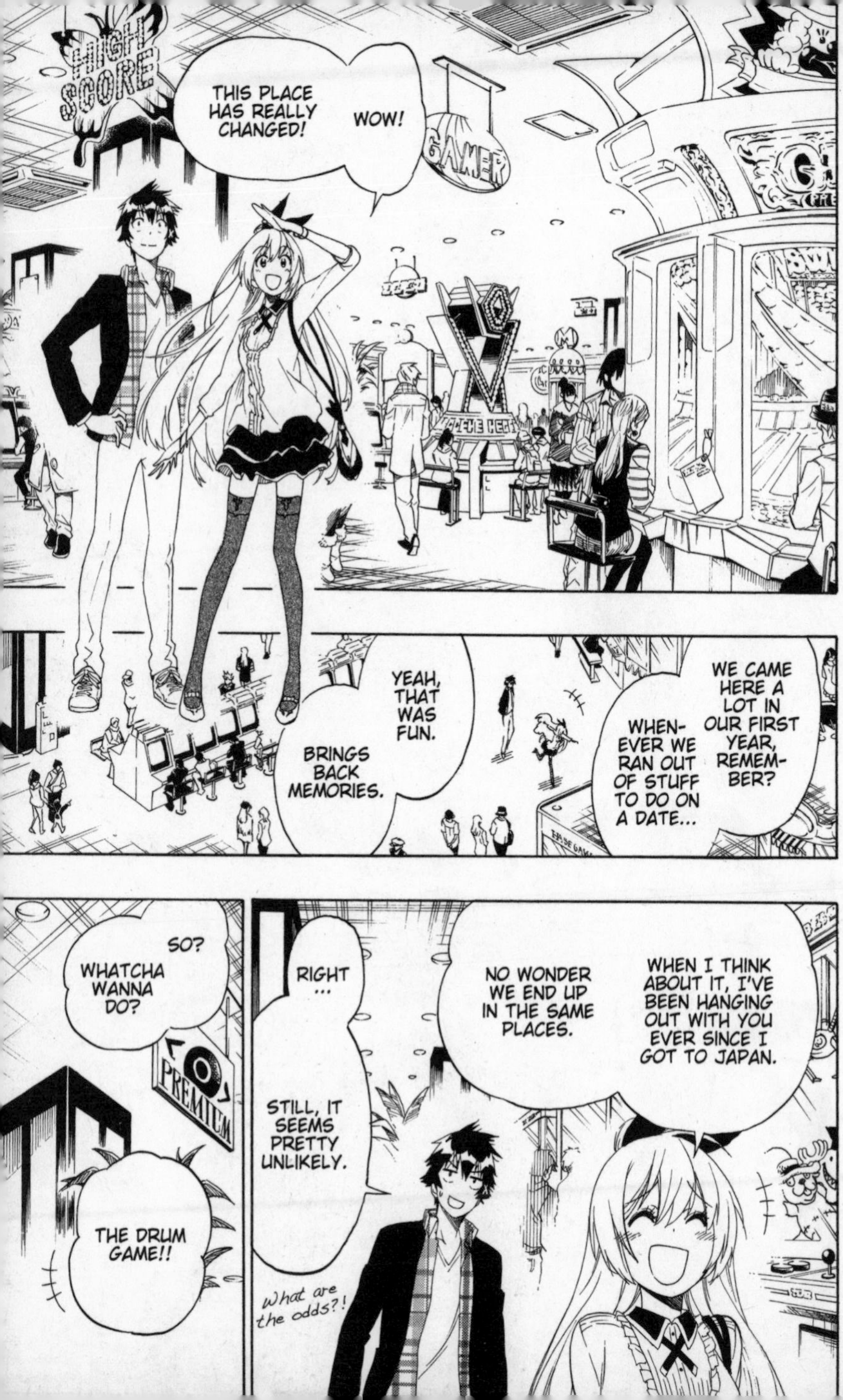
HIGH SCORE
GAMER
WOW!
THIS PLACE HAS REALLY CHANGED!
WE CAME HERE A LOT IN OUR FIRST YEAR, REMEMBER?
WHENEVER WE RAN OUT OF STUFF TO DO ON A DATE...
YEAH, THAT WAS FUN.
BRINGS BACK MEMORIES.
WHEN I THINK ABOUT IT, I'VE BEEN HANGING OUT WITH YOU EVER SINCE I GOT TO JAPAN.
NO WONDER WE END UP IN THE SAME PLACES.
RIGHT...
STILL, IT SEEMS PRETTY UNLIKELY.
What are the odds?!
SO?
WHATCHA WANNA DO?
PREMIUM
THE DRUM GAME!!

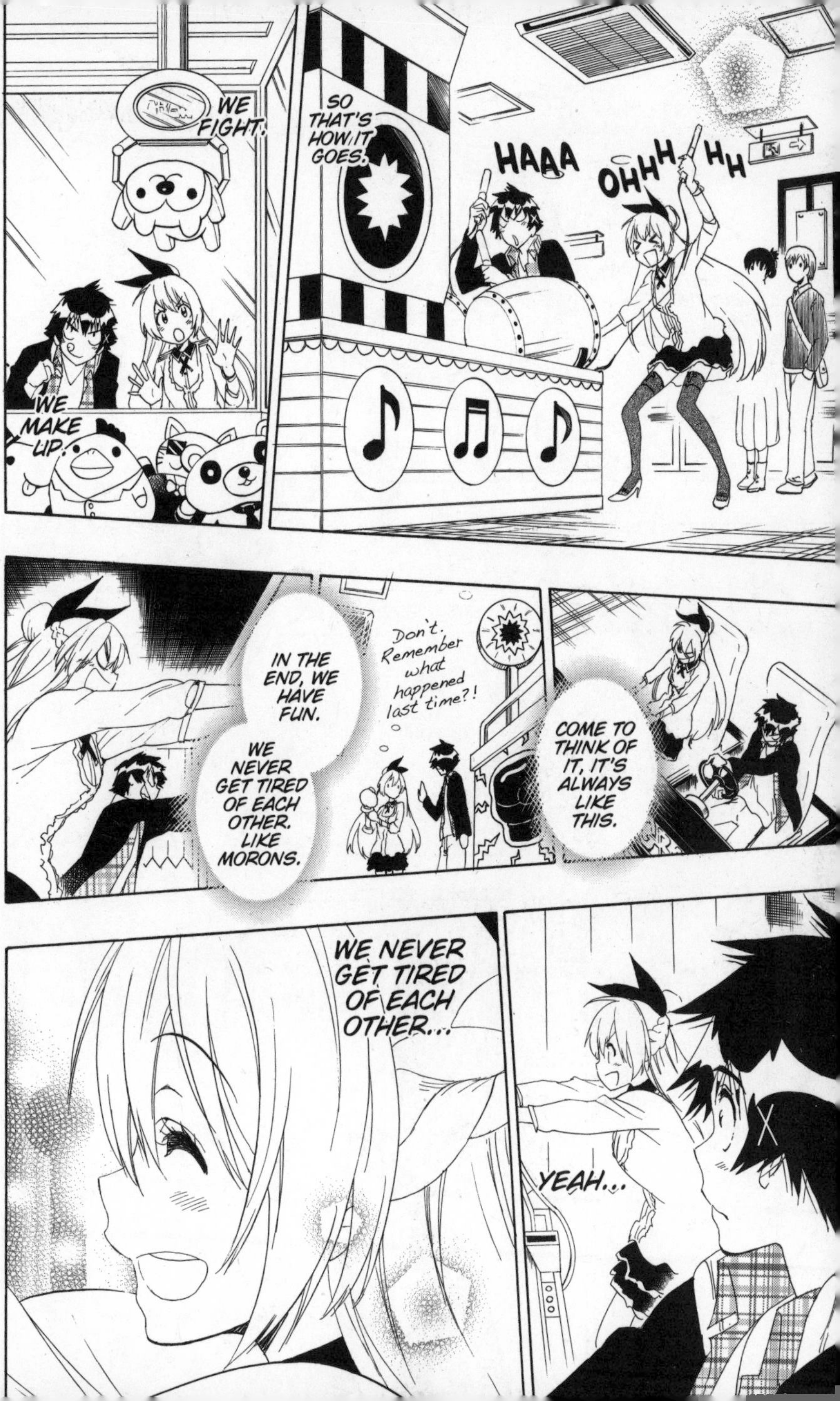
HAAA OHHHHHH
SO THAT'S HOW IT GOES.
WE FIGHT.
WE MAKE UP.
COME TO THINK OF IT, IT'S ALWAYS LIKE THIS.
Don't. Remember what happened last time?!
IN THE END, WE HAVE FUN.
WE NEVER GET TIRED OF EACH OTHER. LIKE MORONS.
YEAH...
WE NEVER GET TIRED OF EACH OTHER...

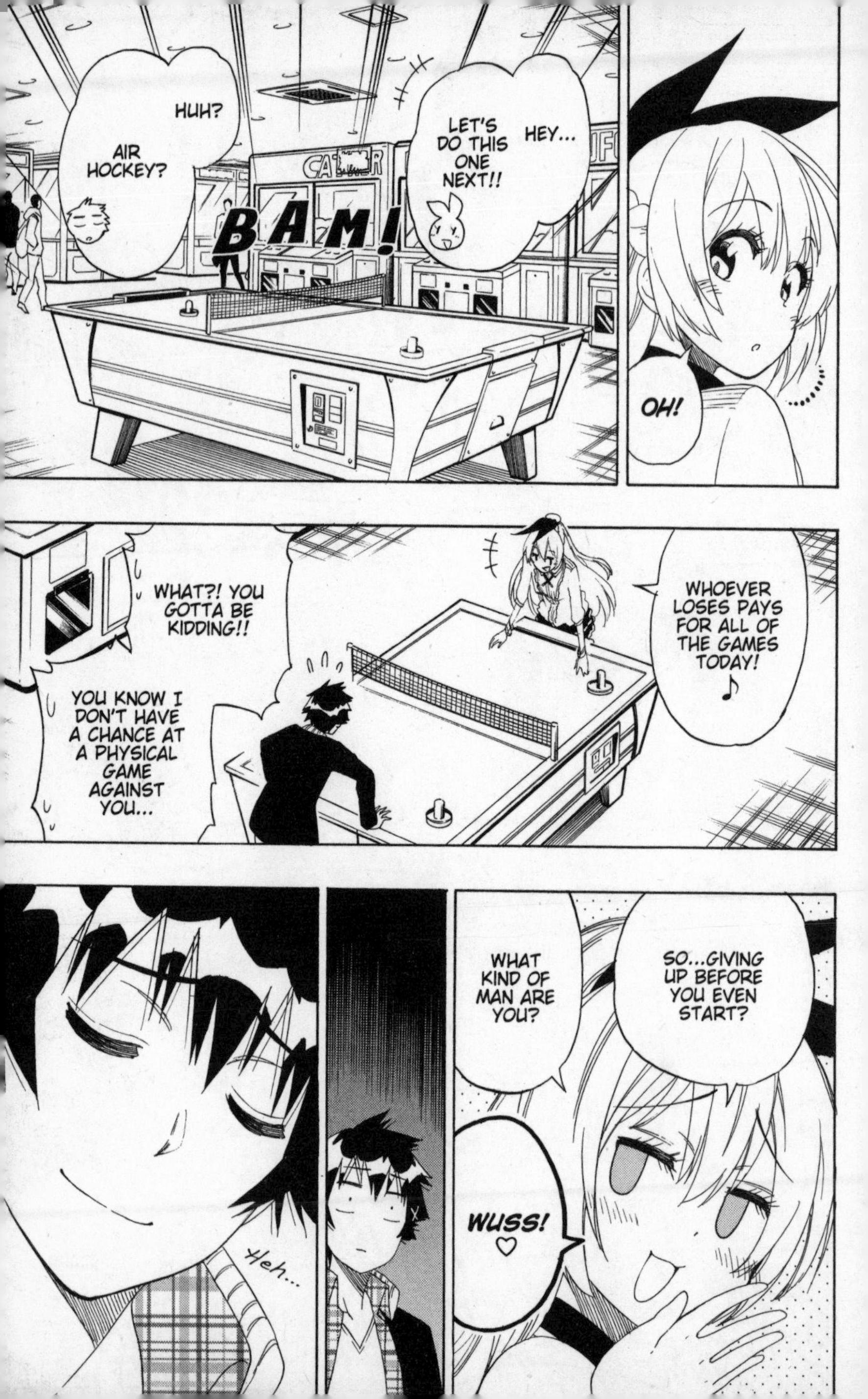
OH!
HEY...
LET'S DO THIS ONE NEXT!!
BAM!
HUH?
AIR HOCKEY?
WHOEVER LOSES PAYS FOR ALL OF THE GAMES TODAY! ♪
WHAT?! YOU GOTTA BE KIDDING!!
YOU KNOW I DON'T HAVE A CHANCE AT A PHYSICAL GAME AGAINST YOU...
SO...GIVING UP BEFORE YOU EVEN START?
WHAT KIND OF MAN ARE YOU?
WUSS! ♡
Heh...

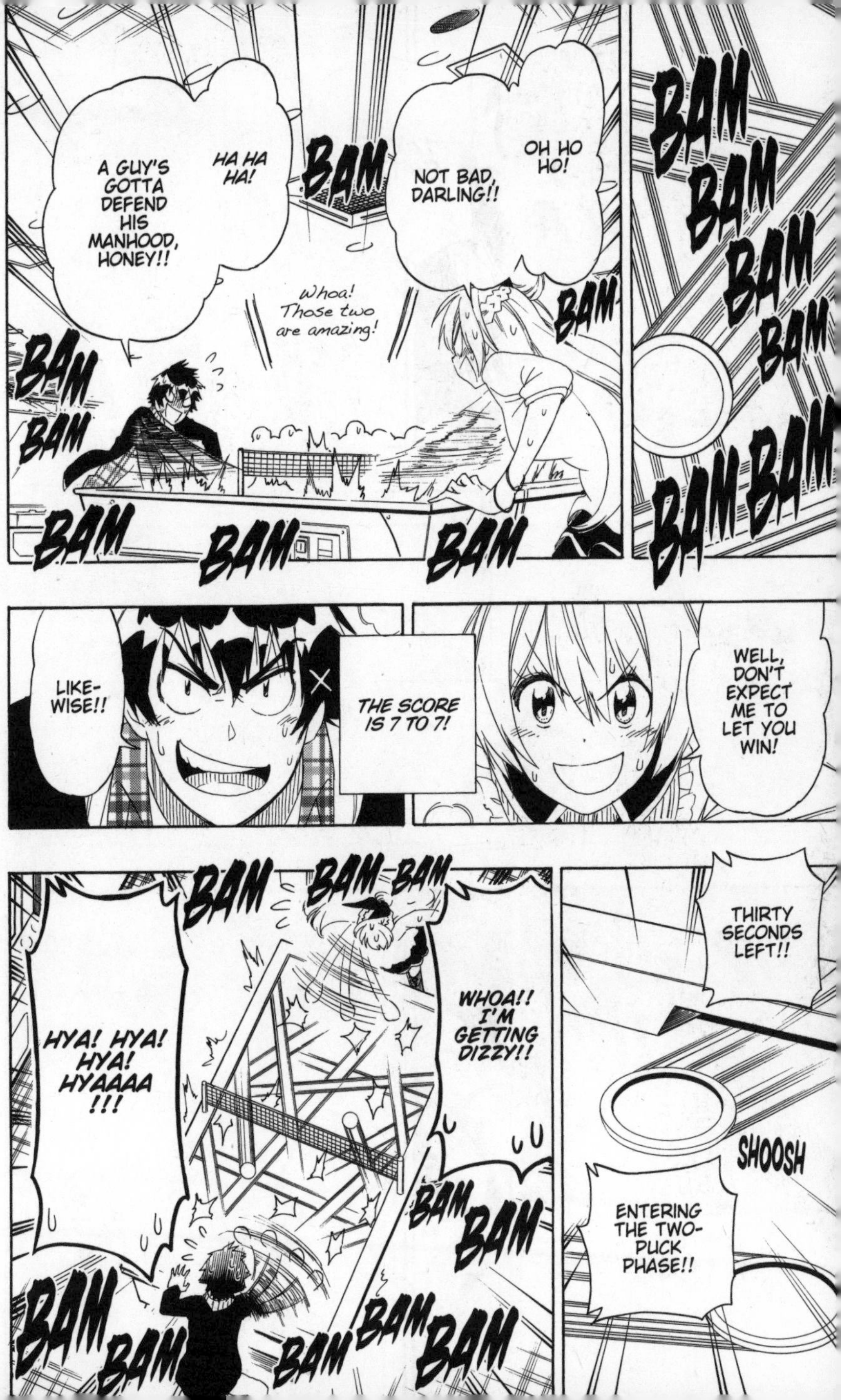
BAM BAM BAM BAM
BAM-BAM BAM-BAM
OH HO HO!
NOT BAD, DARLING!!
BAM
HA HA HA!
A GUY'S GOTTA DEFEND HIS MANHOOD, HONEY!!
BAM
Whoa! Those two are amazing!
BAM BAM
BAM BAM BAM
WELL, DON'T EXPECT ME TO LET YOU WIN!
THE SCORE IS 7 TO 7!
LIKE-WISE!!
THIRTY SECONDS LEFT!!
SHOOSH
ENTERING THE TWO-PUCK PHASE!!
BAM-BAM BAM
WHOA!! I'M GETTING DIZZY!!
HYA! HYA! HYA! HYAAAA!!!
BAM BAM
BAM BAM BAM
BAM BAM

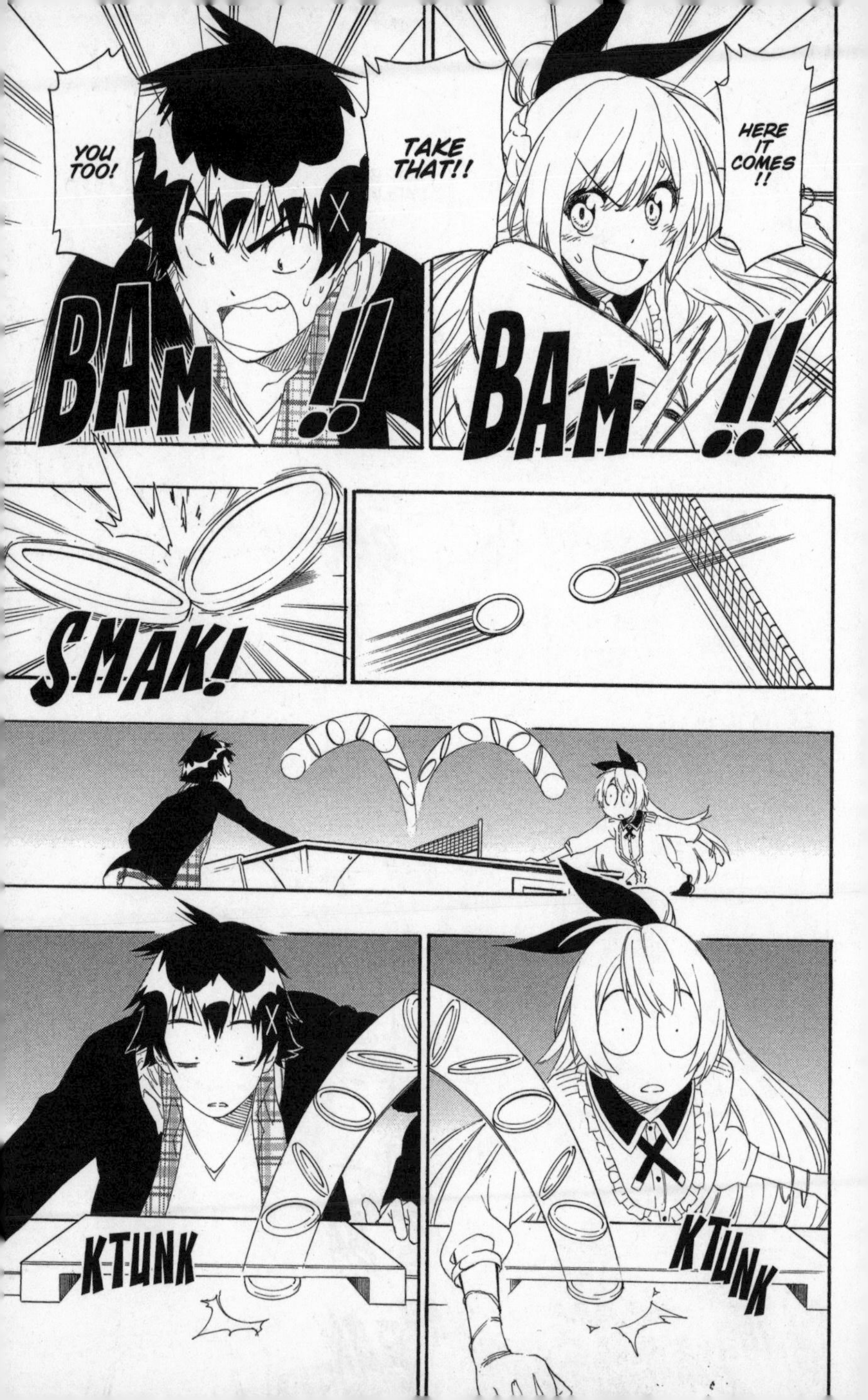

HERE IT COMES!!
BAM!!
TAKE THAT!!
YOU TOO!
BAM!!
SMAK!
KTUNK
KTUNK

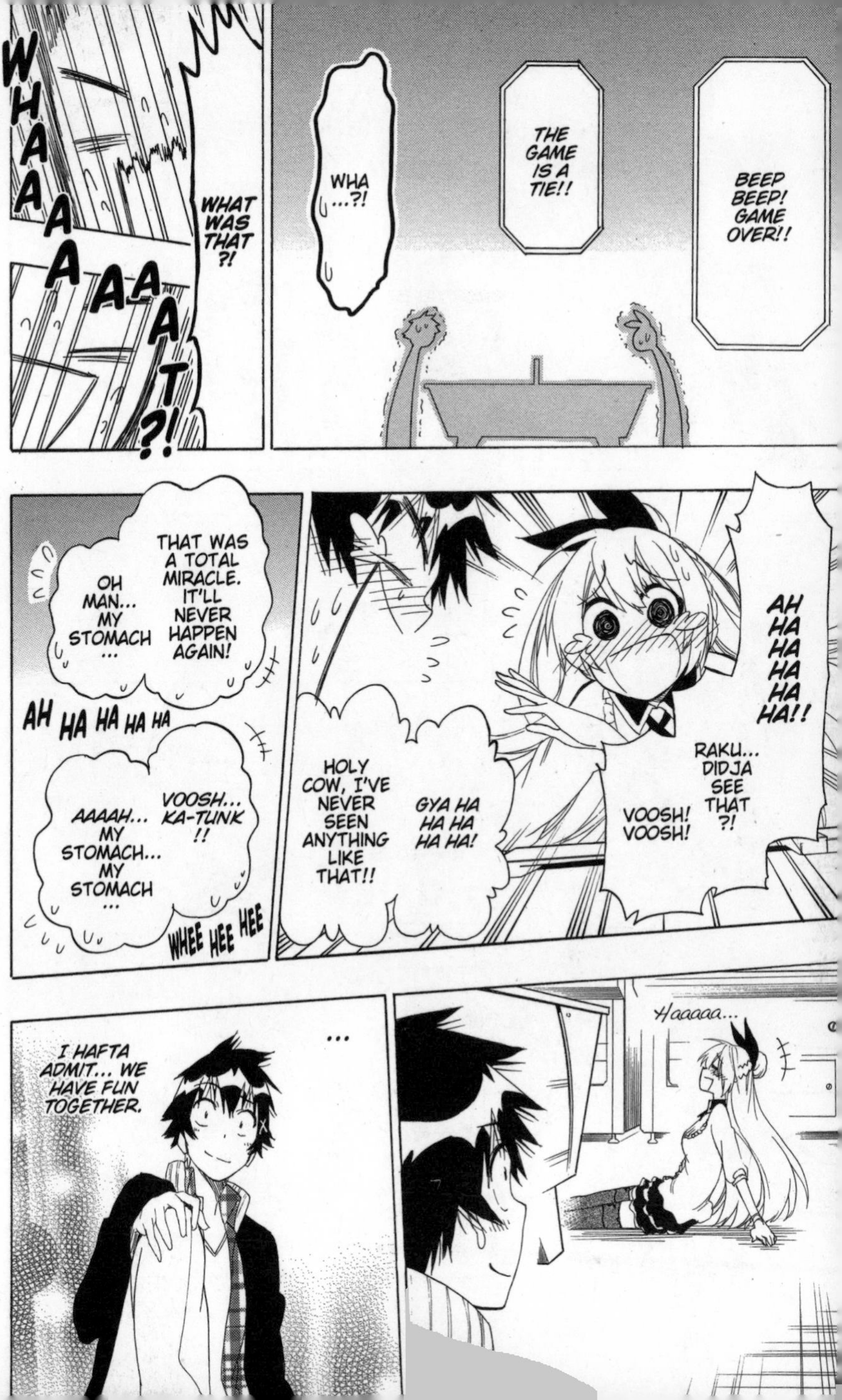

BEEP BEEP! GAME OVER!!
THE GAME IS A TIE!!
WHA ...?!
WHAT WAS THAT ?!
WHAAAAAAAT ?!
AH HA HA HA HA HA HA!!
RAKU... DIDJA SEE THAT ?!
VOOSH! VOOSH!
GYA HA HA HA HA HA!
HOLY COW, I'VE NEVER SEEN ANYTHING LIKE THAT!!
THAT WAS A TOTAL MIRACLE. IT'LL NEVER HAPPEN AGAIN!
OH MAN... MY STOMACH ...
AH HA HA HA HA
VOOSH... KA-TUNK !!
AAAAH... MY STOMACH... MY STOMACH ...
WHEE HEE HEE
Haaaaa...
...
I HAFTA ADMIT... WE HAVE FUN TOGETHER.

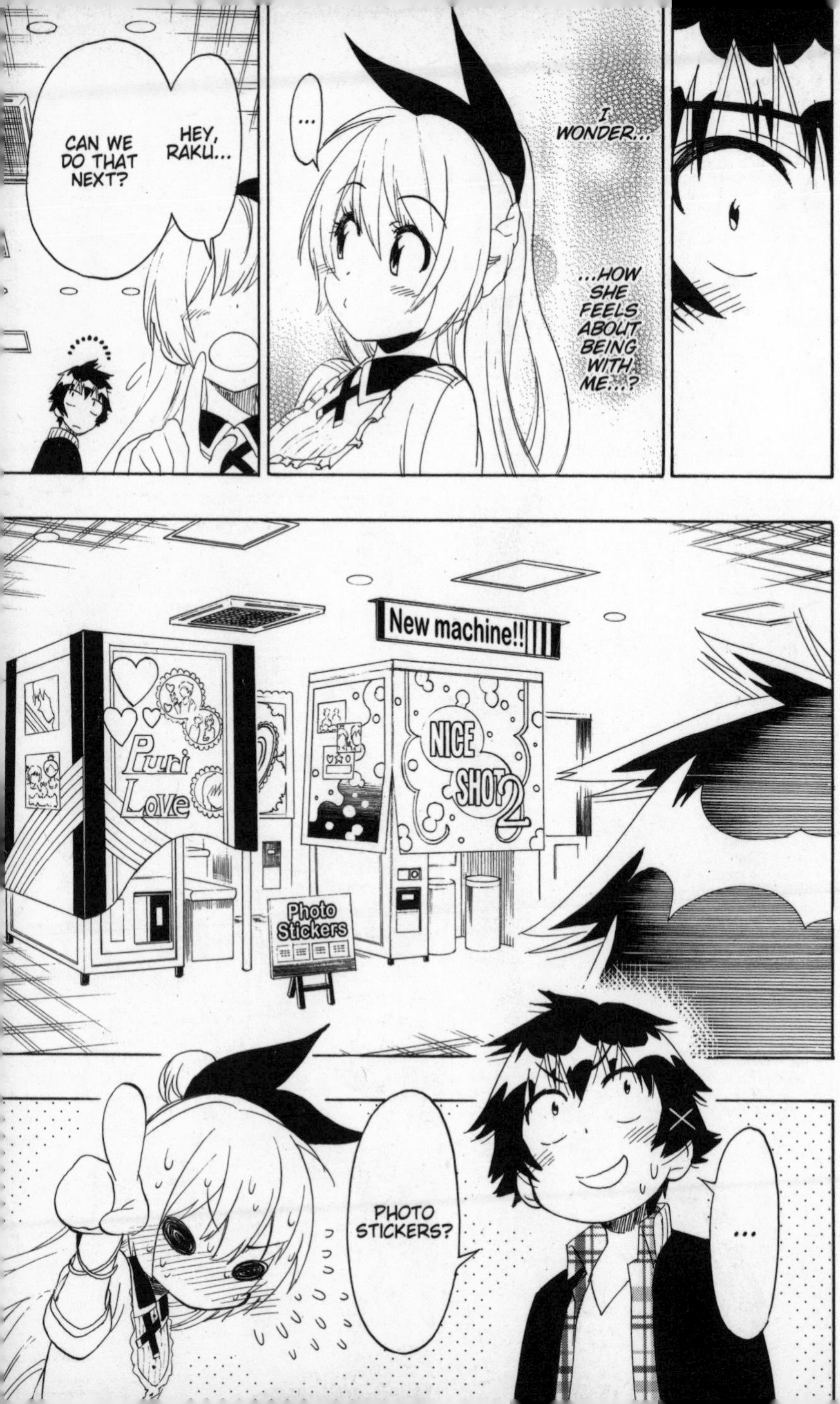
I WONDER...
...HOW SHE FEELS ABOUT BEING WITH ME...?
...
HEY, RAKU...
CAN WE DO THAT NEXT?
New machine!!
NICE SHOT 2
Puri Love
Photo Stickers
...
PHOTO STICKERS?

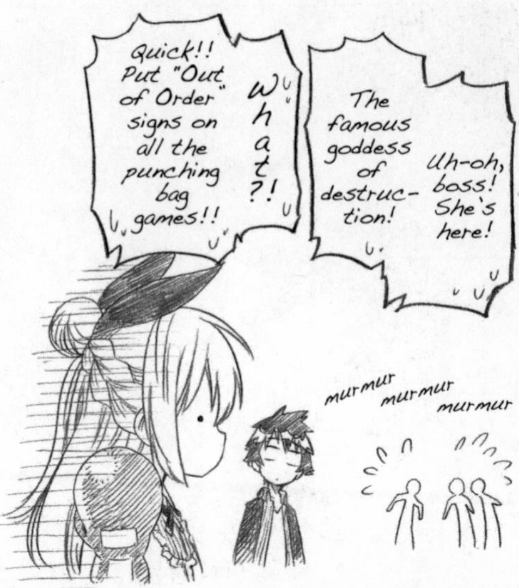
Uh-oh, boss! She's here!
The famous goddess of destruction!
What?!
Quick!! Put "Out of Order" signs on all the punching bag games!!
murmur murmur murmur

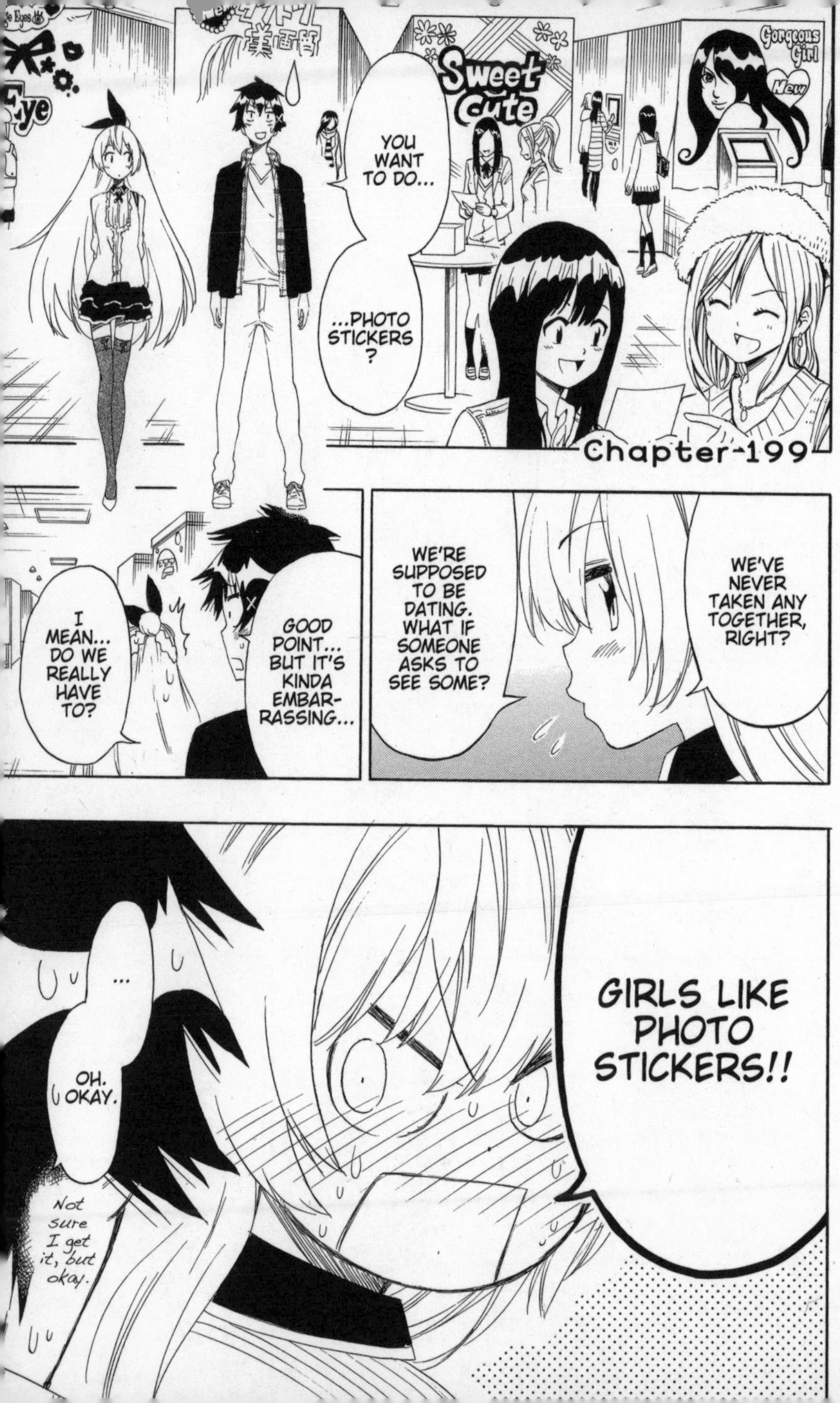
Chapter-199
Gorgeous Girl
New
Sweet Cute
Eye
YOU WANT TO DO...
...PHOTO STICKERS?
WE'VE NEVER TAKEN ANY TOGETHER, RIGHT?
WE'RE SUPPOSED TO BE DATING. WHAT IF SOMEONE ASKS TO SEE SOME?
GOOD POINT... BUT IT'S KINDA EMBARRASSING...
I MEAN... DO WE REALLY HAVE TO?
GIRLS LIKE PHOTO STICKERS!!
...
OH. OKAY.
Not sure I get it, but okay.

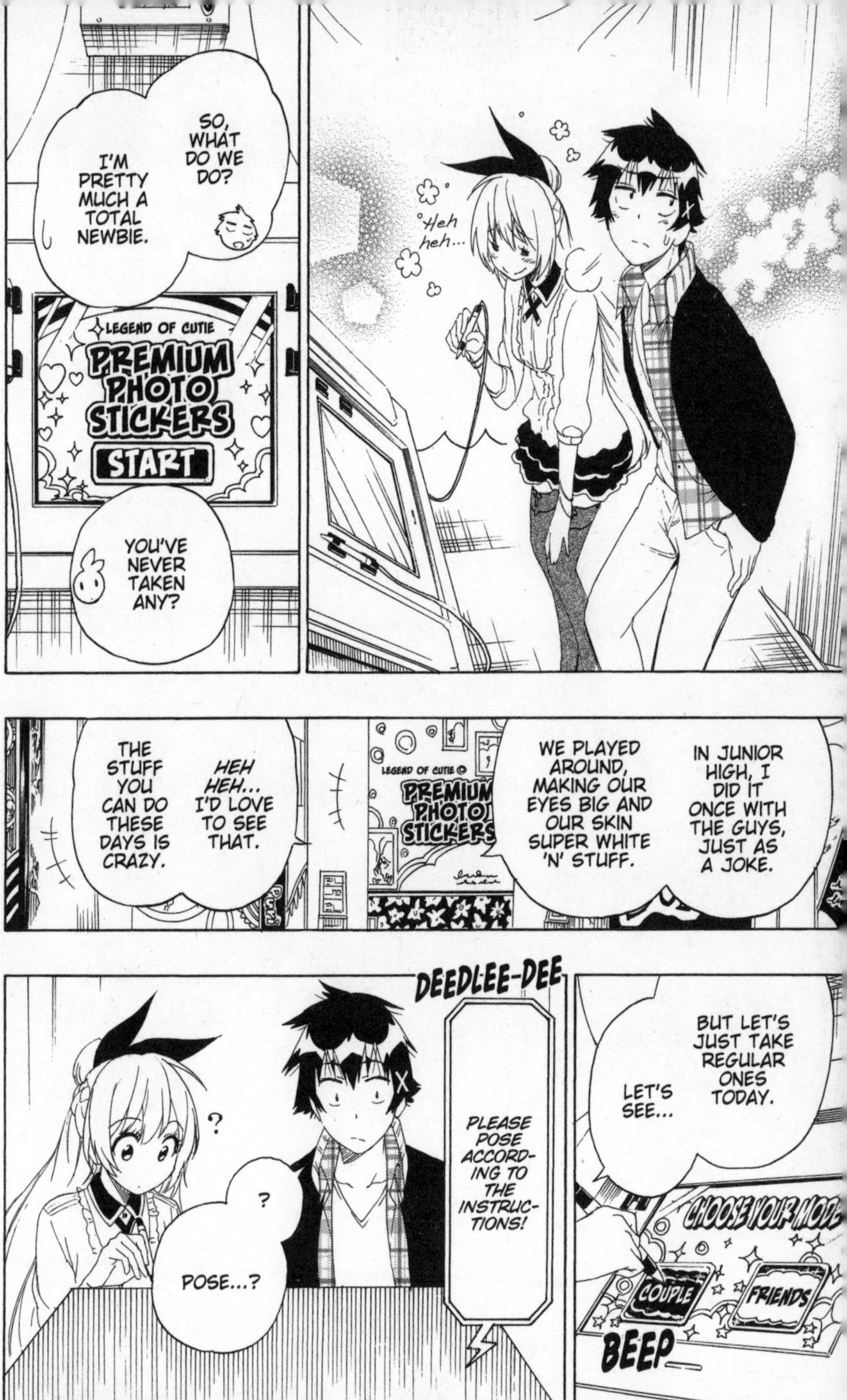
Heh heh...
SO, WHAT DO WE DO?
I'M PRETTY MUCH A TOTAL NEWBIE.
LEGEND OF CUTIE
PREMIUM PHOTO STICKERS
START
YOU'VE NEVER TAKEN ANY?
IN JUNIOR HIGH, I DID IT ONCE WITH THE GUYS, JUST AS A JOKE.
WE PLAYED AROUND, MAKING OUR EYES BIG AND OUR SKIN SUPER WHITE 'N' STUFF.
LEGEND OF CUTIE
PREMIUM PHOTO STICKERS
HEH HEH... I'D LOVE TO SEE THAT.
THE STUFF YOU CAN DO THESE DAYS IS CRAZY.
BUT LET'S JUST TAKE REGULAR ONES TODAY.
LET'S SEE...
CHOOSE YOUR MODE
COUPLE
FRIENDS
BEEP
DEEDLEE-DEE
PLEASE POSE ACCORDING TO THE INSTRUCTIONS!
?
?
POSE...?

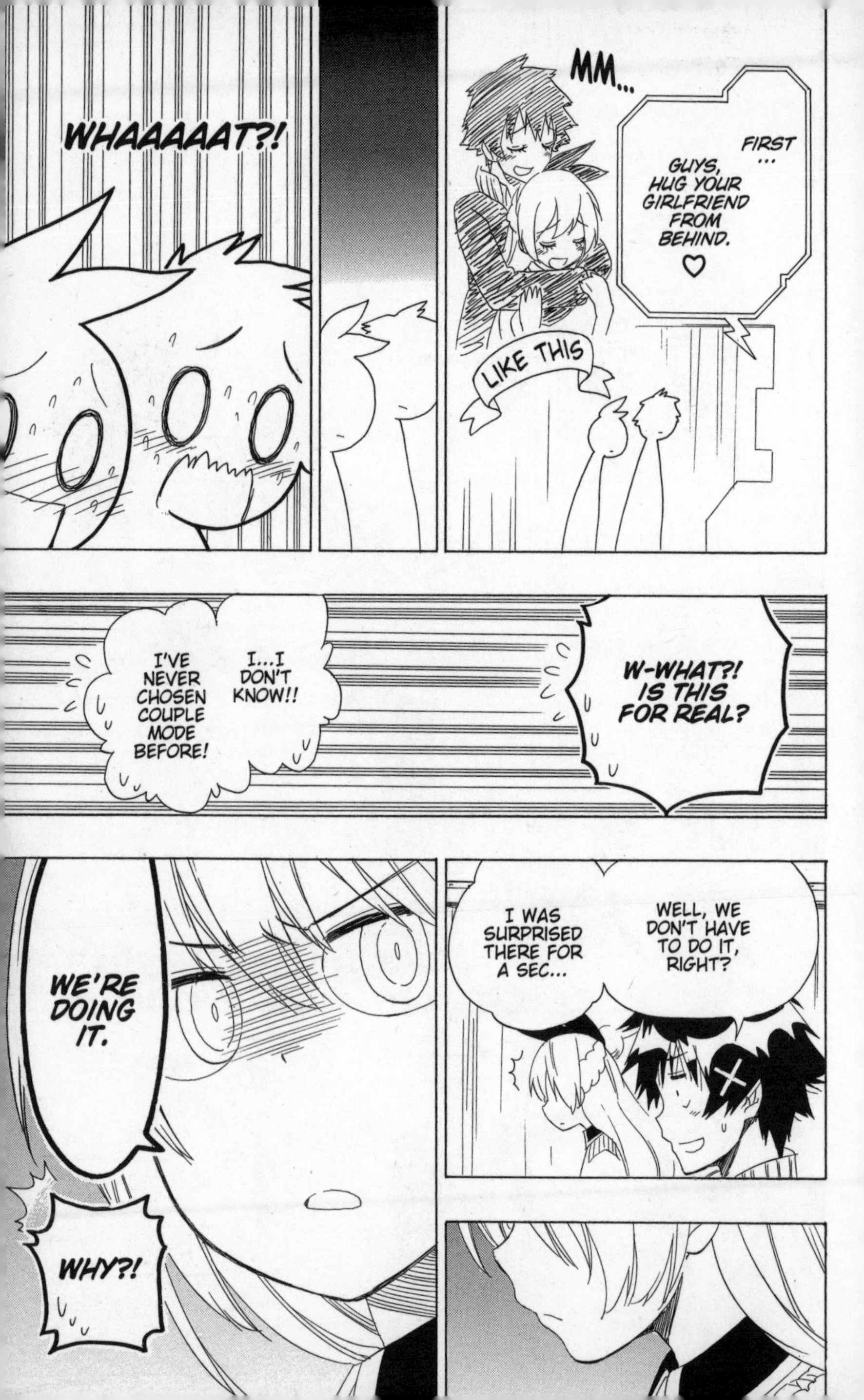
MM...
FIRST...
GUYS, HUG YOUR GIRLFRIEND FROM BEHIND. ♡
LIKE THIS
WHAAAAAT?!
W-WHAT?! IS THIS FOR REAL?
I'VE NEVER CHOSEN COUPLE MODE BEFORE!
I...I DON'T KNOW!!
I WAS SURPRISED THERE FOR A SEC...
WELL, WE DON'T HAVE TO DO IT, RIGHT?
WE'RE DOING IT.
WHY?!

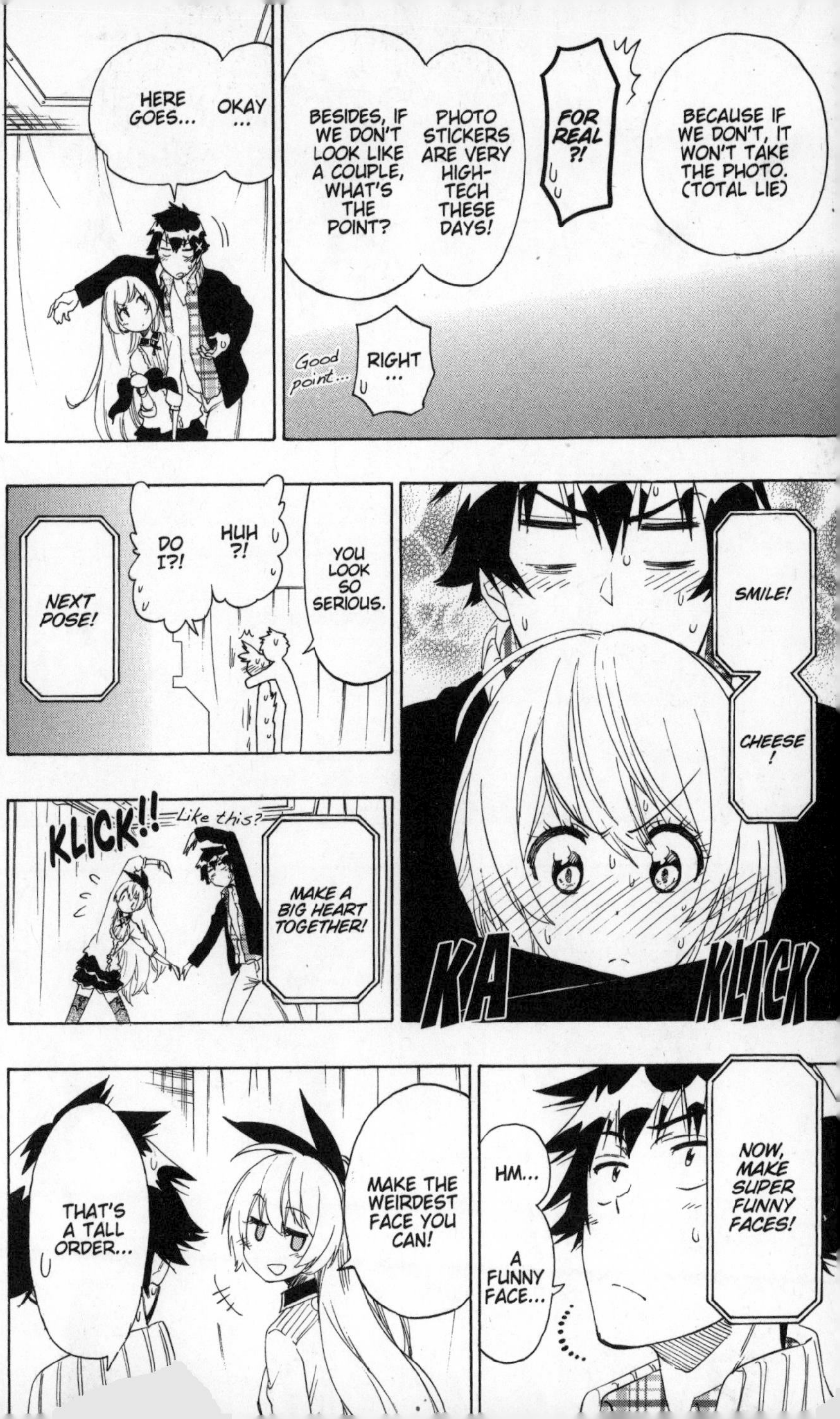
BECAUSE IF WE DON'T, IT WON'T TAKE THE PHOTO. (TOTAL LIE)
FOR REAL?!
PHOTO STICKERS ARE VERY HIGH-TECH THESE DAYS!
BESIDES, IF WE DON'T LOOK LIKE A COUPLE, WHAT'S THE POINT?
RIGHT...
Good point...
OKAY...
HERE GOES...
SMILE!
CHEESE!
KA KLICK
YOU LOOK SO SERIOUS.
HUH?!
DO I?!
NEXT POSE!
MAKE A BIG HEART TOGETHER!
Like this?
KLICK!!
NOW, MAKE SUPER FUNNY FACES!
HM...
A FUNNY FACE...
MAKE THE WEIRDEST FACE YOU CAN!
THAT'S A TALL ORDER...

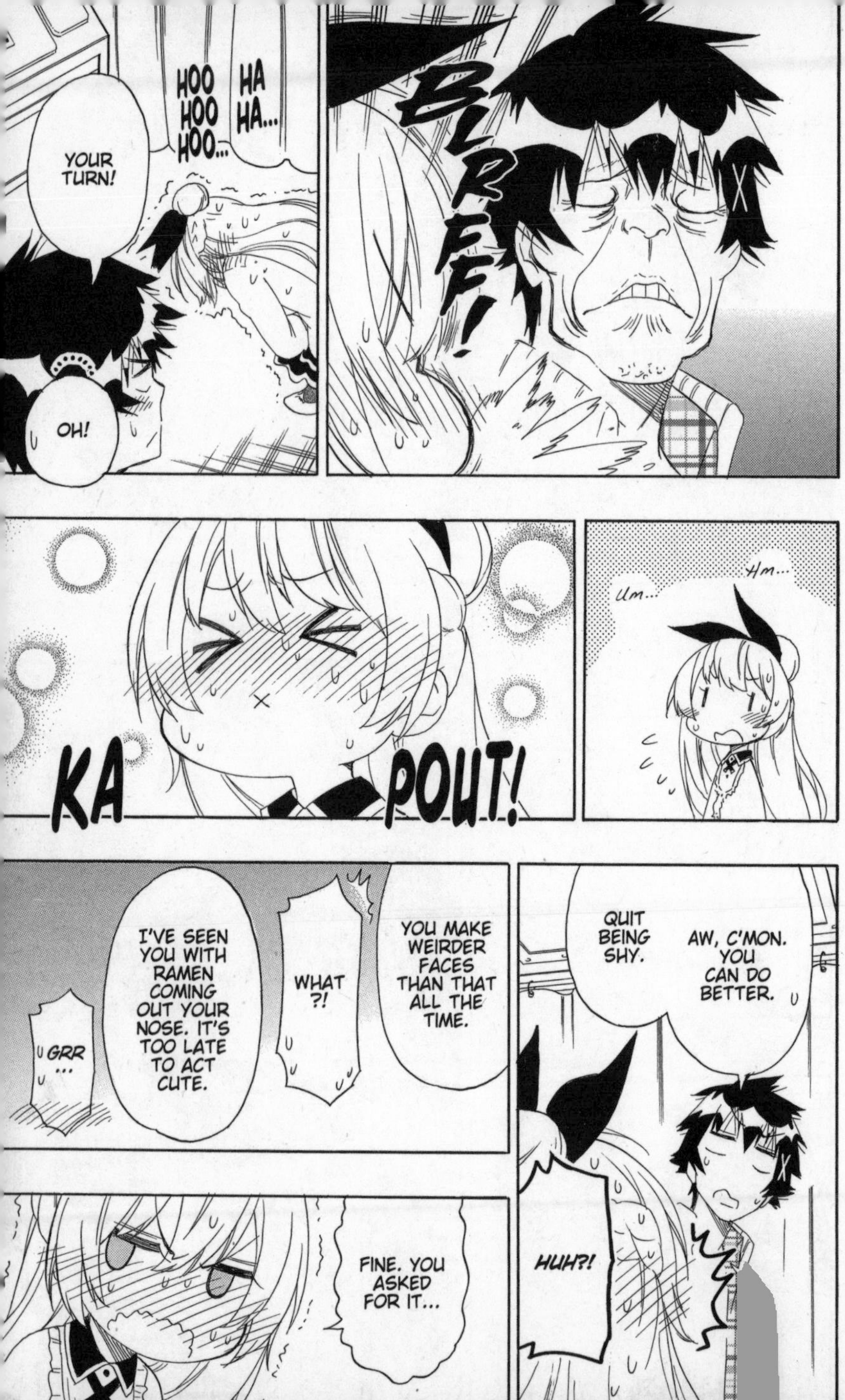
BLRFF!
HA HA...
HOO HOO HOO...
YOUR TURN!
OH!
Hm...
Um...
KA POUT!
AW, C'MON. YOU CAN DO BETTER.
QUIT BEING SHY.
HUH?!
YOU MAKE WEIRDER FACES THAN THAT ALL THE TIME.
WHAT?!
I'VE SEEN YOU WITH RAMEN COMING OUT YOUR NOSE. IT'S TOO LATE TO ACT CUTE.
GRR...
FINE. YOU ASKED FOR IT...

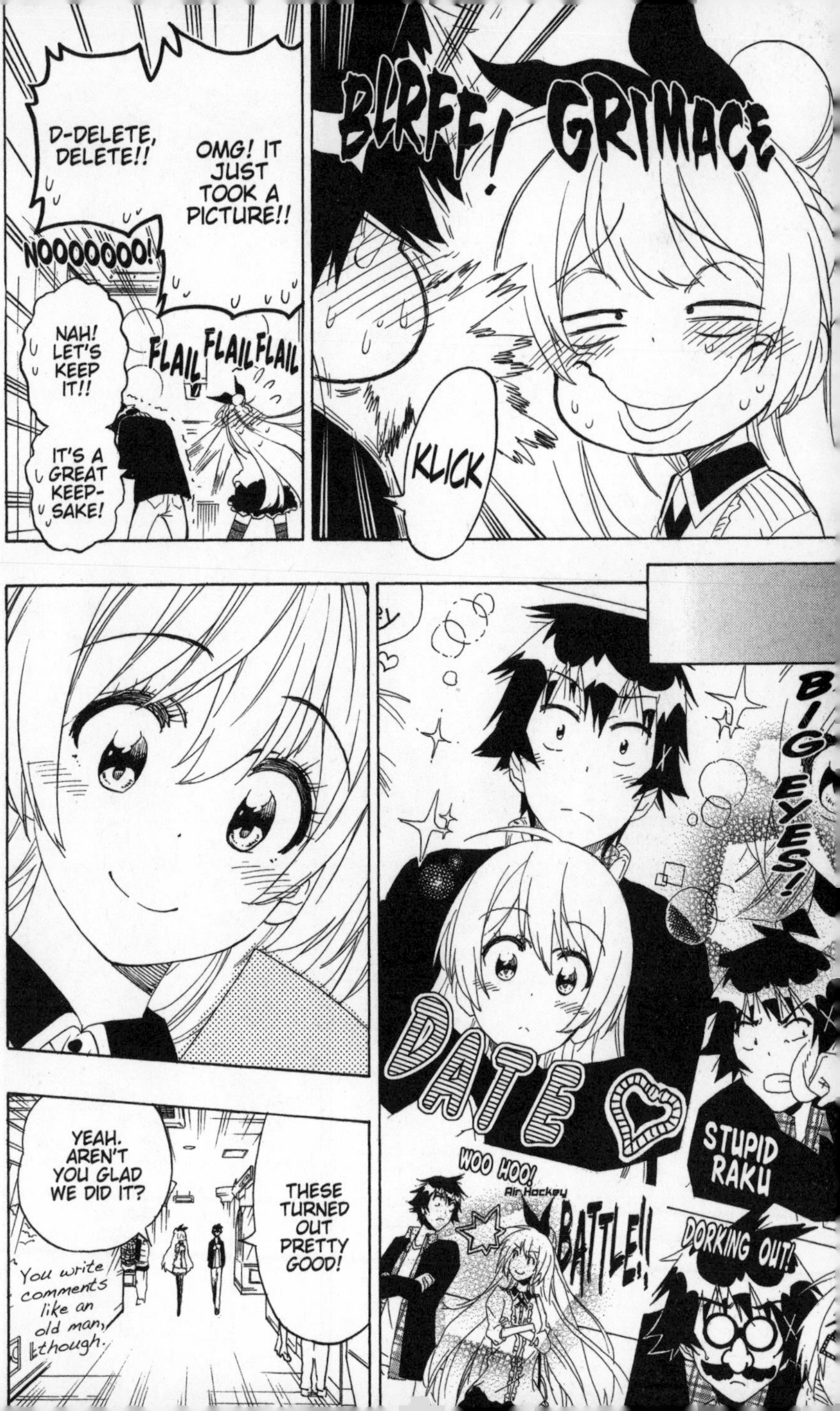
BLRFF!
GRIMACE
KLICK
OMG! IT JUST TOOK A PICTURE!!
D-DELETE, DELETE!!
NOOOOOOO!
FLAIL FLAIL FLAIL
NAH! LET'S KEEP IT!!
IT'S A GREAT KEEP-SAKE!
BIG EYES!
DATE
STUPID RAKU
WOO HOO!
Air Hockey
BATTLE!!
DORKING OUT!
THESE TURNED OUT PRETTY GOOD!
YEAH. AREN'T YOU GLAD WE DID IT?
You write comments like an old man, though.

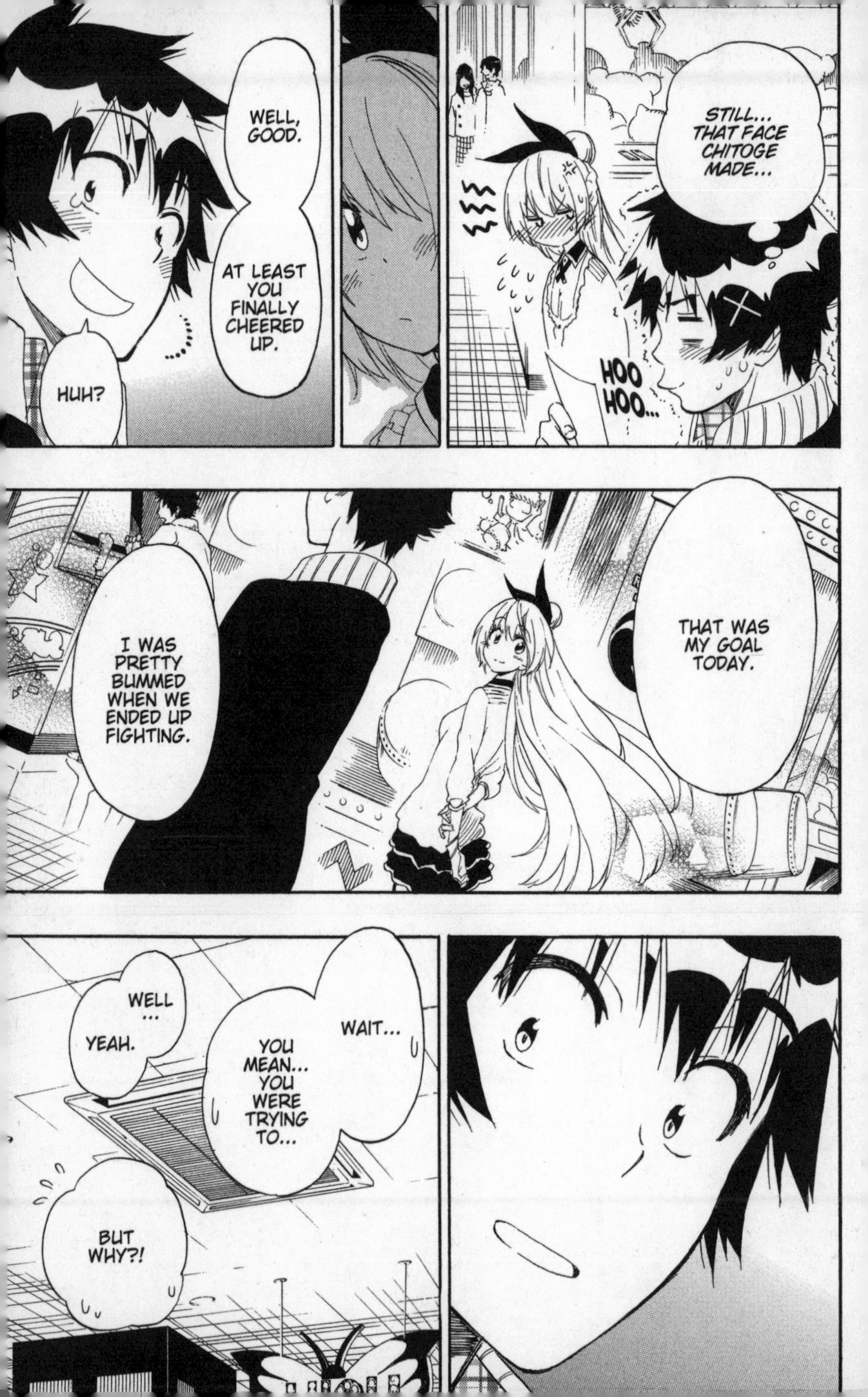
STILL... THAT FACE CHITOGE MADE...
HOO HOO...
WELL, GOOD.
AT LEAST YOU FINALLY CHEERED UP.
HUH?
THAT WAS MY GOAL TODAY.
I WAS PRETTY BUMMED WHEN WE ENDED UP FIGHTING.
WAIT...
YOU MEAN... YOU WERE TRYING TO...
WELL... YEAH.
BUT WHY?!

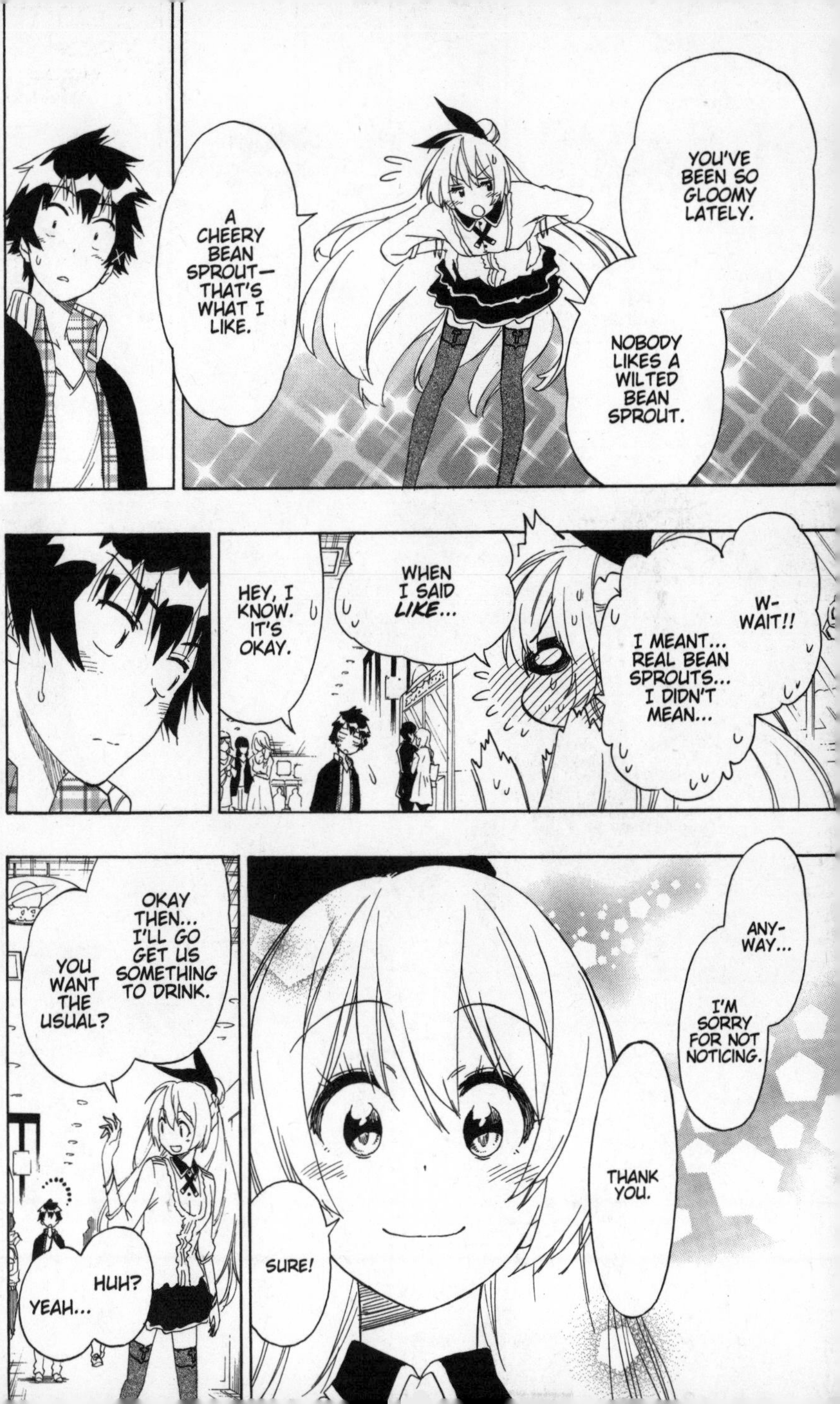
YOU'VE BEEN SO GLOOMY LATELY.
NOBODY LIKES A WILTED BEAN SPROUT.
A CHEERY BEAN SPROUT—THAT'S WHAT I LIKE.
W-WAIT!!
I MEANT... REAL BEAN SPROUTS... I DIDN'T MEAN...
WHEN I SAID *LIKE*...
HEY, I KNOW. IT'S OKAY.
ANY-WAY...
I'M SORRY FOR NOT NOTICING.
THANK YOU.
SURE!
OKAY THEN... I'LL GO GET US SOMETHING TO DRINK.
YOU WANT THE USUAL?
HUH? YEAH...

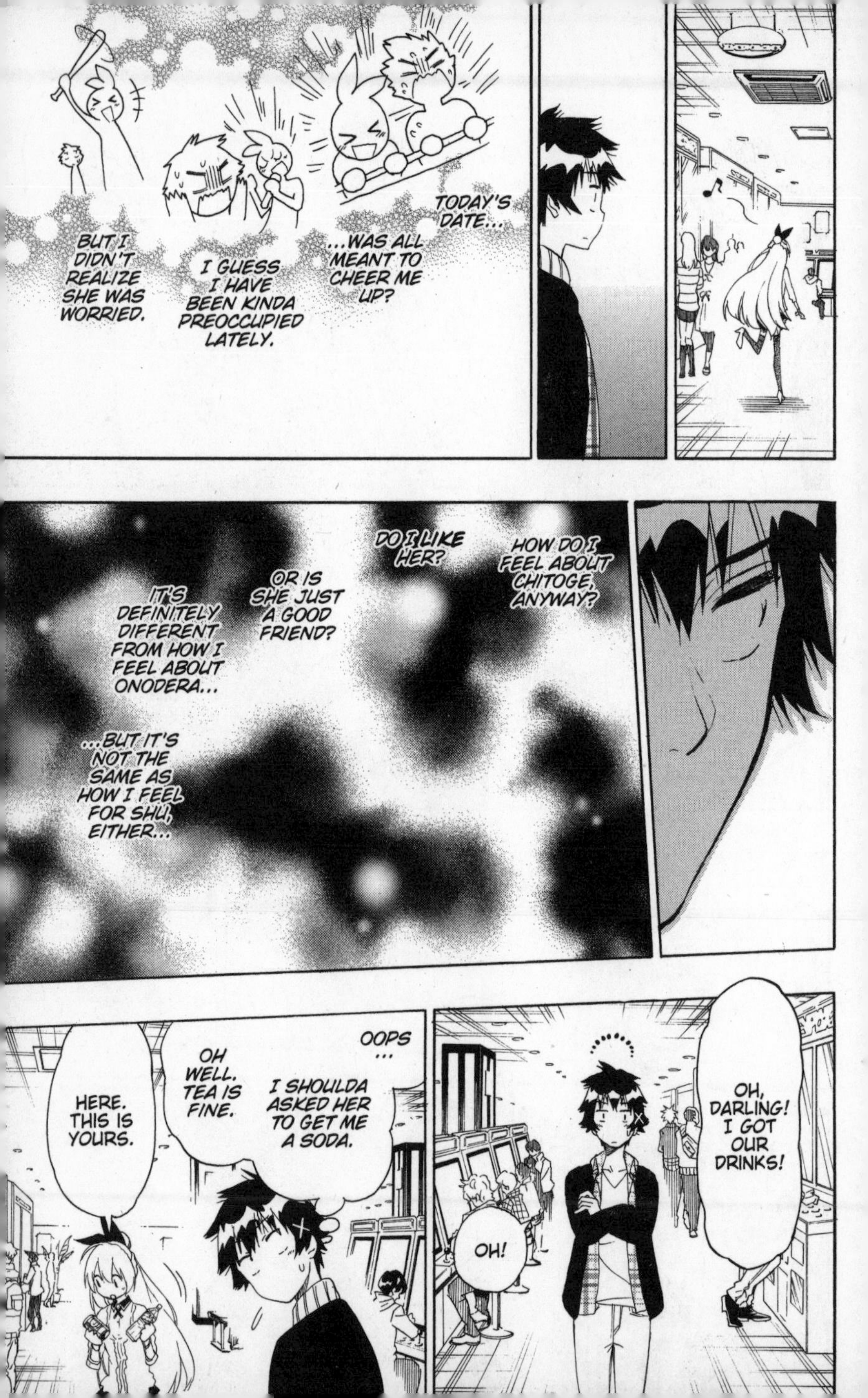
TODAY'S DATE...
...WAS ALL MEANT TO CHEER ME UP?
I GUESS I HAVE BEEN KINDA PREOCCUPIED LATELY.
BUT I DIDN'T REALIZE SHE WAS WORRIED.
HOW DO I FEEL ABOUT CHITOGE, ANYWAY?
DO I LIKE HER?
OR IS SHE JUST A GOOD FRIEND?
IT'S DEFINITELY DIFFERENT FROM HOW I FEEL ABOUT ONODERA...
...BUT IT'S NOT THE SAME AS HOW I FEEL FOR SHU, EITHER...
OH, DARLING! I GOT OUR DRINKS!
OH!
OOPS...
I SHOULDA ASKED HER TO GET ME A SODA.
OH WELL. TEA IS FINE.
HERE. THIS IS YOURS.

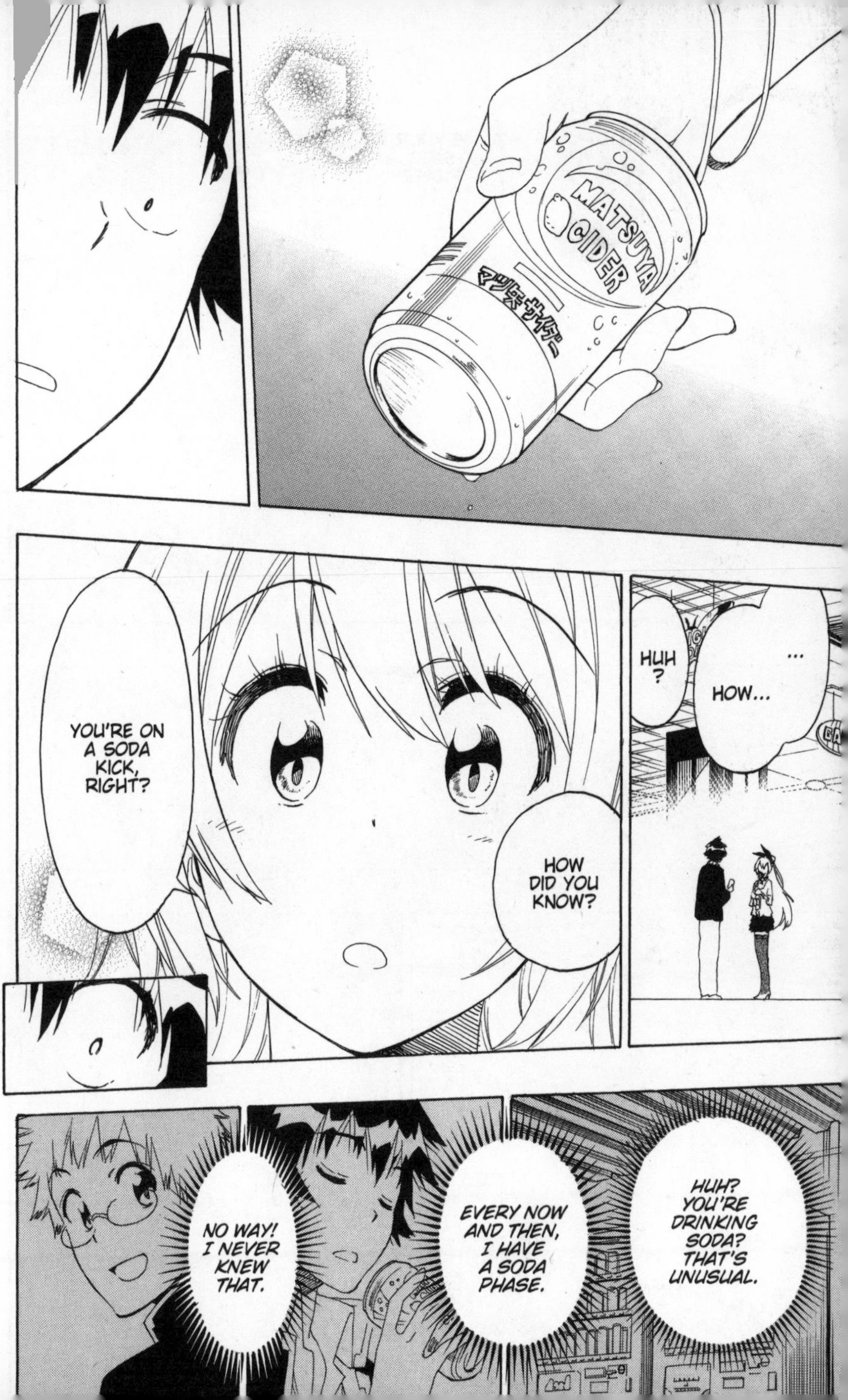
MATSUYA CIDER
... HOW...
HUH?
HOW DID YOU KNOW?
YOU'RE ON A SODA KICK, RIGHT?
HUH? YOU'RE DRINKING SODA? THAT'S UNUSUAL.
EVERY NOW AND THEN, I HAVE A SODA PHASE.
NO WAY! I NEVER KNEW THAT.

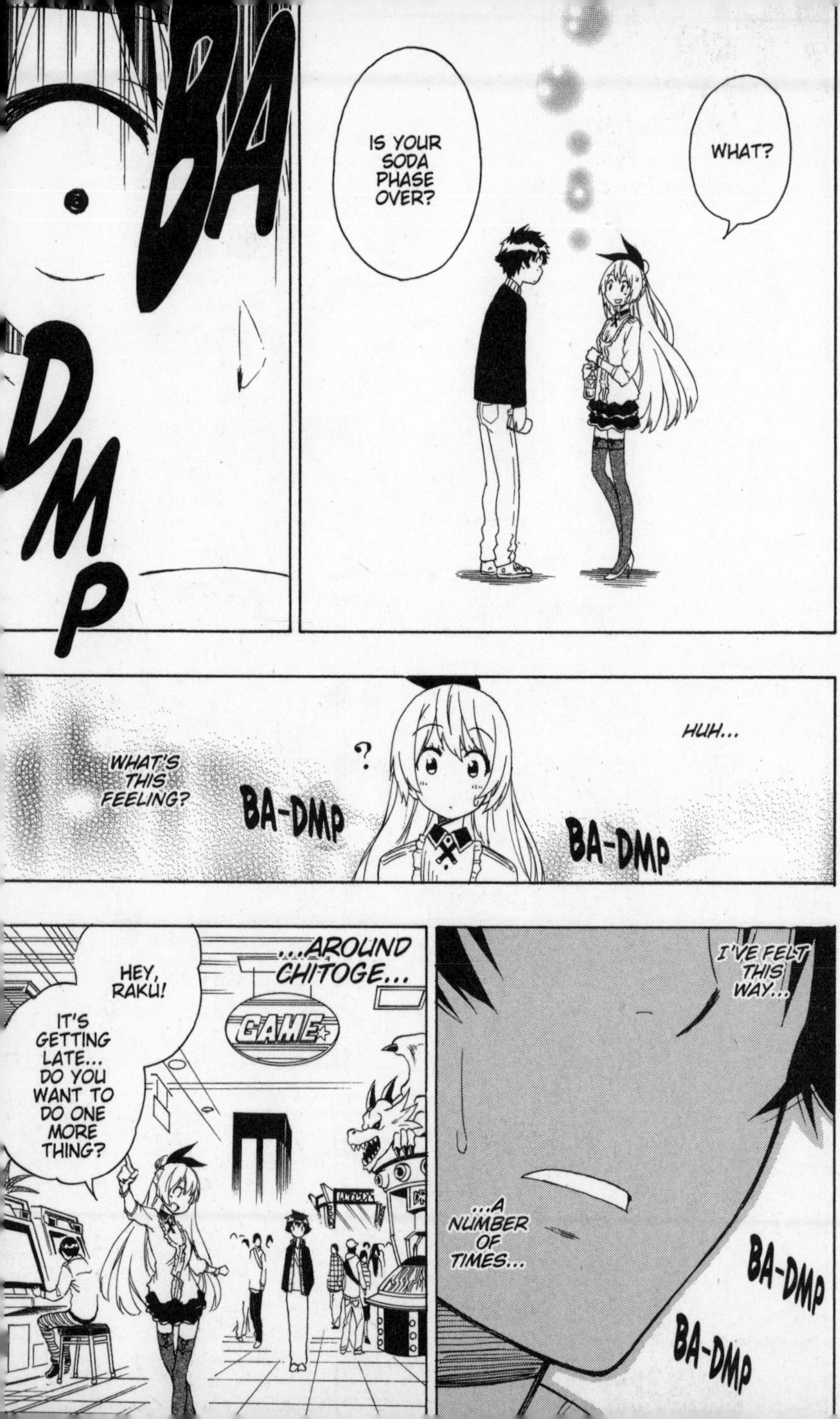
WHAT?
IS YOUR SODA PHASE OVER?
BA DMP
HUH...
BA-DMP
?
BA-DMP
WHAT'S THIS FEELING?
I'VE FELT THIS WAY...
...A NUMBER OF TIMES...
BA-DMP
BA-DMP
...AROUND CHITOGE...
HEY, RAKU!
IT'S GETTING LATE... DO YOU WANT TO DO ONE MORE THING?
GAME

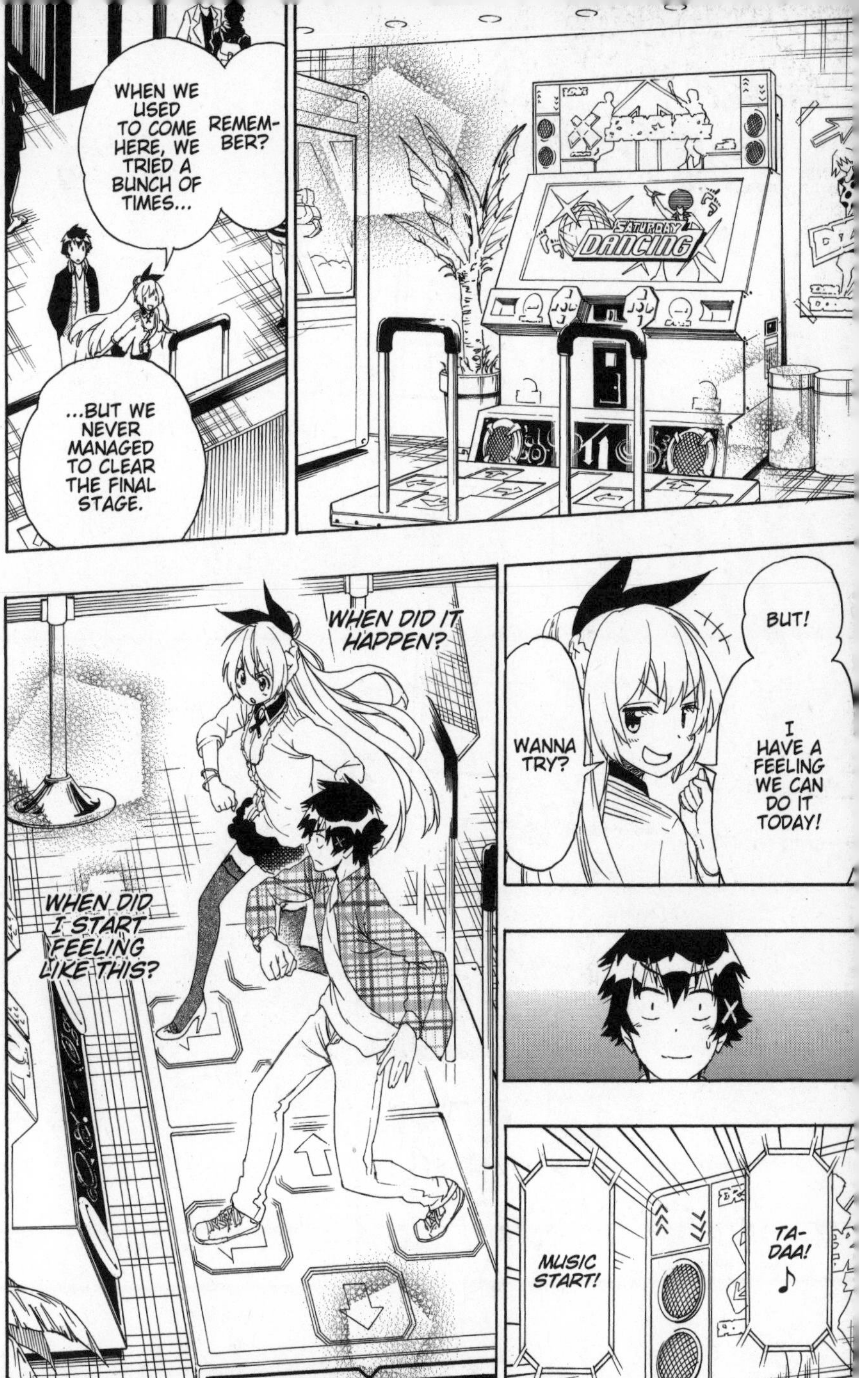
SATURDAY DANCING
REMEM-BER?
WHEN WE USED TO COME HERE, WE TRIED A BUNCH OF TIMES...
...BUT WE NEVER MANAGED TO CLEAR THE FINAL STAGE.
BUT!
I HAVE A FEELING WE CAN DO IT TODAY!
WANNA TRY?
TA-DAA! ♪
MUSIC START!
WHEN DID IT HAPPEN?
WHEN DID I START FEELING LIKE THIS?

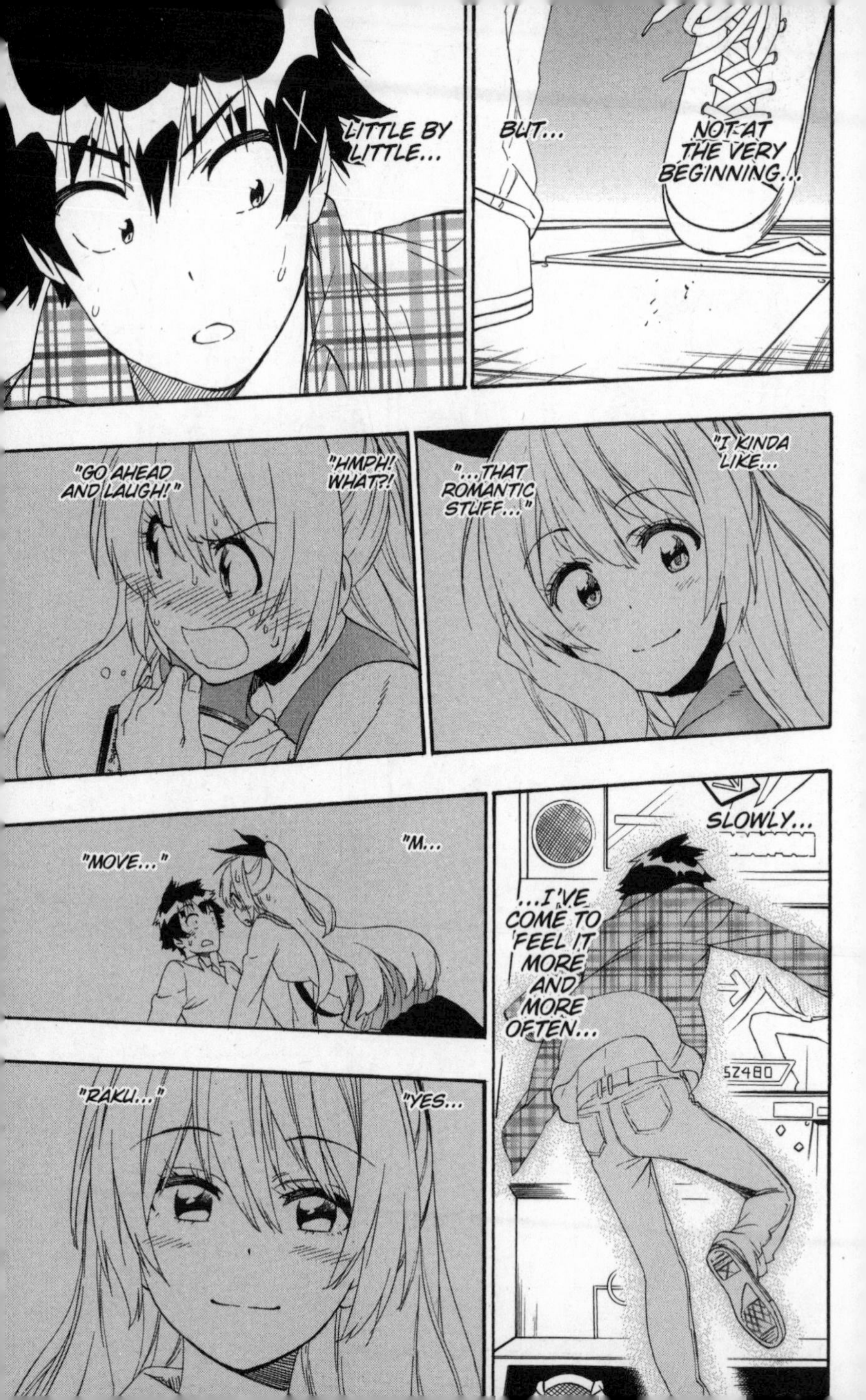
NOT AT THE VERY BEGINNING...
BUT...
LITTLE BY LITTLE...
"I KINDA LIKE...
"...THAT ROMANTIC STUFF..."
"HMPH! WHAT?!
"GO AHEAD AND LAUGH!"
SLOWLY...
...I'VE COME TO FEEL IT MORE AND MORE OFTEN...
SZ480
"M...
"MOVE..."
"YES...
"RAKU..."

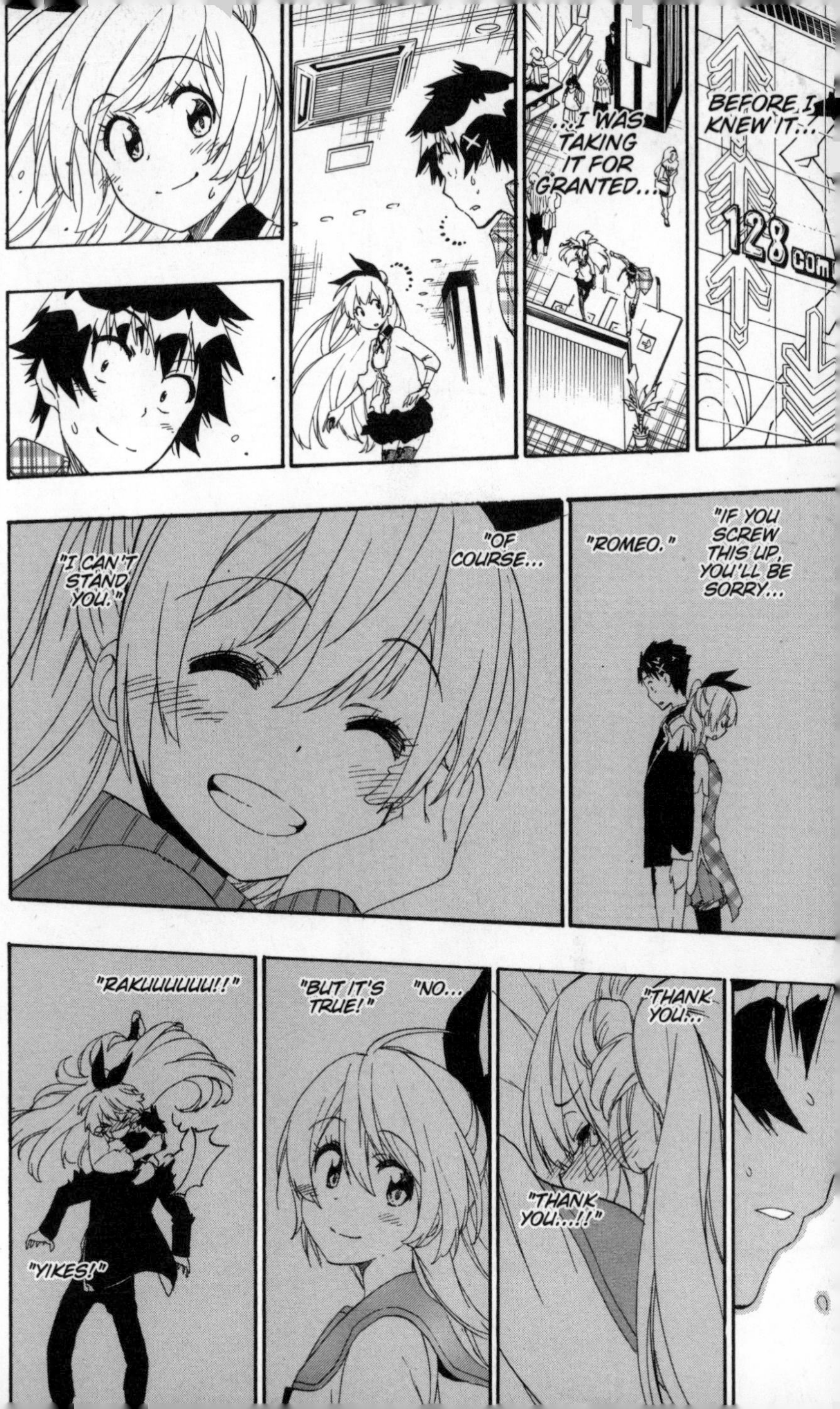
BEFORE I KNEW IT...
...I WAS TAKING IT FOR GRANTED...
"IF YOU SCREW THIS UP, YOU'LL BE SORRY...
"ROMEO."
"OF COURSE...
"I CAN'T STAND YOU."
"THANK YOU...
"THANK YOU...!!"
"NO...
"BUT IT'S TRUE!"
"RAKUUUUUU!!"
"YIKES!"

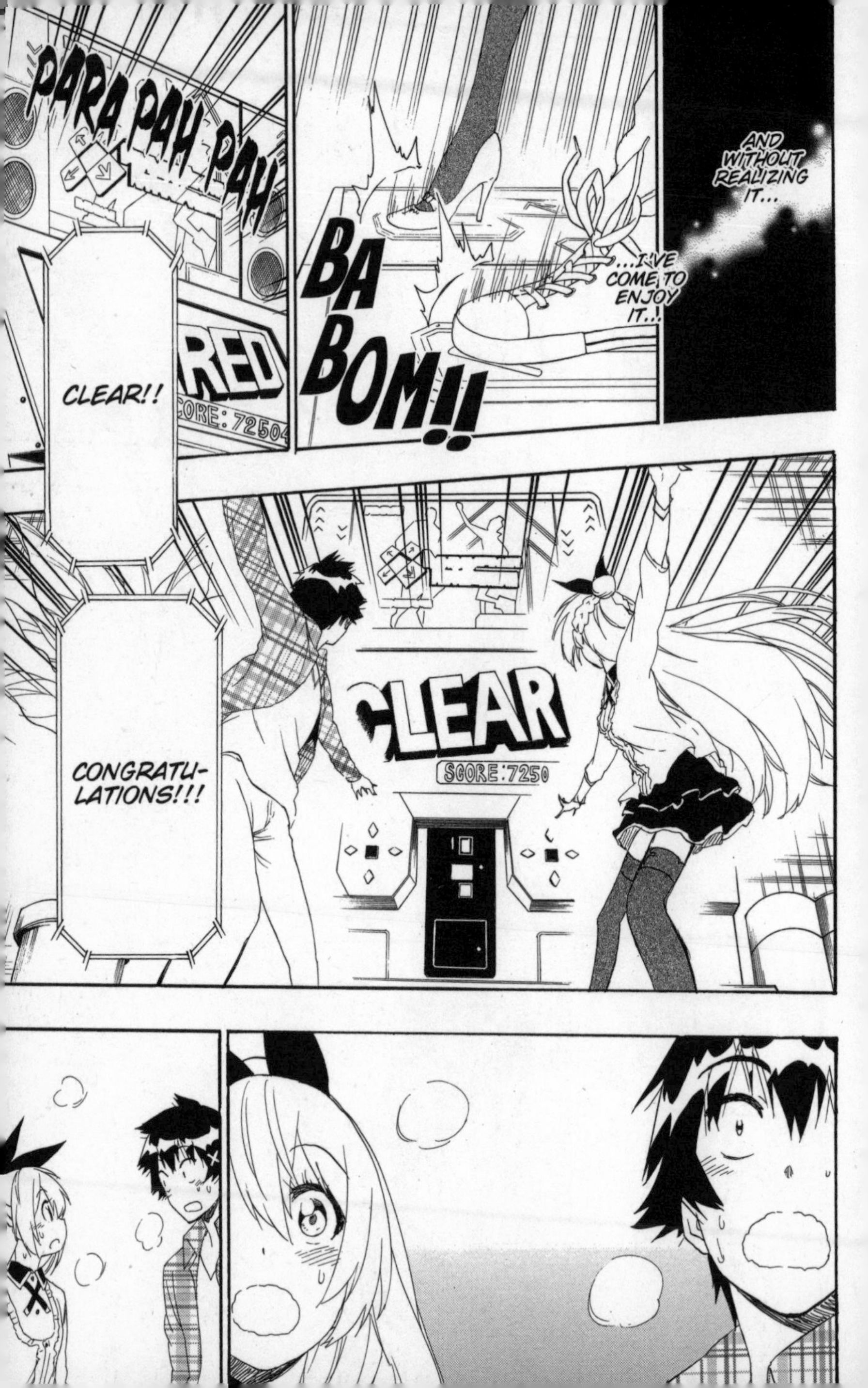
AND WITHOUT REALIZING IT...
...I'VE COME TO ENJOY IT...
BA BOM!!
PARA PAH PAH
RED
SCORE:72504
CLEAR!!
CONGRATU-LATIONS!!!
CLEAR
SCORE:7250

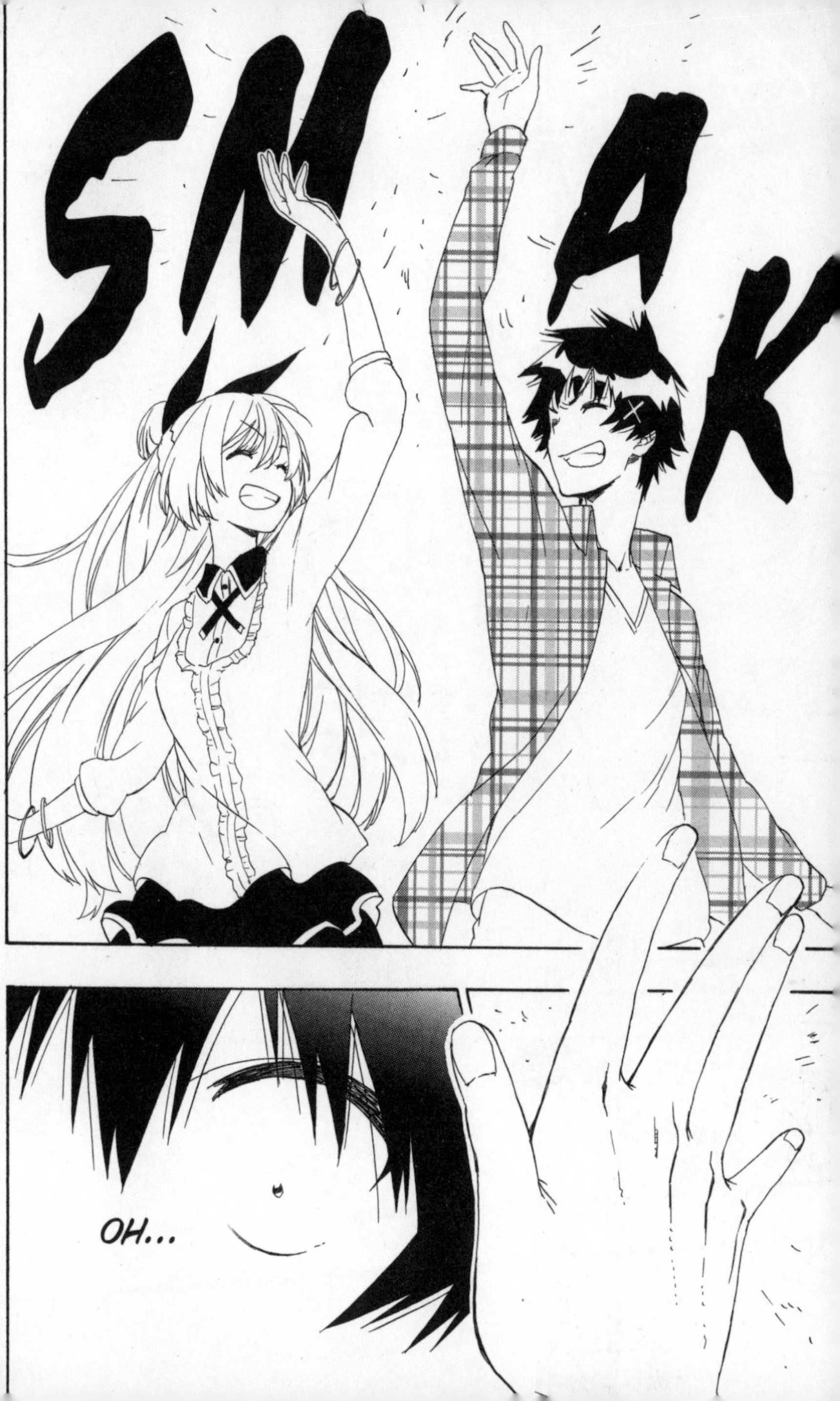
SMAK
OH...

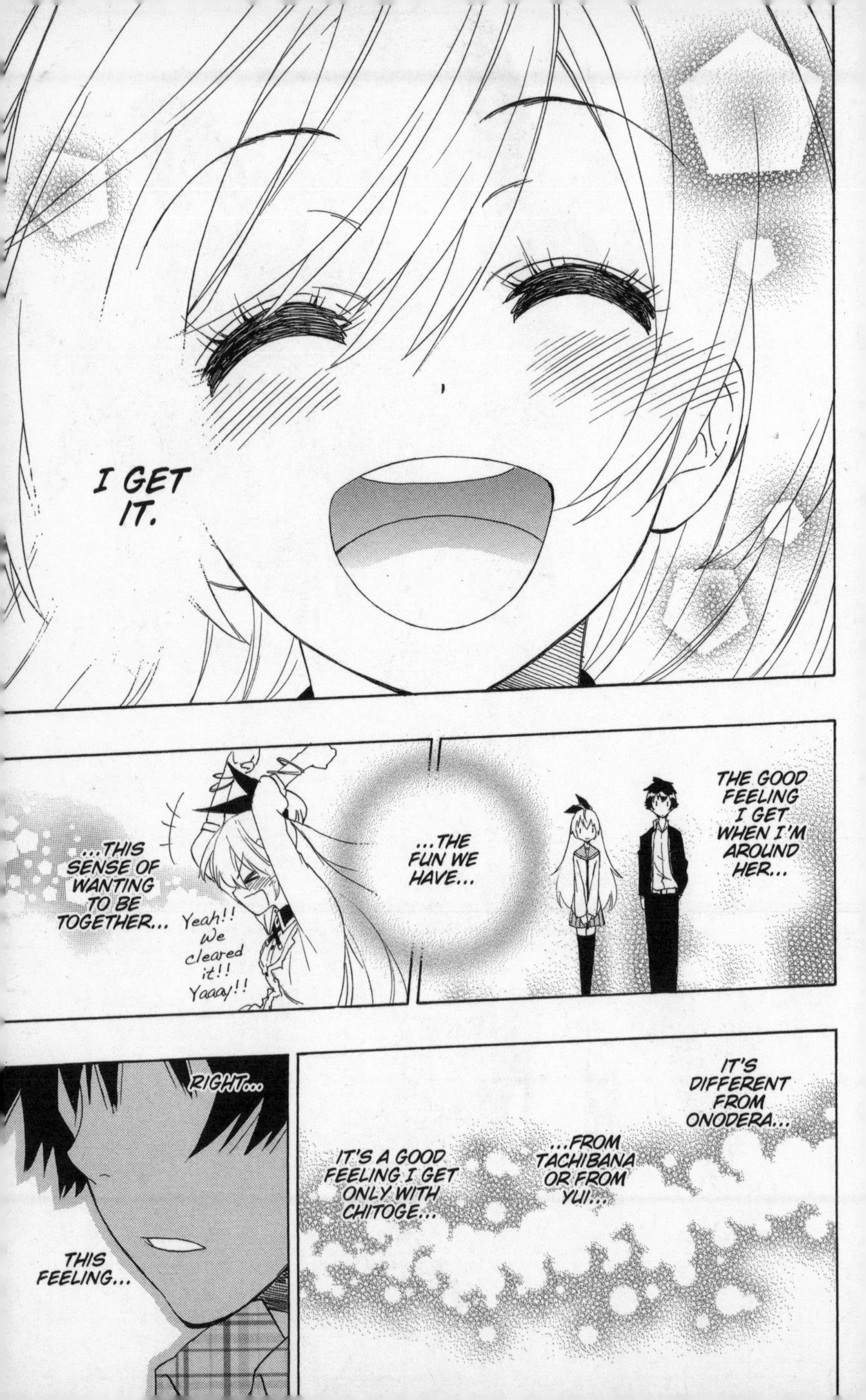
I GET IT.
THE GOOD FEELING I GET WHEN I'M AROUND HER...
...THE FUN WE HAVE...
...THIS SENSE OF WANTING TO BE TOGETHER...
Yeah!! We cleared it!! Yaaay!!
IT'S DIFFERENT FROM ONODERA...
...FROM TACHIBANA OR FROM YUI...
IT'S A GOOD FEELING I GET ONLY WITH CHITOGE...
RIGHT...
THIS FEELING...

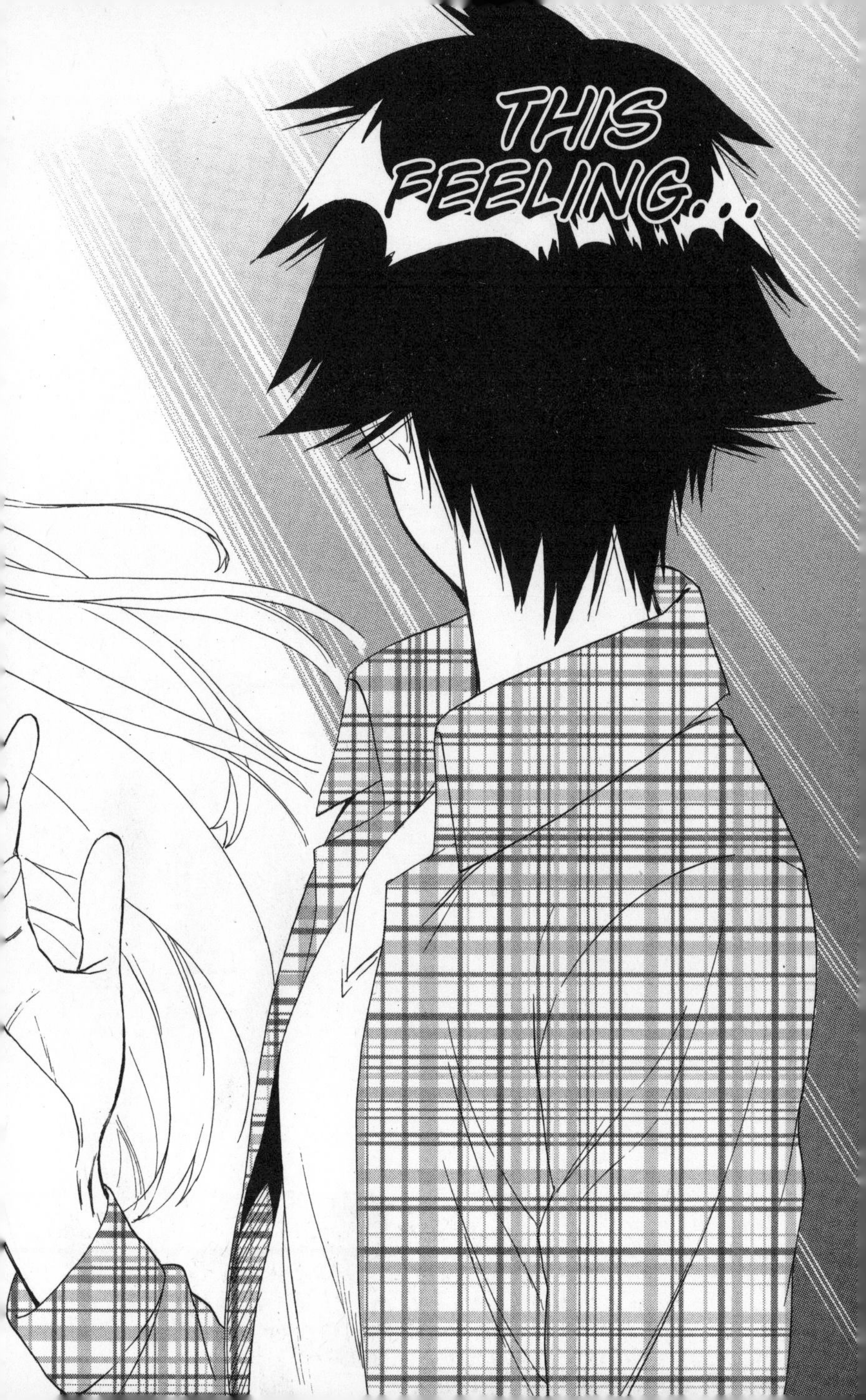
THIS FEELING...

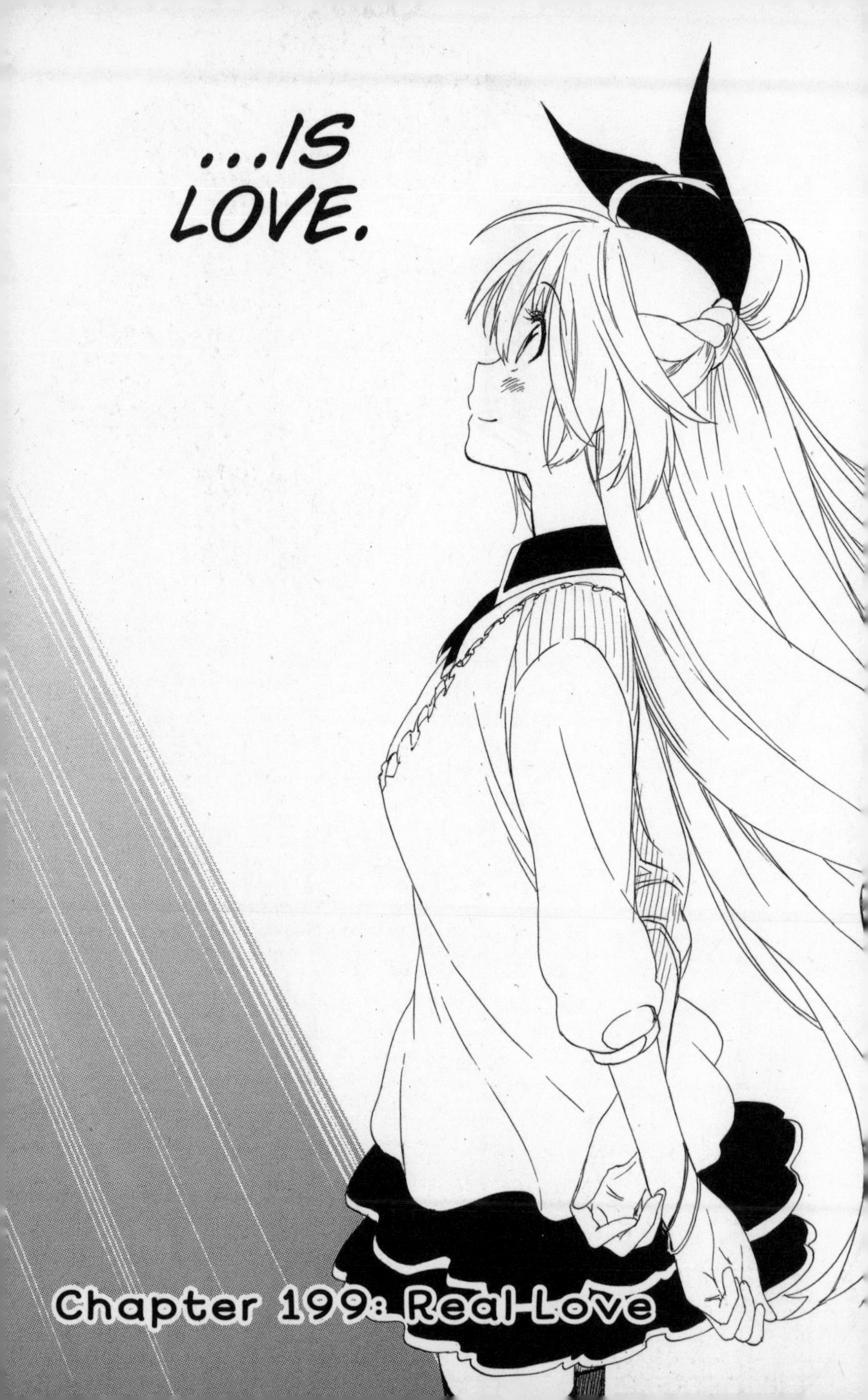
...IS LOVE.
Chapter 199: Real Love

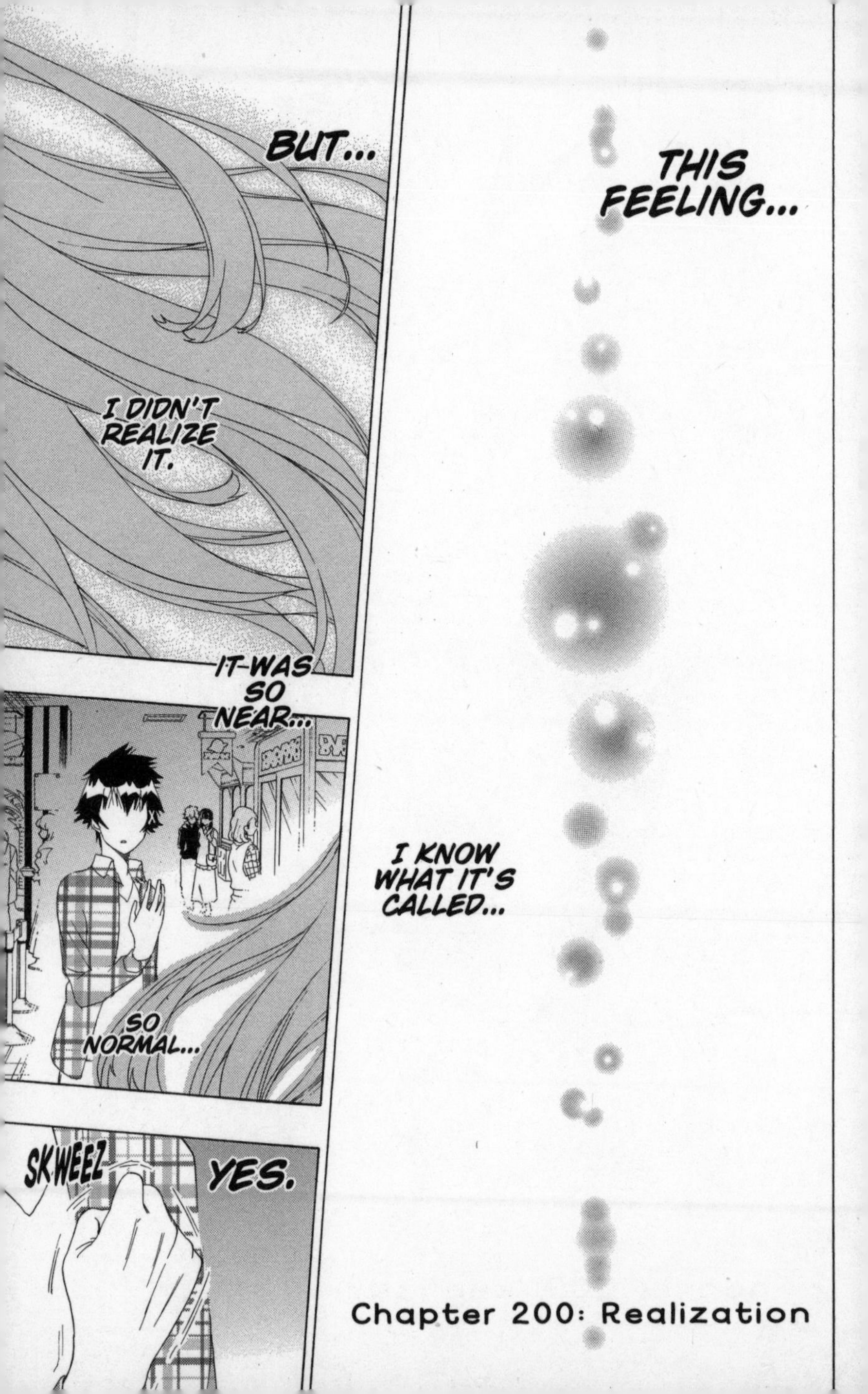
THIS FEELING...
I KNOW WHAT IT'S CALLED...
BUT...
I DIDN'T REALIZE IT.
IT WAS SO NEAR...
SO NORMAL...
YES.
SKWEEZ

Chapter 200: Realization

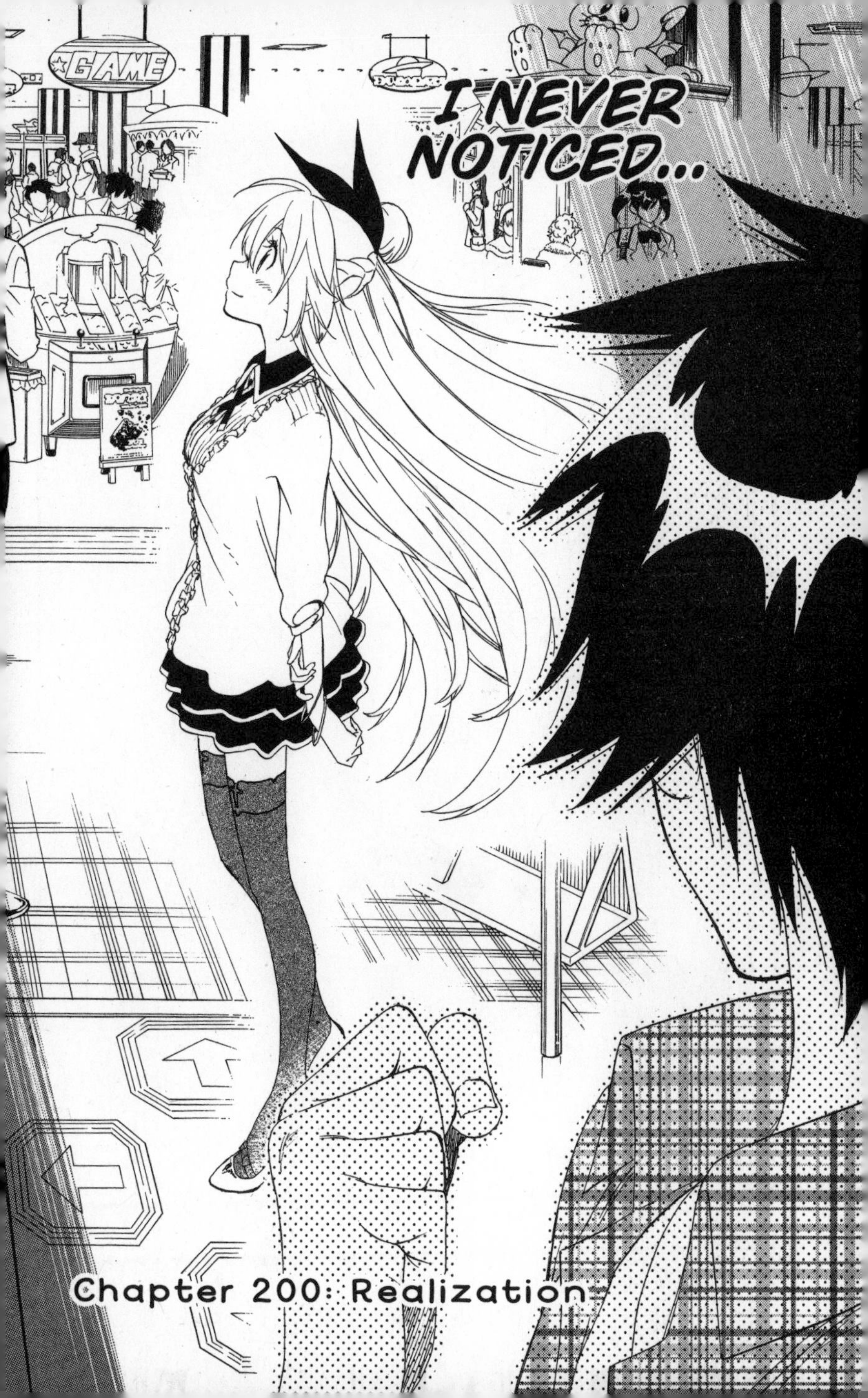
I NEVER NOTICED...
Chapter 200: Realization
GAME

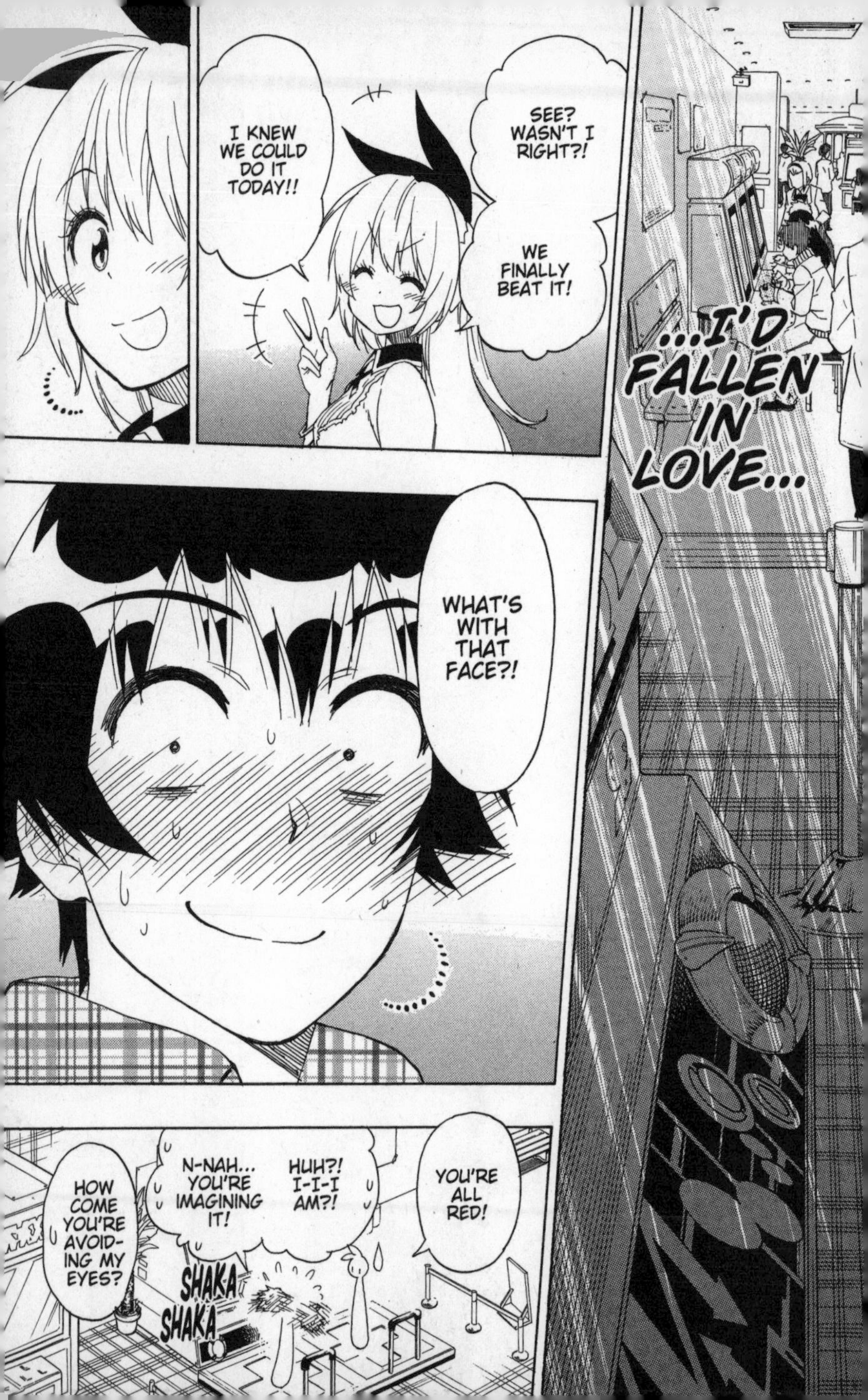
...I'D FALLEN IN LOVE...
SEE? WASN'T I RIGHT?!
WE FINALLY BEAT IT!
I KNEW WE COULD DO IT TODAY!!
WHAT'S WITH THAT FACE?!
YOU'RE ALL RED!
HUH?! I-I-I AM?!
N-NAH... YOU'RE IMAGINING IT!
HOW COME YOU'RE AVOID-ING MY EYES?
SHAKA SHAKA

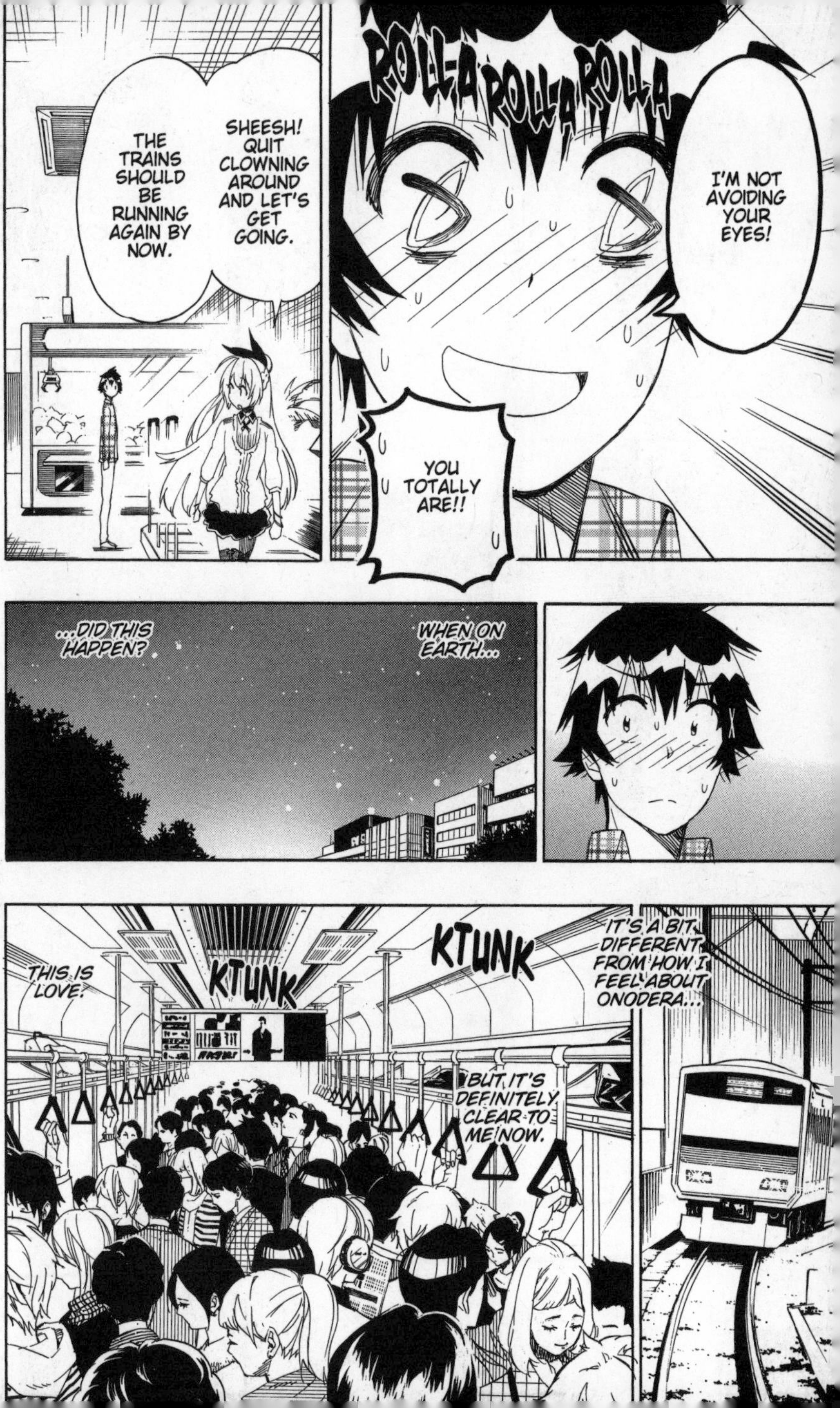
ROLL-A ROLL-A ROLL-A
I'M NOT AVOIDING YOUR EYES!
YOU TOTALLY ARE!!
SHEESH! QUIT CLOWNING AROUND AND LET'S GET GOING.
THE TRAINS SHOULD BE RUNNING AGAIN BY NOW.
WHEN ON EARTH...
...DID THIS HAPPEN?
IT'S A BIT DIFFERENT FROM HOW I FEEL ABOUT ONODERA...
KTUNK
BUT IT'S DEFINITELY CLEAR TO ME NOW.
KTUNK
THIS IS LOVE.

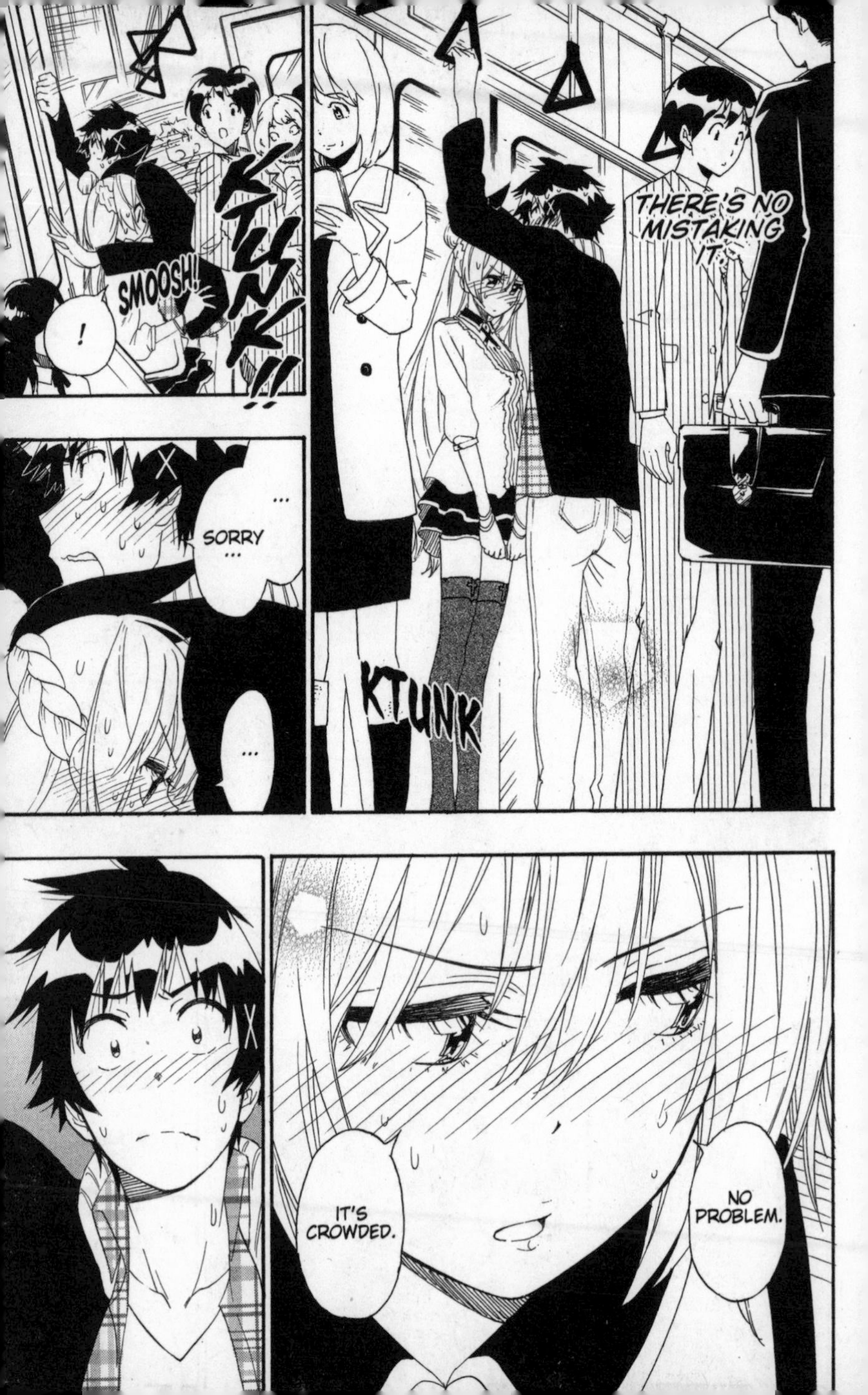
THERE'S NO MISTAKING IT...
KTUNK
KTUNK!!
SMOOSH!
!
... SORRY ...
...
NO PROBLEM.
IT'S CROWDED.

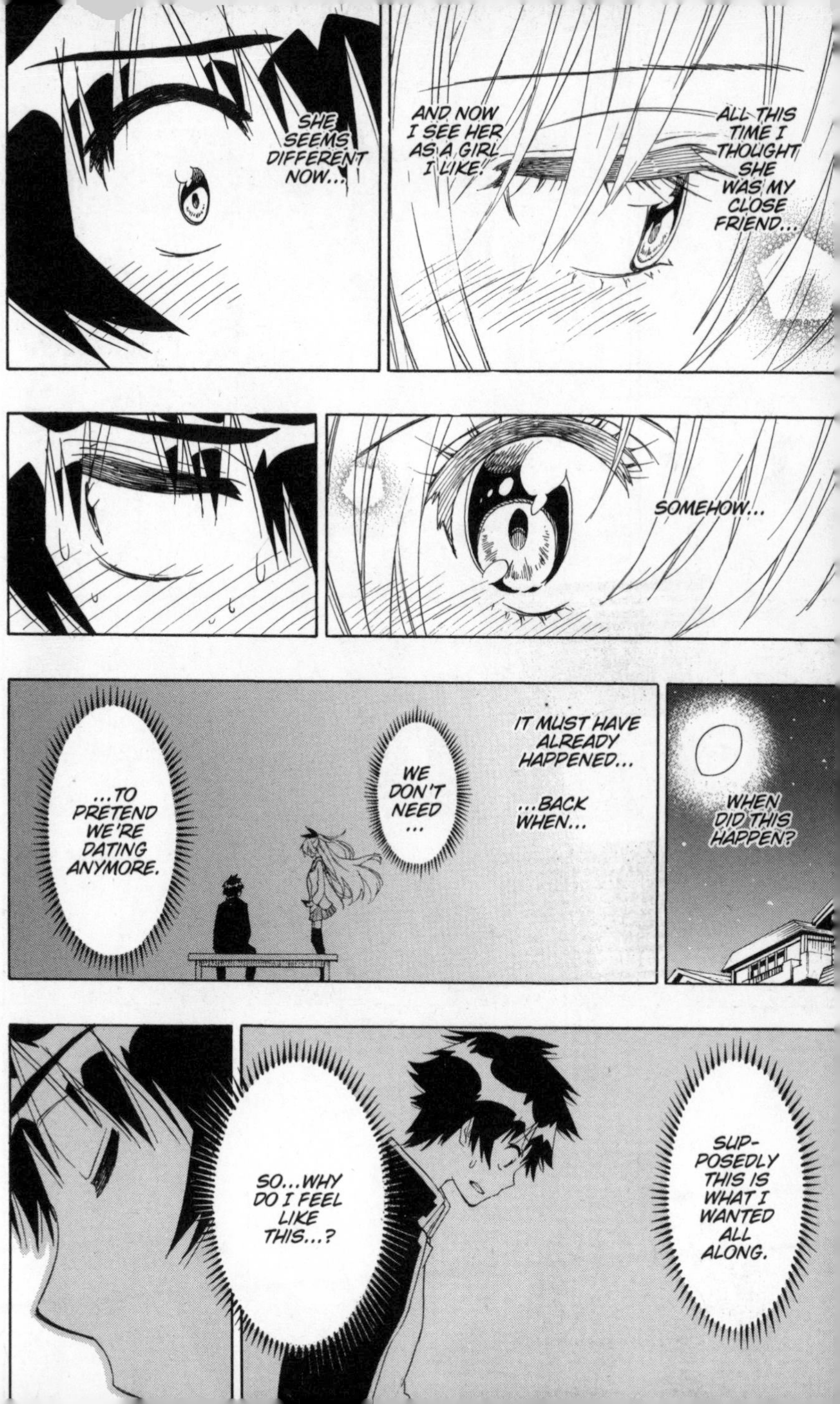
ALL THIS TIME I THOUGHT SHE WAS MY CLOSE FRIEND...
AND NOW I SEE HER AS A GIRL I LIKE.
SHE SEEMS DIFFERENT NOW...
SOMEHOW...
WHEN DID THIS HAPPEN?
IT MUST HAVE ALREADY HAPPENED...
...BACK WHEN...
WE DON'T NEED...
...TO PRETEND WE'RE DATING ANYMORE.
SUP-POSEDLY THIS IS WHAT I WANTED ALL ALONG.
SO...WHY DO I FEEL LIKE THIS...?

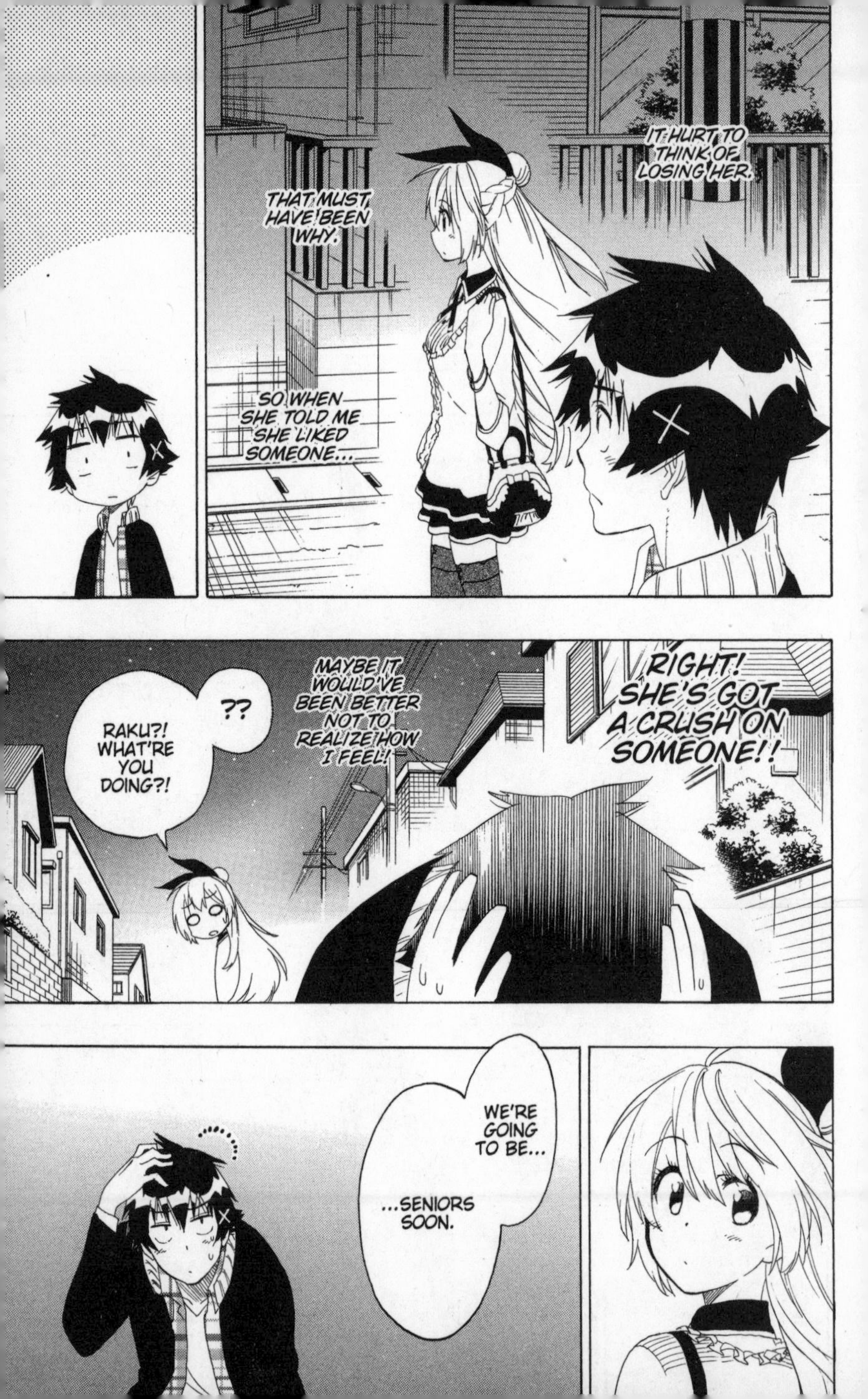
IT HURT TO THINK OF LOSING HER.
THAT MUST HAVE BEEN WHY.
SO WHEN SHE TOLD ME SHE LIKED SOMEONE...
RIGHT! SHE'S GOT A CRUSH ON SOMEONE!!
MAYBE IT WOULD'VE BEEN BETTER NOT TO REALIZE HOW I FEEL!
??
RAKU?! WHAT'RE YOU DOING?!
WE'RE GOING TO BE...
...SENIORS SOON.
....

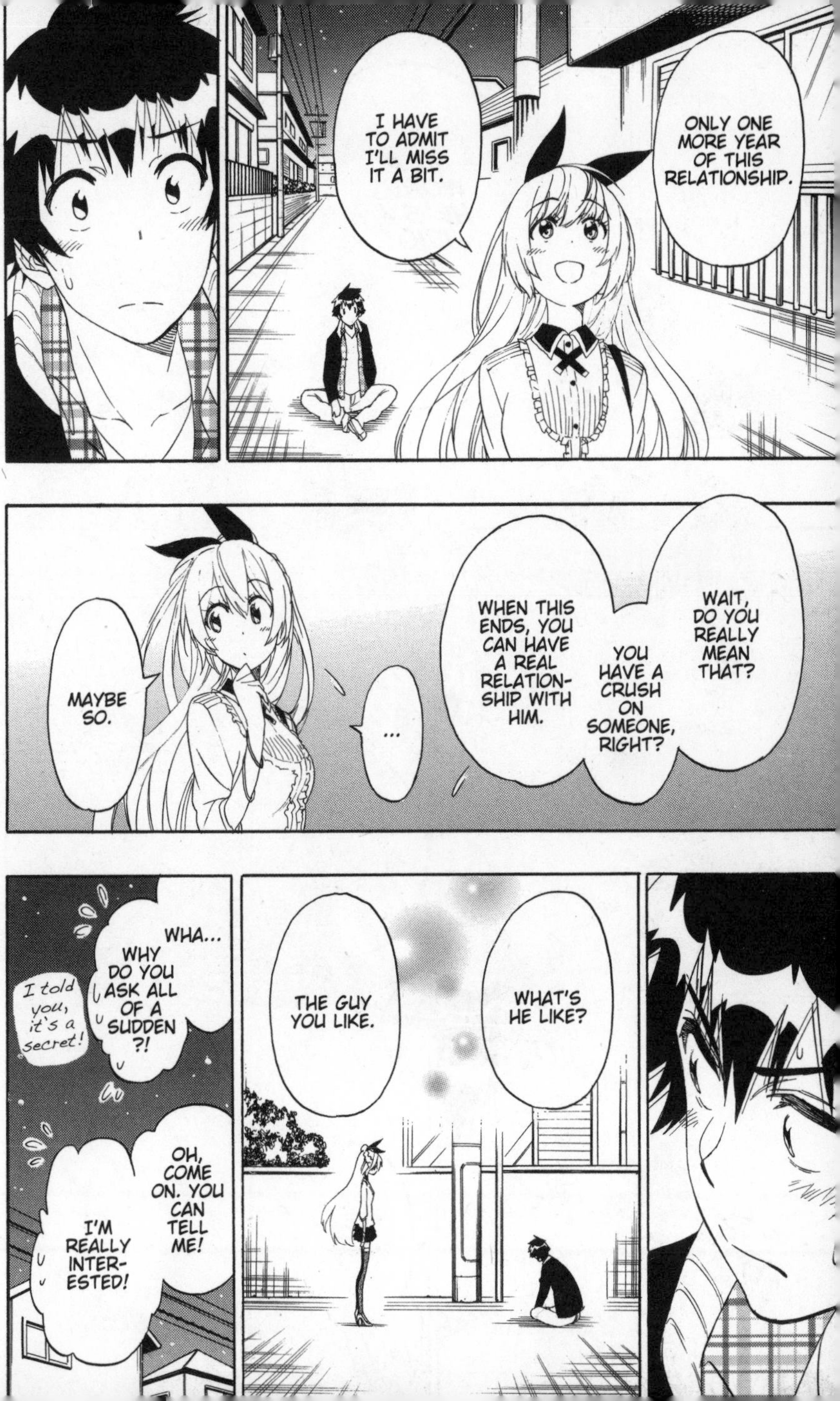
ONLY ONE MORE YEAR OF THIS RELATIONSHIP.
I HAVE TO ADMIT I'LL MISS IT A BIT.
WAIT, DO YOU REALLY MEAN THAT?
YOU HAVE A CRUSH ON SOMEONE, RIGHT?
WHEN THIS ENDS, YOU CAN HAVE A REAL RELATION-SHIP WITH HIM.
...
MAYBE SO.
WHAT'S HE LIKE?
THE GUY YOU LIKE.
WHA... WHY DO YOU ASK ALL OF A SUDDEN?!
I told you, it's a secret!
OH, COME ON. YOU CAN TELL ME!
I'M REALLY INTER-ESTED!

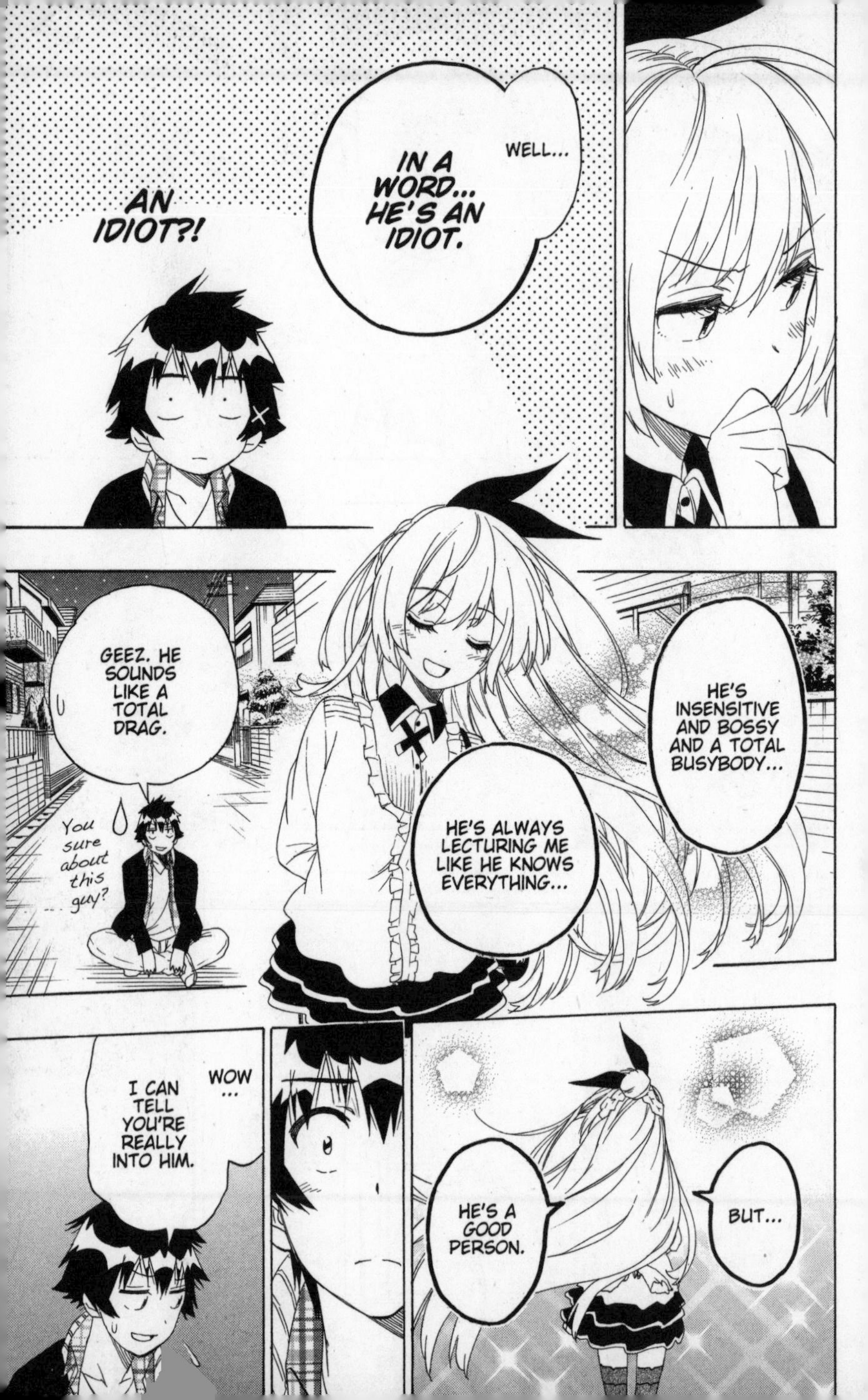
WELL...
IN A WORD... HE'S AN IDIOT.
AN IDIOT?!
HE'S INSENSITIVE AND BOSSY AND A TOTAL BUSYBODY...
HE'S ALWAYS LECTURING ME LIKE HE KNOWS EVERYTHING...
GEEZ. HE SOUNDS LIKE A TOTAL DRAG.
You sure about this guy?
BUT...
HE'S A GOOD PERSON.
WOW...
I CAN TELL YOU'RE REALLY INTO HIM.

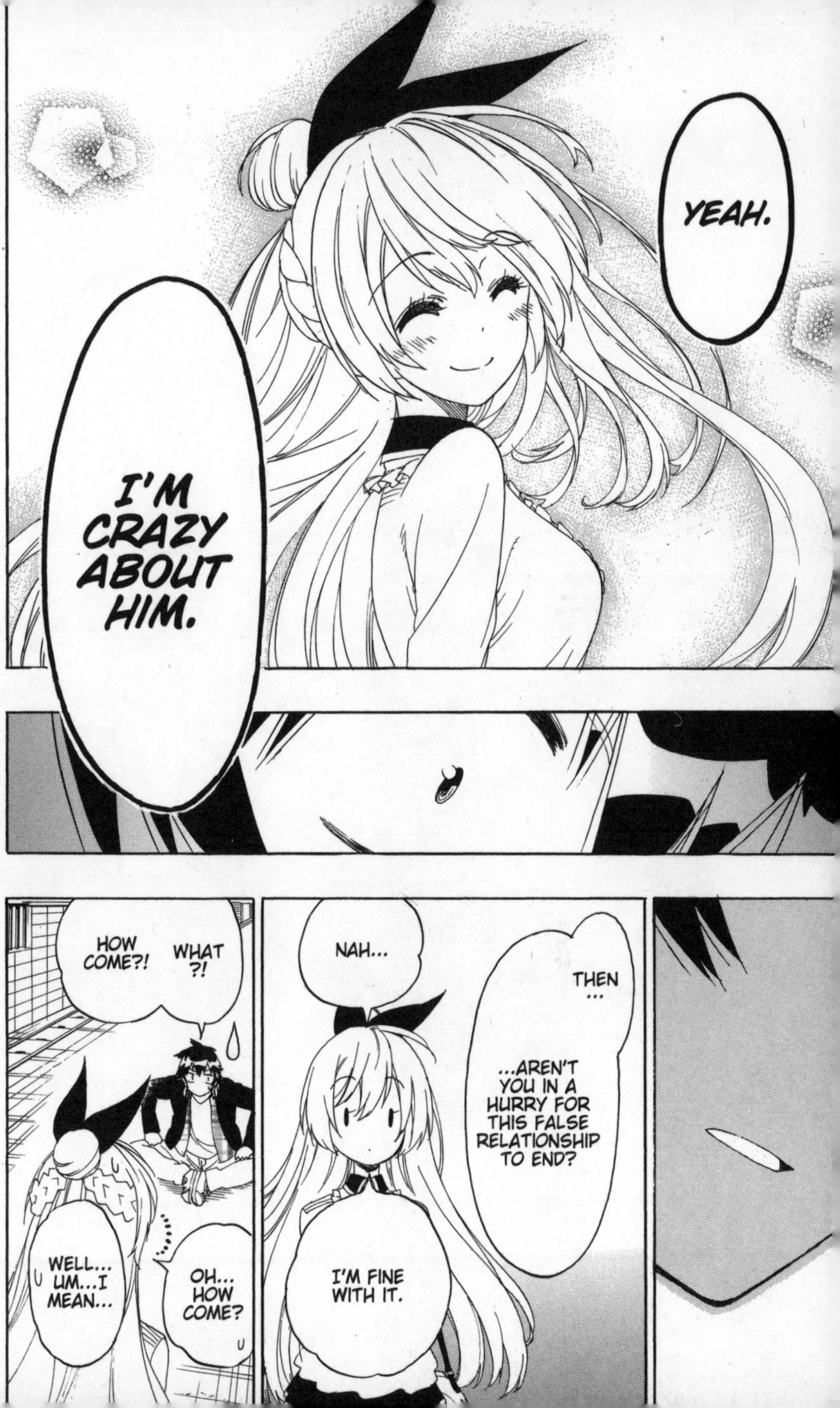
YEAH.
I'M CRAZY ABOUT HIM.
THEN...
...AREN'T YOU IN A HURRY FOR THIS FALSE RELATIONSHIP TO END?
NAH...
I'M FINE WITH IT.
WHAT?!
HOW COME?!
OH... HOW COME?
WELL... UM...I MEAN...

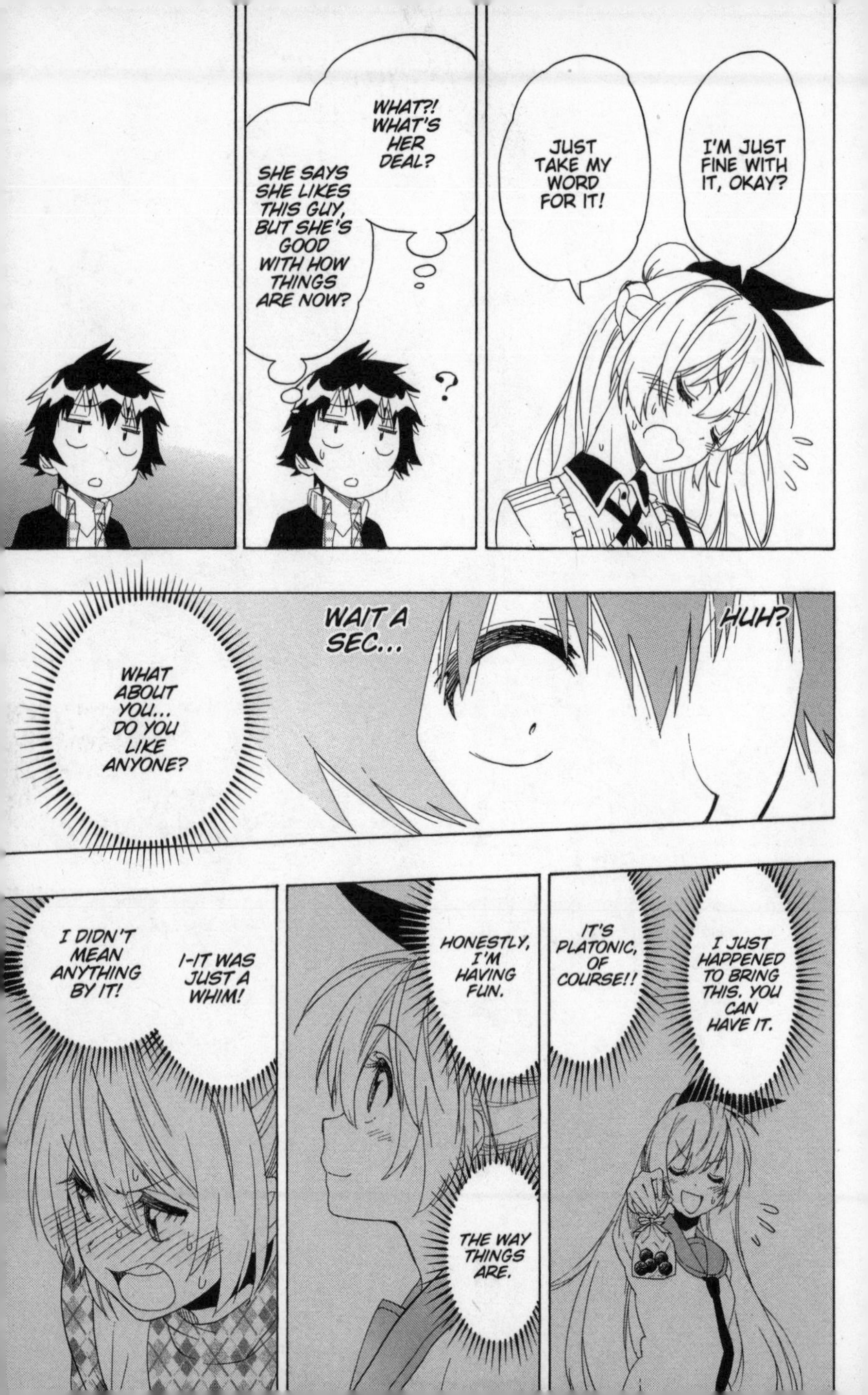
I'M JUST FINE WITH IT, OKAY?
JUST TAKE MY WORD FOR IT!
WHAT?! WHAT'S HER DEAL?
SHE SAYS SHE LIKES THIS GUY, BUT SHE'S GOOD WITH HOW THINGS ARE NOW?
?
HUH?
WAIT A SEC...
WHAT ABOUT YOU... DO YOU LIKE ANYONE?
I JUST HAPPENED TO BRING THIS. YOU CAN HAVE IT.
IT'S PLATONIC, OF COURSE!!
HONESTLY, I'M HAVING FUN.
THE WAY THINGS ARE.
I-IT WAS JUST A WHIM!
I DIDN'T MEAN ANYTHING BY IT!

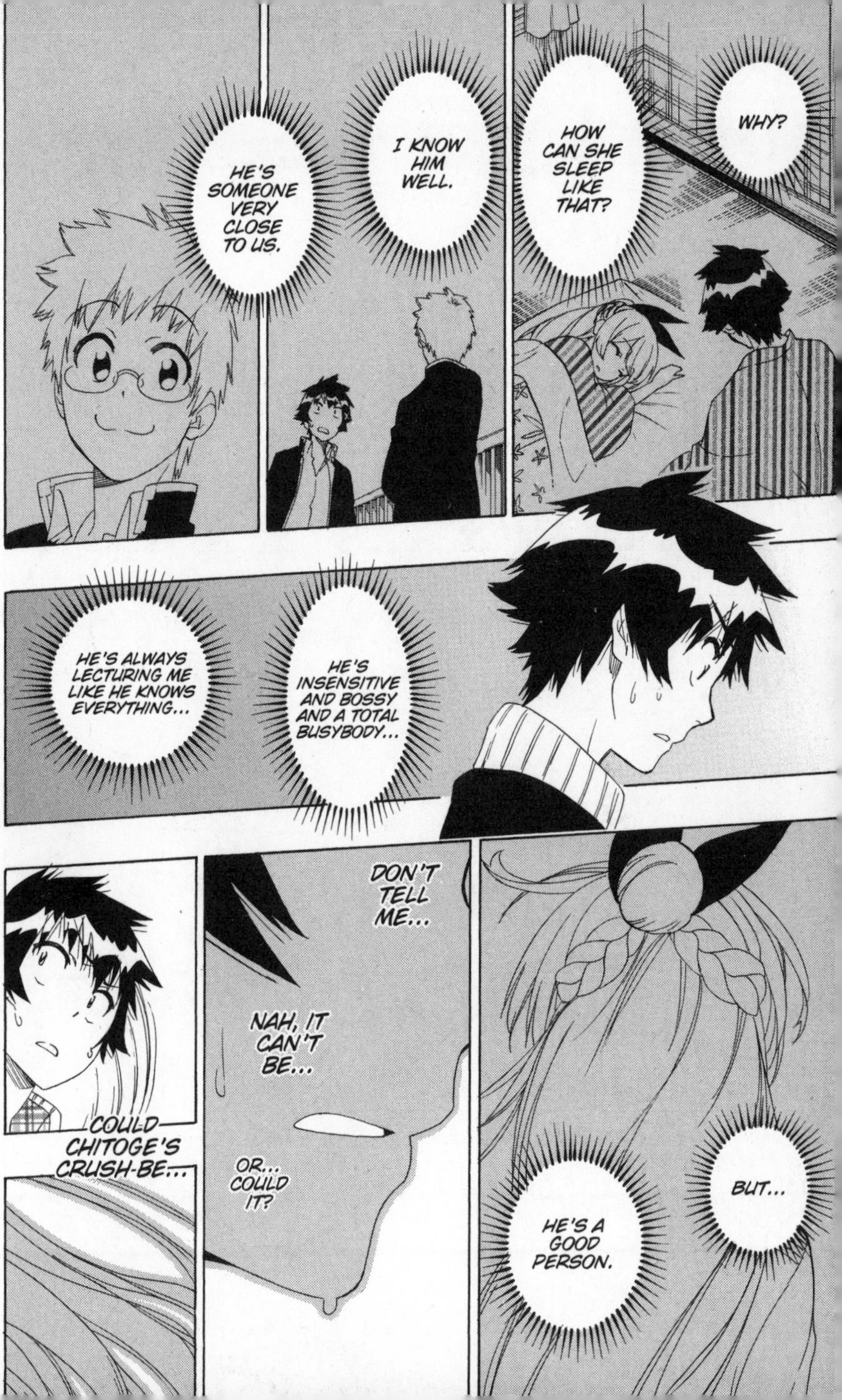
WHY?
HOW CAN SHE SLEEP LIKE THAT?
I KNOW HIM WELL.
HE'S SOMEONE VERY CLOSE TO US.
HE'S INSENSITIVE AND BOSSY AND A TOTAL BUSYBODY...
HE'S ALWAYS LECTURING ME LIKE HE KNOWS EVERYTHING...
BUT...
HE'S A GOOD PERSON.
DON'T TELL ME...
NAH, IT CAN'T BE...
OR... COULD IT?
COULD CHITOGE'S CRUSH BE...

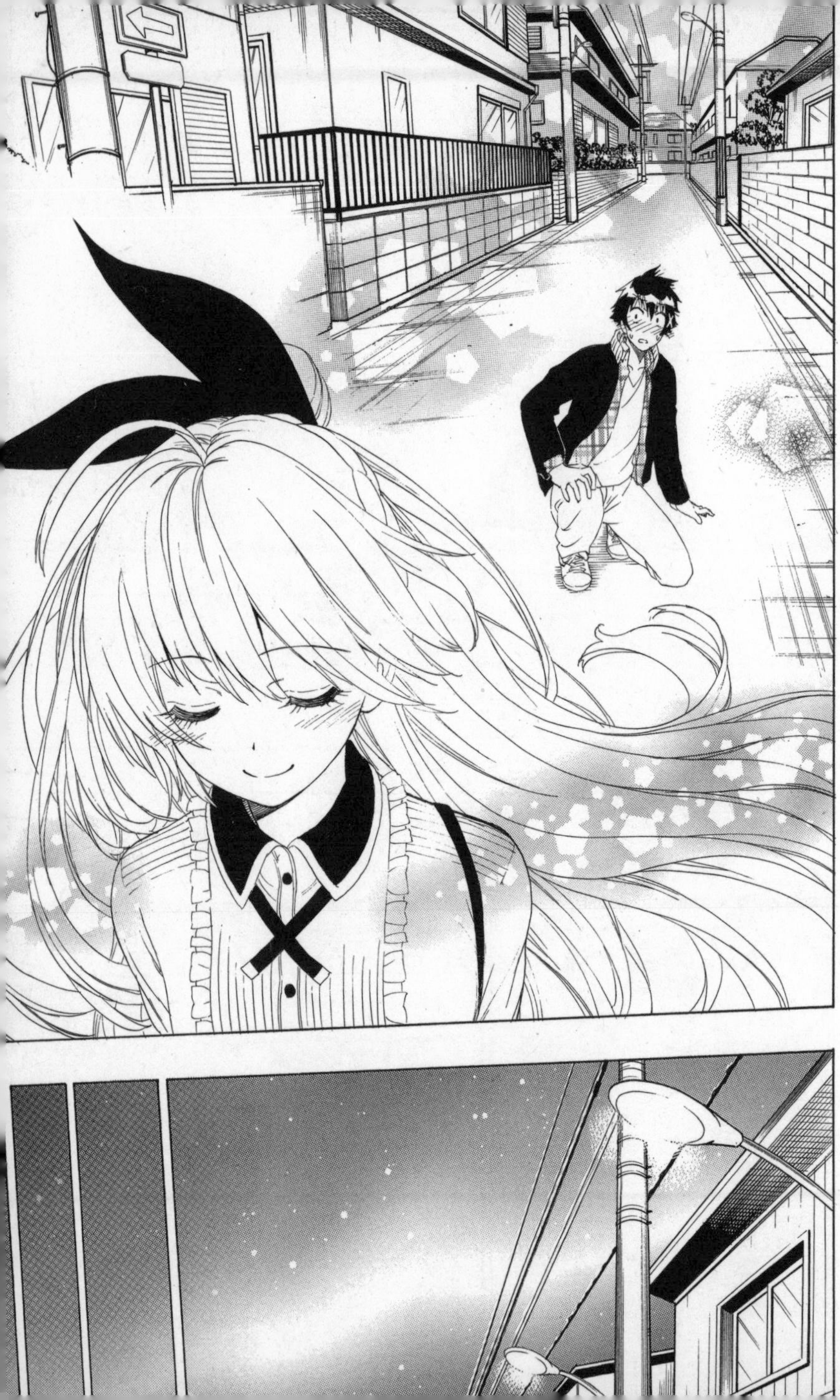

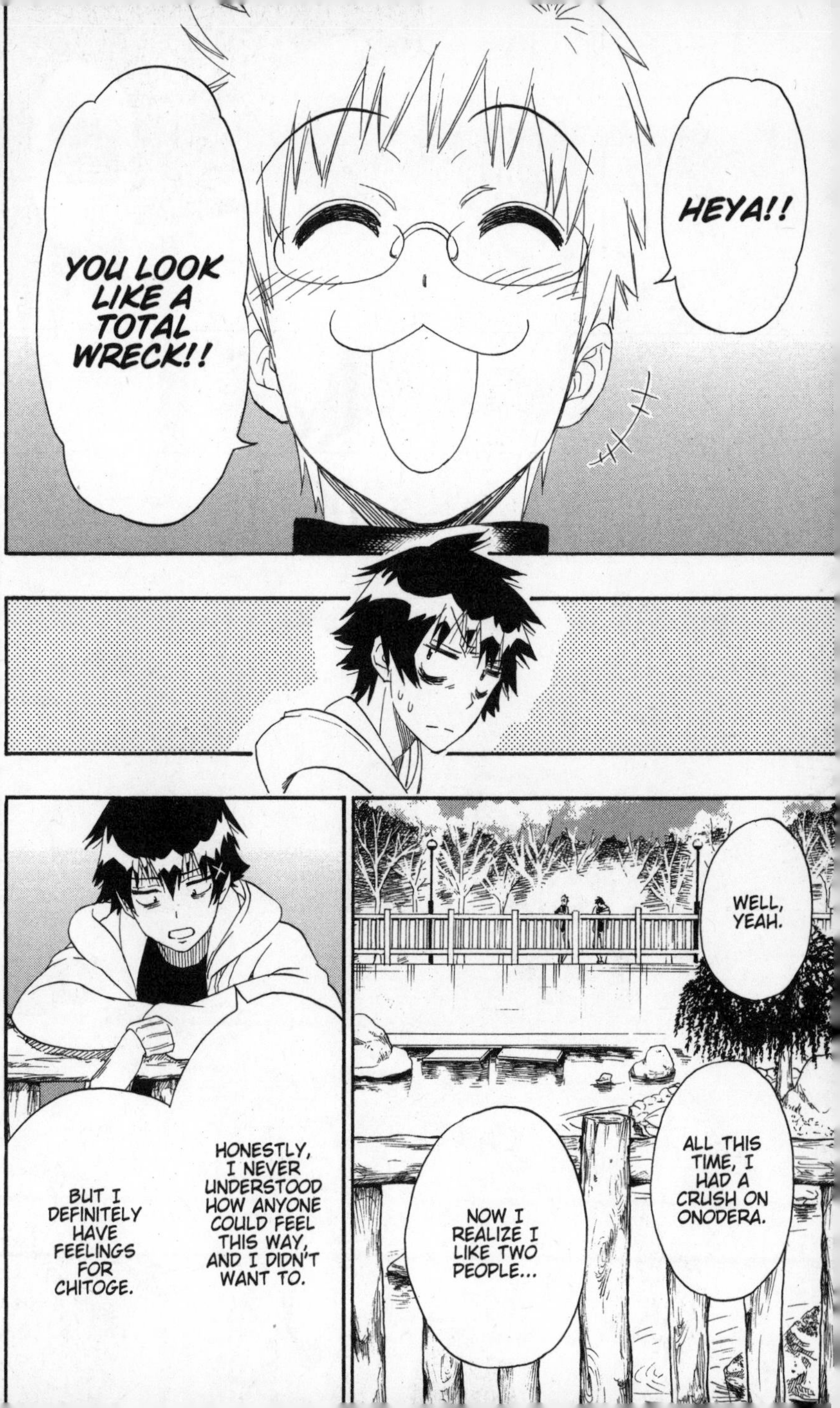
HEYA!!
YOU LOOK LIKE A TOTAL WRECK!!
WELL, YEAH.
ALL THIS TIME, I HAD A CRUSH ON ONODERA.
NOW I REALIZE I LIKE TWO PEOPLE...
HONESTLY, I NEVER UNDERSTOOD HOW ANYONE COULD FEEL THIS WAY, AND I DIDN'T WANT TO.
BUT I DEFINITELY HAVE FEELINGS FOR CHITOGE.

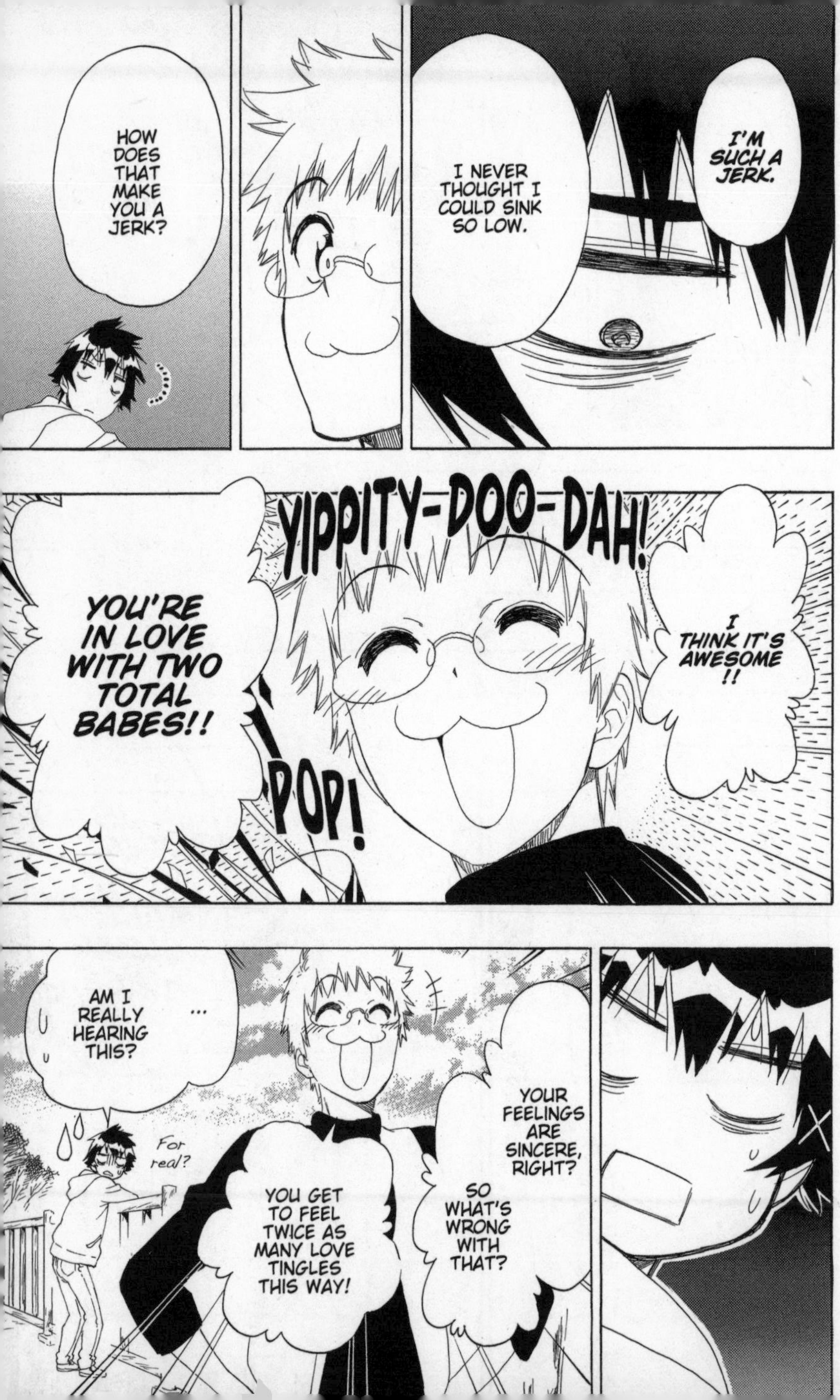

I'M SUCH A JERK.
I NEVER THOUGHT I COULD SINK SO LOW.
HOW DOES THAT MAKE YOU A JERK?
YIPPITY-DOO-DAH!
I THINK IT'S AWESOME!!
YOU'RE IN LOVE WITH TWO TOTAL BABES!!
POP!
YOUR FEELINGS ARE SINCERE, RIGHT?
SO WHAT'S WRONG WITH THAT?
YOU GET TO FEEL TWICE AS MANY LOVE TINGLES THIS WAY!
...
AM I REALLY HEARING THIS?
For real?

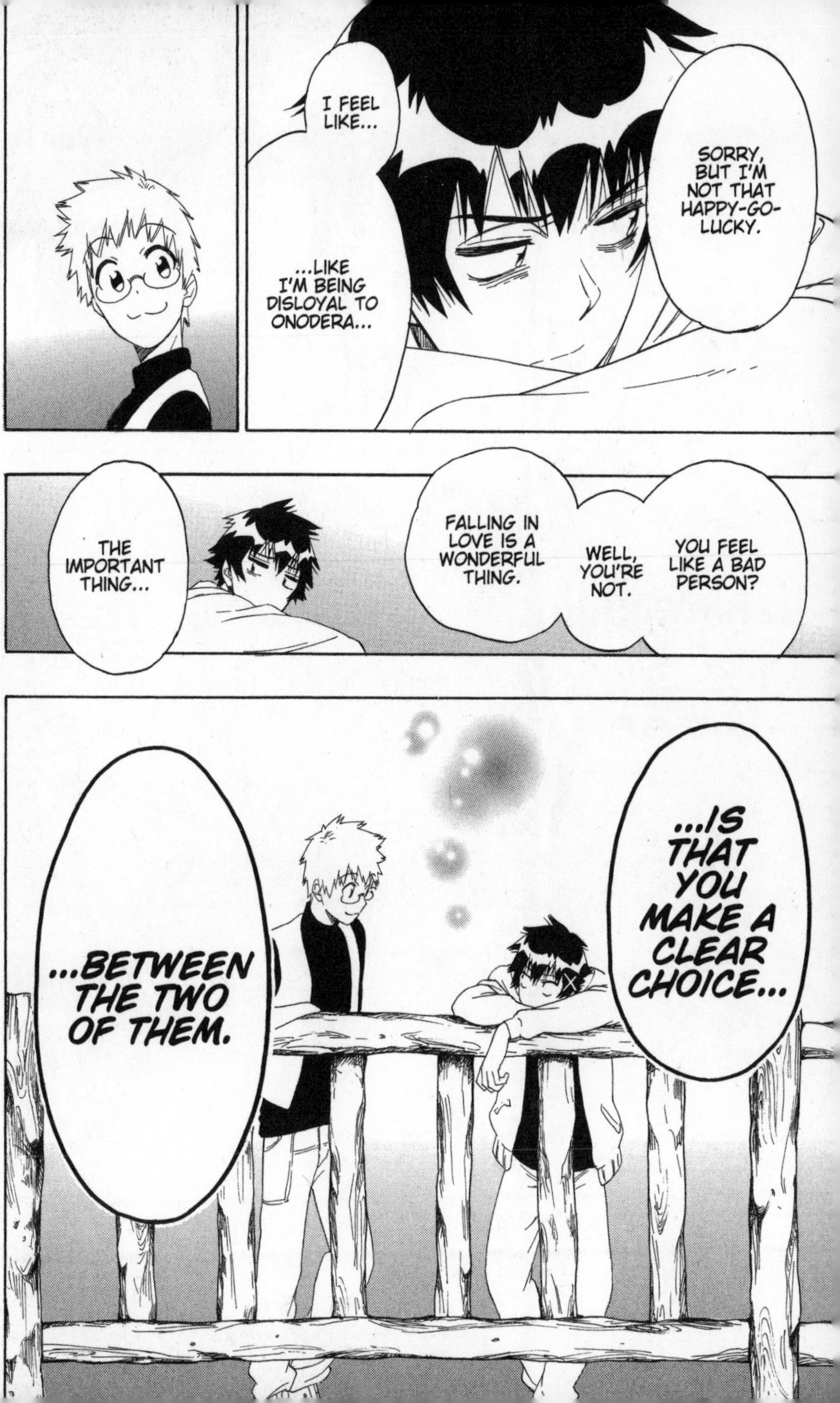
SORRY, BUT I'M NOT THAT HAPPY-GO-LUCKY.
I FEEL LIKE...
...LIKE I'M BEING DISLOYAL TO ONODERA...
YOU FEEL LIKE A BAD PERSON?
WELL, YOU'RE NOT.
FALLING IN LOVE IS A WONDERFUL THING.
THE IMPORTANT THING...
...IS THAT YOU MAKE A CLEAR CHOICE...
...BETWEEN THE TWO OF THEM.

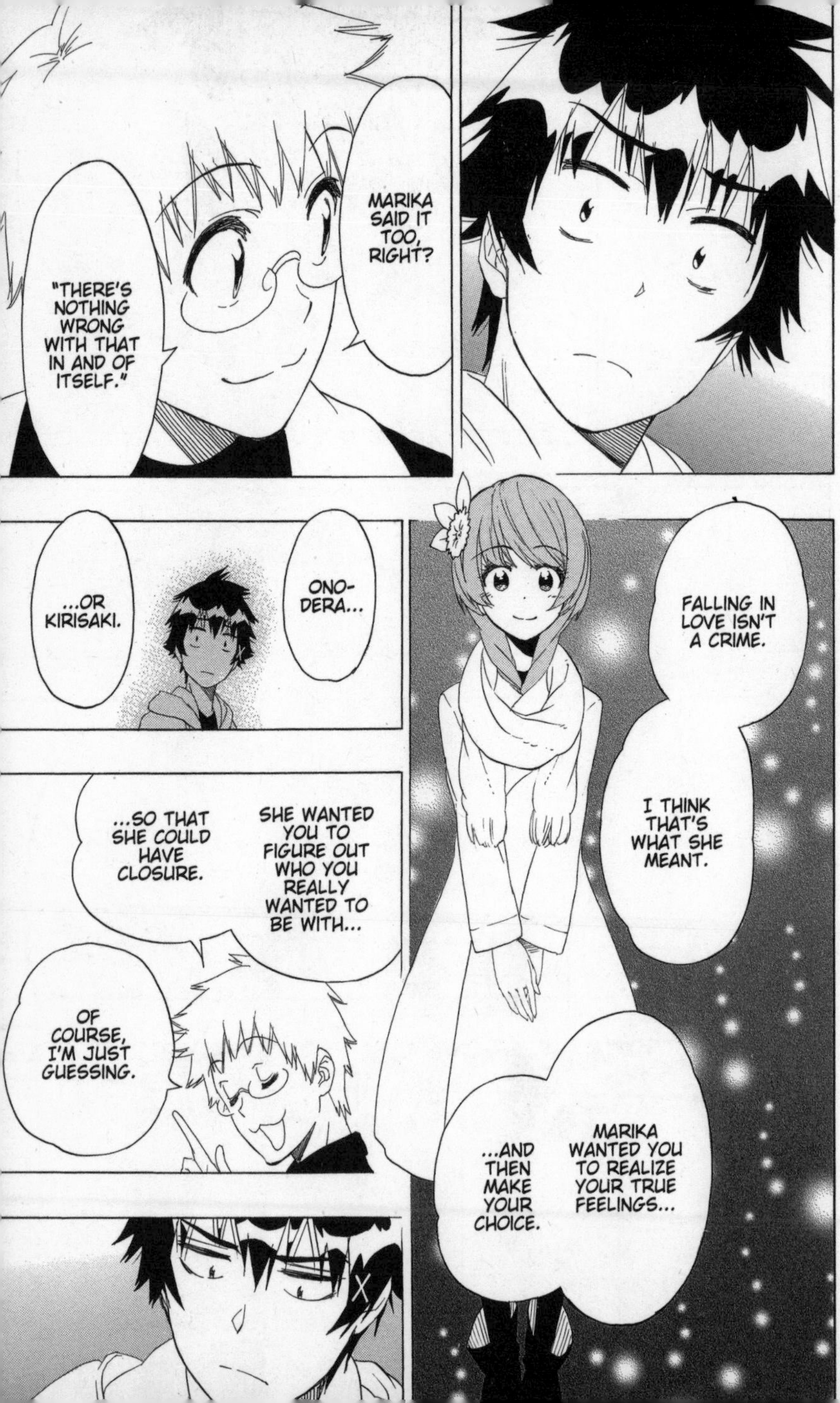
MARIKA SAID IT TOO, RIGHT?
"THERE'S NOTHING WRONG WITH THAT IN AND OF ITSELF."
FALLING IN LOVE ISN'T A CRIME.
I THINK THAT'S WHAT SHE MEANT.
MARIKA WANTED YOU TO REALIZE YOUR TRUE FEELINGS...
...AND THEN MAKE YOUR CHOICE.
ONO-DERA...
...OR KIRISAKI.
SHE WANTED YOU TO FIGURE OUT WHO YOU REALLY WANTED TO BE WITH...
...SO THAT SHE COULD HAVE CLOSURE.
OF COURSE, I'M JUST GUESSING.

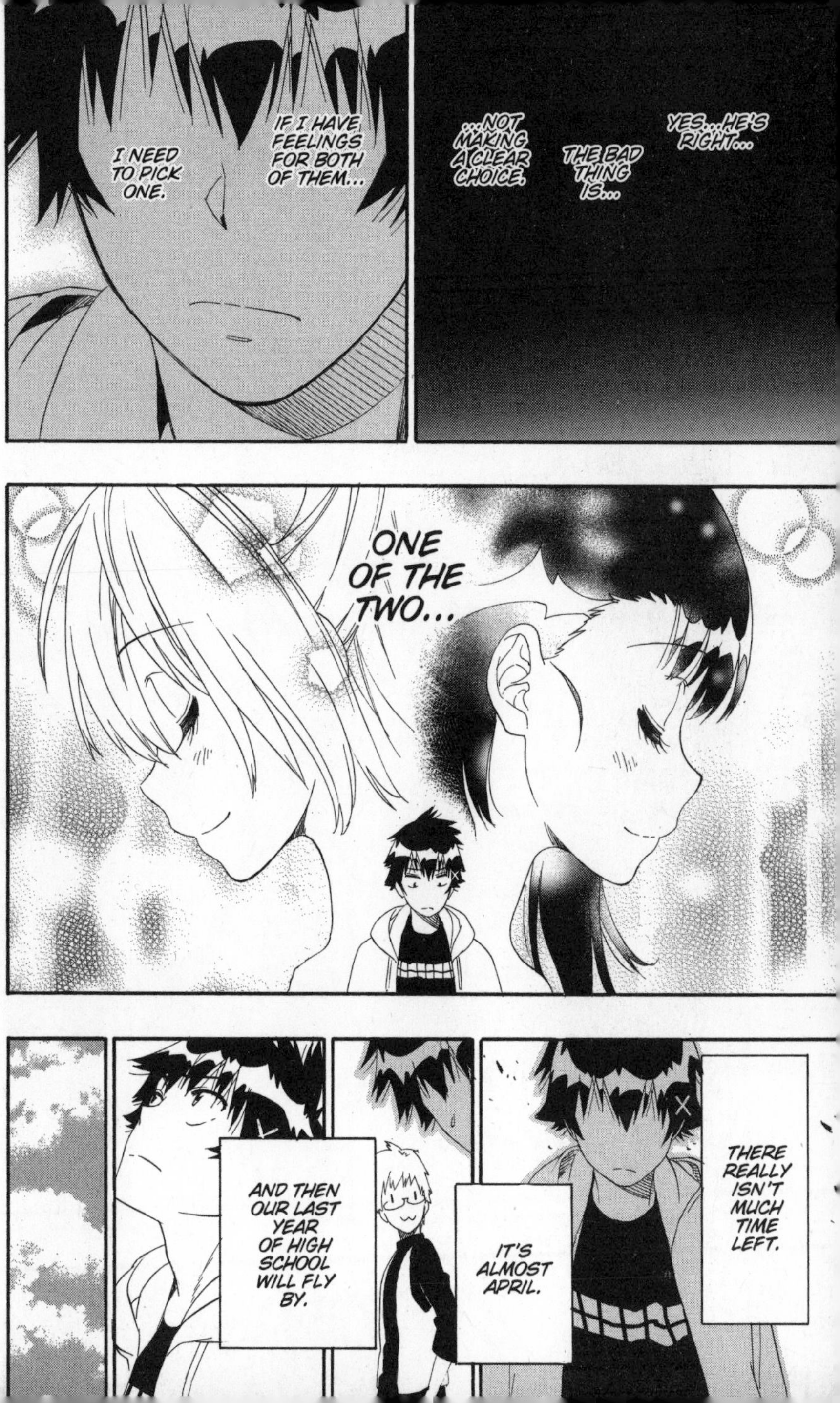
YES...HE'S RIGHT...
THE BAD THING IS...
...NOT MAKING A CLEAR CHOICE.
IF I HAVE FEELINGS FOR BOTH OF THEM...
I NEED TO PICK ONE.
ONE OF THE TWO...
THERE REALLY ISN'T MUCH TIME LEFT.
IT'S ALMOST APRIL.
AND THEN OUR LAST YEAR OF HIGH SCHOOL WILL FLY BY.

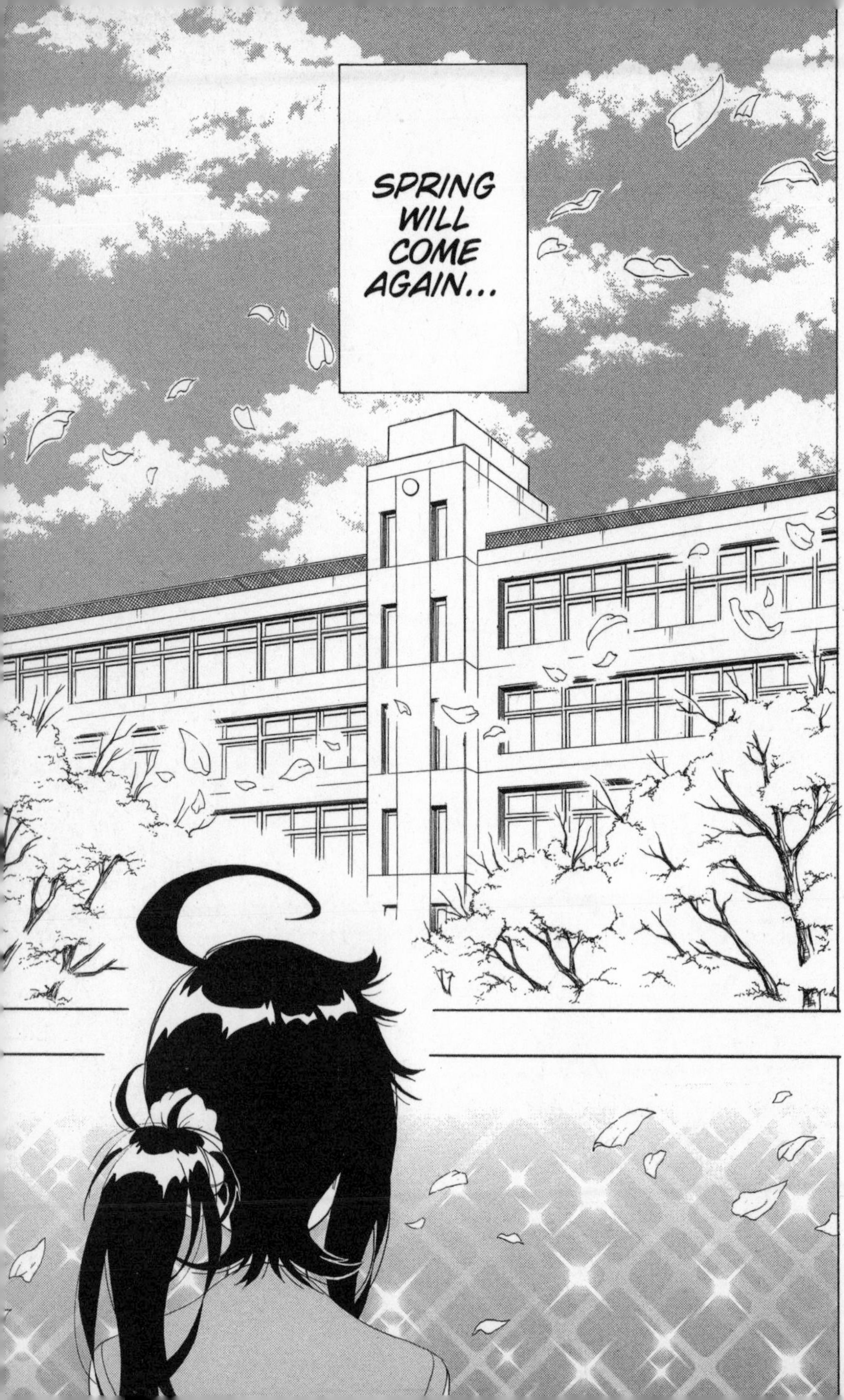
SPRING WILL COME AGAIN...

Was that a pun?

*NOTE: HARU MEANS "SPRING" IN JAPANESE.

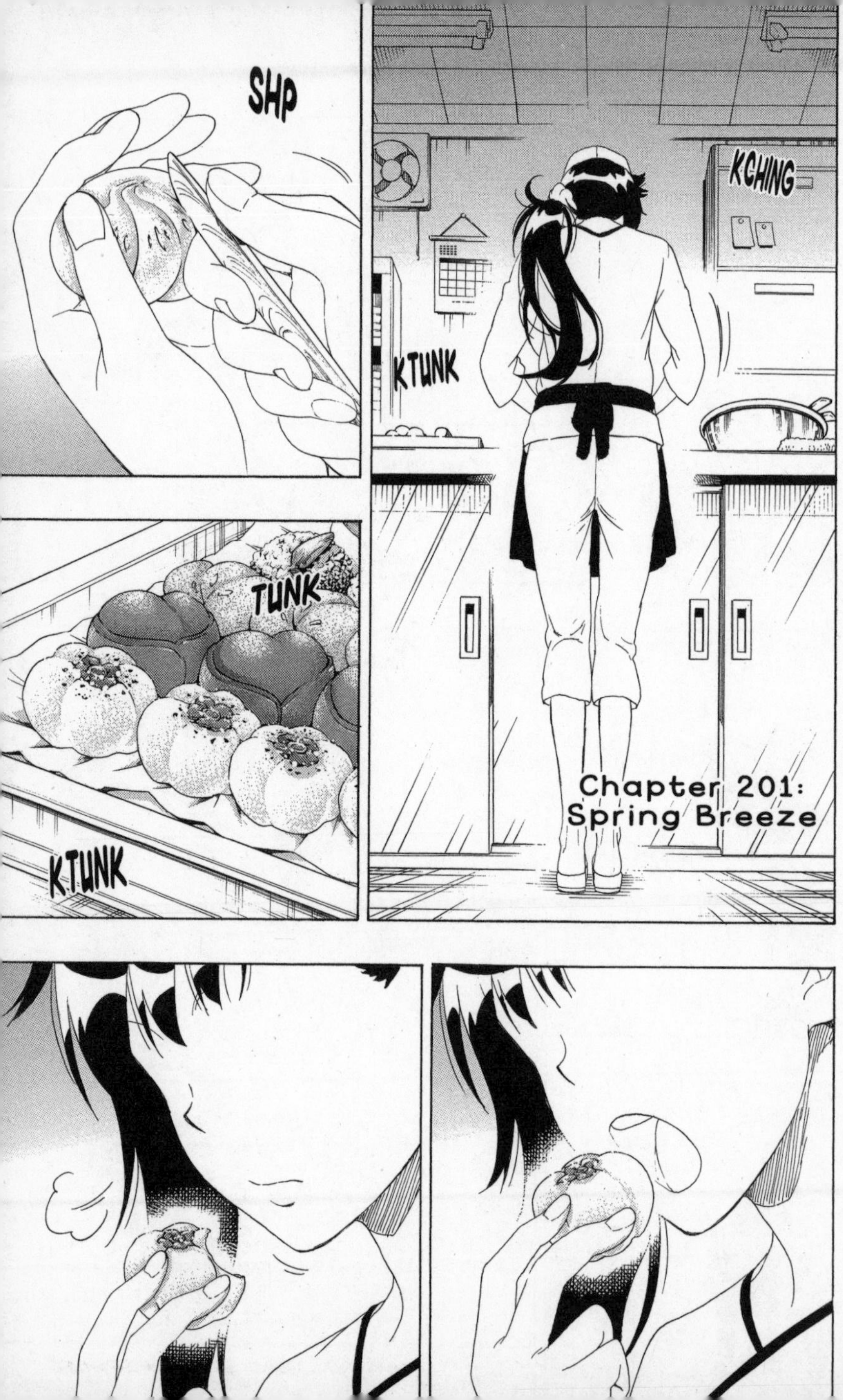
KCHING
KTUNK
Chapter 201:
Spring Breeze
SHP
TUNK
KTUNK

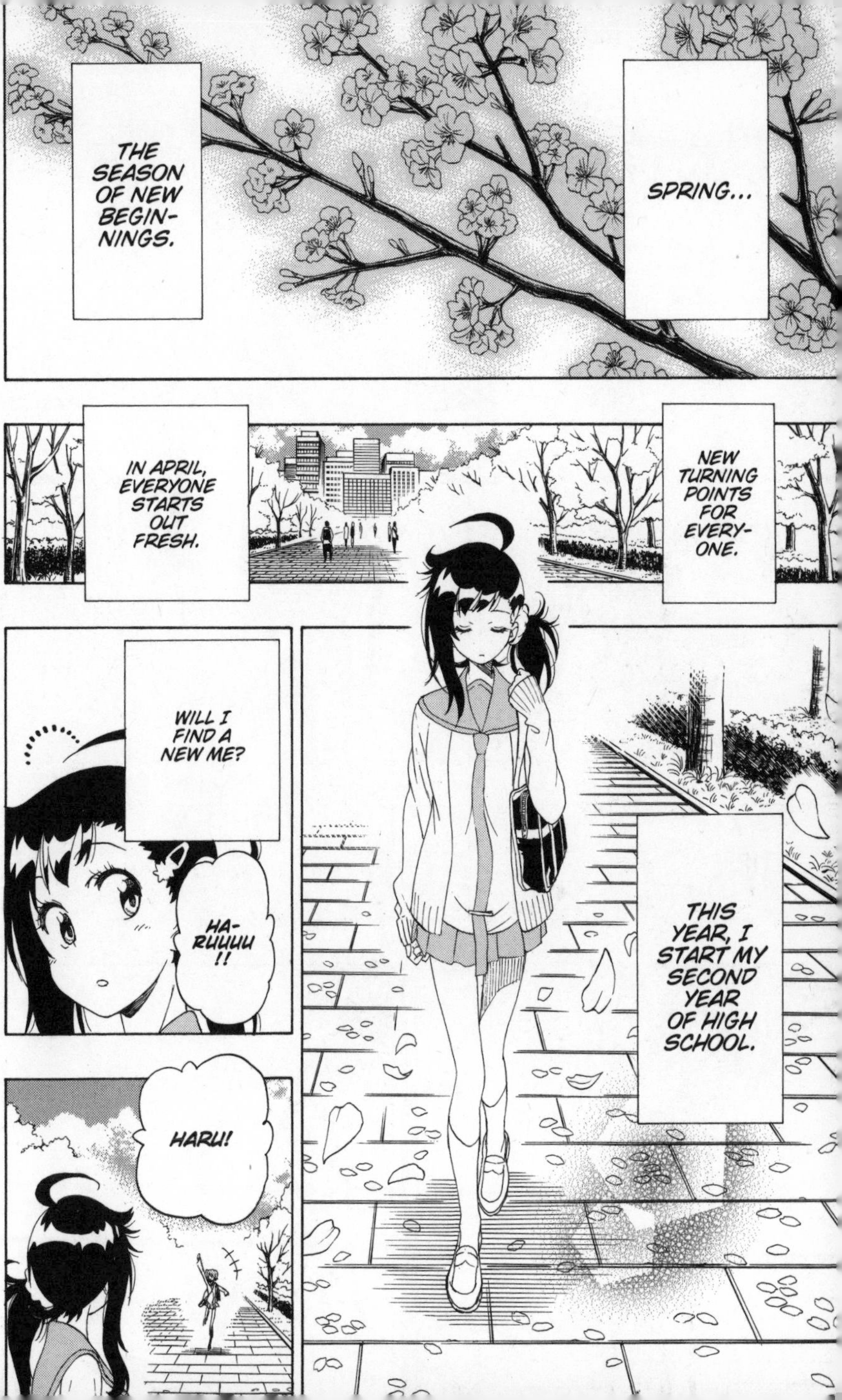

SPRING...
THE SEASON OF NEW BEGIN-NINGS.
NEW TURNING POINTS FOR EVERY-ONE.
IN APRIL, EVERYONE STARTS OUT FRESH.
THIS YEAR, I START MY SECOND YEAR OF HIGH SCHOOL.
WILL I FIND A NEW ME?
......
HA-RUUUU!!
HARU!

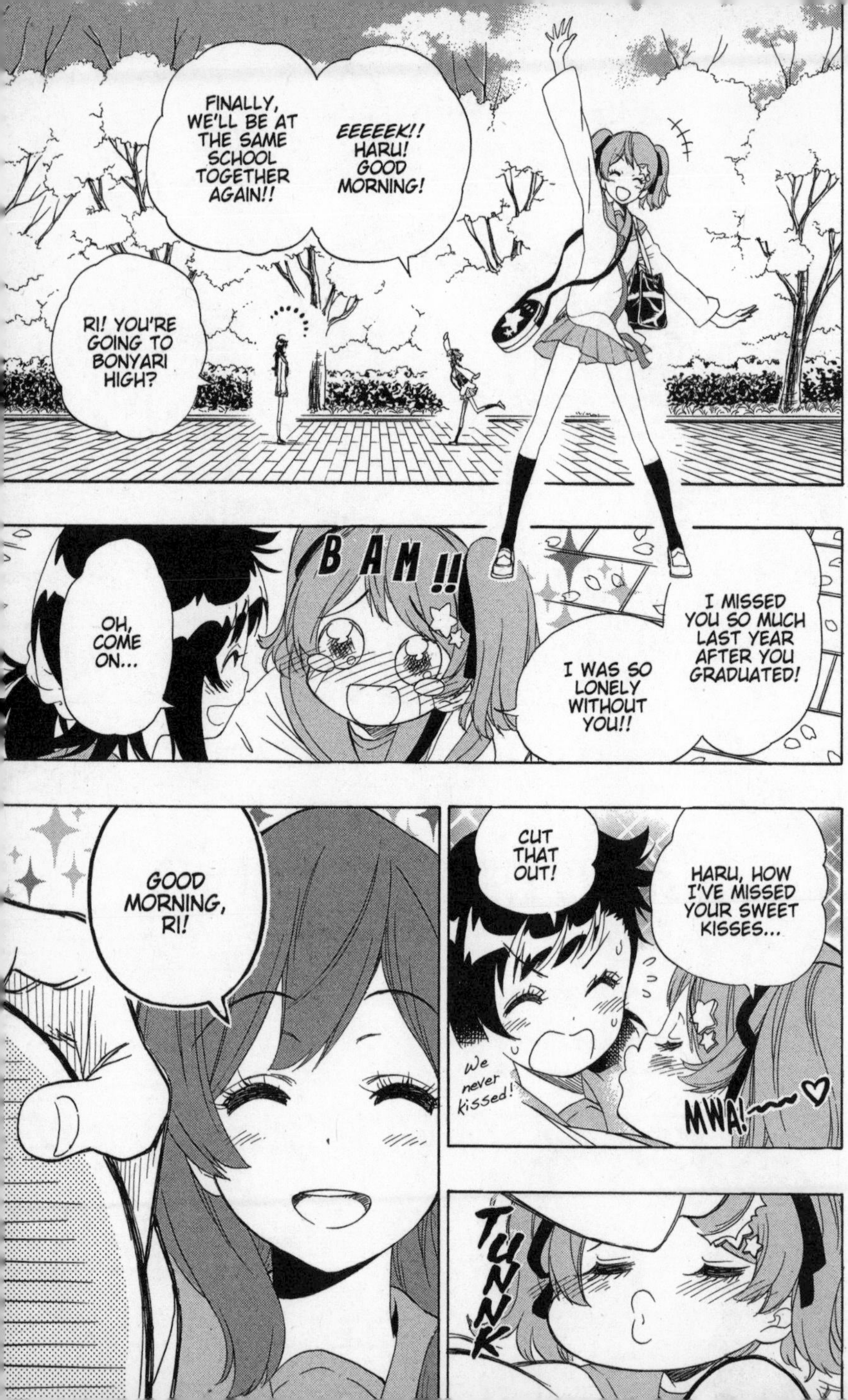
EEEEEK!! HARU! GOOD MORNING!
FINALLY, WE'LL BE AT THE SAME SCHOOL TOGETHER AGAIN!!
RI! YOU'RE GOING TO BONYARI HIGH?
I MISSED YOU SO MUCH LAST YEAR AFTER YOU GRADUATED!
I WAS SO LONELY WITHOUT YOU!!
BAM!!
OH, COME ON...
HARU, HOW I'VE MISSED YOUR SWEET KISSES...
CUT THAT OUT!
We never kissed!
MWA!
TUNNK
GOOD MORNING, RI!

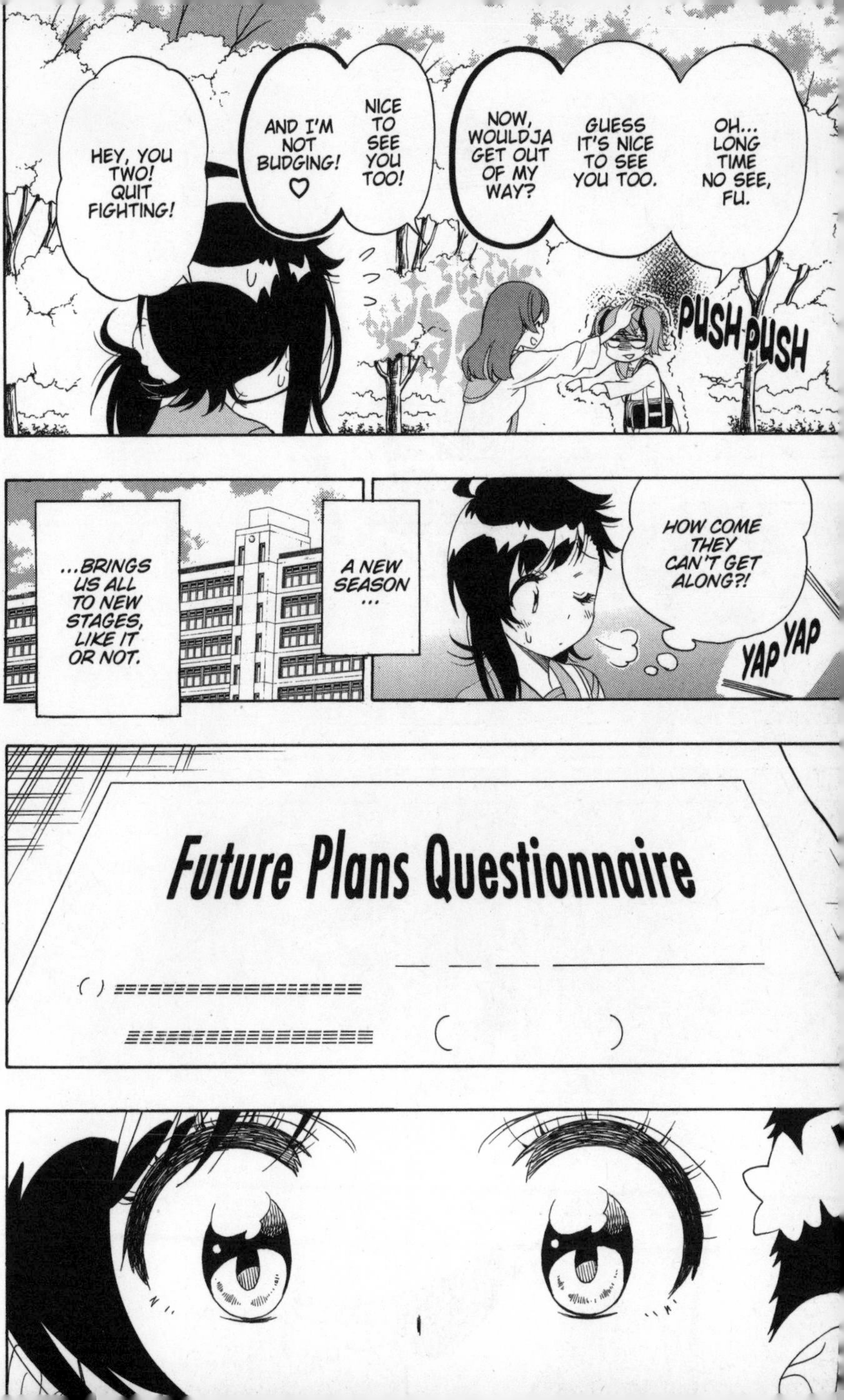
OH... LONG TIME NO SEE, FU.
GUESS IT'S NICE TO SEE YOU TOO.
NOW, WOULDJA GET OUT OF MY WAY?
PUSH PUSH
NICE TO SEE YOU TOO!
AND I'M NOT BUDGING! ♡
HEY, YOU TWO! QUIT FIGHTING!
HOW COME THEY CAN'T GET ALONG?!
YAP YAP
A NEW SEASON...
...BRINGS US ALL TO NEW STAGES, LIKE IT OR NOT.
Future Plans Questionnaire

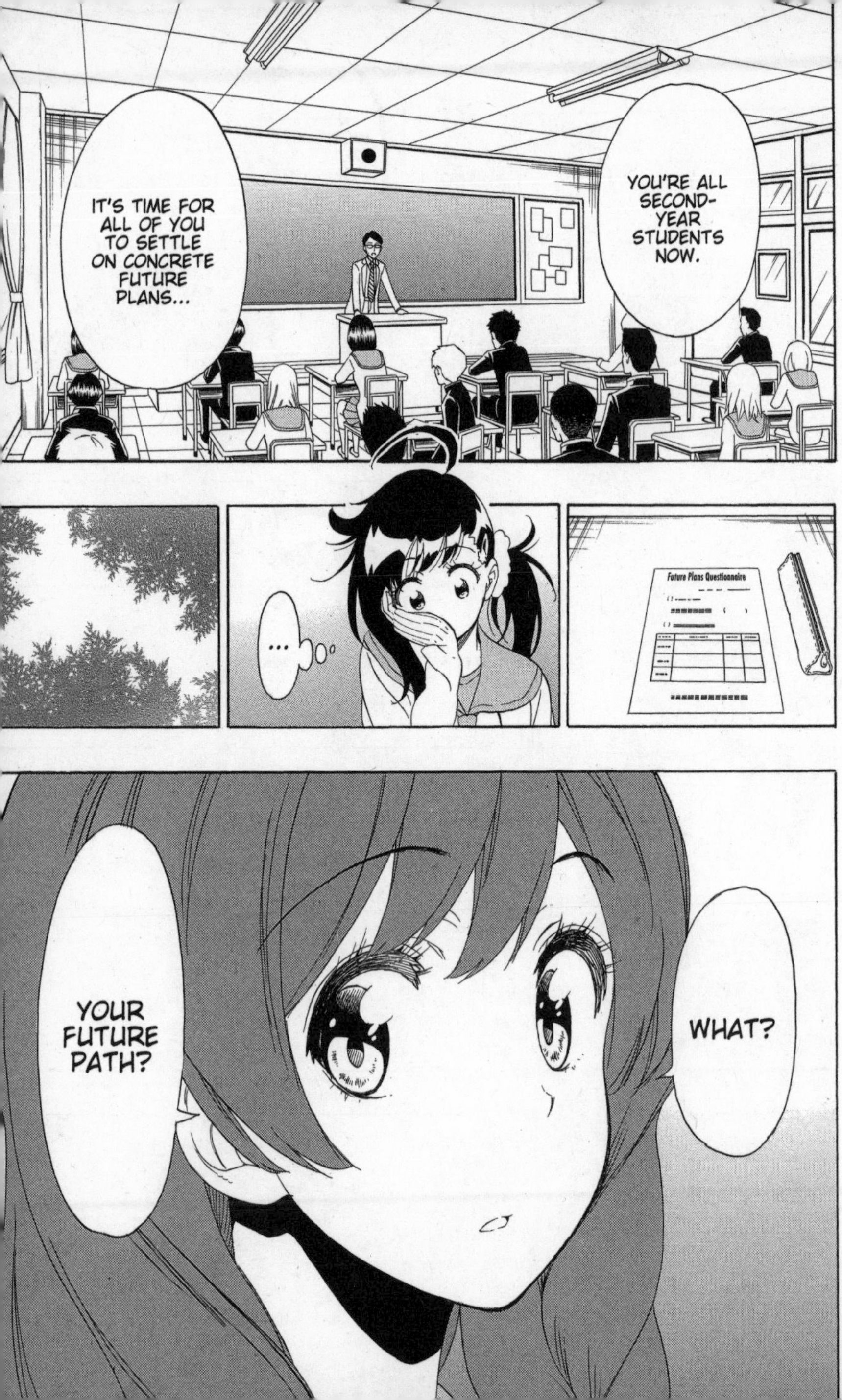
YOU'RE ALL SECOND-YEAR STUDENTS NOW.
IT'S TIME FOR ALL OF YOU TO SETTLE ON CONCRETE FUTURE PLANS...
Future Plans Questionnaire
...
WHAT?
YOUR FUTURE PATH?

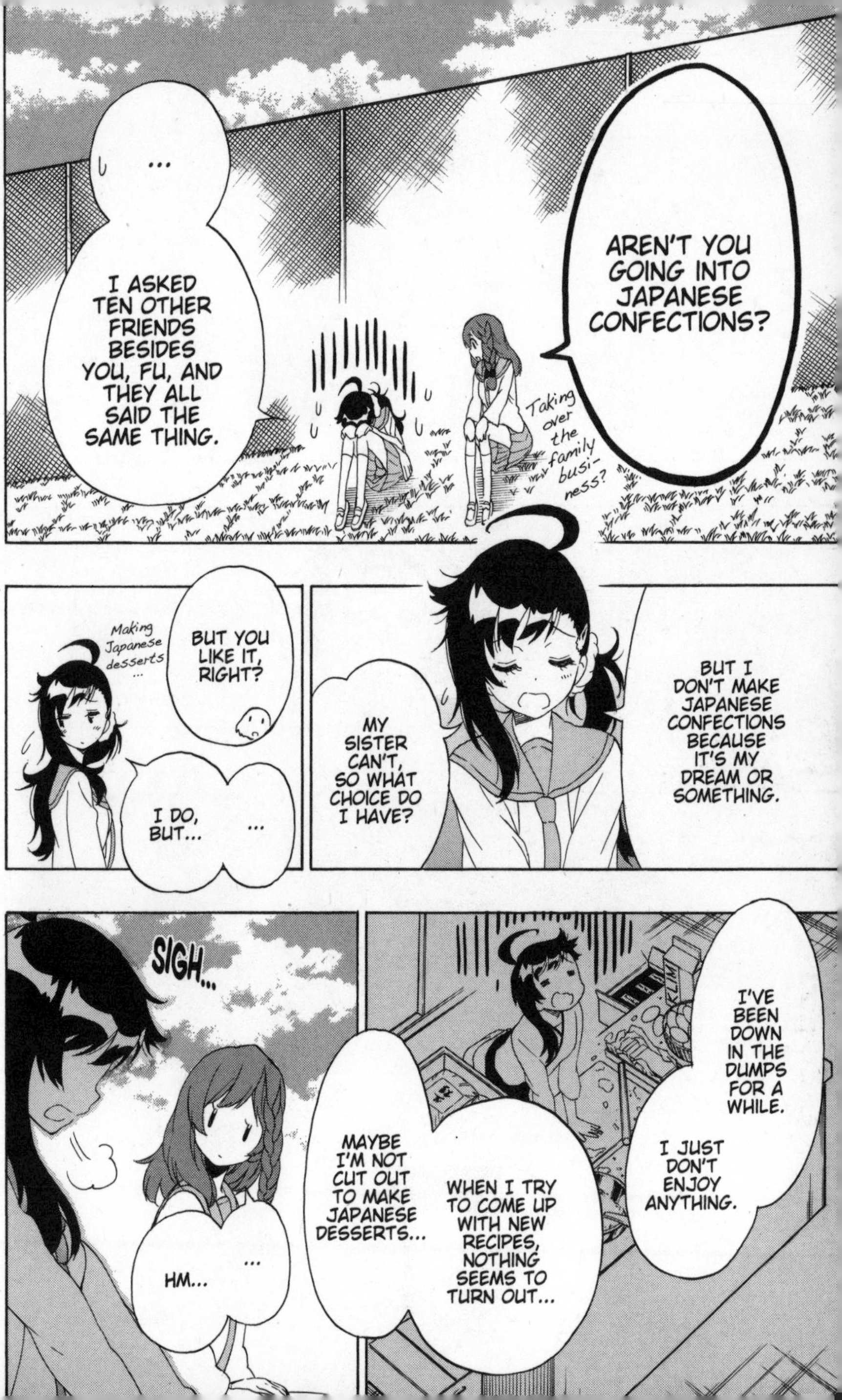

AREN'T YOU GOING INTO JAPANESE CONFECTIONS?
Taking over the family busi-ness?
...
I ASKED TEN OTHER FRIENDS BESIDES YOU, FU, AND THEY ALL SAID THE SAME THING.
BUT I DON'T MAKE JAPANESE CONFECTIONS BECAUSE IT'S MY DREAM OR SOMETHING.
MY SISTER CAN'T, SO WHAT CHOICE DO I HAVE?
BUT YOU LIKE IT, RIGHT?
Making Japanese desserts ...
...
I DO, BUT...
I'VE BEEN DOWN IN THE DUMPS FOR A WHILE.
I JUST DON'T ENJOY ANYTHING.
WHEN I TRY TO COME UP WITH NEW RECIPES, NOTHING SEEMS TO TURN OUT...
MAYBE I'M NOT CUT OUT TO MAKE JAPANESE DESSERTS...
SIGH...
...
HM...

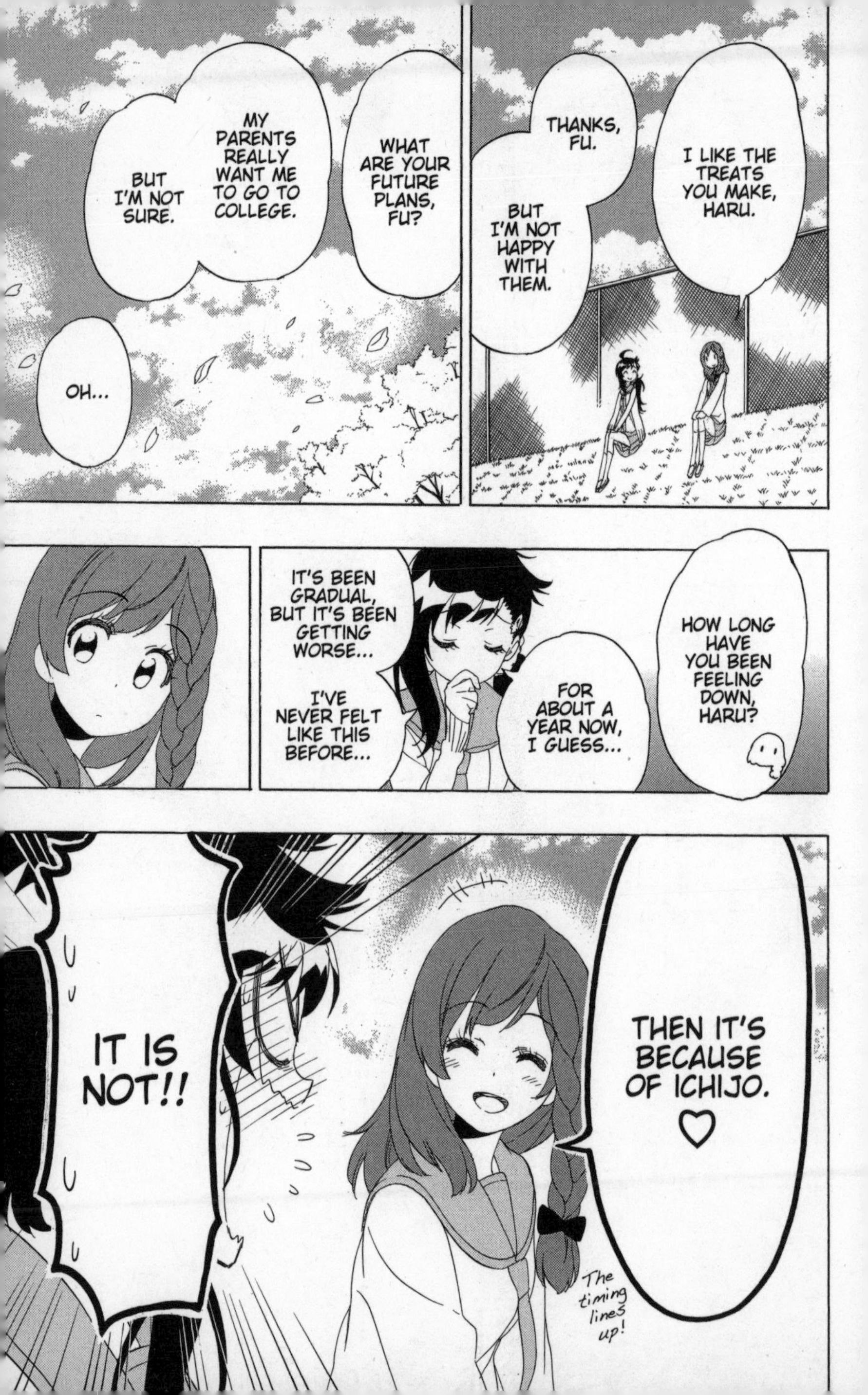
I LIKE THE TREATS YOU MAKE, HARU.
THANKS, FU.
BUT I'M NOT HAPPY WITH THEM.
WHAT ARE YOUR FUTURE PLANS, FU?
MY PARENTS REALLY WANT ME TO GO TO COLLEGE.
BUT I'M NOT SURE.
OH...
HOW LONG HAVE YOU BEEN FEELING DOWN, HARU?
FOR ABOUT A YEAR NOW, I GUESS...
IT'S BEEN GRADUAL, BUT IT'S BEEN GETTING WORSE...
I'VE NEVER FELT LIKE THIS BEFORE...
THEN IT'S BECAUSE OF ICHIJO. ♡
The timing lines up!
IT IS NOT!!

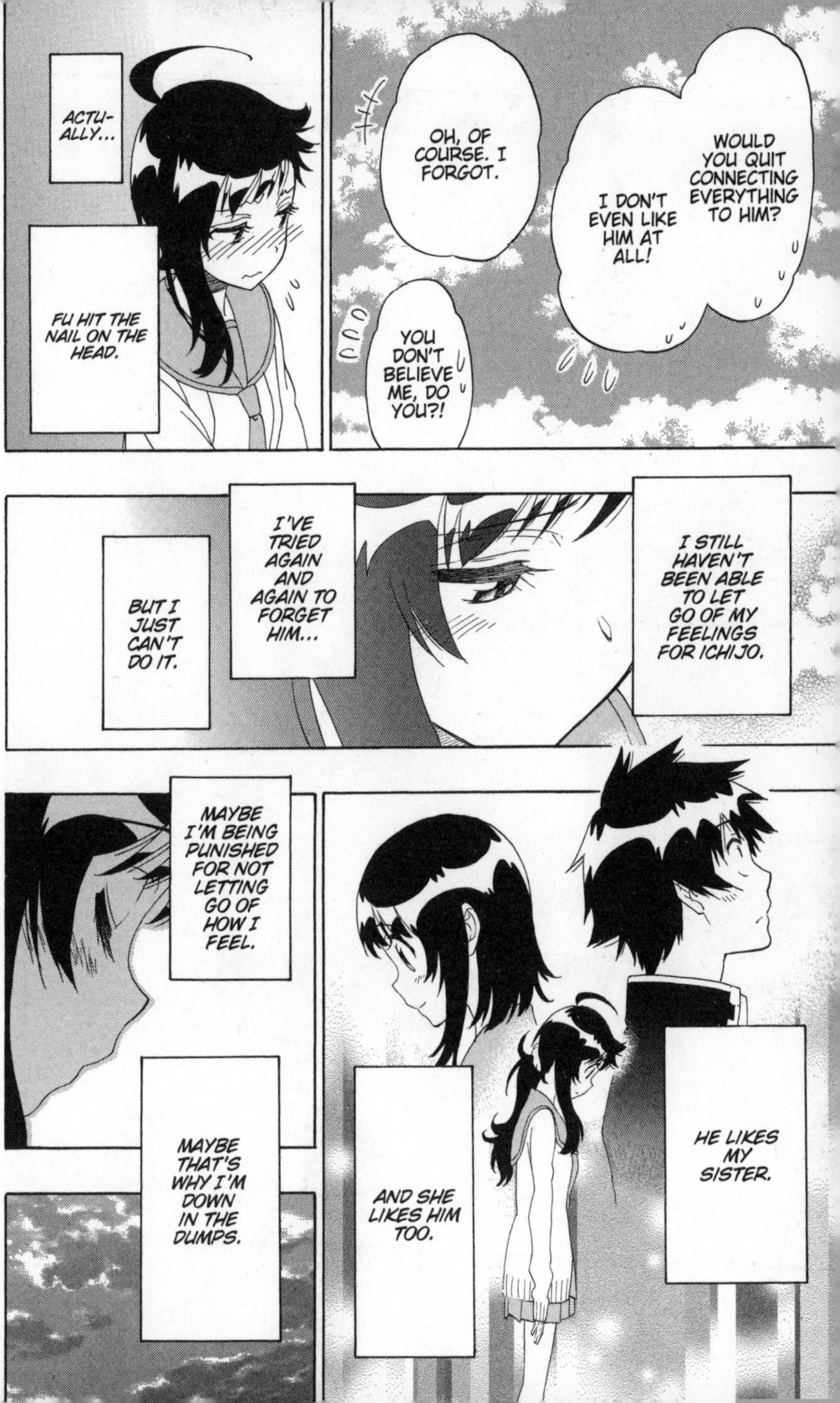
WOULD YOU QUIT CONNECTING EVERYTHING TO HIM?
I DON'T EVEN LIKE HIM AT ALL!
OH, OF COURSE. I FORGOT.
YOU DON'T BELIEVE ME, DO YOU?!
ACTU-ALLY...
FU HIT THE NAIL ON THE HEAD.
I STILL HAVEN'T BEEN ABLE TO LET GO OF MY FEELINGS FOR ICHIJO.
I'VE TRIED AGAIN AND AGAIN TO FORGET HIM...
BUT I JUST CAN'T DO IT.
HE LIKES MY SISTER.
AND SHE LIKES HIM TOO.
MAYBE I'M BEING PUNISHED FOR NOT LETTING GO OF HOW I FEEL.
MAYBE THAT'S WHY I'M DOWN IN THE DUMPS.

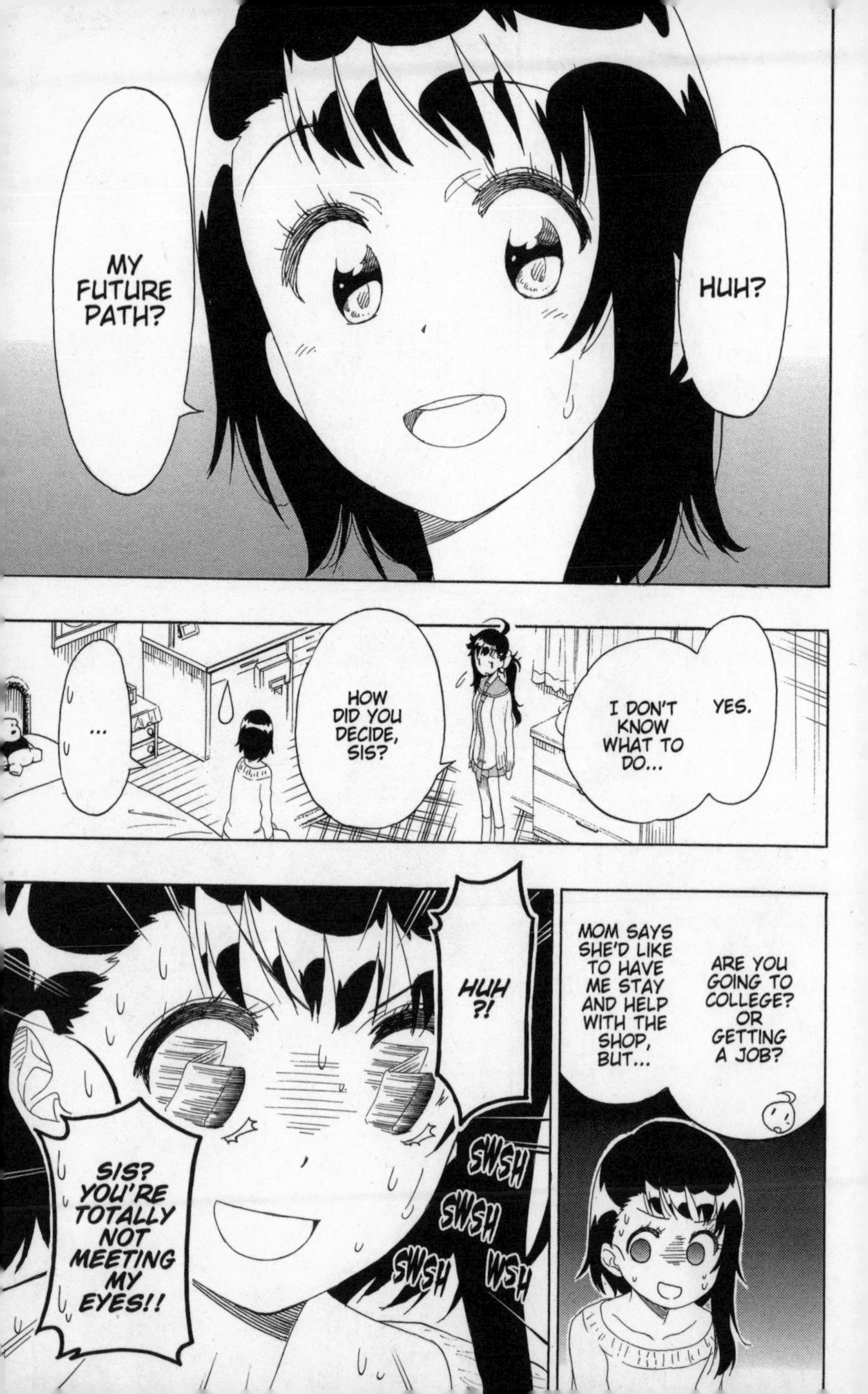
HUH?
MY FUTURE PATH?
YES.
I DON'T KNOW WHAT TO DO...
HOW DID YOU DECIDE, SIS?
...
ARE YOU GOING TO COLLEGE? OR GETTING A JOB?
MOM SAYS SHE'D LIKE TO HAVE ME STAY AND HELP WITH THE SHOP, BUT...
HUH ?!
SWSH
SWSH
SWSH
WSH
SIS? YOU'RE TOTALLY NOT MEETING MY EYES!!

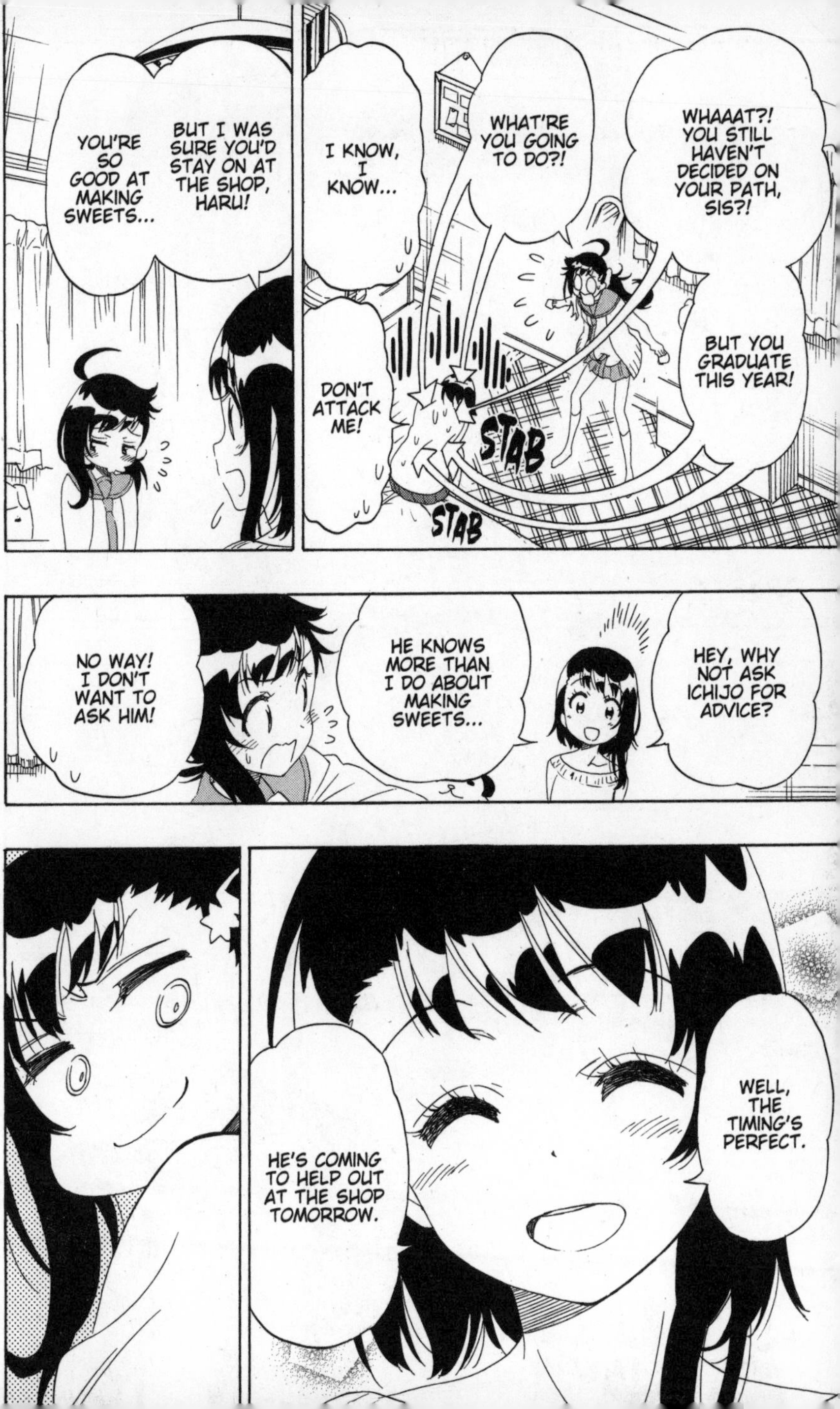
WHAAAT?! YOU STILL HAVEN'T DECIDED ON YOUR PATH, SIS?!
BUT YOU GRADUATE THIS YEAR!
WHAT'RE YOU GOING TO DO?!
STAB
STAB
I KNOW, I KNOW...
DON'T ATTACK ME!
BUT I WAS SURE YOU'D STAY ON AT THE SHOP, HARU!
YOU'RE SO GOOD AT MAKING SWEETS...
HEY, WHY NOT ASK ICHIJO FOR ADVICE?
HE KNOWS MORE THAN I DO ABOUT MAKING SWEETS...
NO WAY! I DON'T WANT TO ASK HIM!
WELL, THE TIMING'S PERFECT.
HE'S COMING TO HELP OUT AT THE SHOP TOMORROW.

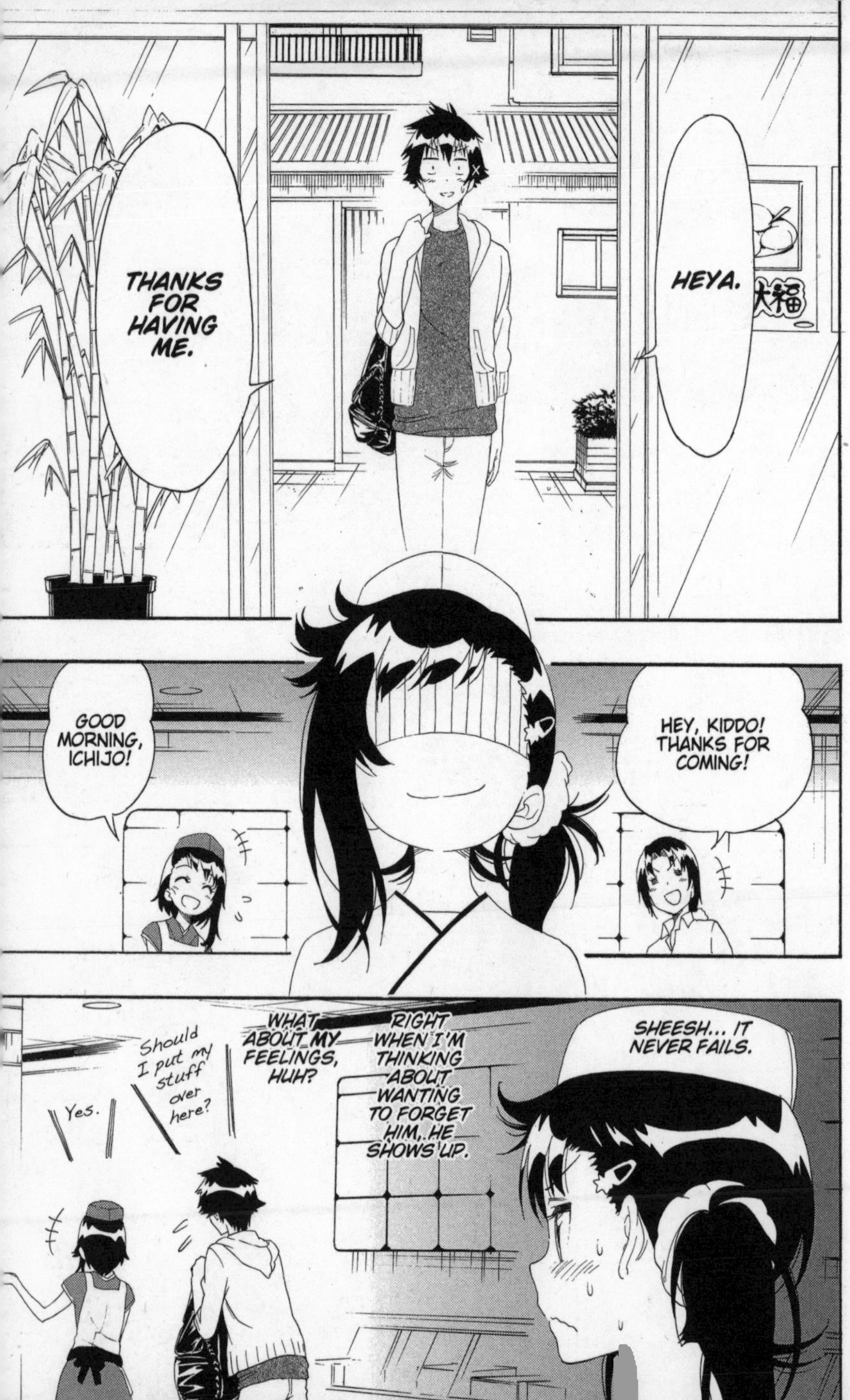
HEYA.
THANKS FOR HAVING ME.
HEY, KIDDO! THANKS FOR COMING!
GOOD MORNING, ICHIJO!
SHEESH... IT NEVER FAILS.
RIGHT WHEN I'M THINKING ABOUT WANTING TO FORGET HIM, HE SHOWS UP.
WHAT ABOUT MY FEELINGS, HUH?
Should I put my stuff over here?
Yes.

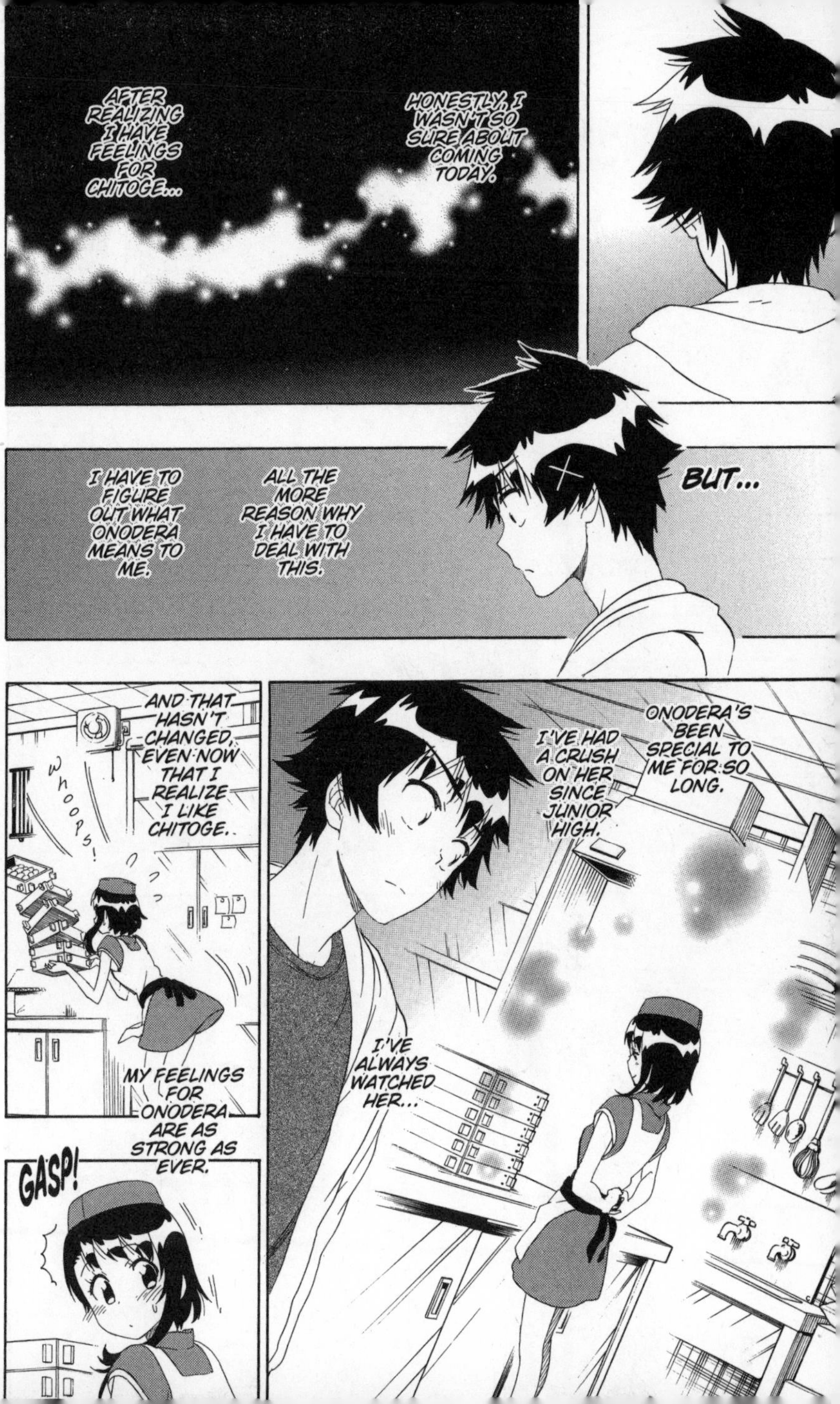

HONESTLY, I WASN'T SO SURE ABOUT COMING TODAY.
AFTER REALIZING I HAVE FEELINGS FOR CHITOGE...
BUT...
ALL THE MORE REASON WHY I HAVE TO DEAL WITH THIS.
I HAVE TO FIGURE OUT WHAT ONODERA MEANS TO ME.
ONODERA'S BEEN SPECIAL TO ME FOR SO LONG.
I'VE HAD A CRUSH ON HER SINCE JUNIOR HIGH.
I'VE ALWAYS WATCHED HER...
AND THAT HASN'T CHANGED, EVEN NOW THAT I REALIZE I LIKE CHITOGE.
Whoops!
MY FEELINGS FOR ONODERA ARE AS STRONG AS EVER.
GASP!

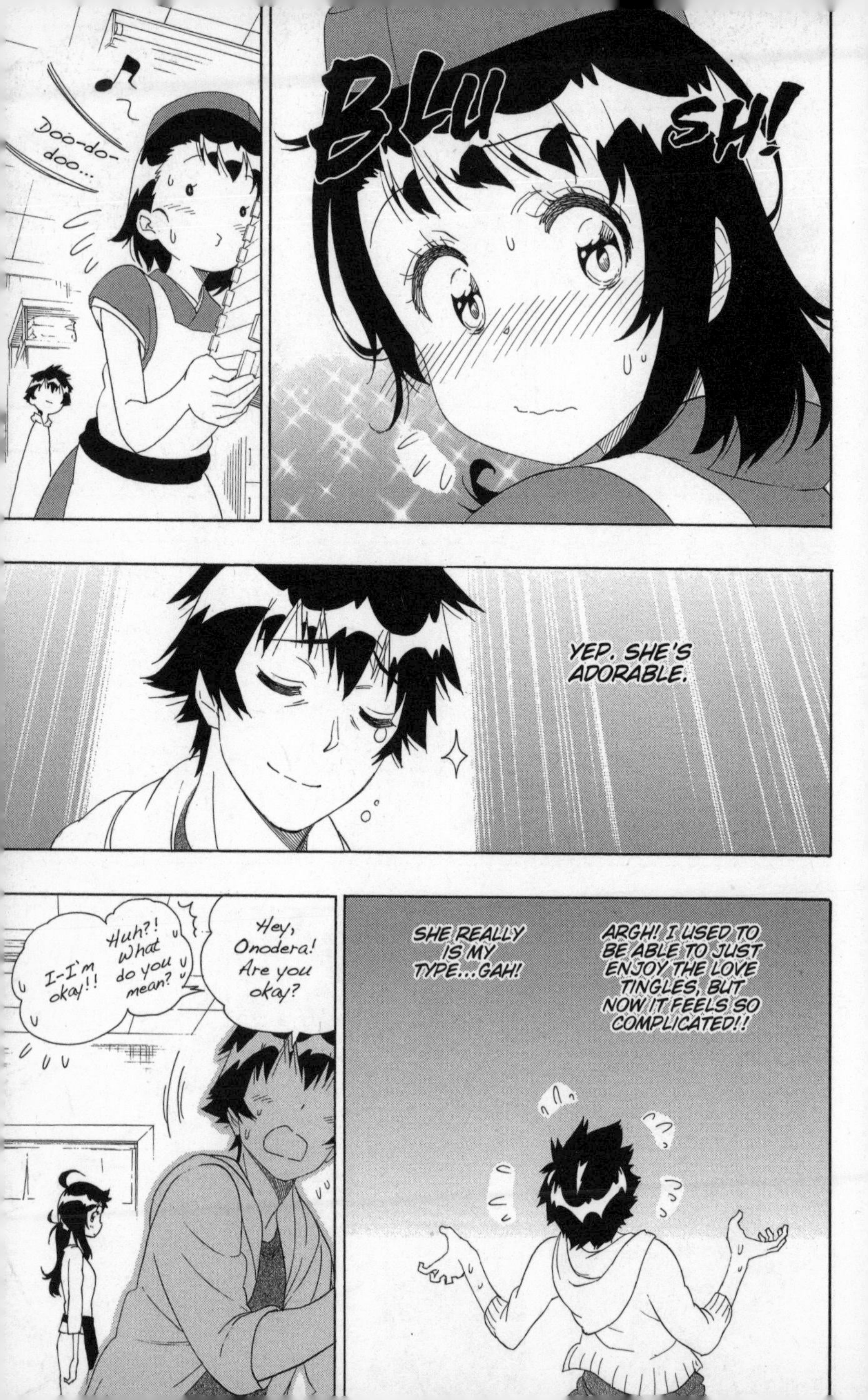
BLUSH!
Doo-do-doo...
YEP. SHE'S ADORABLE.
ARGH! I USED TO BE ABLE TO JUST ENJOY THE LOVE TINGLES, BUT NOW IT FEELS SO COMPLICATED!!
SHE REALLY IS MY TYPE...GAH!
Hey, Onodera! Are you okay?
Huh?! What do you mean?
I-I'm okay!!

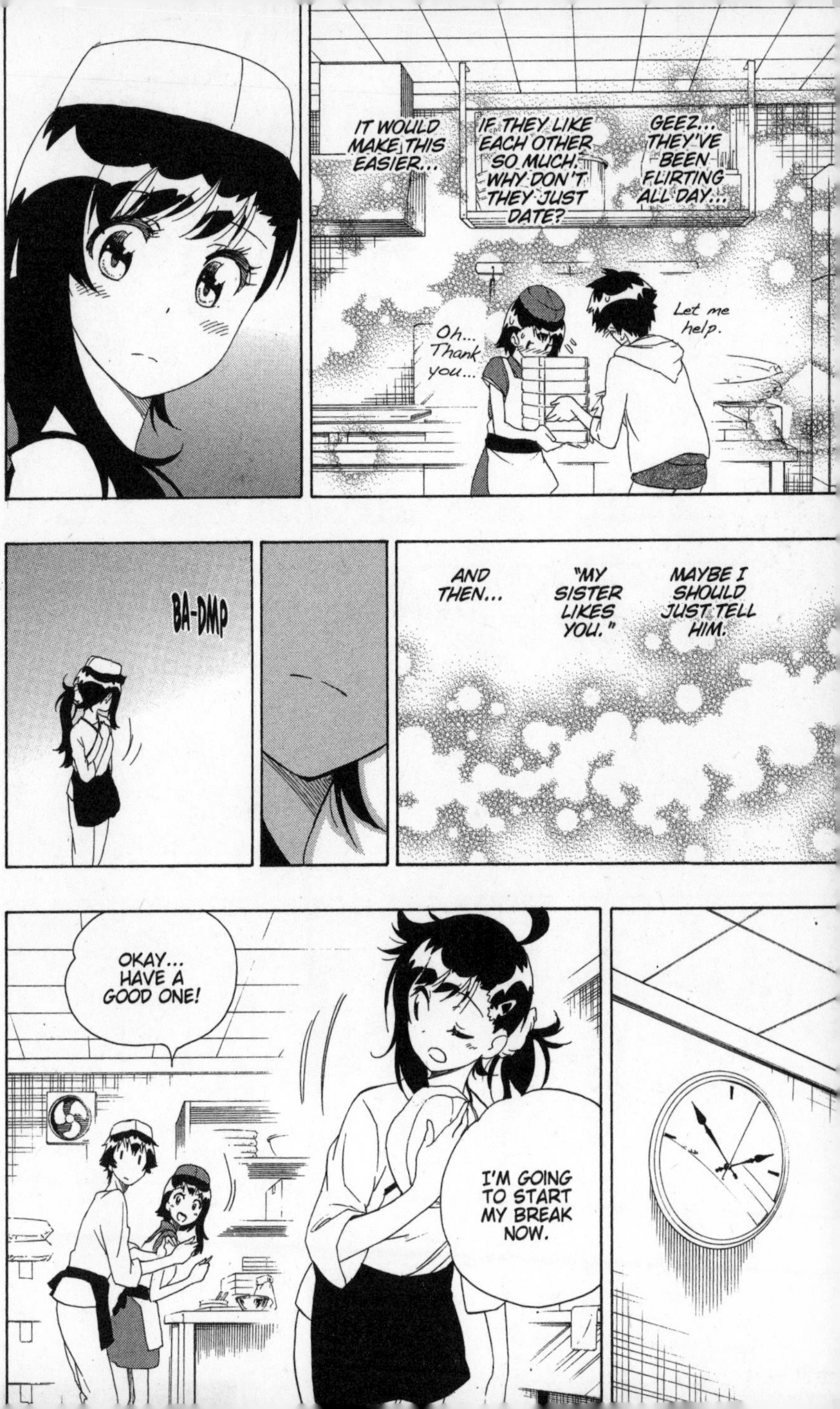
GEEZ... THEY'VE BEEN FLIRTING ALL DAY...
IF THEY LIKE EACH OTHER SO MUCH, WHY DON'T THEY JUST DATE?
IT WOULD MAKE THIS EASIER...
Let me help.
Oh... Thank you...
MAYBE I SHOULD JUST TELL HIM.
"MY SISTER LIKES YOU."
AND THEN...
BA-DMP
I'M GOING TO START MY BREAK NOW.
OKAY... HAVE A GOOD ONE!

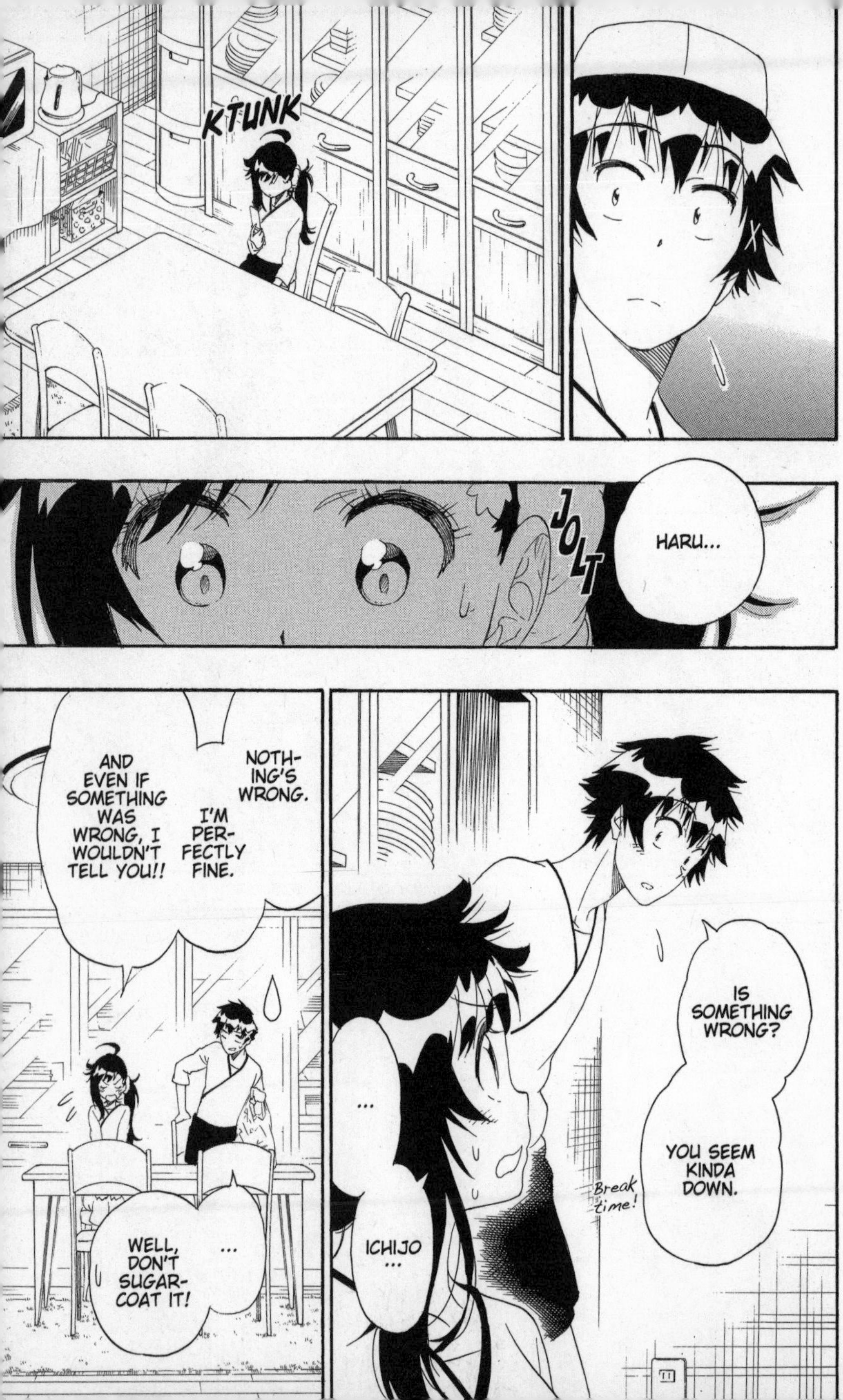
KTUNK
JOLT
HARU...
IS SOMETHING WRONG?
YOU SEEM KINDA DOWN.
Break time!
...
ICHIJO...
NOTHING'S WRONG.
I'M PERFECTLY FINE.
AND EVEN IF SOMETHING WAS WRONG, I WOULDN'T TELL YOU!!
...
WELL, DON'T SUGARCOAT IT!

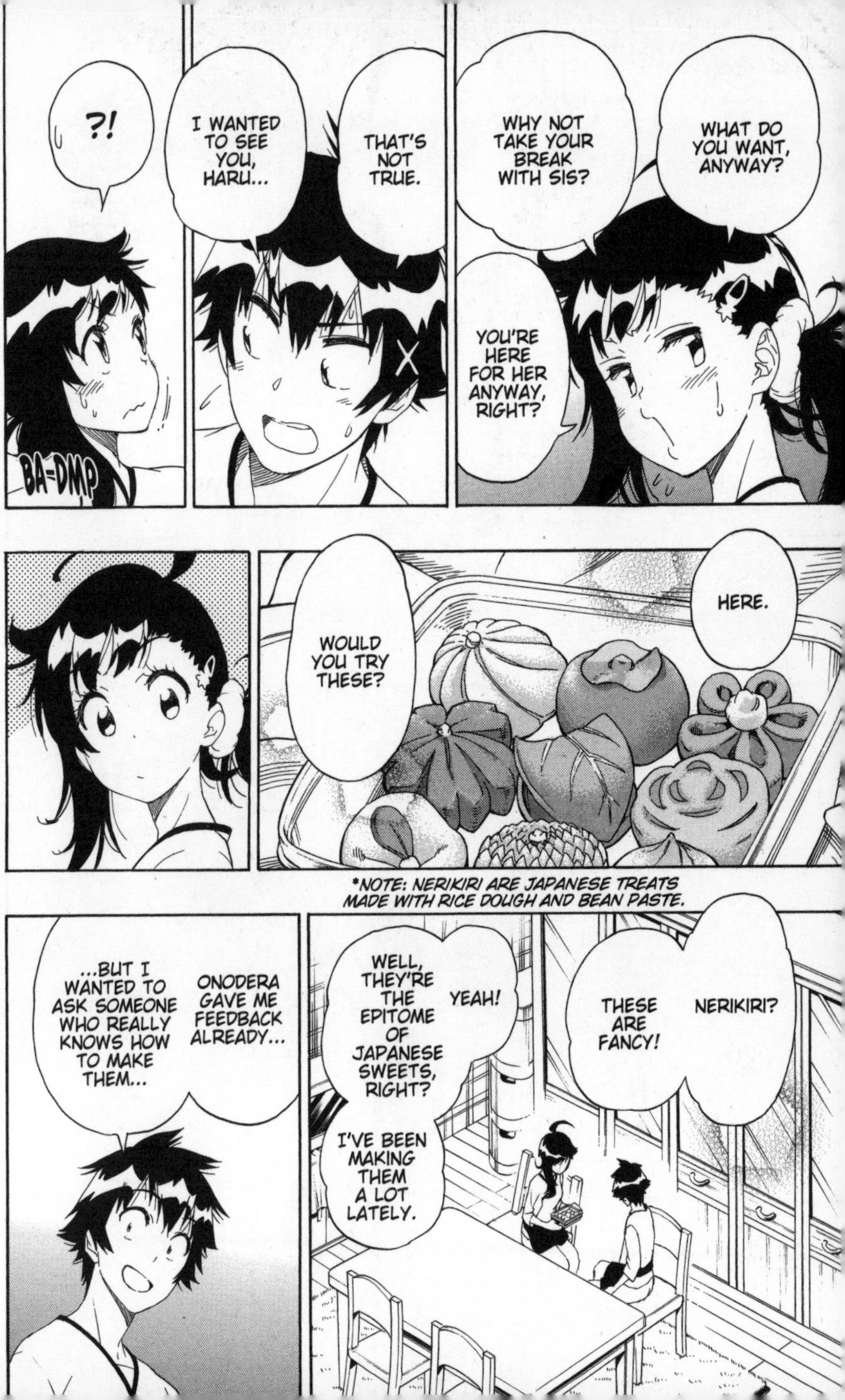
WHAT DO YOU WANT, ANYWAY?
WHY NOT TAKE YOUR BREAK WITH SIS?
YOU'RE HERE FOR HER ANYWAY, RIGHT?
THAT'S NOT TRUE.
I WANTED TO SEE YOU, HARU...
?!
BA-DMP
HERE.
WOULD YOU TRY THESE?
*NOTE: NERIKIRI ARE JAPANESE TREATS MADE WITH RICE DOUGH AND BEAN PASTE.
NERIKIRI?
THESE ARE FANCY!
YEAH!
WELL, THEY'RE THE EPITOME OF JAPANESE SWEETS, RIGHT?
I'VE BEEN MAKING THEM A LOT LATELY.
ONODERA GAVE ME FEEDBACK ALREADY...
...BUT I WANTED TO ASK SOMEONE WHO REALLY KNOWS HOW TO MAKE THEM...

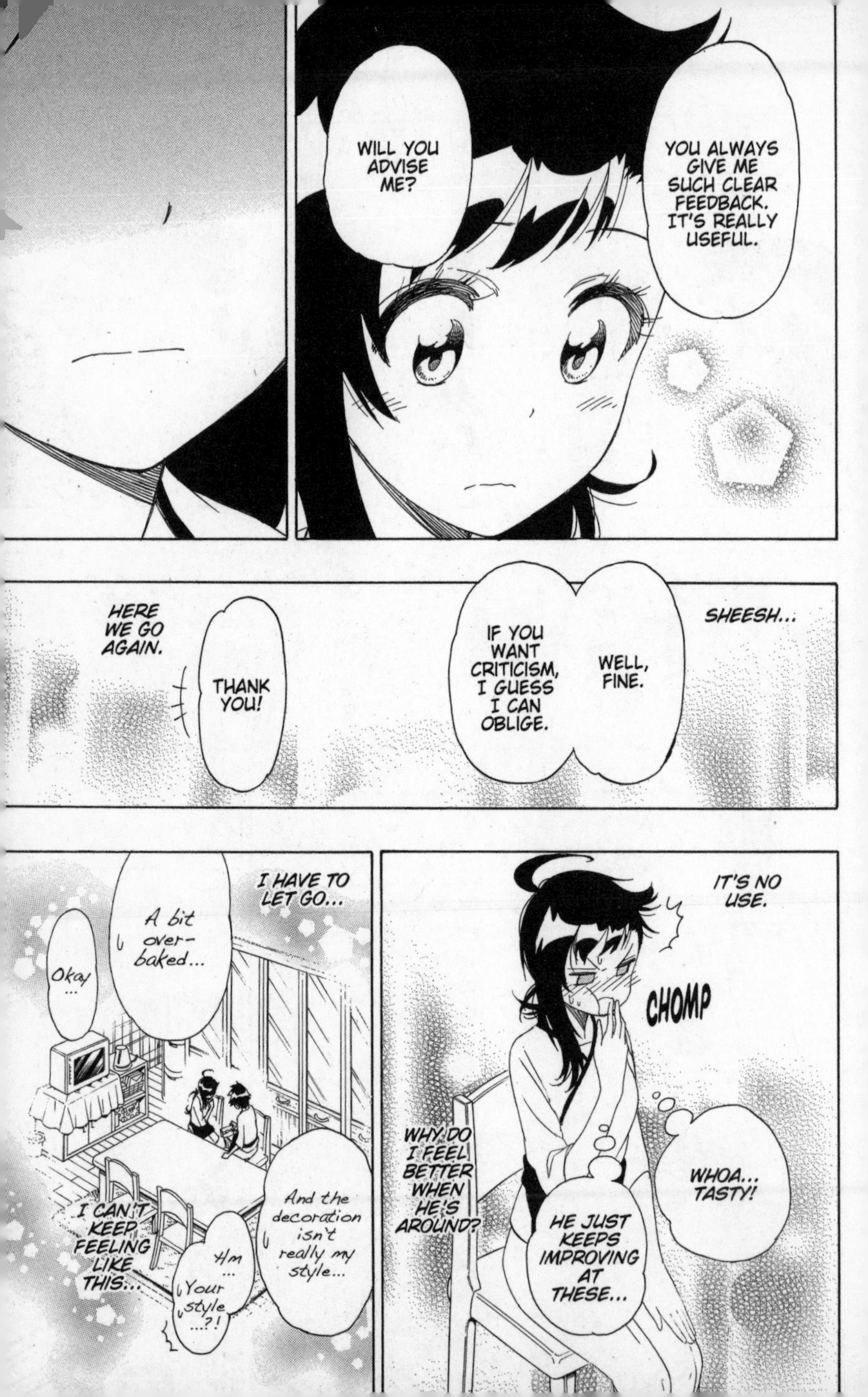
YOU ALWAYS GIVE ME SUCH CLEAR FEEDBACK. IT'S REALLY USEFUL.
WILL YOU ADVISE ME?
SHEESH...
WELL, FINE.
IF YOU WANT CRITICISM, I GUESS I CAN OBLIGE.
THANK YOU!
HERE WE GO AGAIN.
IT'S NO USE.
CHOMP
WHOA... TASTY!
HE JUST KEEPS IMPROVING AT THESE...
WHY DO I FEEL BETTER WHEN HE'S AROUND?
I HAVE TO LET GO...
A bit over-baked...
Okay...
And the decoration isn't really my style...
Hm... Your style...?!
I CAN'T KEEP FEELING LIKE THIS...

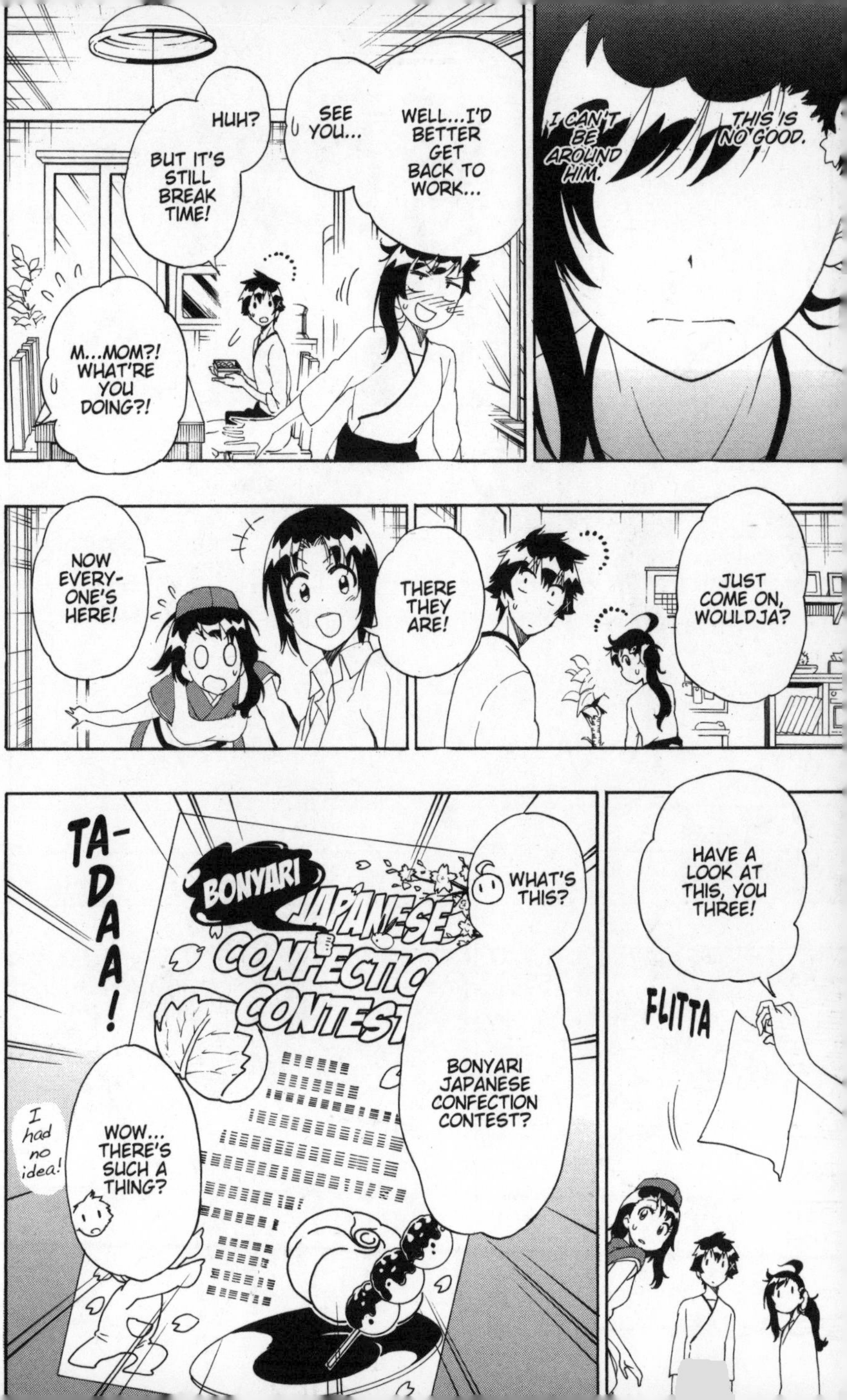
THIS IS NO GOOD.
I CAN'T BE AROUND HIM.
WELL...I'D BETTER GET BACK TO WORK...
SEE YOU...
HUH?
BUT IT'S STILL BREAK TIME!
M...MOM?! WHAT'RE YOU DOING?!
JUST COME ON, WOULDJA?
THERE THEY ARE!
NOW EVERY-ONE'S HERE!
HAVE A LOOK AT THIS, YOU THREE!
FLITTA
TA-DAAA!
BONYARI JAPANESE CONFECTION CONTEST
WHAT'S THIS?
BONYARI JAPANESE CONFECTION CONTEST?
WOW... THERE'S SUCH A THING?
I had no idea!

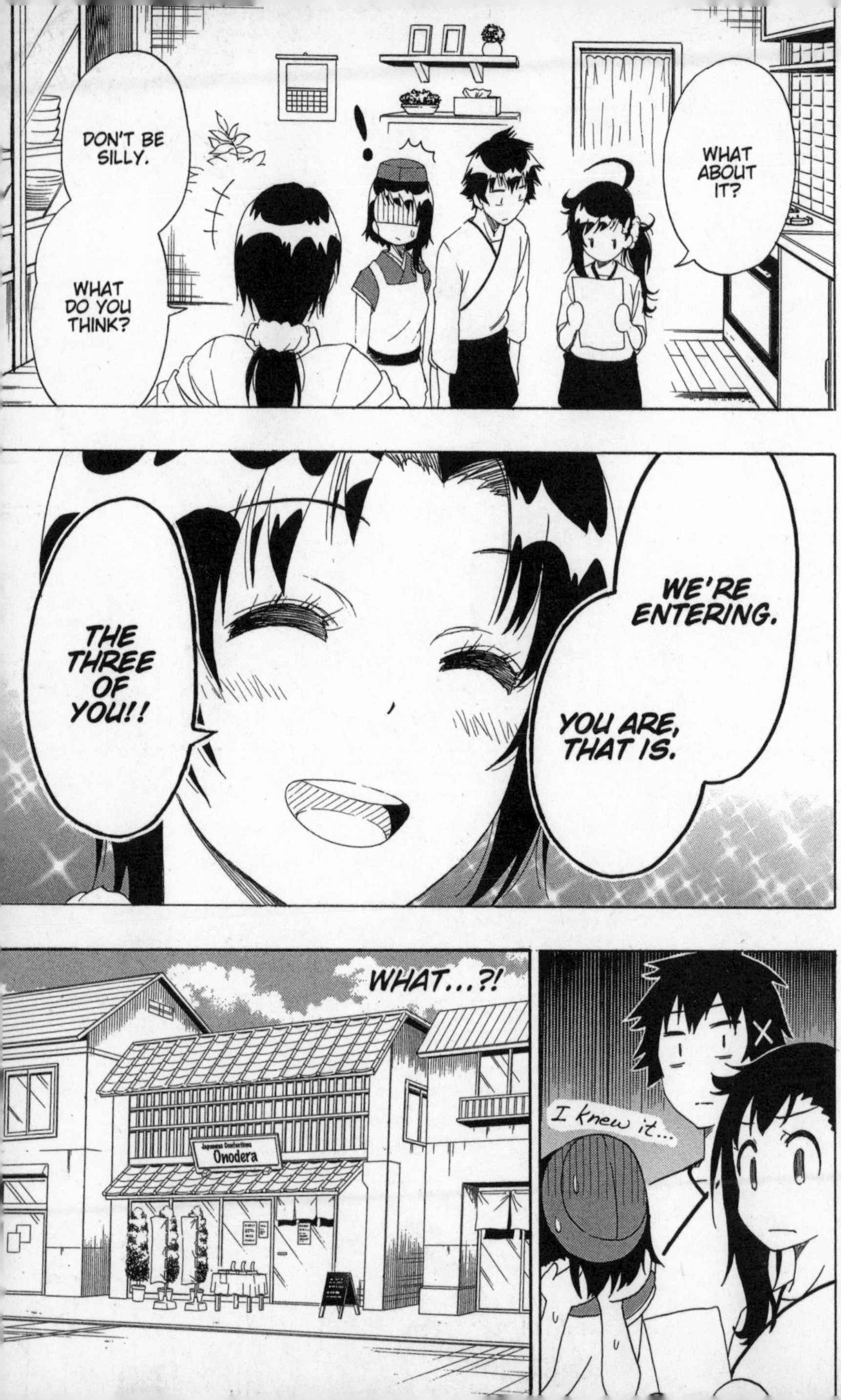
WHAT ABOUT IT?
DON'T BE SILLY.
WHAT DO YOU THINK?
WE'RE ENTERING.
YOU ARE, THAT IS.
THE THREE OF YOU!!
I knew it...
WHAT...?!
Japanese Confections
Onodera

Ritsu Hoshihara

Attended Hannari Junior High with Haru. Currently a first-year at Bonyari High. Former member of the archery club. Haru and Fu were in the archery club too. Has a big crush on Haru—apparently she was pierced with a love arrow watching Haru draw her bowstring. She and Fu fight like cats and dogs. The reason is unclear. Why? Because it is, okay?

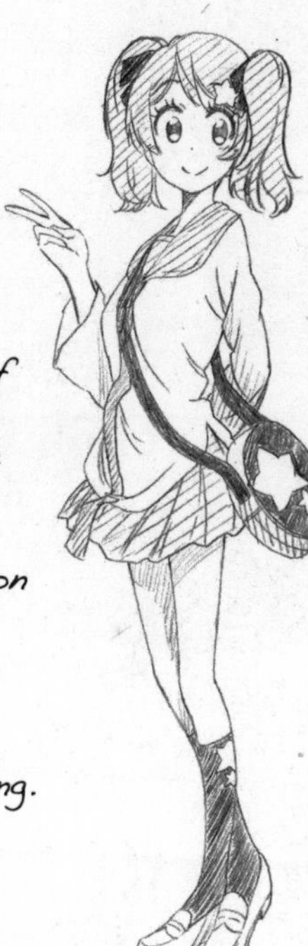

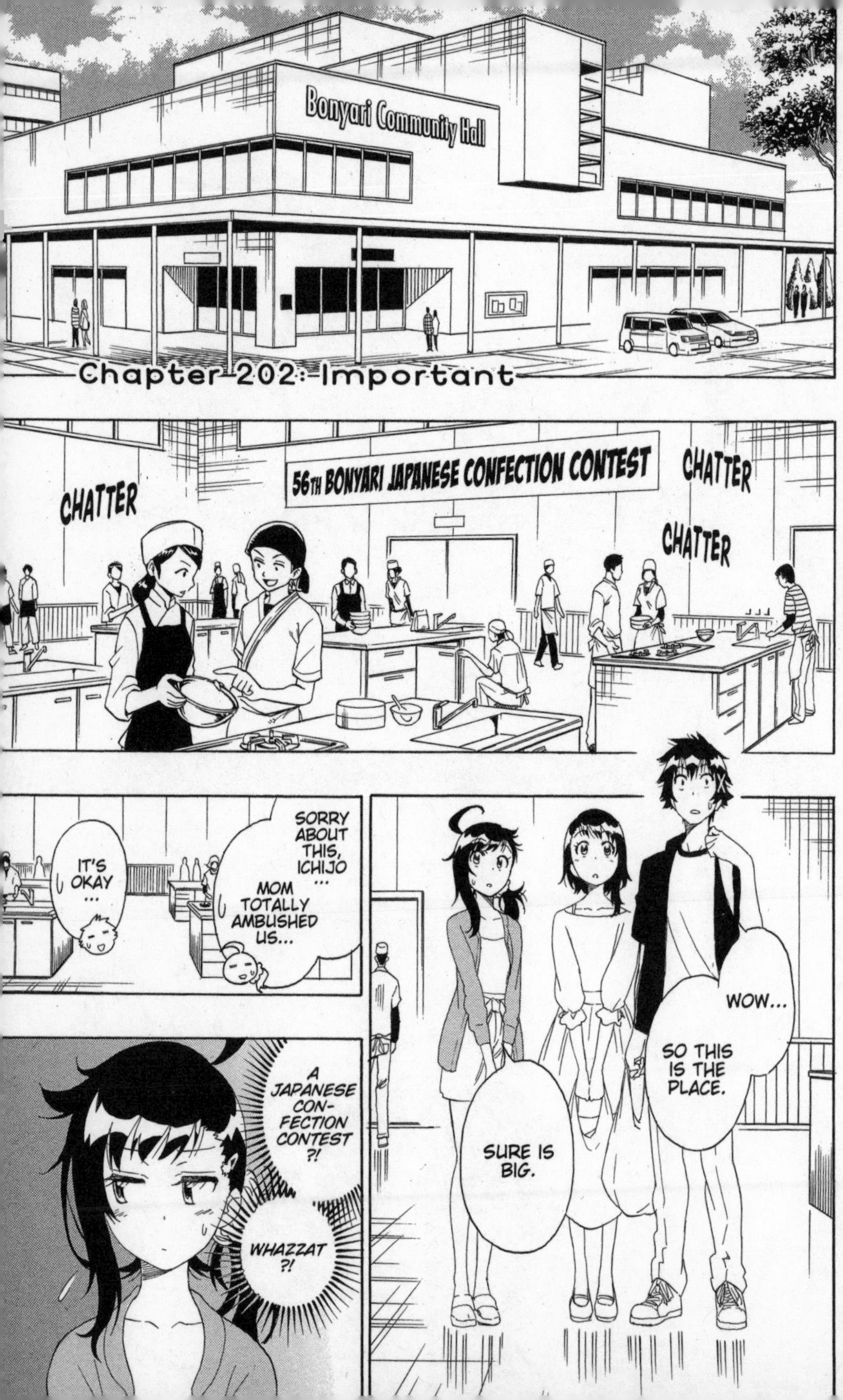
Bonyari Community Hall
Chapter 202: Important
CHATTER
56TH BONYARI JAPANESE CONFECTION CONTEST
CHATTER
CHATTER
WOW... SO THIS IS THE PLACE.
SURE IS BIG.
SORRY ABOUT THIS, ICHIJO... MOM TOTALLY AMBUSHED US...
IT'S OKAY...
A JAPANESE CONFECTION CONTEST?!
WHAZZAT?!

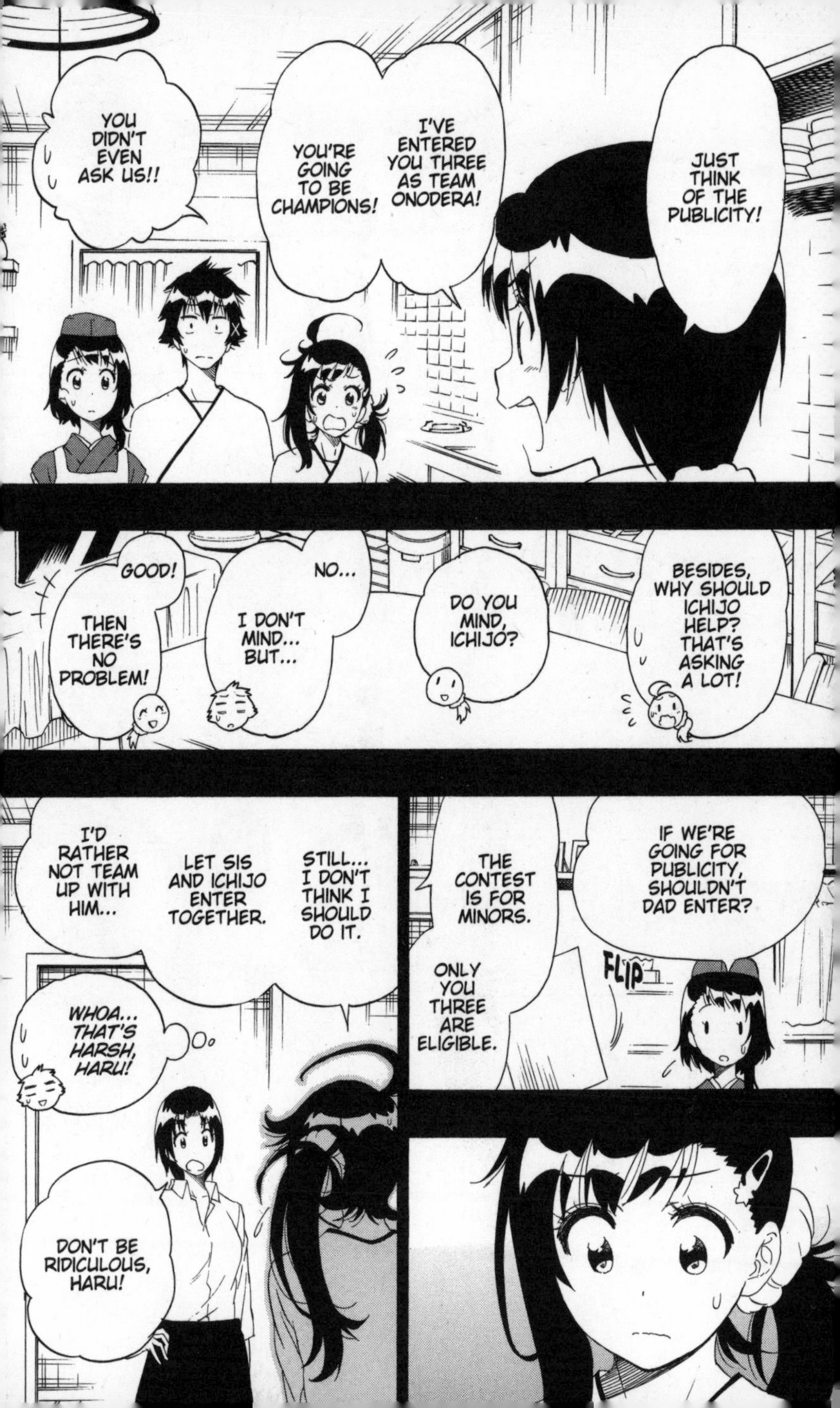
JUST THINK OF THE PUBLICITY!
I'VE ENTERED YOU THREE AS TEAM ONODERA!
YOU'RE GOING TO BE CHAMPIONS!
YOU DIDN'T EVEN ASK US!!
BESIDES, WHY SHOULD ICHIJO HELP? THAT'S ASKING A LOT!
DO YOU MIND, ICHIJO?
NO...
I DON'T MIND... BUT...
GOOD!
THEN THERE'S NO PROBLEM!
IF WE'RE GOING FOR PUBLICITY, SHOULDN'T DAD ENTER?
FLIP
THE CONTEST IS FOR MINORS.
ONLY YOU THREE ARE ELIGIBLE.
STILL... I DON'T THINK I SHOULD DO IT.
LET SIS AND ICHIJO ENTER TOGETHER.
I'D RATHER NOT TEAM UP WITH HIM...
WHOA... THAT'S HARSH, HARU!
DON'T BE RIDICULOUS, HARU!

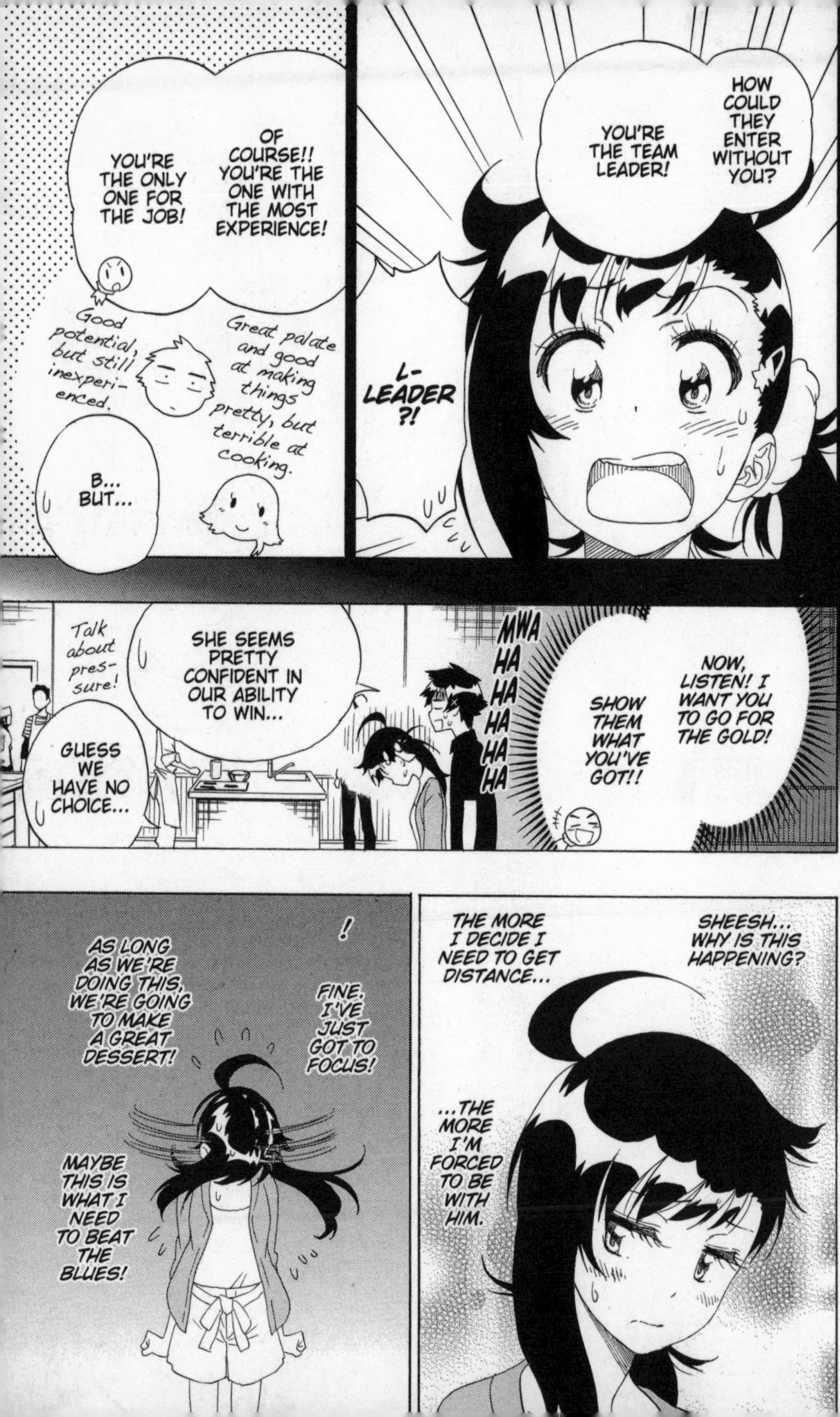
HOW COULD THEY ENTER WITHOUT YOU?
YOU'RE THE TEAM LEADER!
L-LEADER?!
OF COURSE!! YOU'RE THE ONE WITH THE MOST EXPERIENCE!
YOU'RE THE ONLY ONE FOR THE JOB!
Great palate and good at making things pretty, but terrible at cooking.
Good potential, but still inexperienced.
B... BUT...
MWA HA HA HA HA HA HA
NOW, LISTEN! I WANT YOU TO GO FOR THE GOLD!
SHOW THEM WHAT YOU'VE GOT!!
SHE SEEMS PRETTY CONFIDENT IN OUR ABILITY TO WIN...
Talk about pressure!
GUESS WE HAVE NO CHOICE...
SHEESH... WHY IS THIS HAPPENING?
THE MORE I DECIDE I NEED TO GET DISTANCE...
...THE MORE I'M FORCED TO BE WITH HIM.
!
FINE. I'VE JUST GOT TO FOCUS!
AS LONG AS WE'RE DOING THIS, WE'RE GOING TO MAKE A GREAT DESSERT!
MAYBE THIS IS WHAT I NEED TO BEAT THE BLUES!

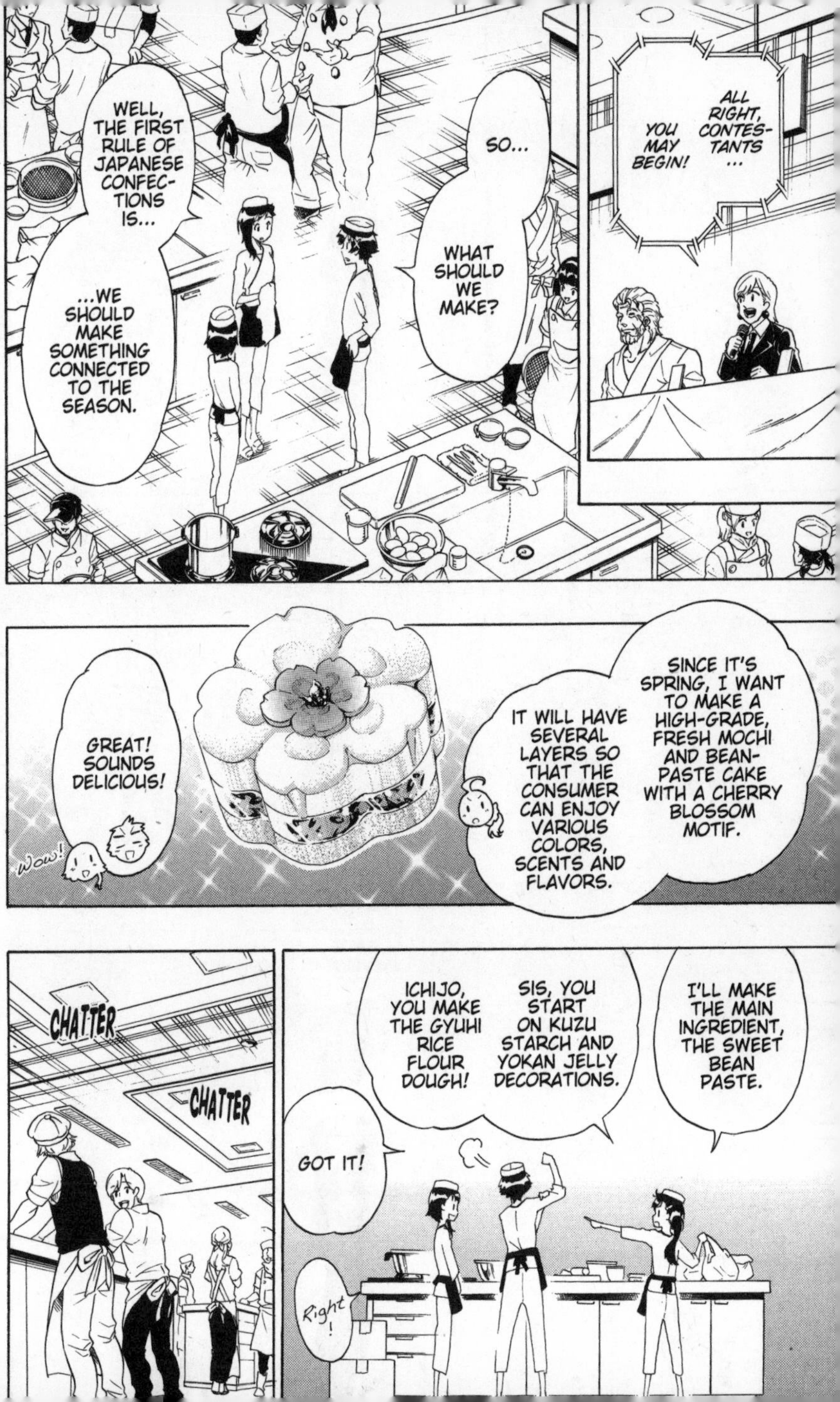
ALL RIGHT, CONTESTANTS... YOU MAY BEGIN!
SO...
WHAT SHOULD WE MAKE?
WELL, THE FIRST RULE OF JAPANESE CONFECTIONS IS...
...WE SHOULD MAKE SOMETHING CONNECTED TO THE SEASON.
SINCE IT'S SPRING, I WANT TO MAKE A HIGH-GRADE, FRESH MOCHI AND BEAN-PASTE CAKE WITH A CHERRY BLOSSOM MOTIF.
IT WILL HAVE SEVERAL LAYERS SO THAT THE CONSUMER CAN ENJOY VARIOUS COLORS, SCENTS AND FLAVORS.
GREAT! SOUNDS DELICIOUS!
Wow!
I'LL MAKE THE MAIN INGREDIENT, THE SWEET BEAN PASTE.
SIS, YOU START ON KUZU STARCH AND YOKAN JELLY DECORATIONS.
ICHIJO, YOU MAKE THE GYUHI RICE FLOUR DOUGH!
GOT IT!
Right!
CHATTER
CHATTER

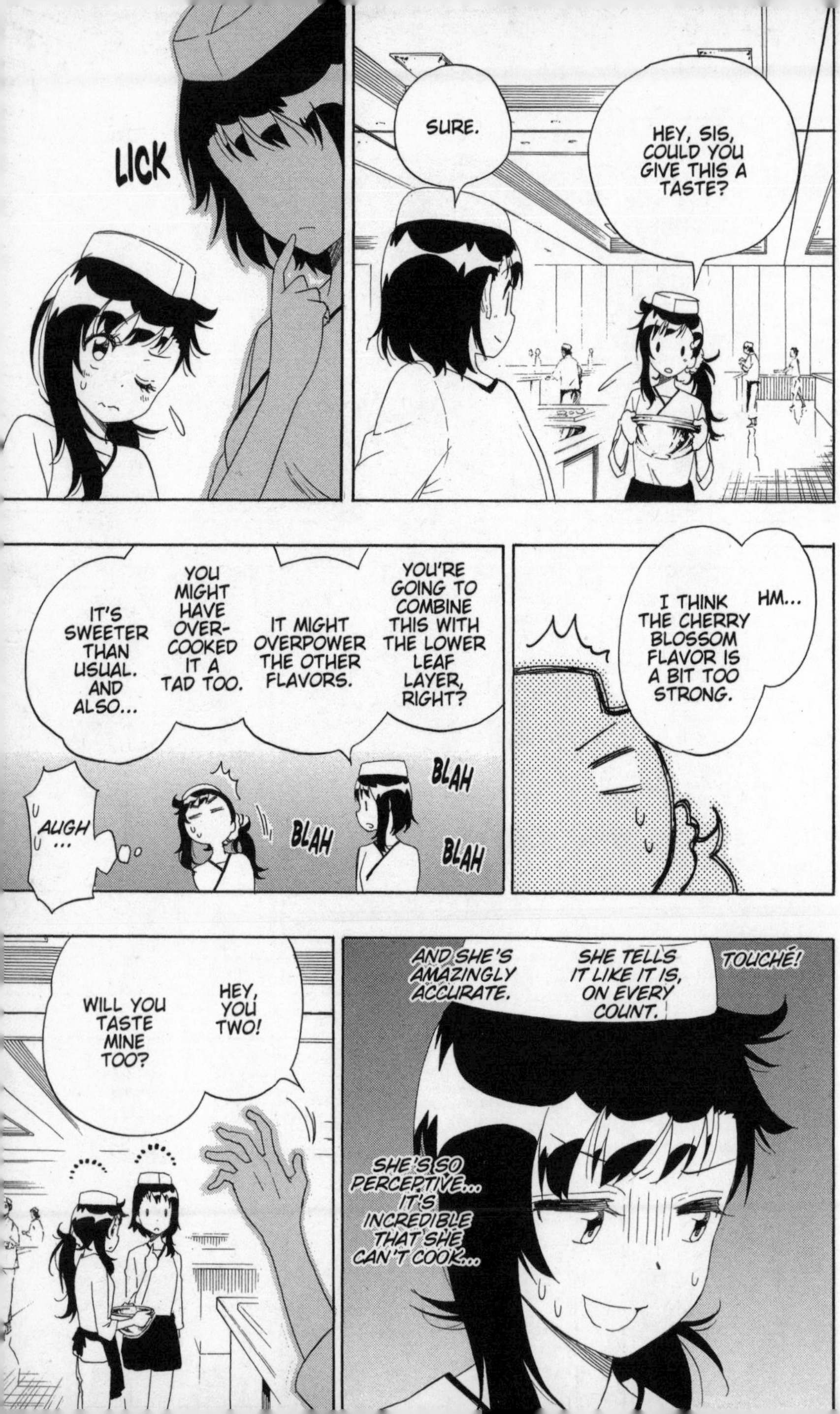
HEY, SIS, COULD YOU GIVE THIS A TASTE?
SURE.
LICK
HM...
I THINK THE CHERRY BLOSSOM FLAVOR IS A BIT TOO STRONG.
YOU'RE GOING TO COMBINE THIS WITH THE LOWER LEAF LAYER, RIGHT?
IT MIGHT OVERPOWER THE OTHER FLAVORS.
YOU MIGHT HAVE OVER-COOKED IT A TAD TOO.
IT'S SWEETER THAN USUAL. AND ALSO...
BLAH
BLAH
BLAH
AUGH...
TOUCHÉ!
SHE TELLS IT LIKE IT IS, ON EVERY COUNT.
AND SHE'S AMAZINGLY ACCURATE.
SHE'S SO PERCEPTIVE... IT'S INCREDIBLE THAT SHE CAN'T COOK...
HEY, YOU TWO!
WILL YOU TASTE MINE TOO?

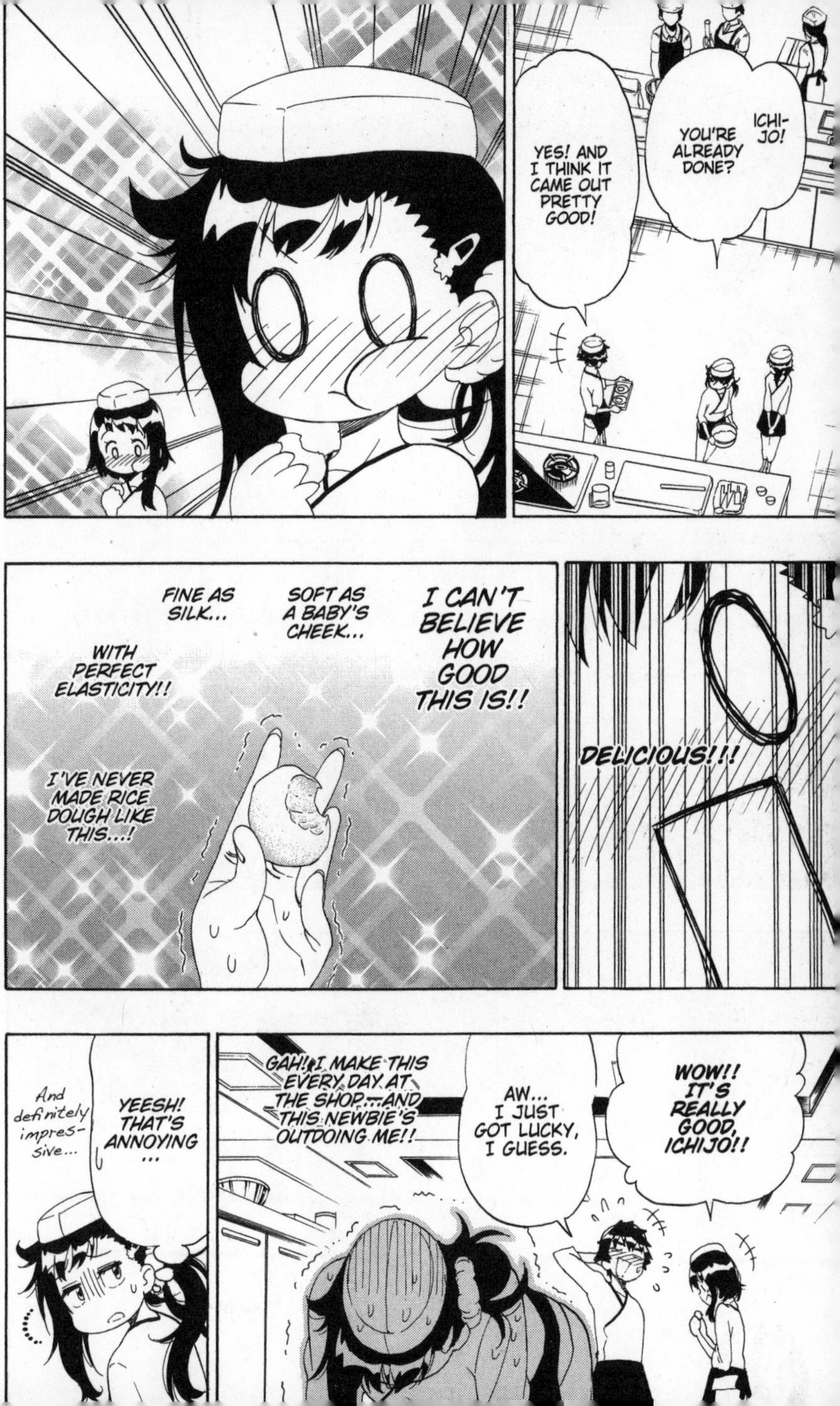
ICHI-JO!
YOU'RE ALREADY DONE?
YES! AND I THINK IT CAME OUT PRETTY GOOD!
DELICIOUS!!!
I CAN'T BELIEVE HOW GOOD THIS IS!!
SOFT AS A BABY'S CHEEK...
FINE AS SILK...
WITH PERFECT ELASTICITY!!
I'VE NEVER MADE RICE DOUGH LIKE THIS...!
WOW!! IT'S REALLY GOOD, ICHIJO!!
AW... I JUST GOT LUCKY, I GUESS.
GAH! I MAKE THIS EVERY DAY AT THE SHOP... AND THIS NEWBIE'S OUTDOING ME!!
YEESH! THAT'S ANNOYING...
And definitely impres-sive...

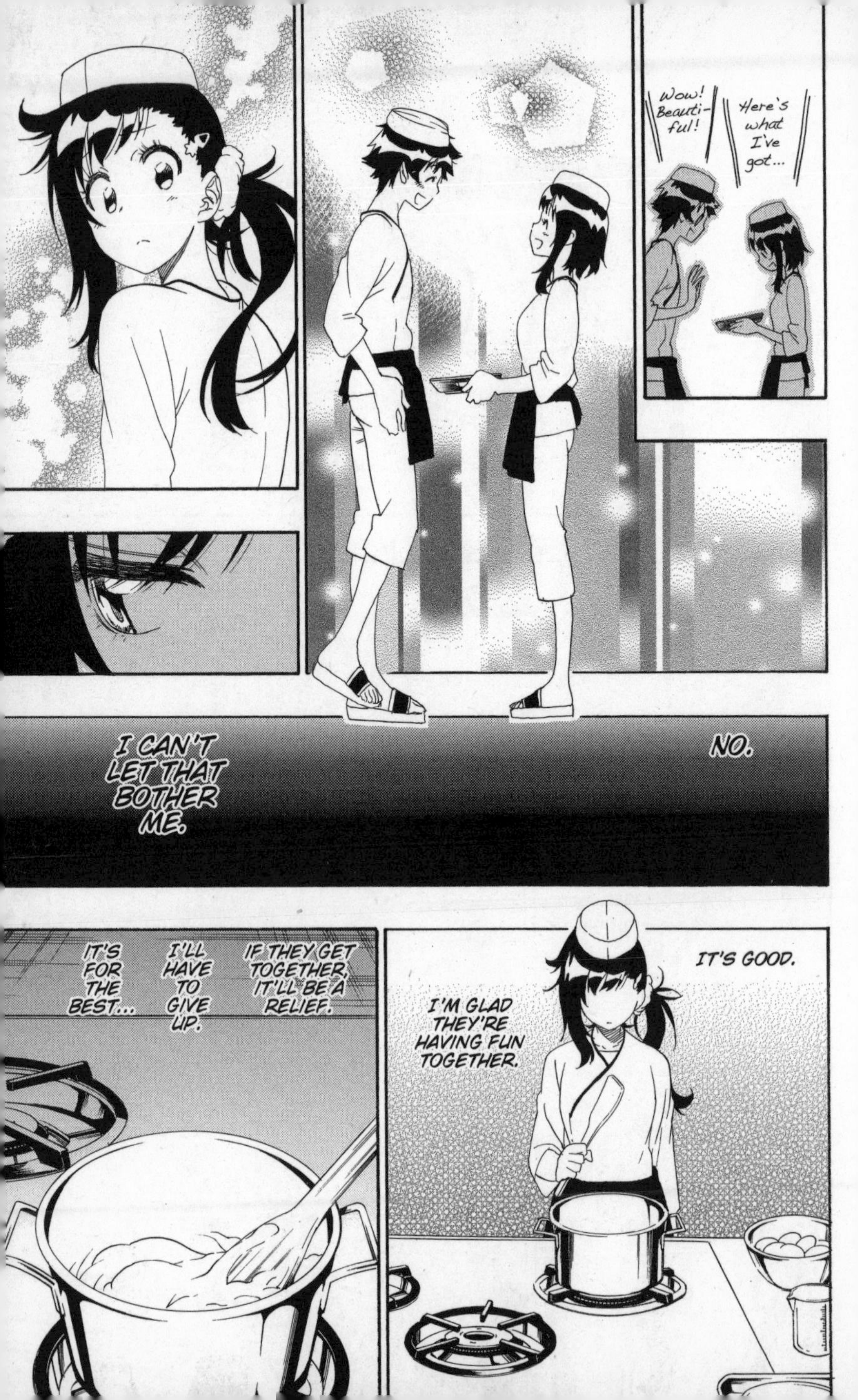
Here's what I've got...
Wow! Beautiful!
NO.
I CAN'T LET THAT BOTHER ME.
IT'S GOOD.
I'M GLAD THEY'RE HAVING FUN TOGETHER.
IF THEY GET TOGETHER, IT'LL BE A RELIEF.
I'LL HAVE TO GIVE UP.
IT'S FOR THE BEST...

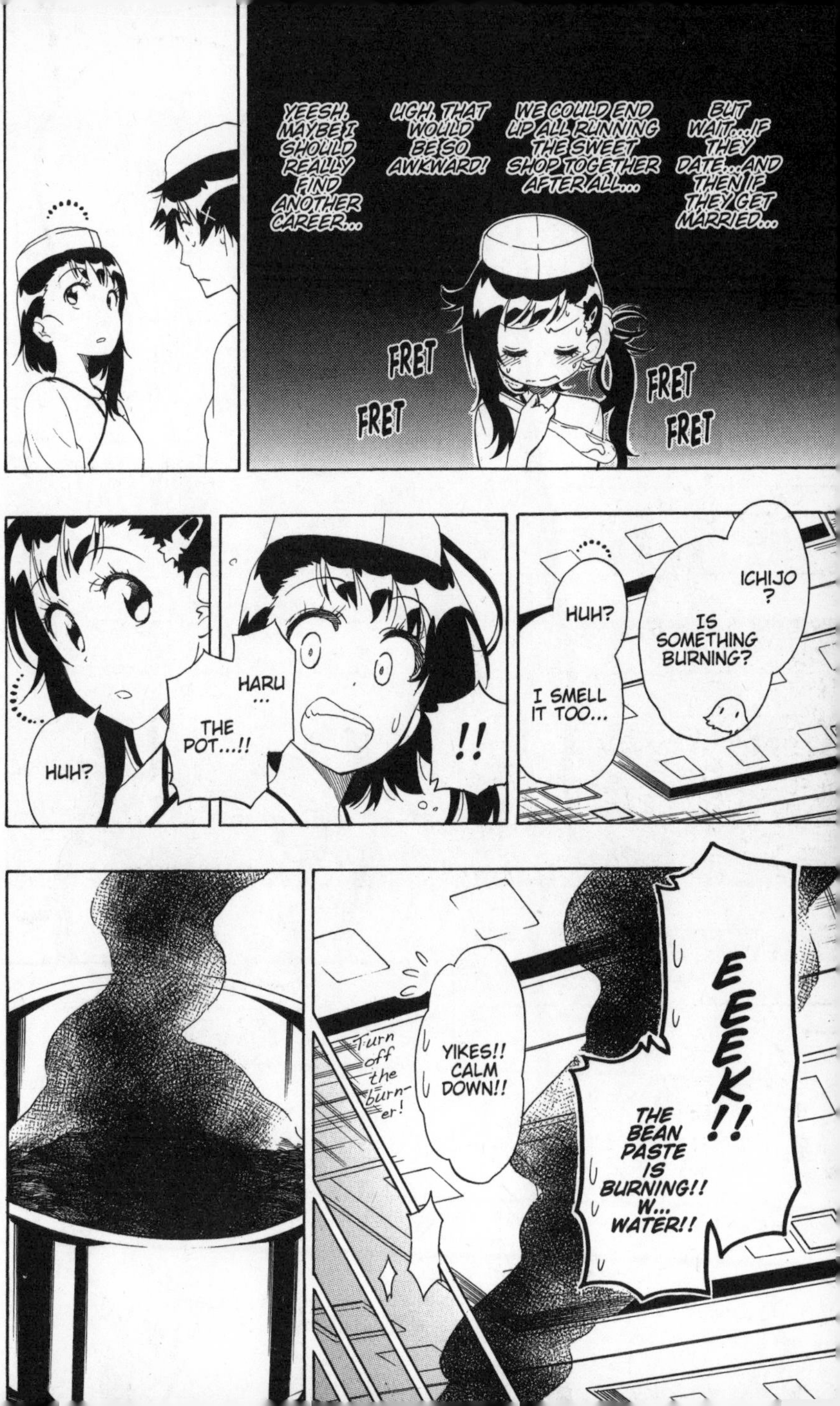
BUT WAIT...IF THEY DATE...AND THEN IF THEY GET MARRIED...
WE COULD END UP ALL RUNNING THE SWEET SHOP TOGETHER AFTER ALL...
UGH, THAT WOULD BE SO AWKWARD!
YEESH. MAYBE I SHOULD REALLY FIND ANOTHER CAREER...
FRET
FRET
FRET
FRET
ICHIJO?
IS SOMETHING BURNING?
HUH?
I SMELL IT TOO...
!!
HARU...
THE POT...!!
HUH?
EEEK!!
THE BEAN PASTE IS BURNING!! W... WATER!!
YIKES!! CALM DOWN!!
Turn off the burner!

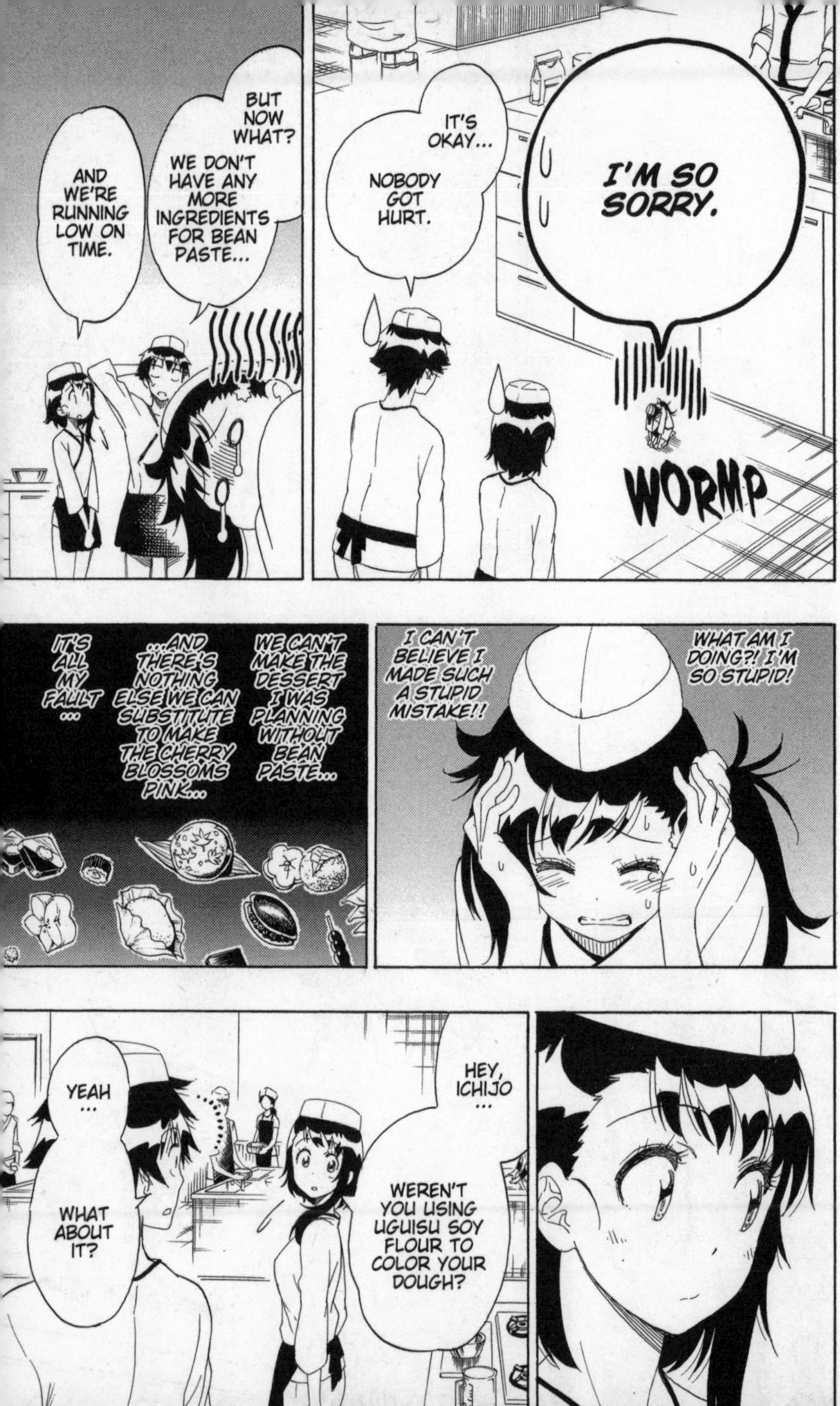
I'M SO SORRY.
IT'S OKAY...
NOBODY GOT HURT.
WORMP
BUT NOW WHAT?
WE DON'T HAVE ANY MORE INGREDIENTS FOR BEAN PASTE...
AND WE'RE RUNNING LOW ON TIME.
WHAT AM I DOING?! I'M SO STUPID!
I CAN'T BELIEVE I MADE SUCH A STUPID MISTAKE!!
WE CAN'T MAKE THE DESSERT I WAS PLANNING WITHOUT BEAN PASTE...
...AND THERE'S NOTHING ELSE WE CAN SUBSTITUTE TO MAKE THE CHERRY BLOSSOMS PINK...
IT'S ALL MY FAULT...
HEY, ICHIJO...
WEREN'T YOU USING UGUISU SOY FLOUR TO COLOR YOUR DOUGH?
YEAH...
WHAT ABOUT IT?

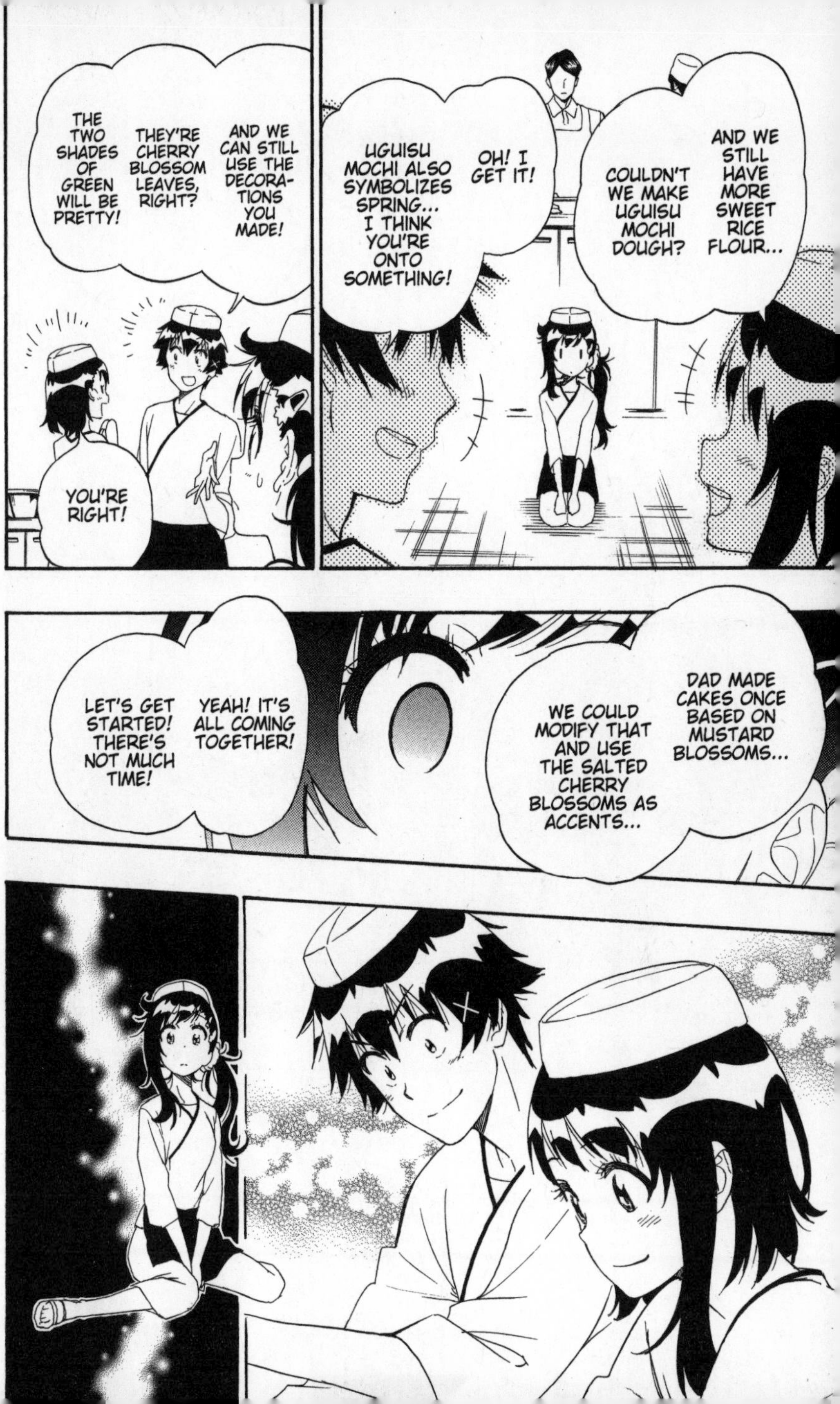
AND WE STILL HAVE MORE SWEET RICE FLOUR...
COULDN'T WE MAKE UGUISU MOCHI DOUGH?
OH! I GET IT!
UGUISU MOCHI ALSO SYMBOLIZES SPRING... I THINK YOU'RE ONTO SOMETHING!
AND WE CAN STILL USE THE DECORA-TIONS YOU MADE!
THEY'RE CHERRY BLOSSOM LEAVES, RIGHT?
THE TWO SHADES OF GREEN WILL BE PRETTY!
YOU'RE RIGHT!
DAD MADE CAKES ONCE BASED ON MUSTARD BLOSSOMS...
WE COULD MODIFY THAT AND USE THE SALTED CHERRY BLOSSOMS AS ACCENTS...
YEAH! IT'S ALL COMING TOGETHER!
LET'S GET STARTED! THERE'S NOT MUCH TIME!

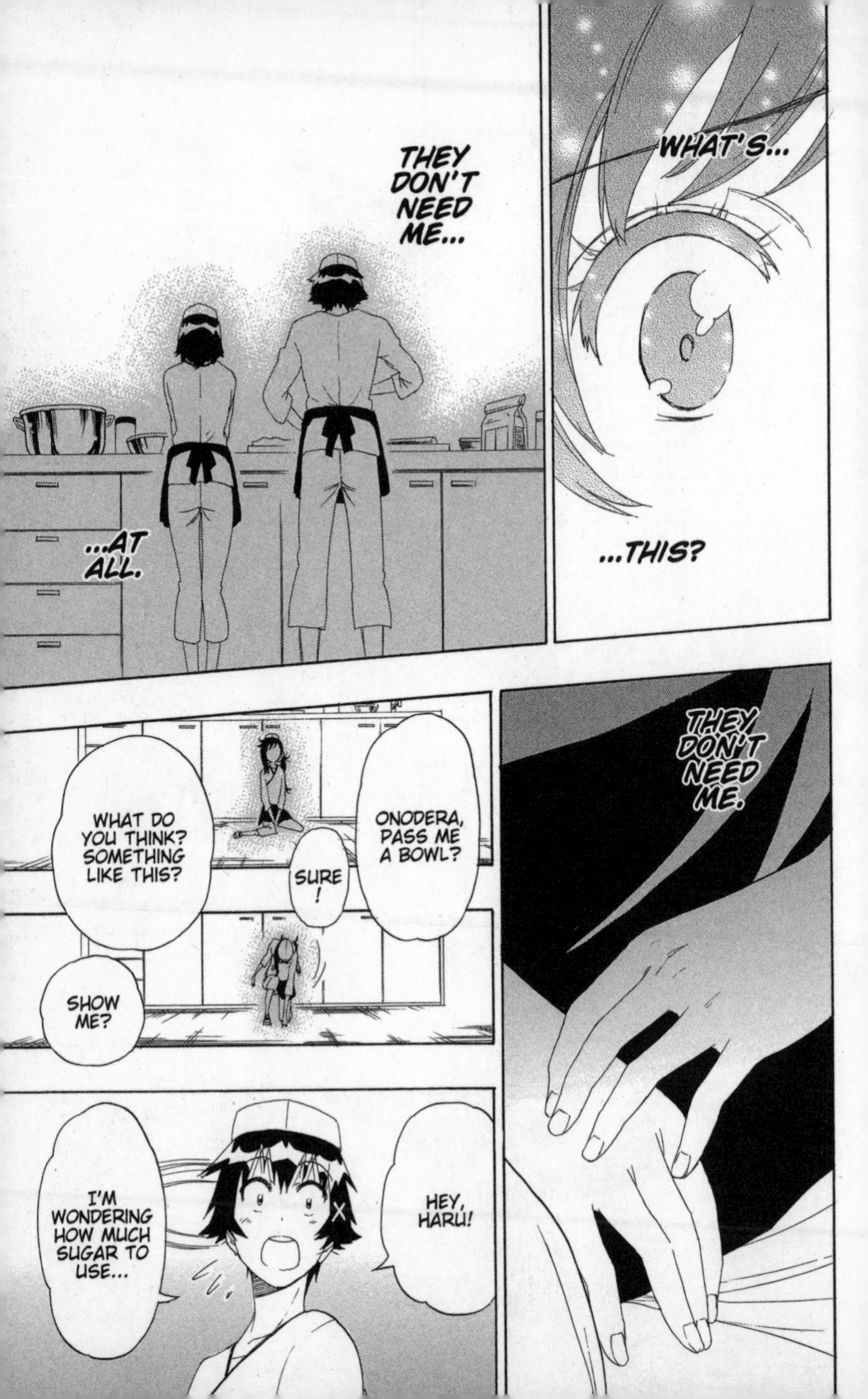
WHAT'S...
...THIS?
THEY DON'T NEED ME...
...AT ALL.
THEY DON'T NEED ME.
ONODERA, PASS ME A BOWL?
SURE!
WHAT DO YOU THINK? SOMETHING LIKE THIS?
SHOW ME?
HEY, HARU!
I'M WONDERING HOW MUCH SUGAR TO USE...

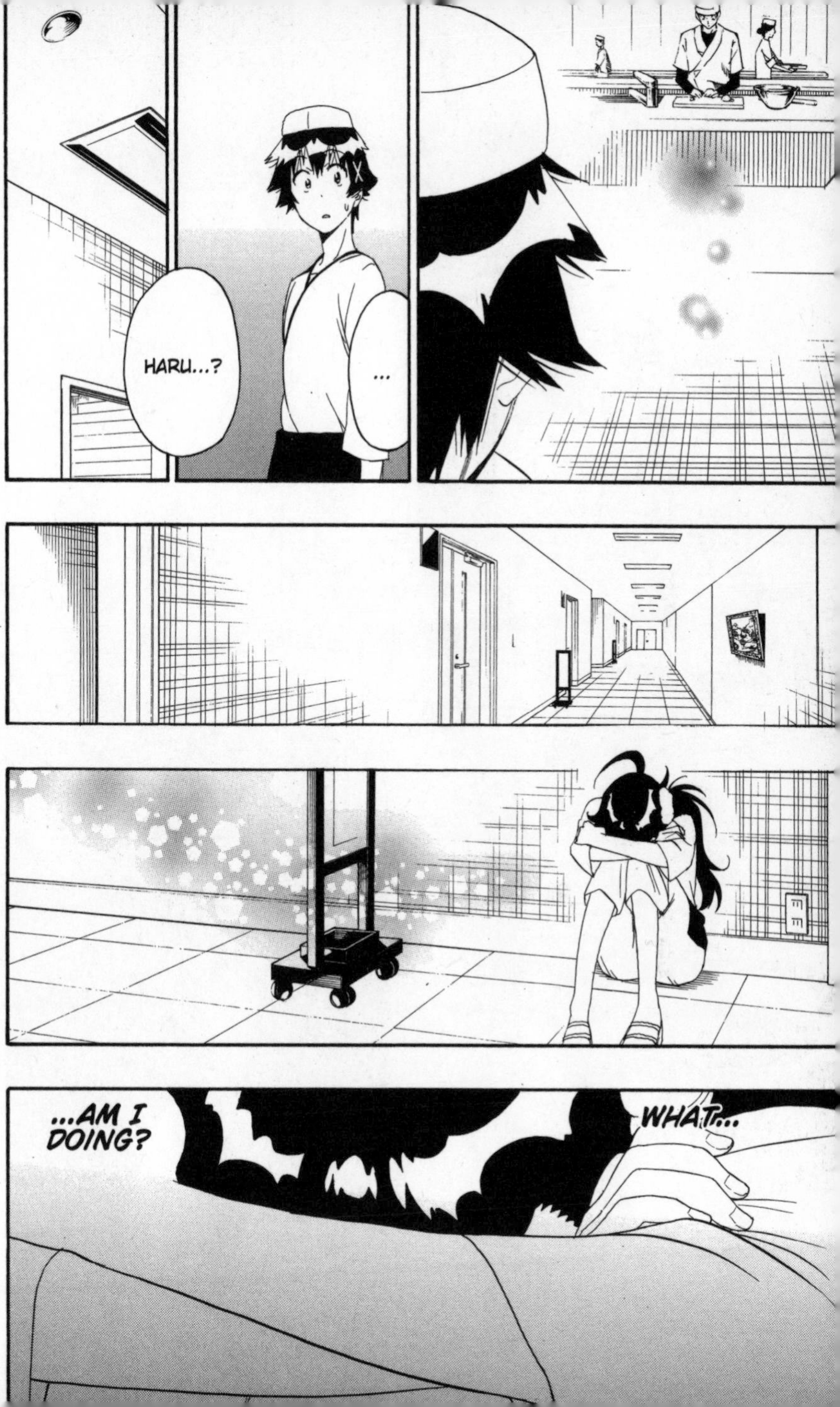
...
HARU...?
WHAT...
...AM I DOING?

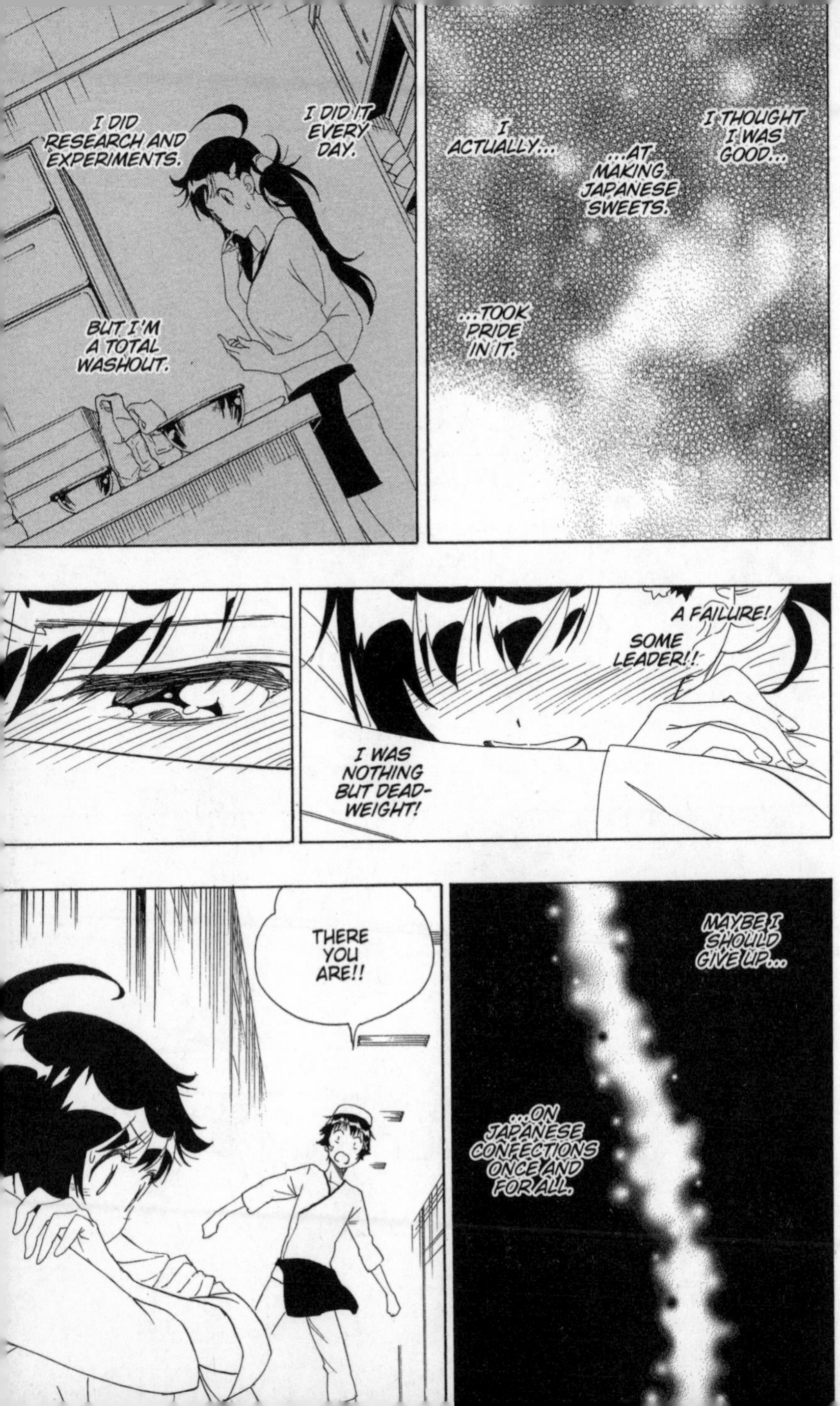
I THOUGHT I WAS GOOD...
...AT MAKING JAPANESE SWEETS.
I ACTUALLY...
...TOOK PRIDE IN IT.
I DID IT EVERY DAY.
I DID RESEARCH AND EXPERIMENTS.
BUT I'M A TOTAL WASHOUT.
A FAILURE!
SOME LEADER!!
I WAS NOTHING BUT DEAD-WEIGHT!
MAYBE I SHOULD GIVE UP...
...ON JAPANESE CONFECTIONS ONCE AND FOR ALL.
THERE YOU ARE!!

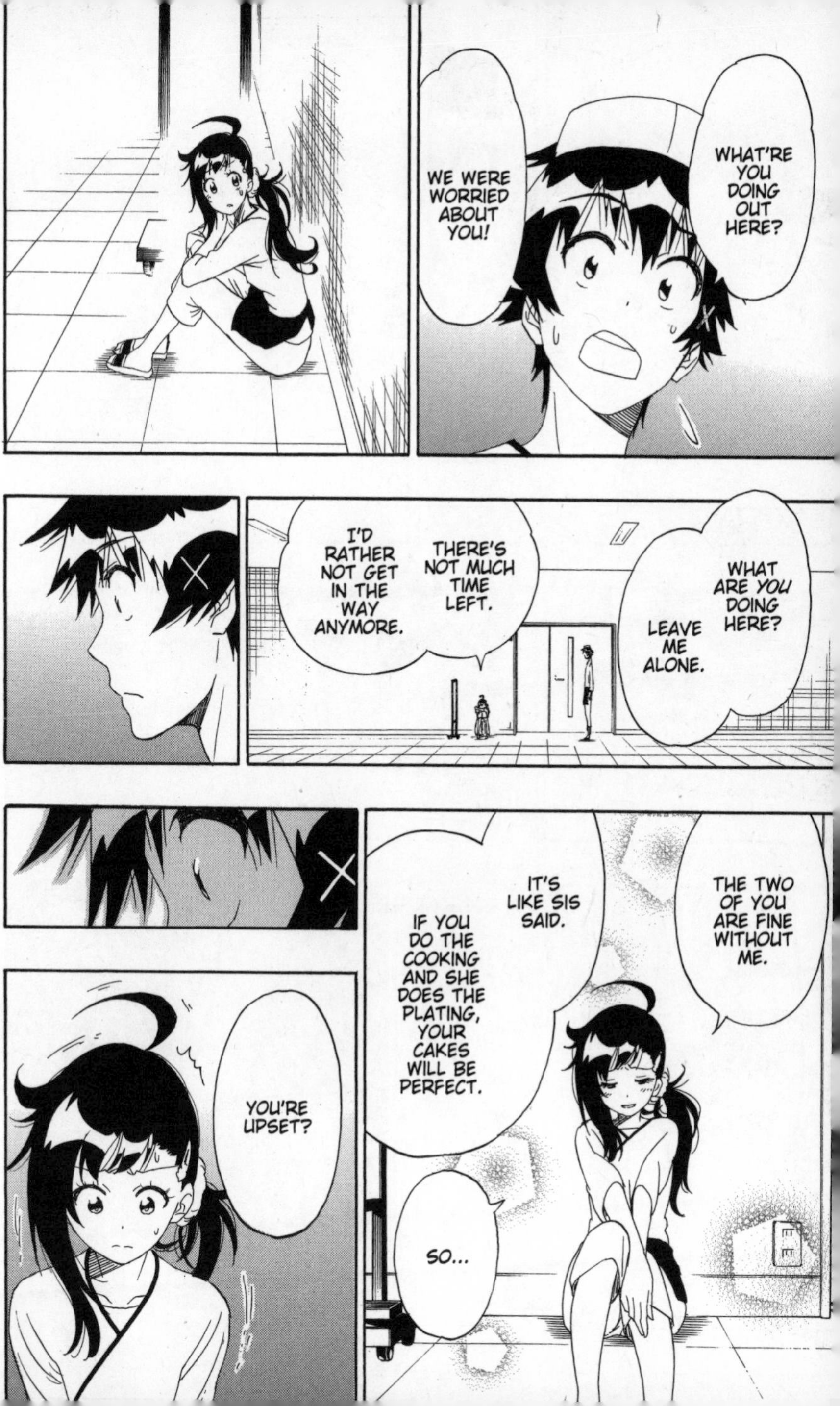
WHAT'RE YOU DOING OUT HERE?
WE WERE WORRIED ABOUT YOU!
WHAT ARE *YOU* DOING HERE?
LEAVE ME ALONE.
THERE'S NOT MUCH TIME LEFT.
I'D RATHER NOT GET IN THE WAY ANYMORE.
THE TWO OF YOU ARE FINE WITHOUT ME.
IT'S LIKE SIS SAID.
IF YOU DO THE COOKING AND SHE DOES THE PLATING, YOUR CAKES WILL BE PERFECT.
SO...
YOU'RE UPSET?

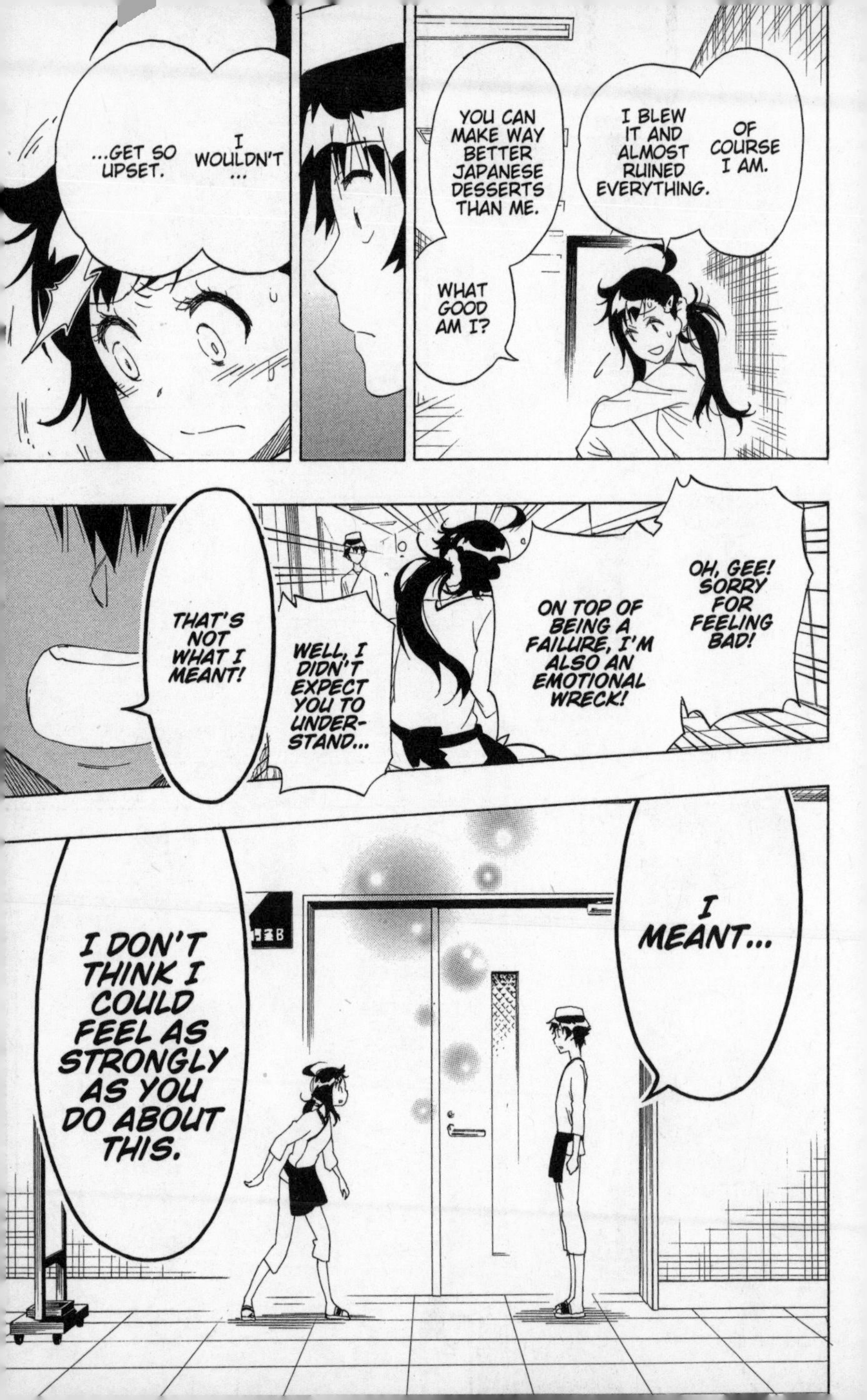
OF COURSE I AM.
I BLEW IT AND ALMOST RUINED EVERYTHING.
YOU CAN MAKE WAY BETTER JAPANESE DESSERTS THAN ME.
WHAT GOOD AM I?
I WOULDN'T ...
...GET SO UPSET.
OH, GEE! SORRY FOR FEELING BAD!
ON TOP OF BEING A FAILURE, I'M ALSO AN EMOTIONAL WRECK!
WELL, I DIDN'T EXPECT YOU TO UNDER-STAND...
THAT'S NOT WHAT I MEANT!
I MEANT...
I DON'T THINK I COULD FEEL AS STRONGLY AS YOU DO ABOUT THIS.

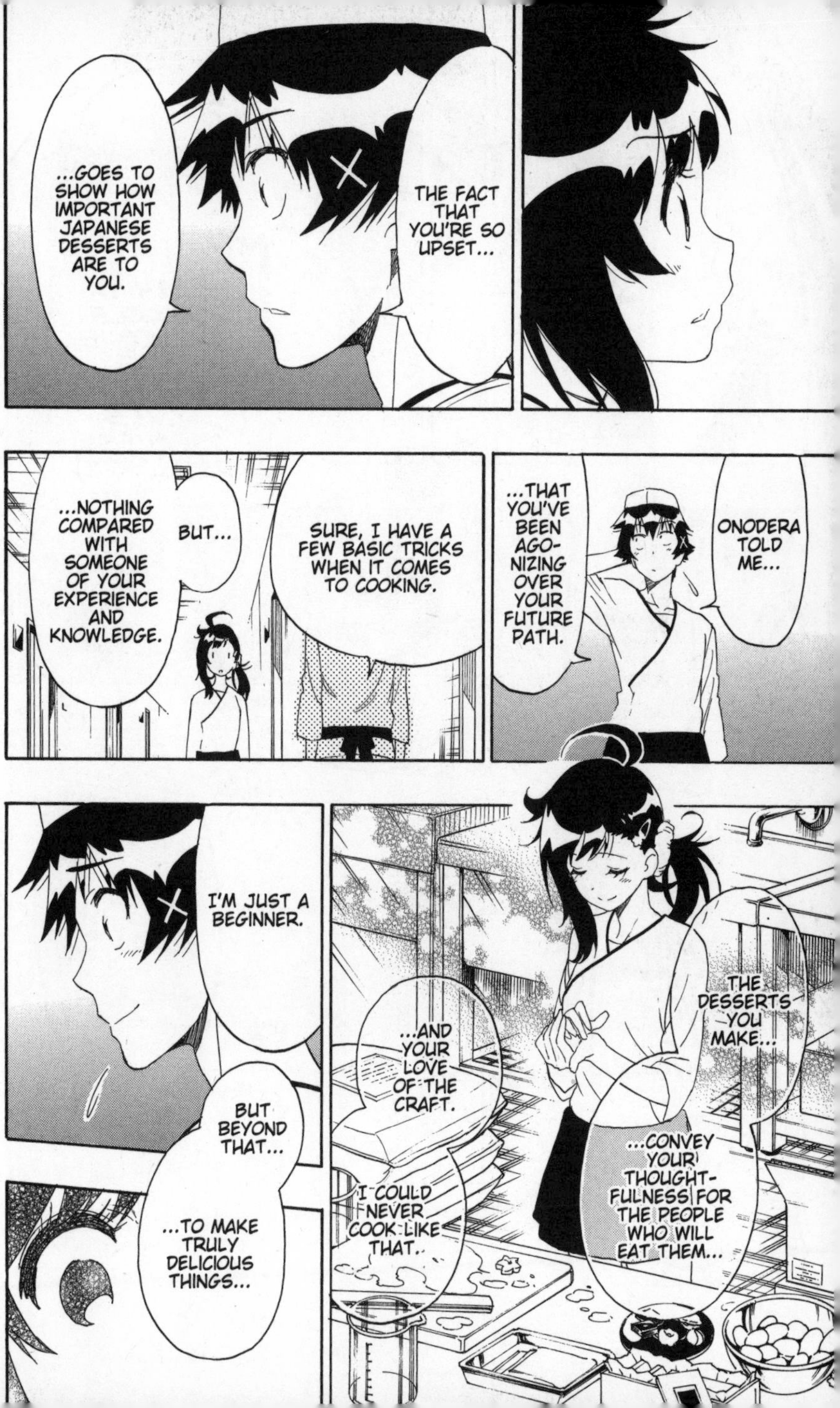
THE FACT THAT YOU'RE SO UPSET...
...GOES TO SHOW HOW IMPORTANT JAPANESE DESSERTS ARE TO YOU.
ONODERA TOLD ME...
...THAT YOU'VE BEEN AGO-NIZING OVER YOUR FUTURE PATH.
SURE, I HAVE A FEW BASIC TRICKS WHEN IT COMES TO COOKING.
BUT...
...NOTHING COMPARED WITH SOMEONE OF YOUR EXPERIENCE AND KNOWLEDGE.
THE DESSERTS YOU MAKE...
...CONVEY YOUR THOUGHT-FULNESS FOR THE PEOPLE WHO WILL EAT THEM...
...AND YOUR LOVE OF THE CRAFT.
I COULD NEVER COOK LIKE THAT.
I'M JUST A BEGINNER.
BUT BEYOND THAT...
...TO MAKE TRULY DELICIOUS THINGS...

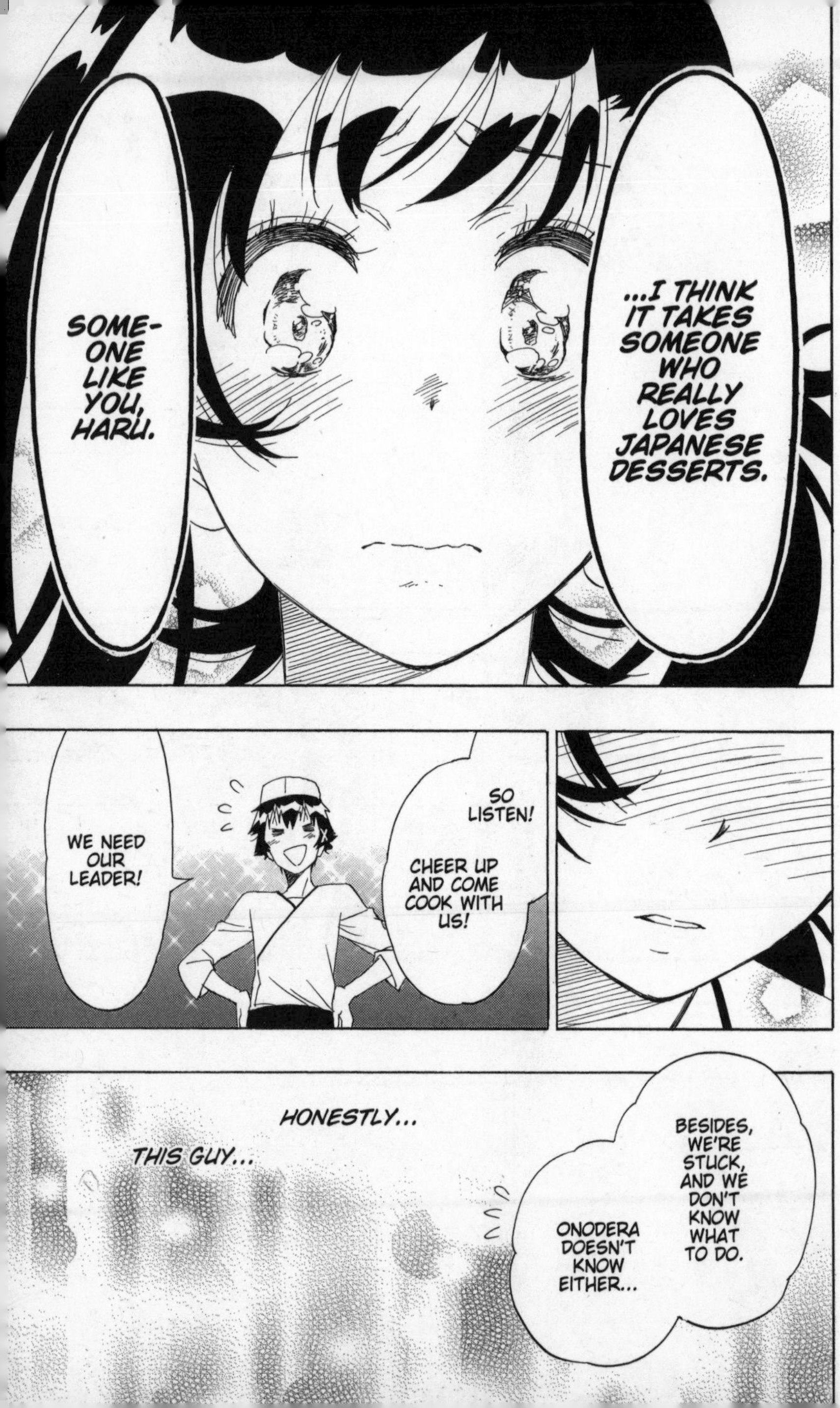
...I THINK IT TAKES SOMEONE WHO REALLY LOVES JAPANESE DESSERTS.
SOME-ONE LIKE YOU, HARU.
SO LISTEN!
CHEER UP AND COME COOK WITH US!
WE NEED OUR LEADER!
BESIDES, WE'RE STUCK, AND WE DON'T KNOW WHAT TO DO.
ONODERA DOESN'T KNOW EITHER...
HONESTLY...
THIS GUY...

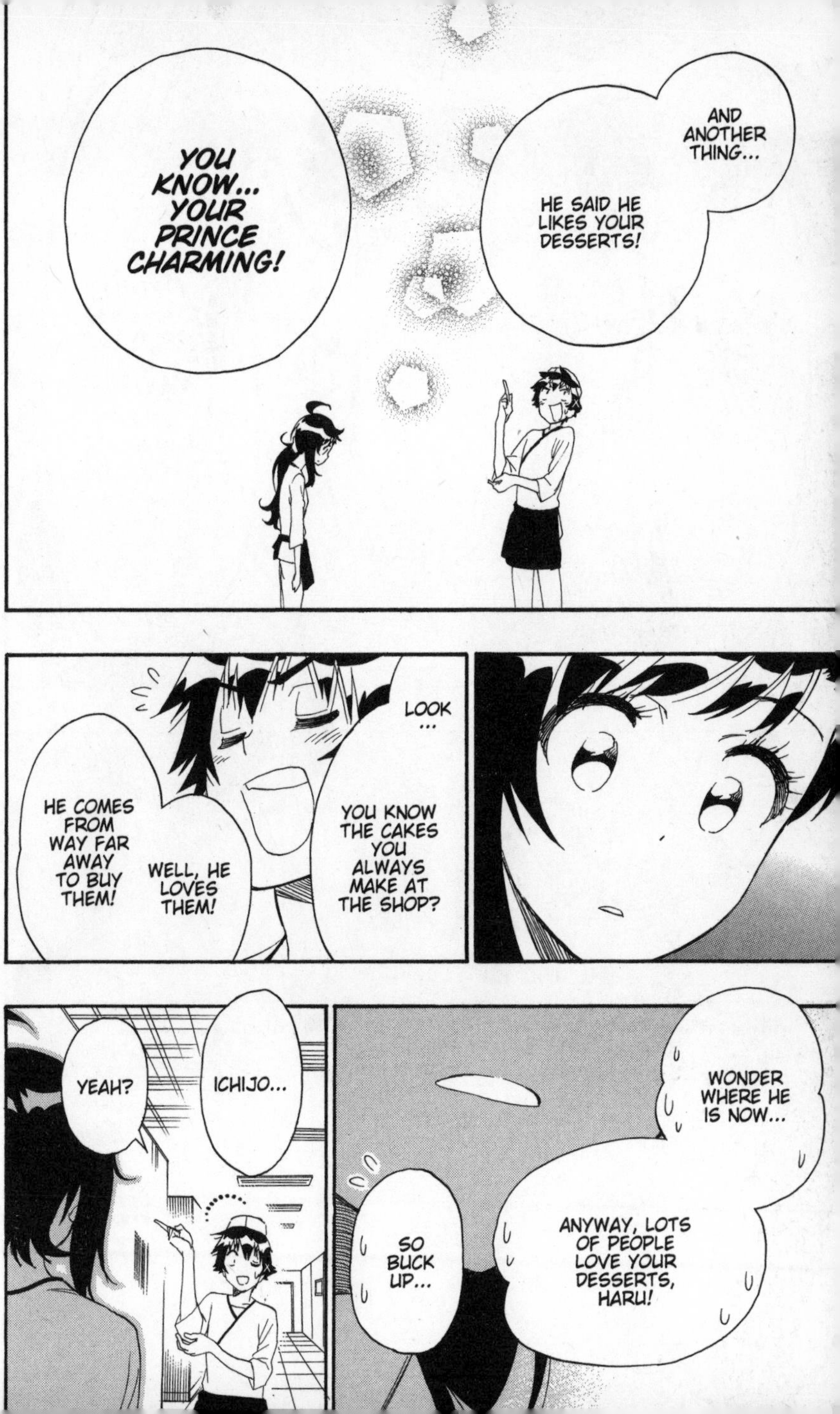
AND ANOTHER THING...
HE SAID HE LIKES YOUR DESSERTS!
YOU KNOW... YOUR PRINCE CHARMING!
LOOK...
YOU KNOW THE CAKES YOU ALWAYS MAKE AT THE SHOP?
WELL, HE LOVES THEM!
HE COMES FROM WAY FAR AWAY TO BUY THEM!
WONDER WHERE HE IS NOW...
ANYWAY, LOTS OF PEOPLE LOVE YOUR DESSERTS, HARU!
SO BUCK UP...
ICHIJO...
YEAH?

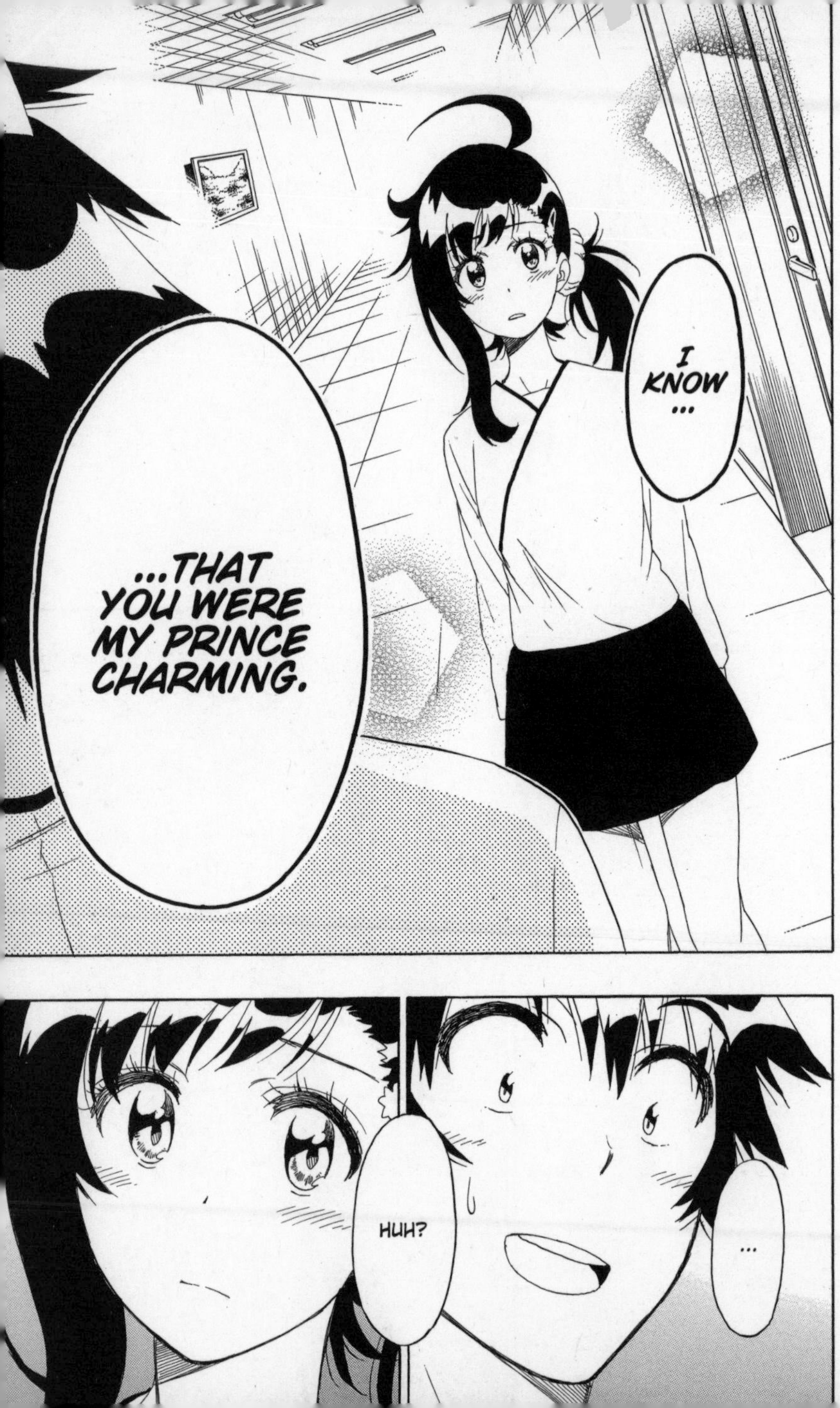
I KNOW...
...THAT YOU WERE MY PRINCE CHARMING.
...
HUH?

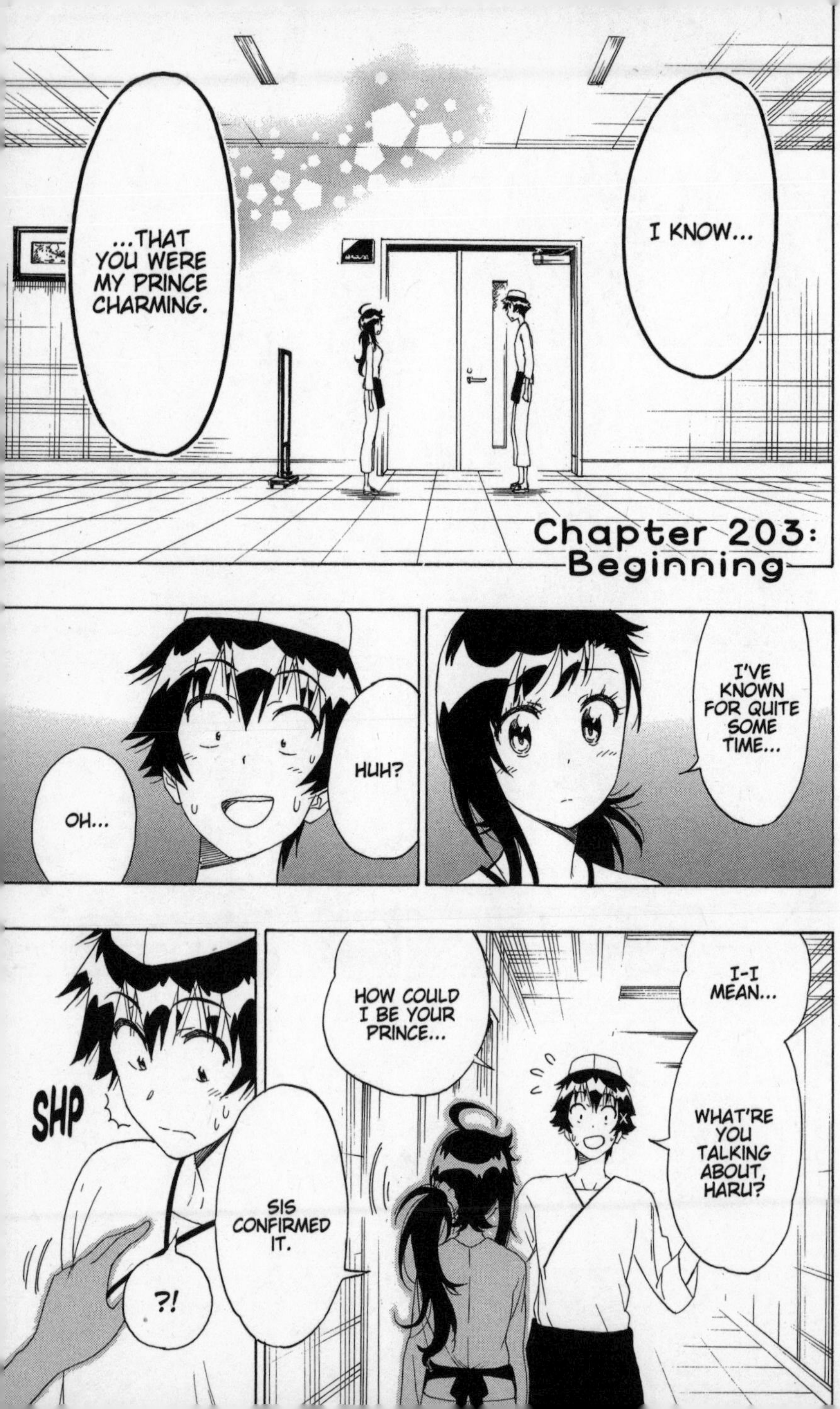
I KNOW...
...THAT YOU WERE MY PRINCE CHARMING.
Chapter 203: Beginning
I'VE KNOWN FOR QUITE SOME TIME...
HUH?
OH...
I-I MEAN...
WHAT'RE YOU TALKING ABOUT, HARU?
HOW COULD I BE YOUR PRINCE...
SIS CONFIRMED IT.
SHP
?!

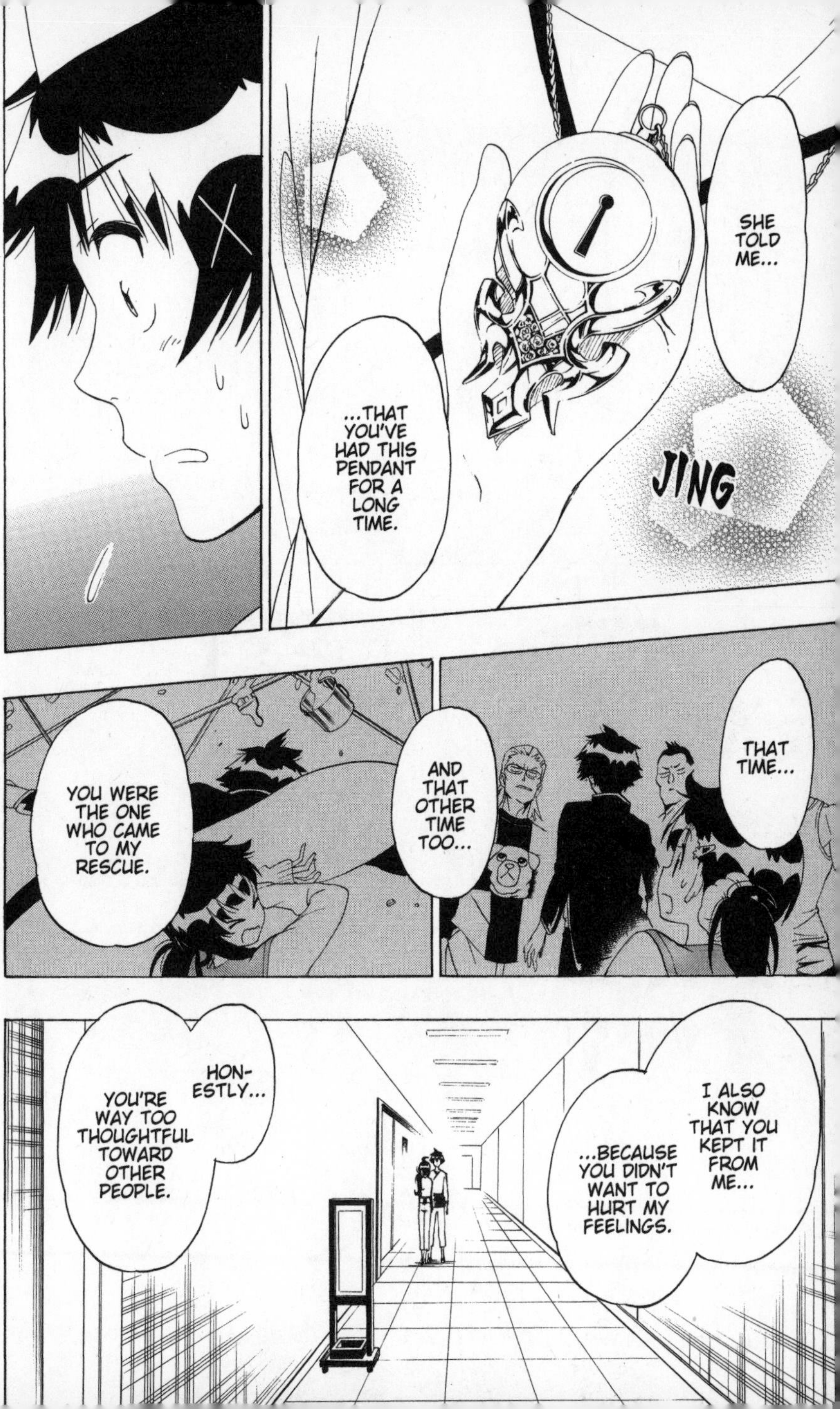
SHE TOLD ME...
JING
...THAT YOU'VE HAD THIS PENDANT FOR A LONG TIME.
THAT TIME...
AND THAT OTHER TIME TOO...
YOU WERE THE ONE WHO CAME TO MY RESCUE.
I ALSO KNOW THAT YOU KEPT IT FROM ME...
...BECAUSE YOU DIDN'T WANT TO HURT MY FEELINGS.
HON-ESTLY...
YOU'RE WAY TOO THOUGHTFUL TOWARD OTHER PEOPLE.

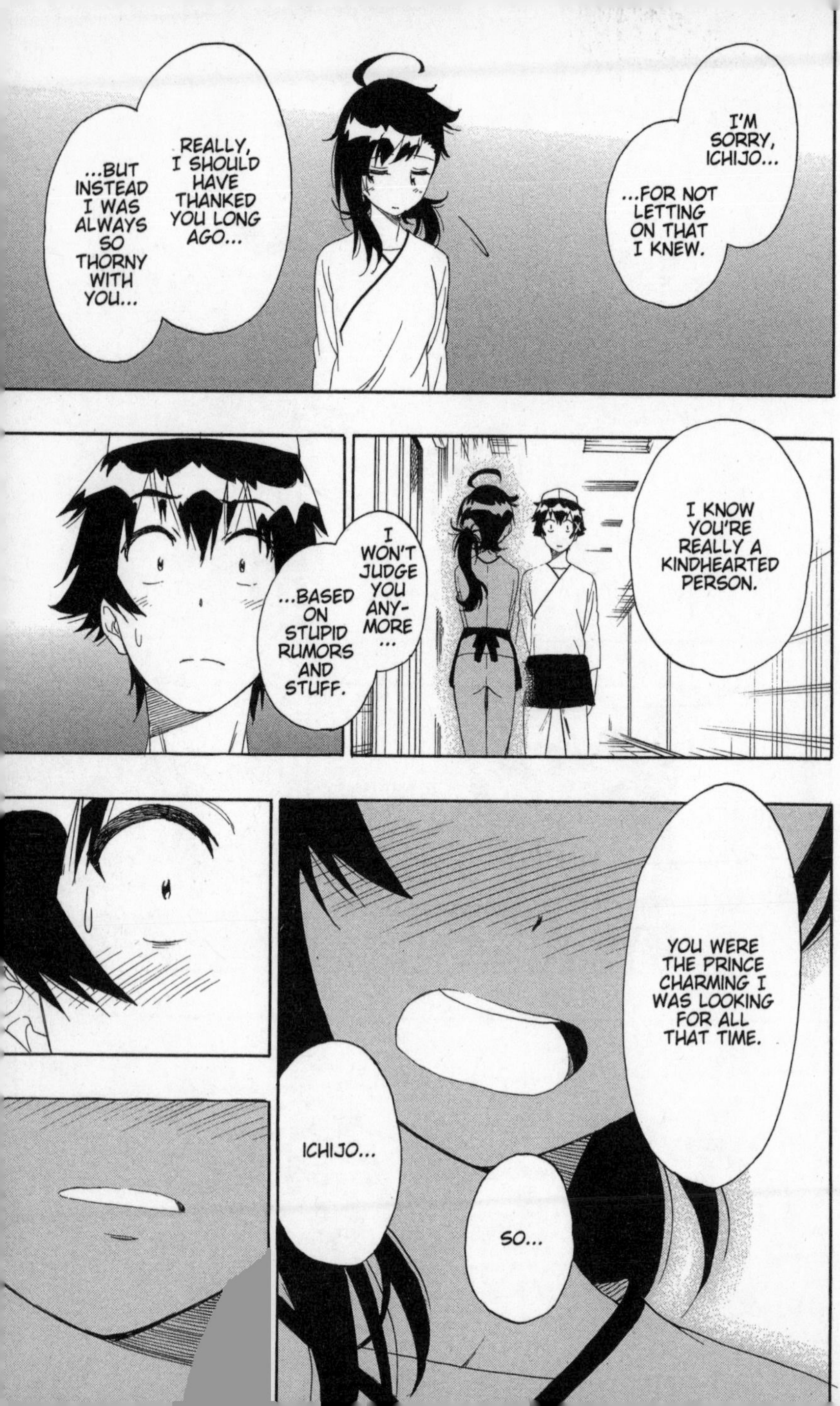
I'M SORRY, ICHIJO...
...FOR NOT LETTING ON THAT I KNEW.
REALLY, I SHOULD HAVE THANKED YOU LONG AGO...
...BUT INSTEAD I WAS ALWAYS SO THORNY WITH YOU...
I KNOW YOU'RE REALLY A KINDHEARTED PERSON.
I WON'T JUDGE YOU ANYMORE...
...BASED ON STUPID RUMORS AND STUFF.
YOU WERE THE PRINCE CHARMING I WAS LOOKING FOR ALL THAT TIME.
SO...
ICHIJO...

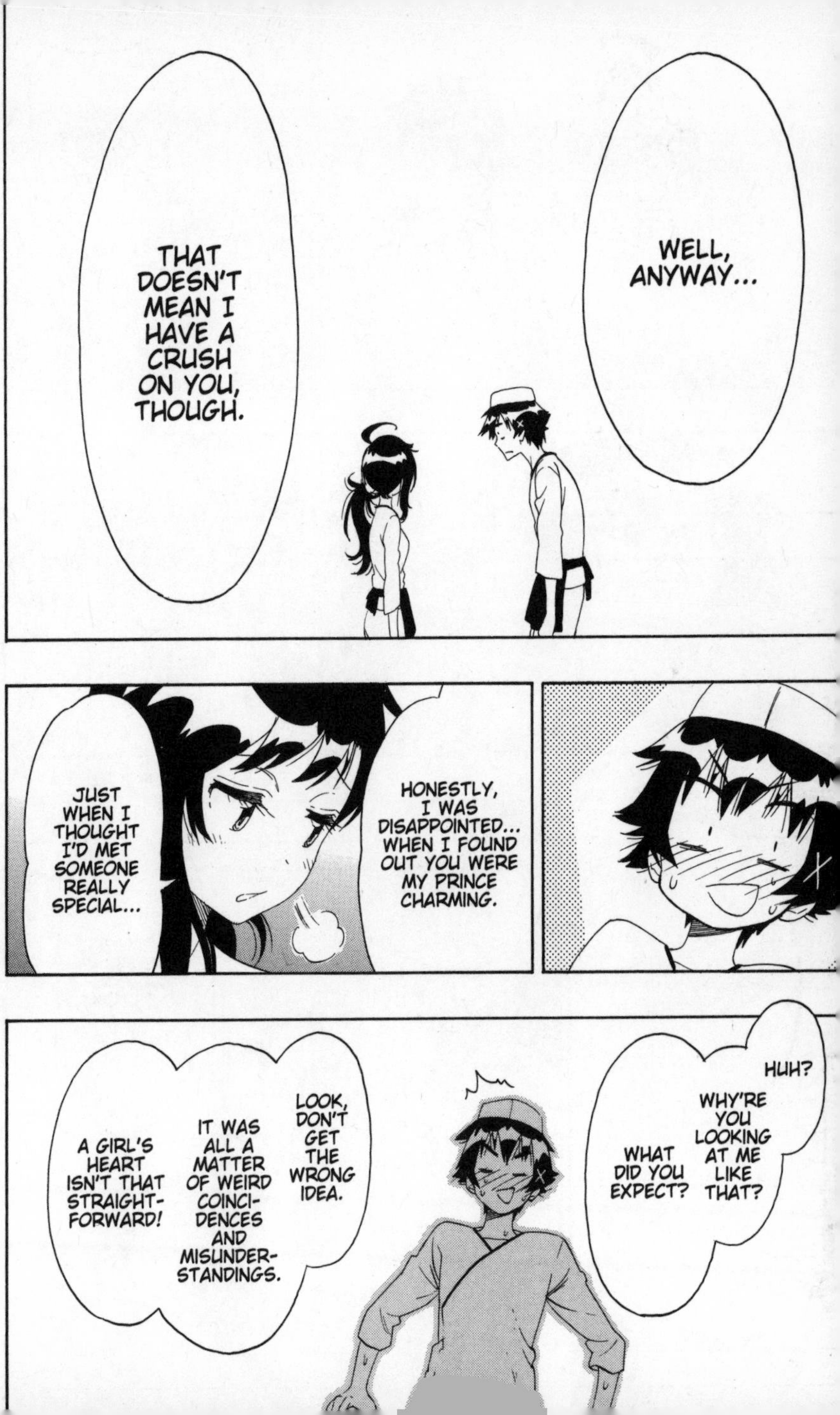
WELL, ANYWAY...
THAT DOESN'T MEAN I HAVE A CRUSH ON YOU, THOUGH.
HONESTLY, I WAS DISAPPOINTED... WHEN I FOUND OUT YOU WERE MY PRINCE CHARMING.
JUST WHEN I THOUGHT I'D MET SOMEONE REALLY SPECIAL...
HUH?
WHY'RE YOU LOOKING AT ME LIKE THAT?
WHAT DID YOU EXPECT?
LOOK, DON'T GET THE WRONG IDEA.
IT WAS ALL A MATTER OF WEIRD COINCI-DENCES AND MISUNDER-STANDINGS.
A GIRL'S HEART ISN'T THAT STRAIGHT-FORWARD!

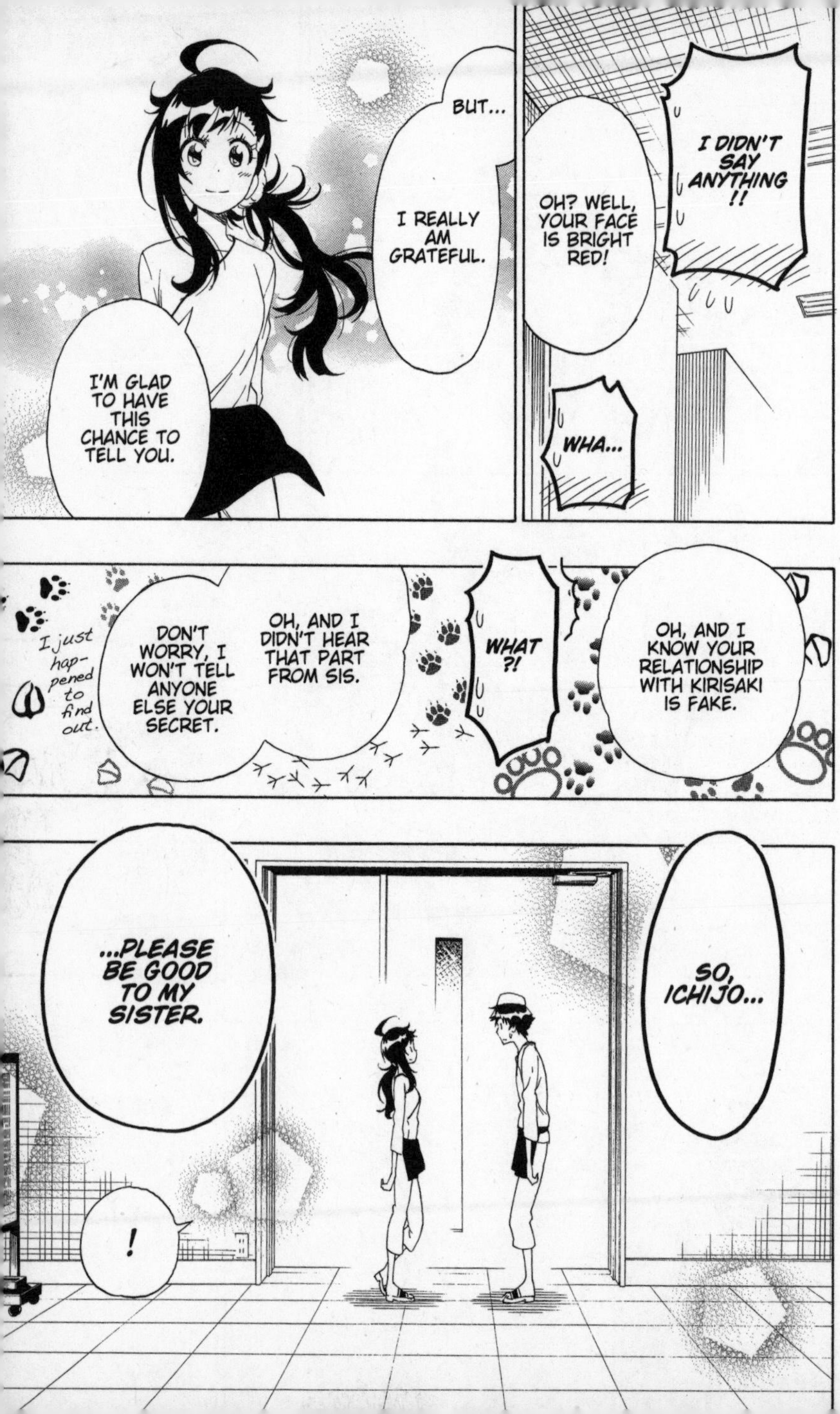
I DIDN'T SAY ANYTHING!!
OH? WELL, YOUR FACE IS BRIGHT RED!
WHA...
BUT...
I REALLY AM GRATEFUL.
I'M GLAD TO HAVE THIS CHANCE TO TELL YOU.
OH, AND I KNOW YOUR RELATIONSHIP WITH KIRISAKI IS FAKE.
WHAT?!
OH, AND I DIDN'T HEAR THAT PART FROM SIS.
DON'T WORRY, I WON'T TELL ANYONE ELSE YOUR SECRET.
I just happened to find out.
SO, ICHIJO...
...PLEASE BE GOOD TO MY SISTER.
!

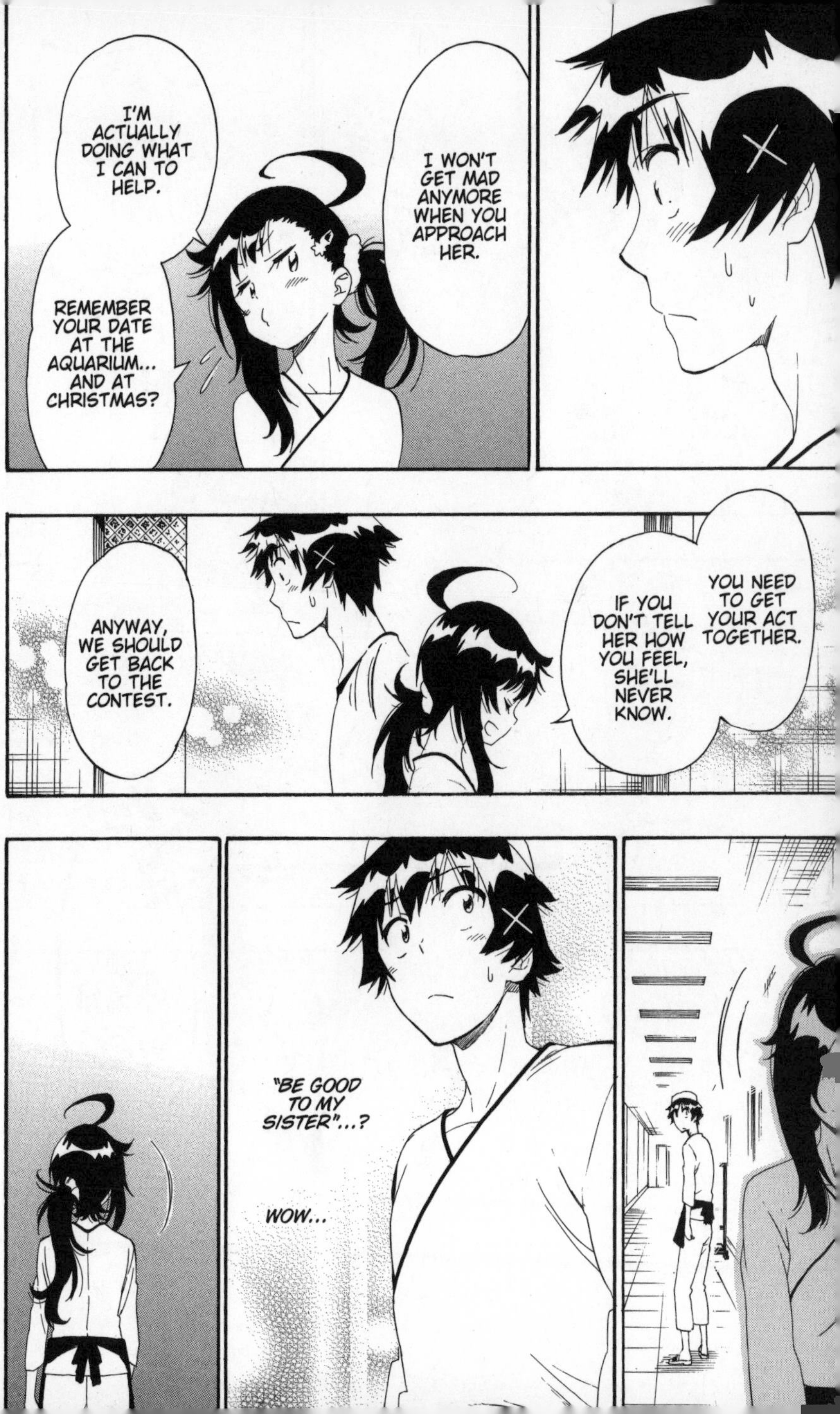
I WON'T GET MAD ANYMORE WHEN YOU APPROACH HER.
I'M ACTUALLY DOING WHAT I CAN TO HELP.
REMEMBER YOUR DATE AT THE AQUARIUM... AND AT CHRISTMAS?
YOU NEED TO GET YOUR ACT TOGETHER.
IF YOU DON'T TELL HER HOW YOU FEEL, SHE'LL NEVER KNOW.
ANYWAY, WE SHOULD GET BACK TO THE CONTEST.
"BE GOOD TO MY SISTER"...?
WOW...

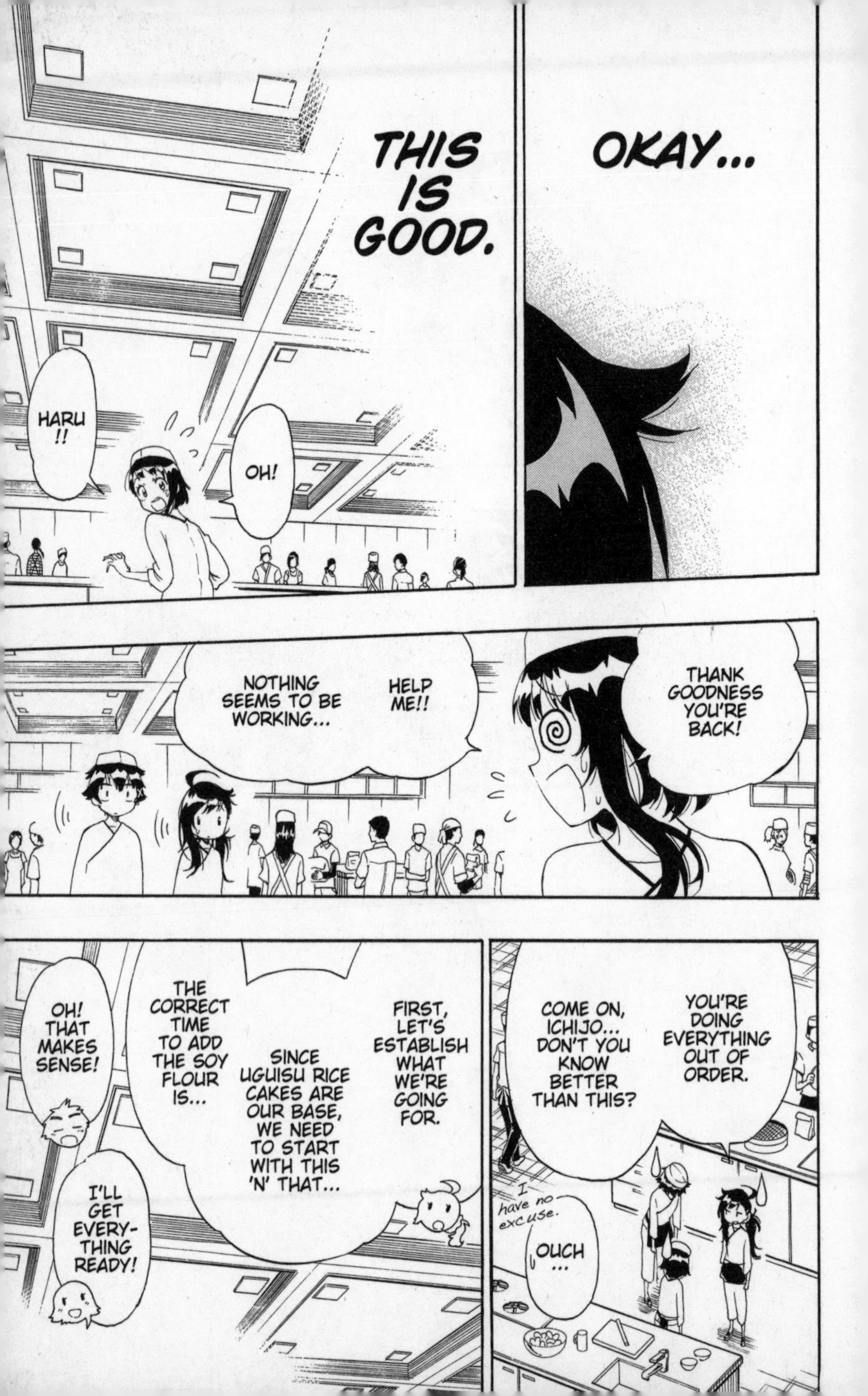
OKAY...
THIS IS GOOD.
OH!
HARU!!
THANK GOODNESS YOU'RE BACK!
HELP ME!!
NOTHING SEEMS TO BE WORKING...
YOU'RE DOING EVERYTHING OUT OF ORDER.
COME ON, ICHIJO... DON'T YOU KNOW BETTER THAN THIS?
I have no excuse.
OUCH...
FIRST, LET'S ESTABLISH WHAT WE'RE GOING FOR.
SINCE UGUISU RICE CAKES ARE OUR BASE, WE NEED TO START WITH THIS 'N' THAT...
THE CORRECT TIME TO ADD THE SOY FLOUR IS...
OH! THAT MAKES SENSE!
I'LL GET EVERY-THING READY!

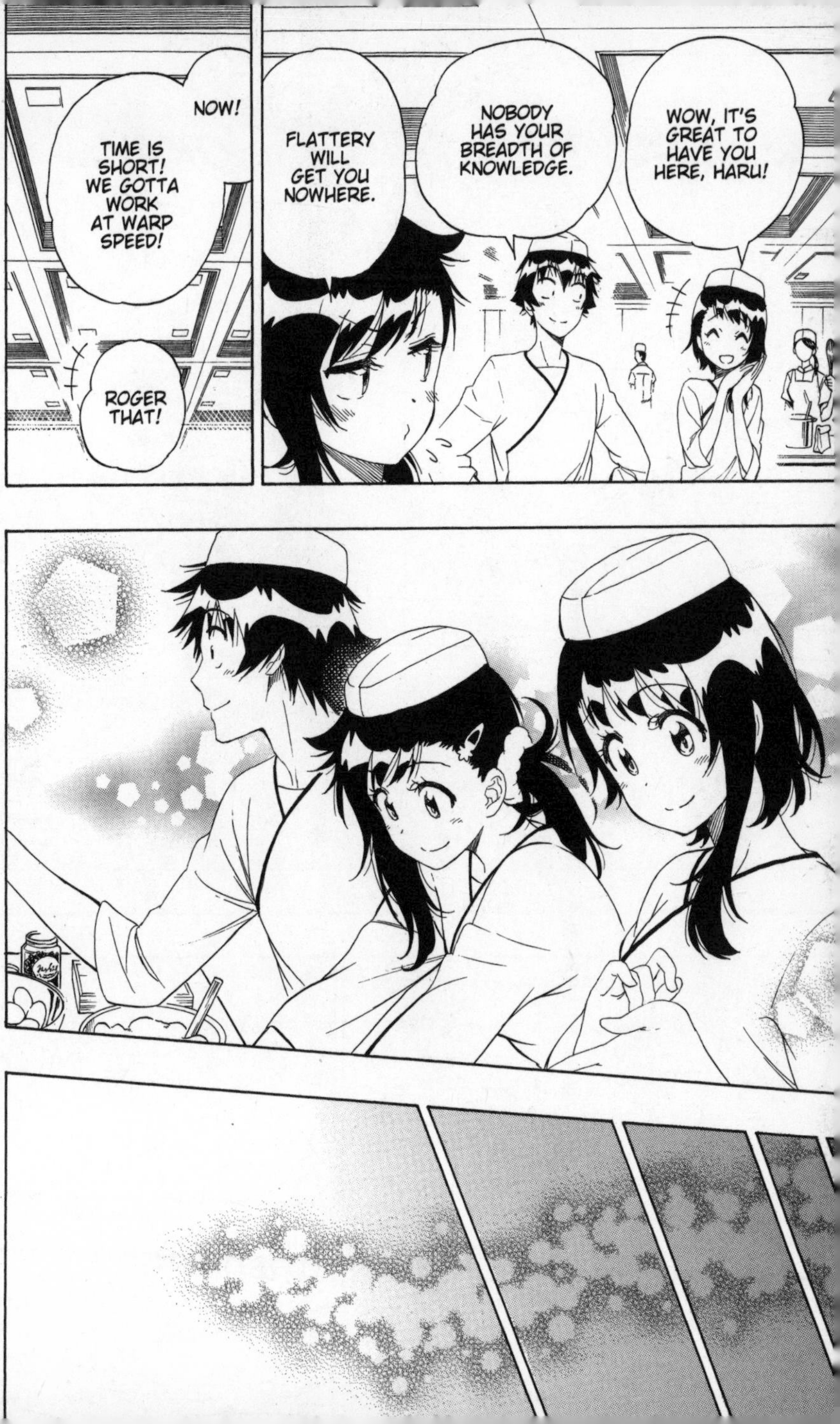
WOW, IT'S GREAT TO HAVE YOU HERE, HARU!
NOBODY HAS YOUR BREADTH OF KNOWLEDGE.
FLATTERY WILL GET YOU NOWHERE.
NOW!
TIME IS SHORT! WE GOTTA WORK AT WARP SPEED!
ROGER THAT!

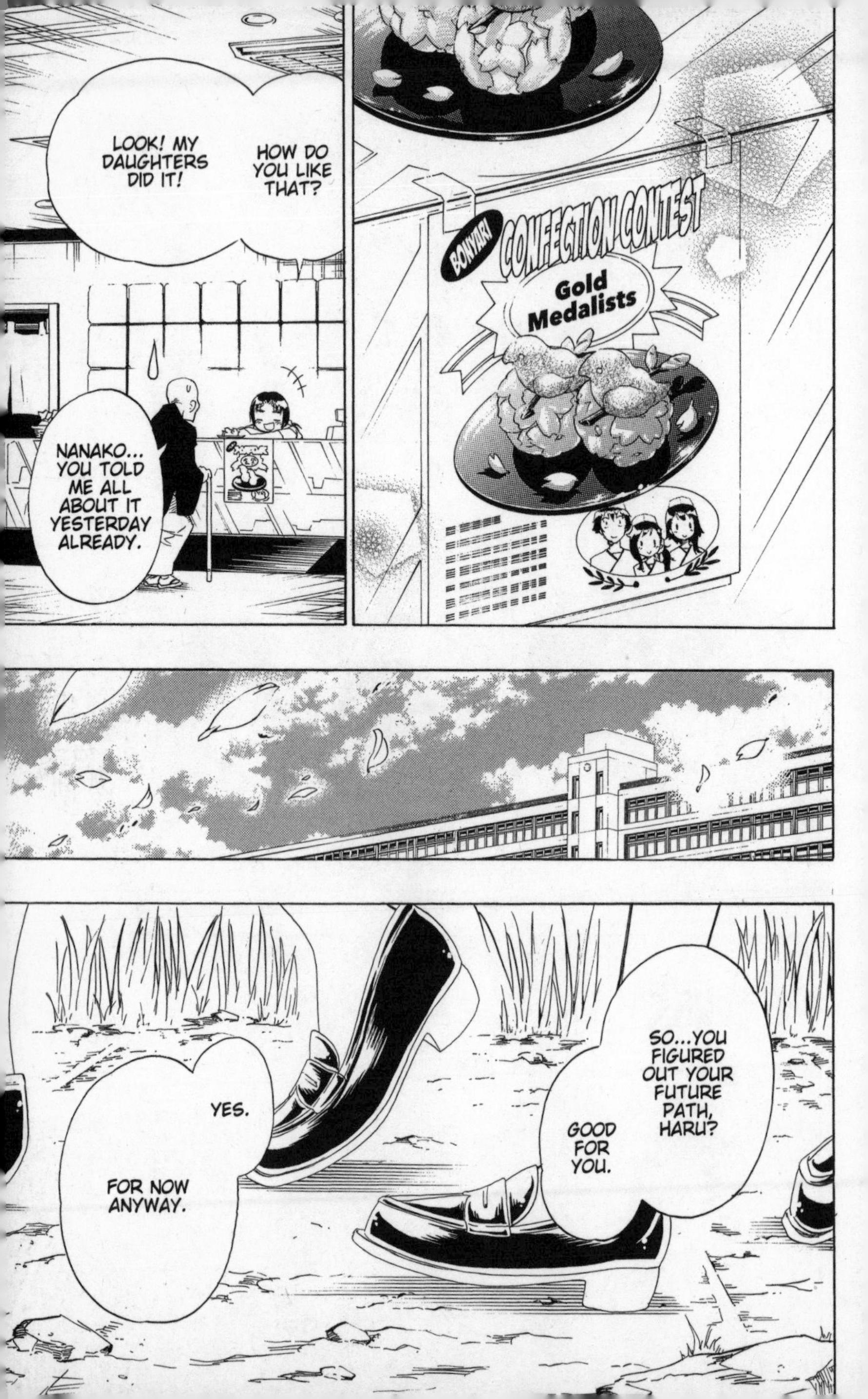
BONYARI
CONFECTION CONTEST
Gold Medalists
HOW DO YOU LIKE THAT?
LOOK! MY DAUGHTERS DID IT!
NANAKO... YOU TOLD ME ALL ABOUT IT YESTERDAY ALREADY.
SO...YOU FIGURED OUT YOUR FUTURE PATH, HARU?
GOOD FOR YOU.
YES.
FOR NOW ANYWAY.

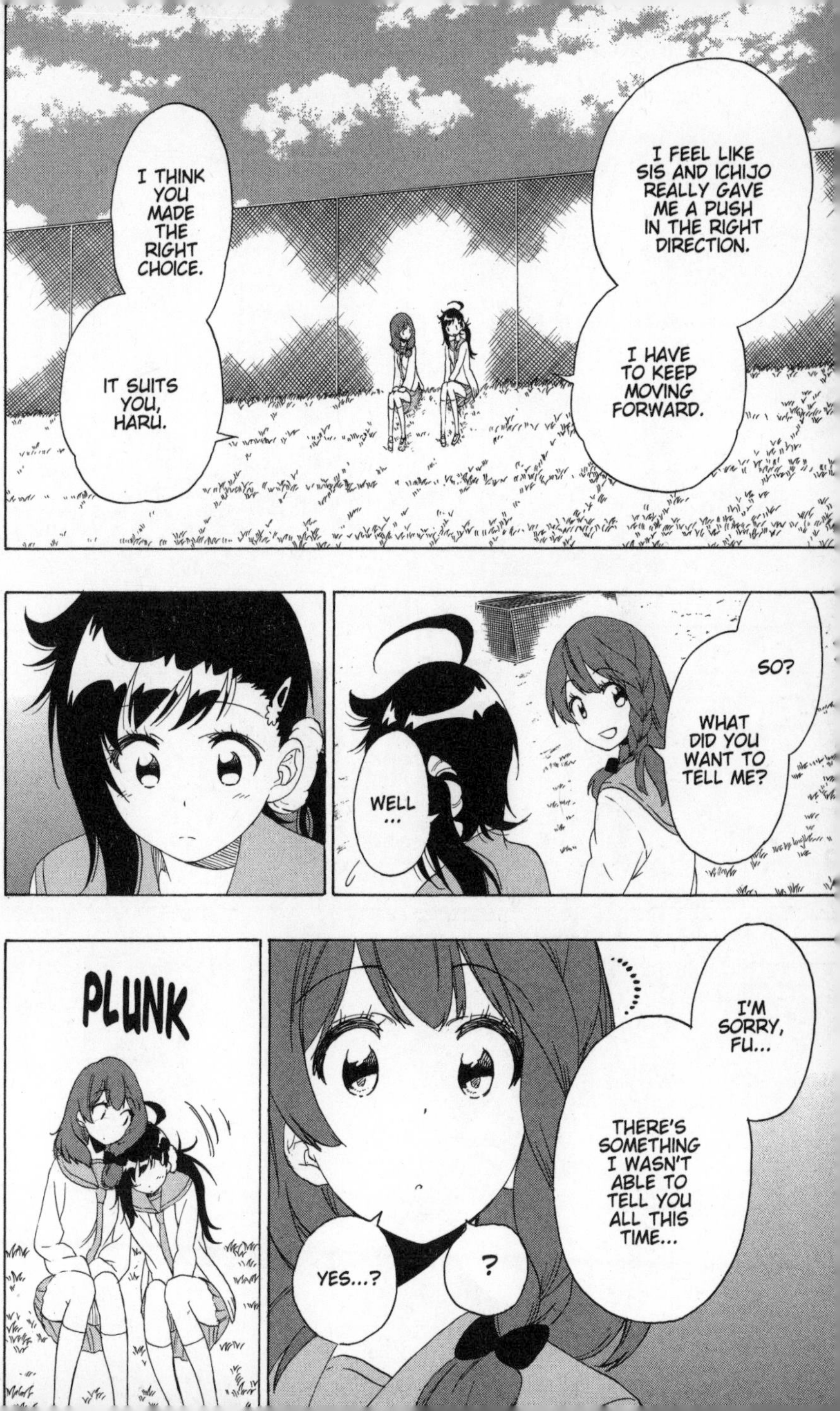
I FEEL LIKE SIS AND ICHIJO REALLY GAVE ME A PUSH IN THE RIGHT DIRECTION.
I HAVE TO KEEP MOVING FORWARD.
I THINK YOU MADE THE RIGHT CHOICE.
IT SUITS YOU, HARU.
SO?
WHAT DID YOU WANT TO TELL ME?
WELL...
...
I'M SORRY, FU...
THERE'S SOMETHING I WASN'T ABLE TO TELL YOU ALL THIS TIME...
?
YES...?
PLUNK

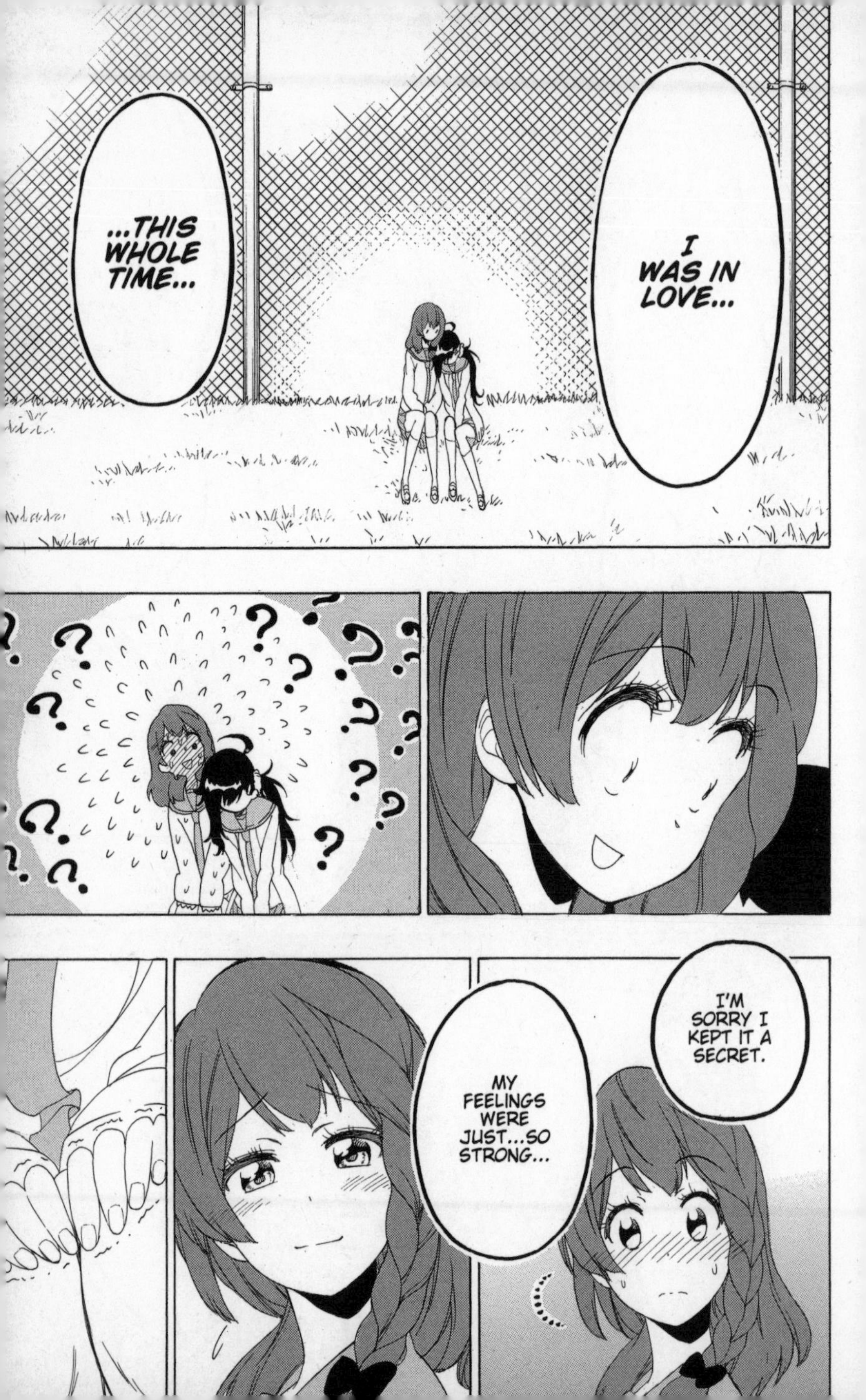
I WAS IN LOVE...
...THIS WHOLE TIME...
I'M SORRY I KEPT IT A SECRET.
MY FEELINGS WERE JUST...SO STRONG...

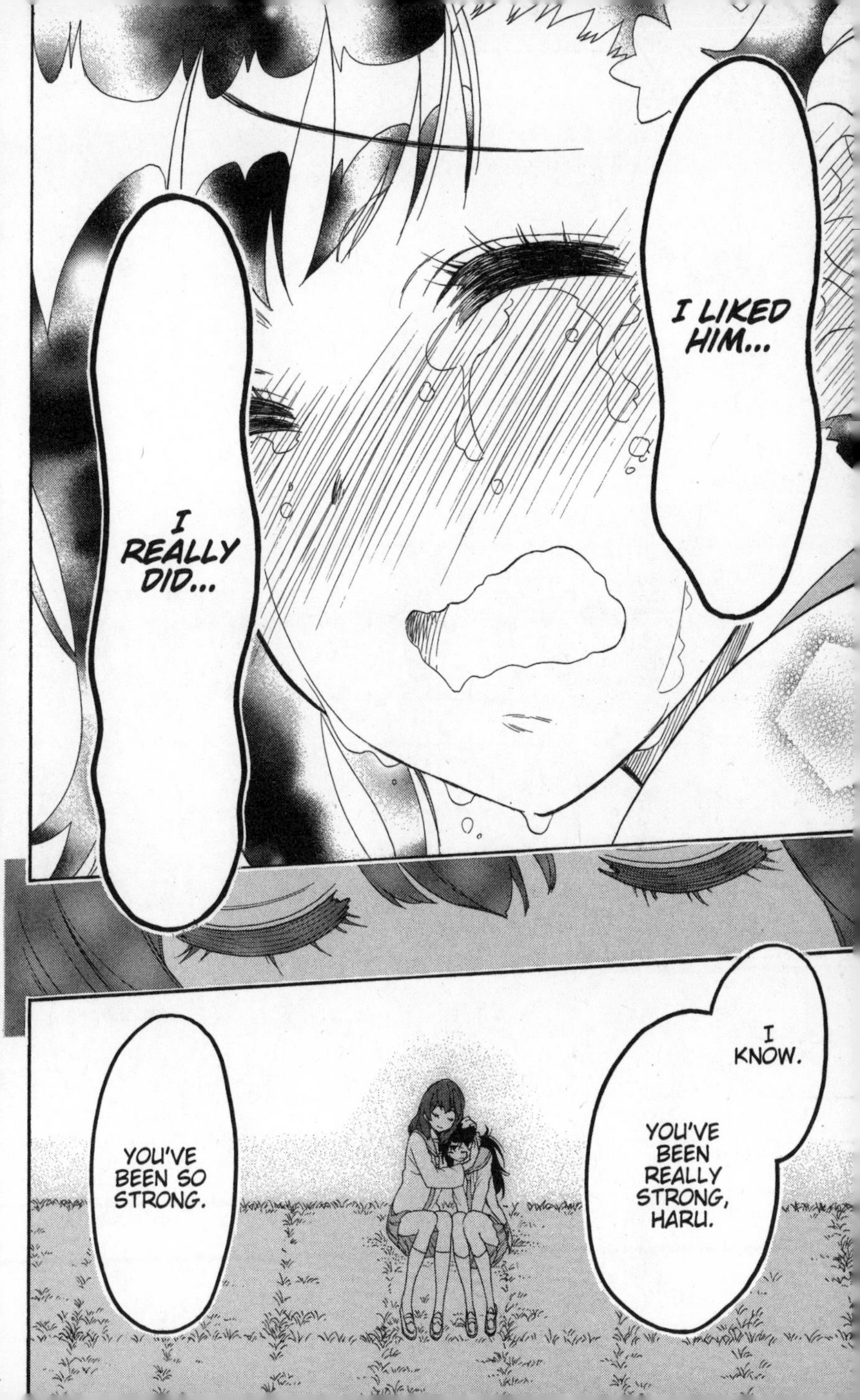
I LIKED HIM...
I REALLY DID...
I KNOW.
YOU'VE BEEN REALLY STRONG, HARU.
YOU'VE BEEN SO STRONG.

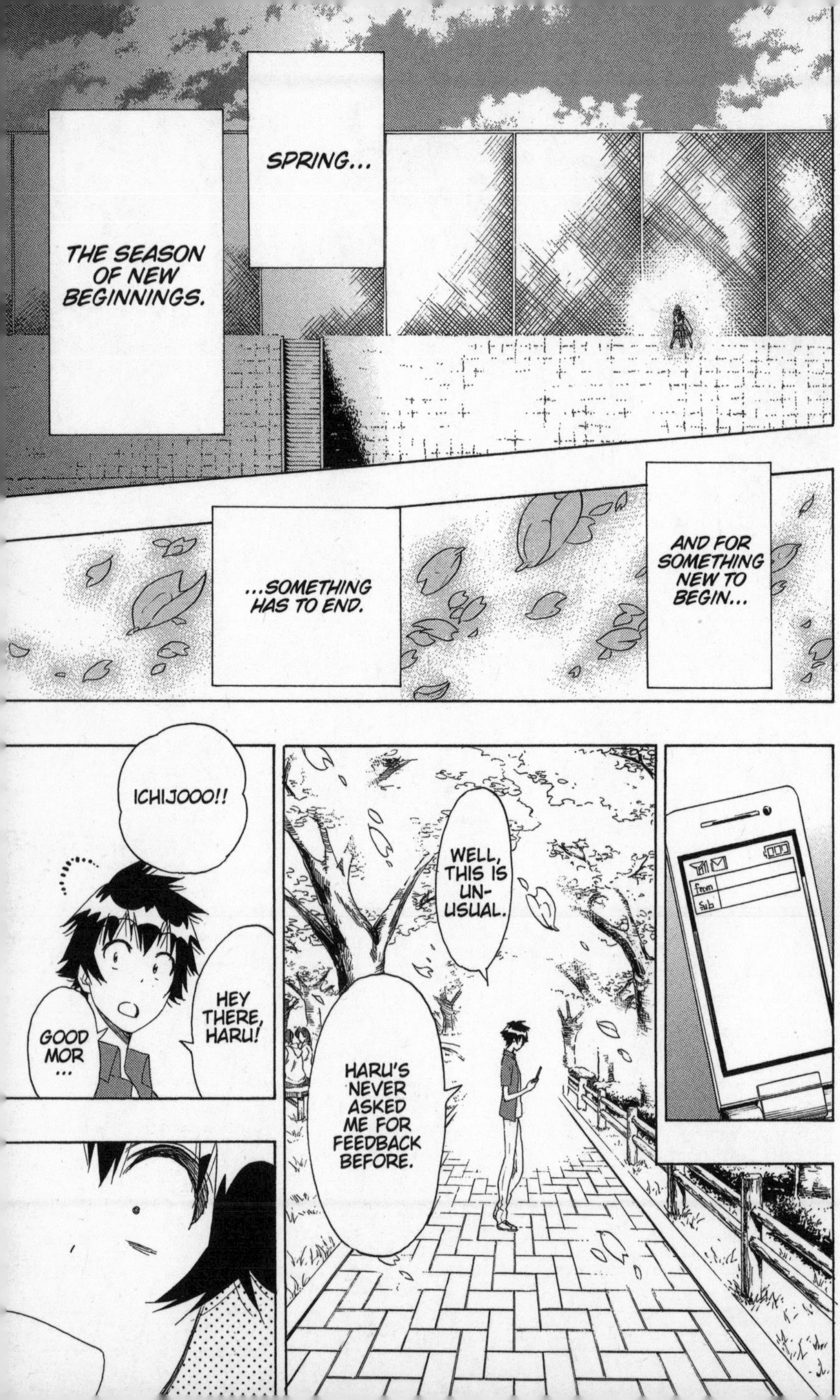
SPRING...
THE SEASON OF NEW BEGINNINGS.
AND FOR SOMETHING NEW TO BEGIN...
...SOMETHING HAS TO END.
from
Sub
WELL, THIS IS UN-USUAL.
HARU'S NEVER ASKED ME FOR FEEDBACK BEFORE.
ICHIJOOO!!
HEY THERE, HARU!
GOOD MOR...

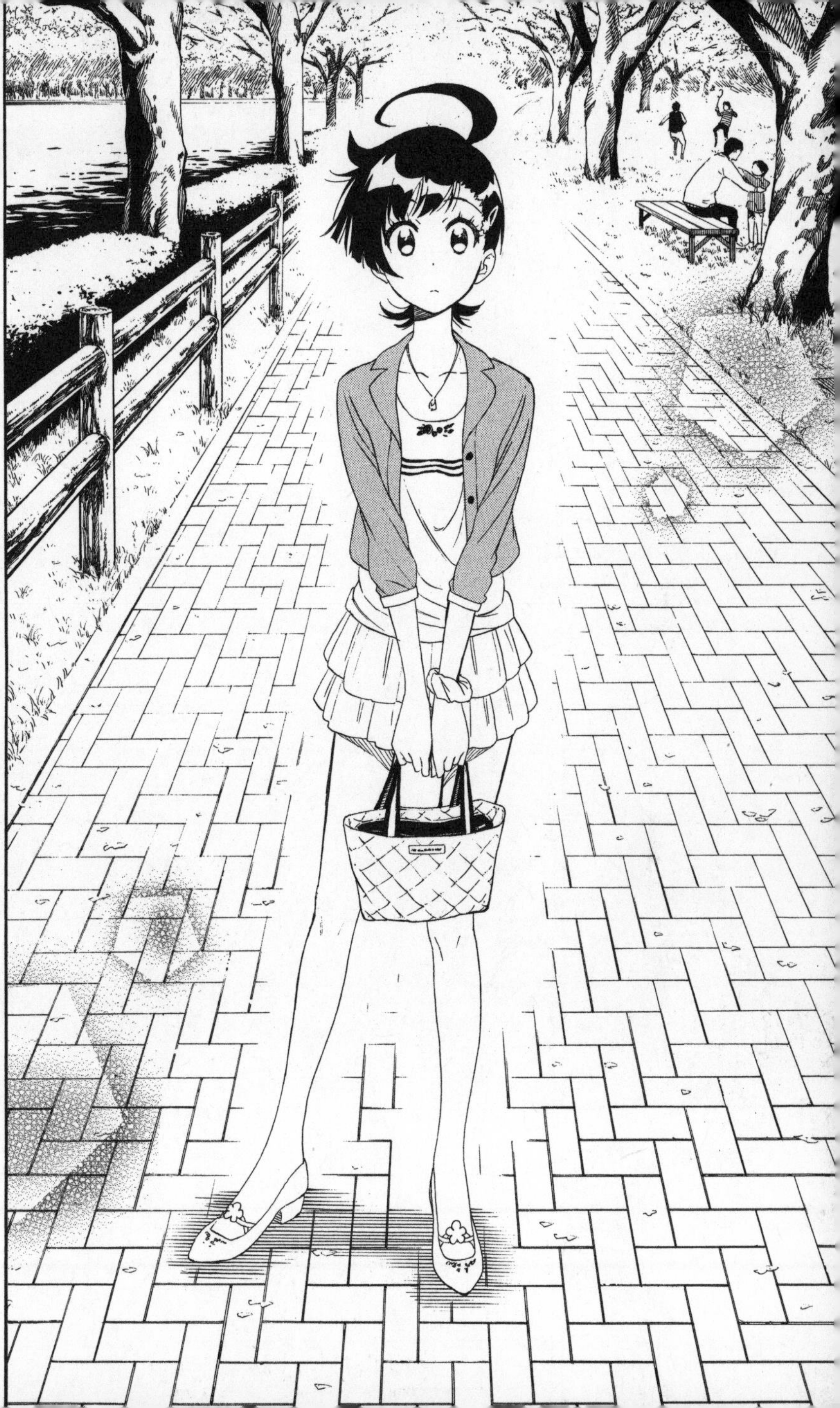

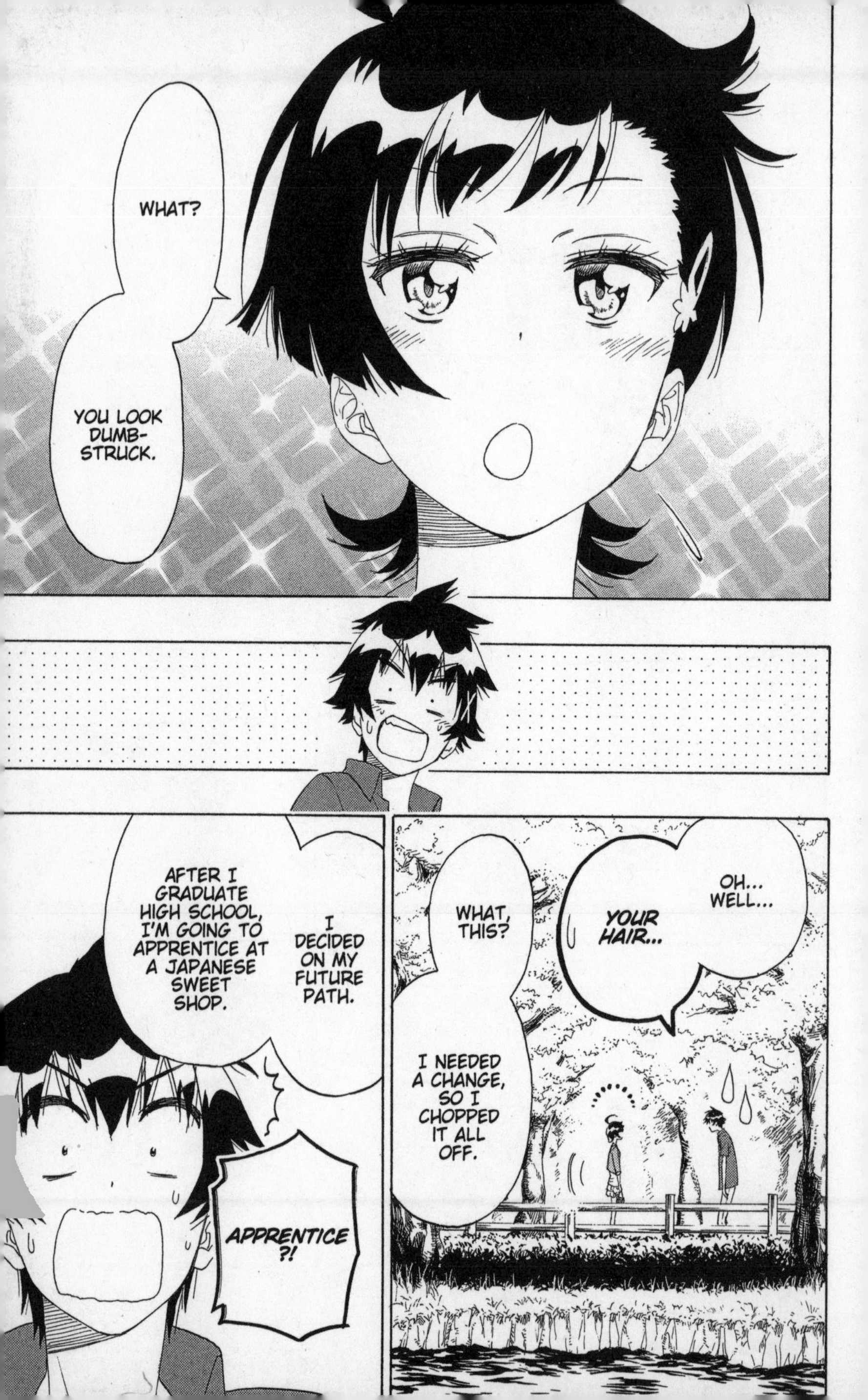
WHAT?
YOU LOOK DUMB-STRUCK.
OH... WELL...
YOUR HAIR...
WHAT, THIS?
I NEEDED A CHANGE, SO I CHOPPED IT ALL OFF.
I DECIDED ON MY FUTURE PATH.
AFTER I GRADUATE HIGH SCHOOL, I'M GOING TO APPRENTICE AT A JAPANESE SWEET SHOP.
APPRENTICE?!

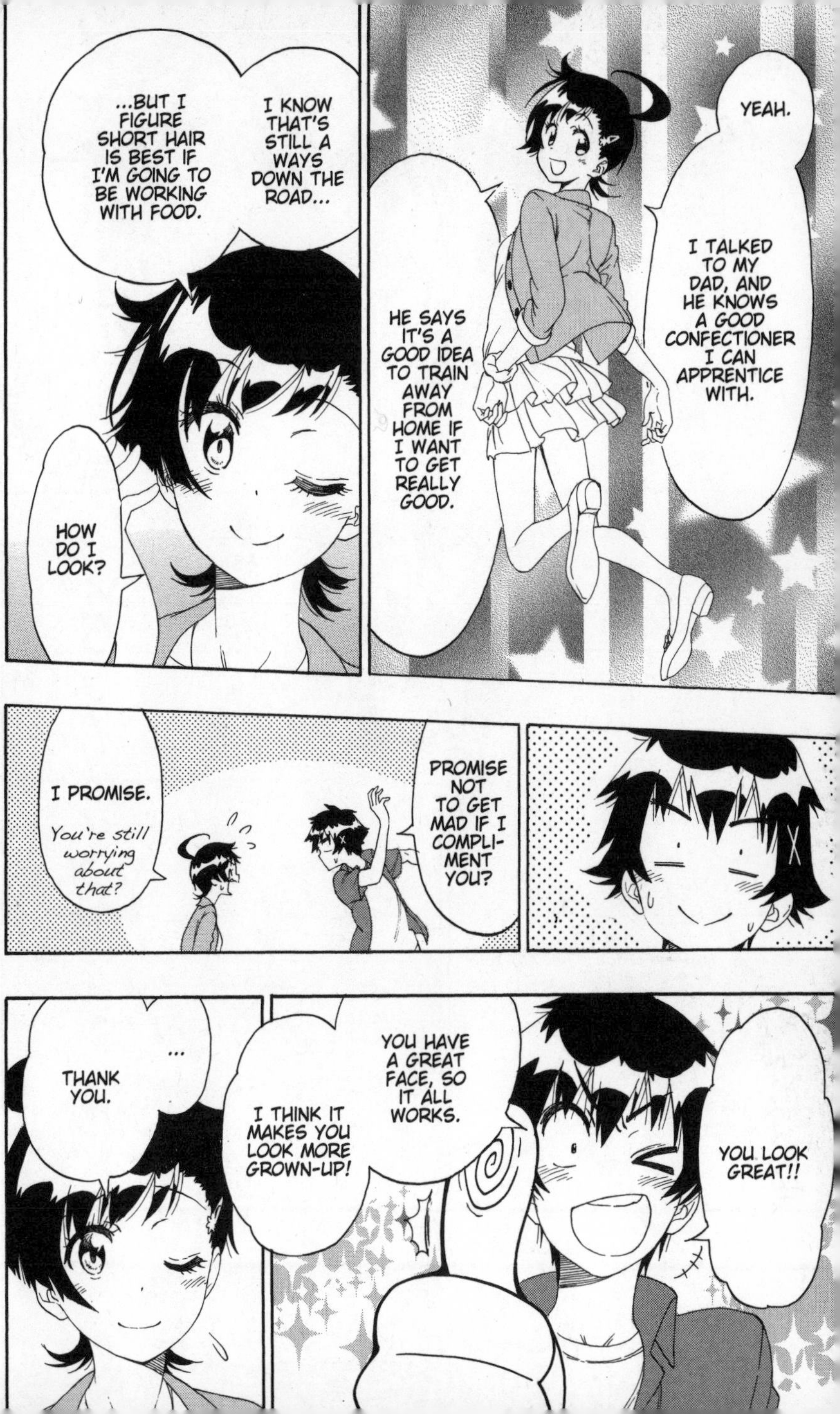
YEAH.
I TALKED TO MY DAD, AND HE KNOWS A GOOD CONFECTIONER I CAN APPRENTICE WITH.
HE SAYS IT'S A GOOD IDEA TO TRAIN AWAY FROM HOME IF I WANT TO GET REALLY GOOD.
I KNOW THAT'S STILL A WAYS DOWN THE ROAD...
...BUT I FIGURE SHORT HAIR IS BEST IF I'M GOING TO BE WORKING WITH FOOD.
HOW DO I LOOK?
PROMISE NOT TO GET MAD IF I COMPLIMENT YOU?
I PROMISE.
You're still worrying about that?
YOU LOOK GREAT!!
YOU HAVE A GREAT FACE, SO IT ALL WORKS.
I THINK IT MAKES YOU LOOK MORE GROWN-UP!
...
THANK YOU.

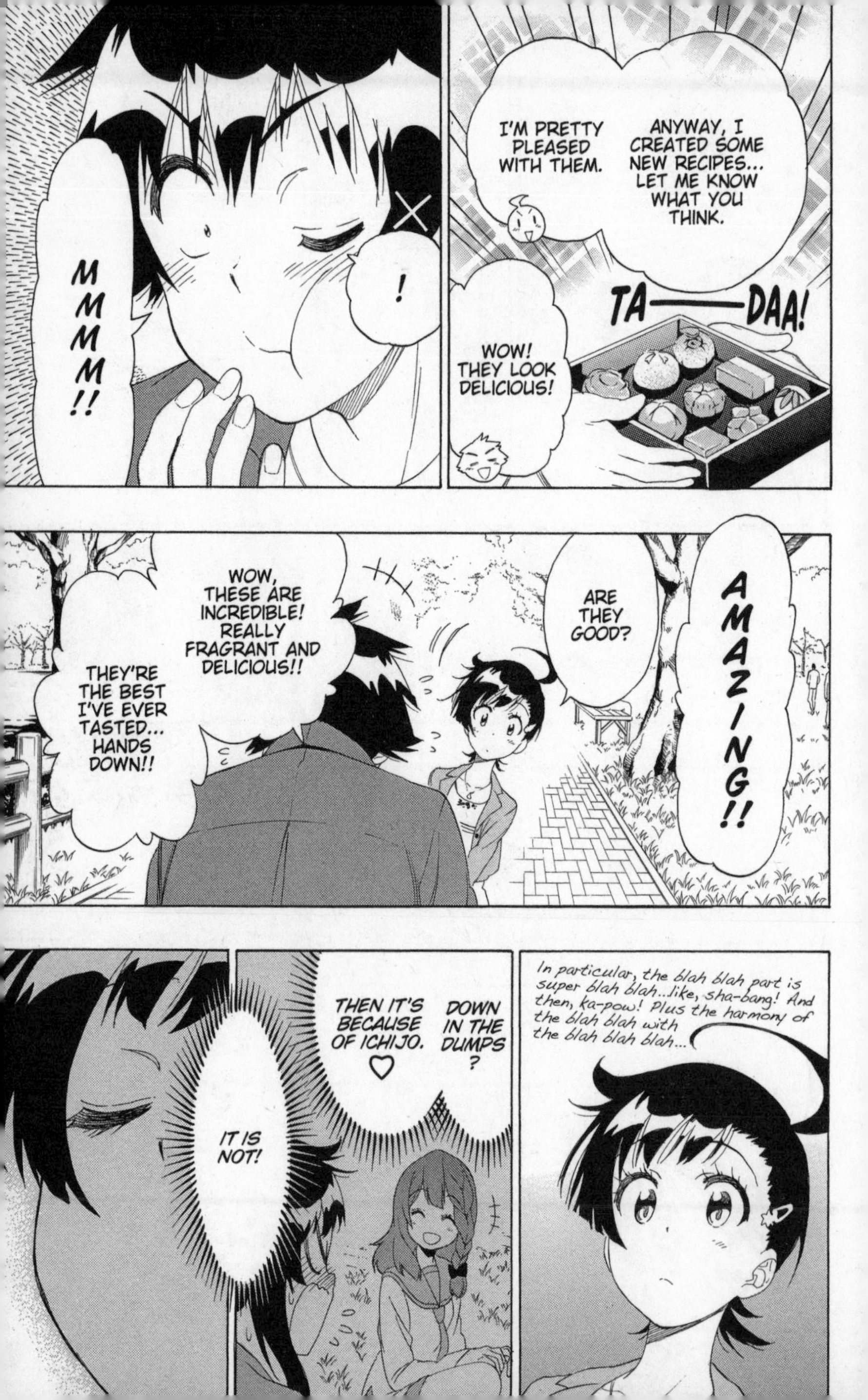
ANYWAY, I CREATED SOME NEW RECIPES... LET ME KNOW WHAT YOU THINK.
I'M PRETTY PLEASED WITH THEM.
TA—DAA!
WOW! THEY LOOK DELICIOUS!
!
MMMMM!!
AMAZING!!
ARE THEY GOOD?
WOW, THESE ARE INCREDIBLE! REALLY FRAGRANT AND DELICIOUS!!
THEY'RE THE BEST I'VE EVER TASTED... HANDS DOWN!!
In particular, the blah blah part is super blah blah...like, sha-bang! And then, ka-pow! Plus the harmony of the blah blah with the blah blah blah...
DOWN IN THE DUMPS?
THEN IT'S BECAUSE OF ICHIJO. ♡
IT IS NOT!

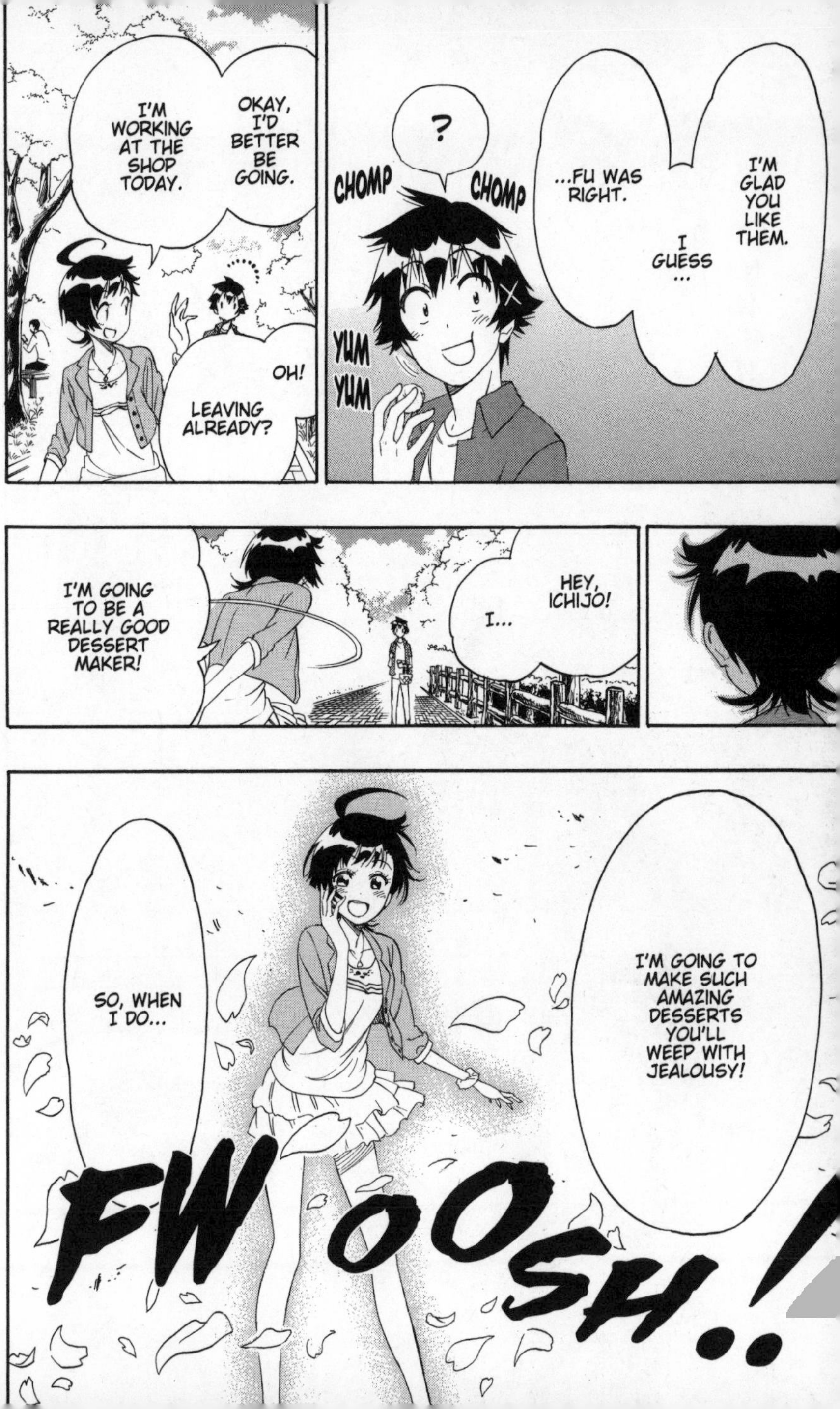
I'M GLAD YOU LIKE THEM.
I GUESS...
...FU WAS RIGHT.
?
CHOMP CHOMP
YUM YUM
OKAY, I'D BETTER BE GOING.
I'M WORKING AT THE SHOP TODAY.
OH!
LEAVING ALREADY?
HEY, ICHIJO!
I...
I'M GOING TO BE A REALLY GOOD DESSERT MAKER!
I'M GOING TO MAKE SUCH AMAZING DESSERTS YOU'LL WEEP WITH JEALOUSY!
SO, WHEN I DO...
FWOOSH..!!

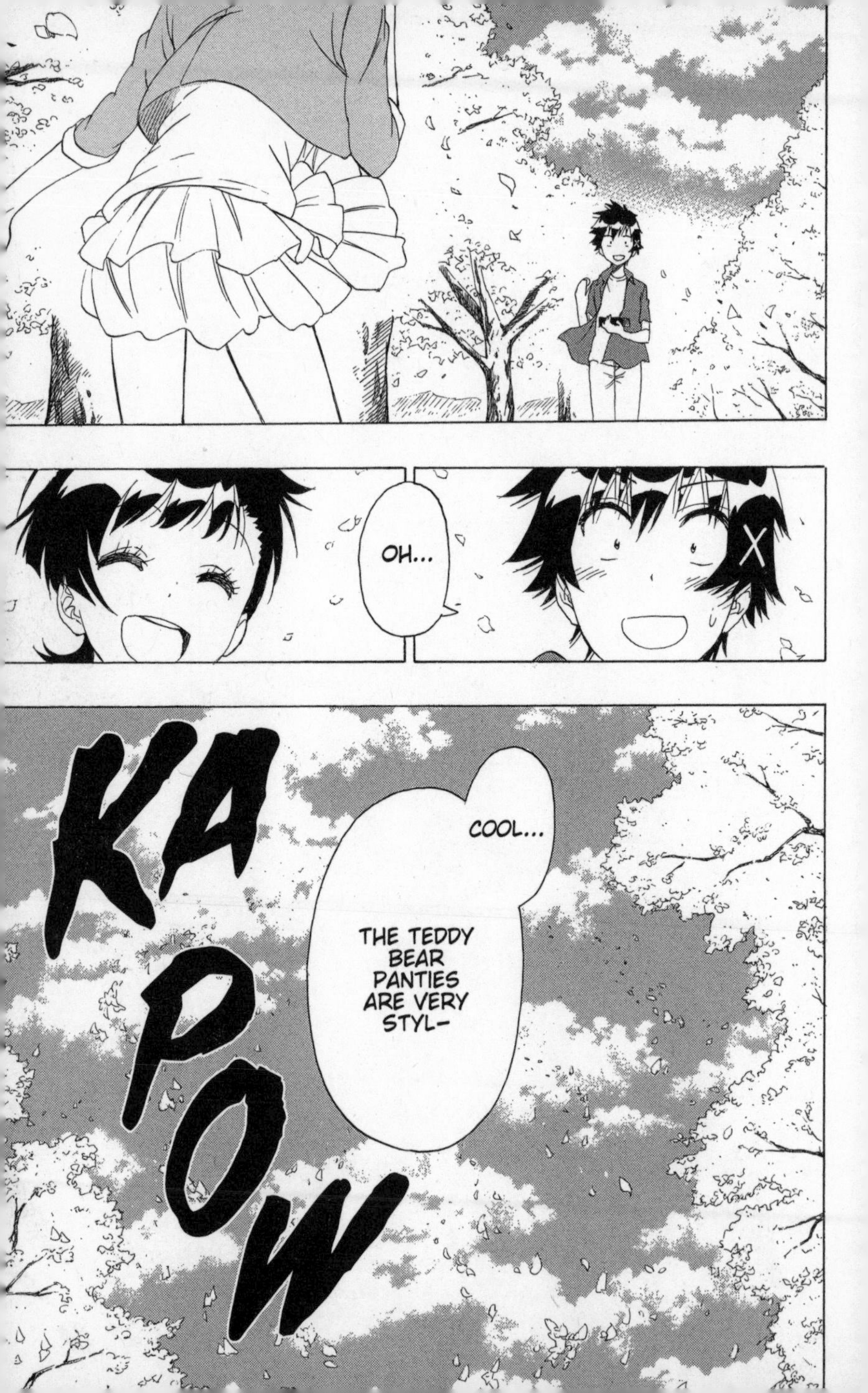
OH...
COOL...
THE TEDDY BEAR PANTIES ARE VERY STYL-
KAPOW

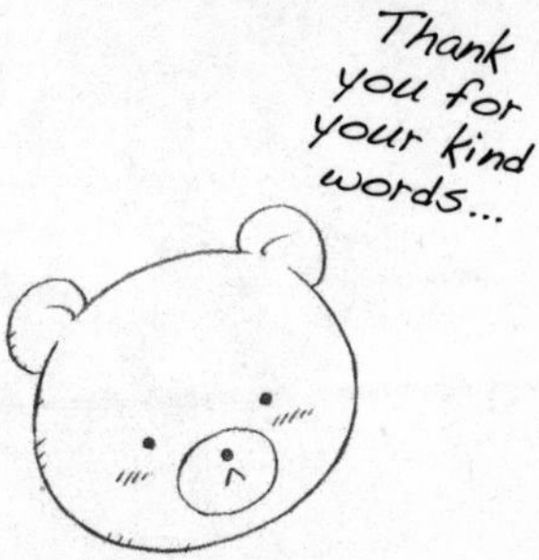
Thank you for your kind words...

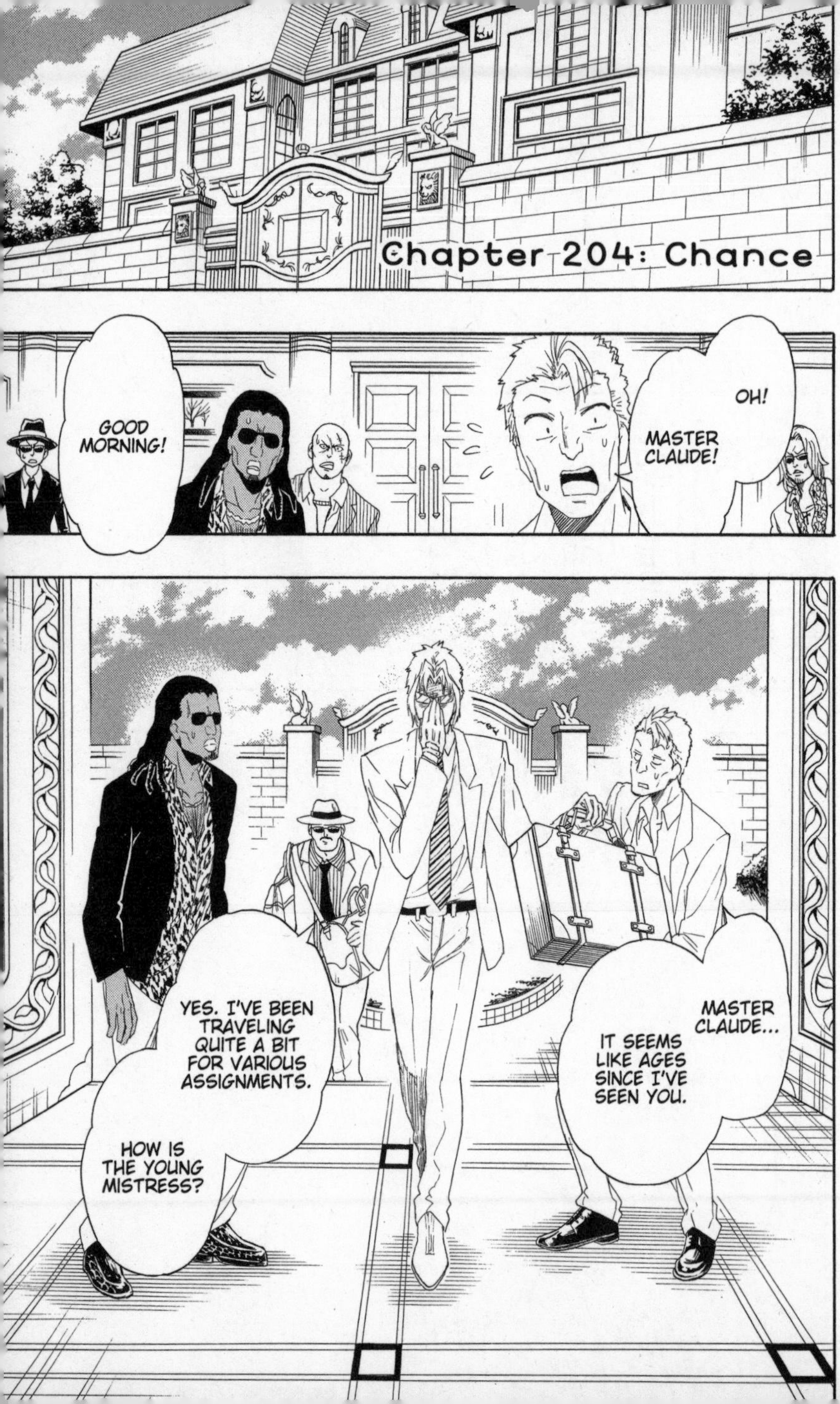
Chapter 204: Chance
OH! MASTER CLAUDE!
GOOD MORNING!
MASTER CLAUDE... IT SEEMS LIKE AGES SINCE I'VE SEEN YOU.
YES. I'VE BEEN TRAVELING QUITE A BIT FOR VARIOUS ASSIGNMENTS.
HOW IS THE YOUNG MISTRESS?

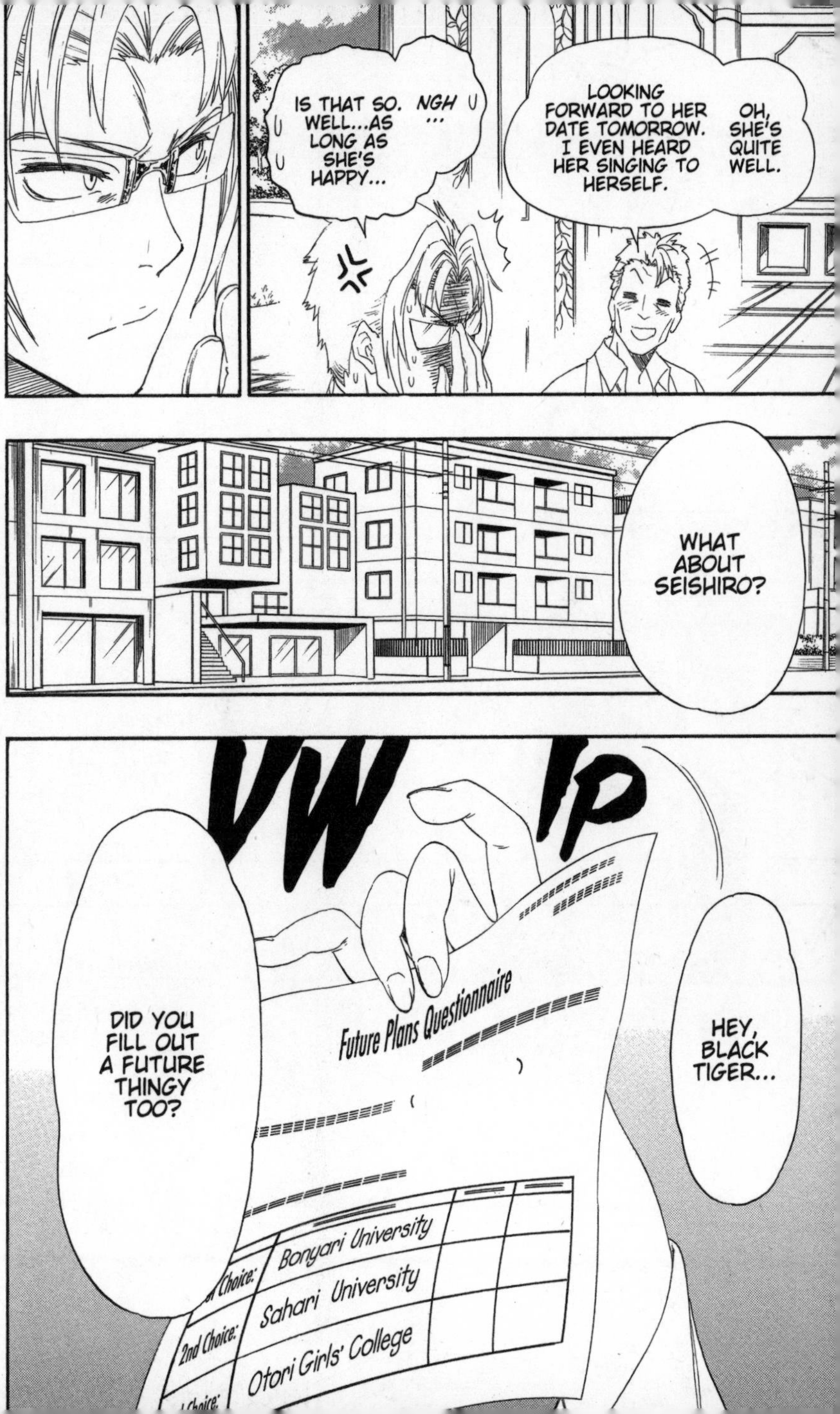
OH, SHE'S QUITE WELL.
LOOKING FORWARD TO HER DATE TOMORROW. I EVEN HEARD HER SINGING TO HERSELF.
IS THAT SO. WELL...AS LONG AS SHE'S HAPPY... NGH ...
WHAT ABOUT SEISHIRO?
VWIP
HEY, BLACK TIGER...
DID YOU FILL OUT A FUTURE THINGY TOO?
Future Plans Questionnaire
Bonyari University
Sahari University
2nd Choice:
Otori Girls' College

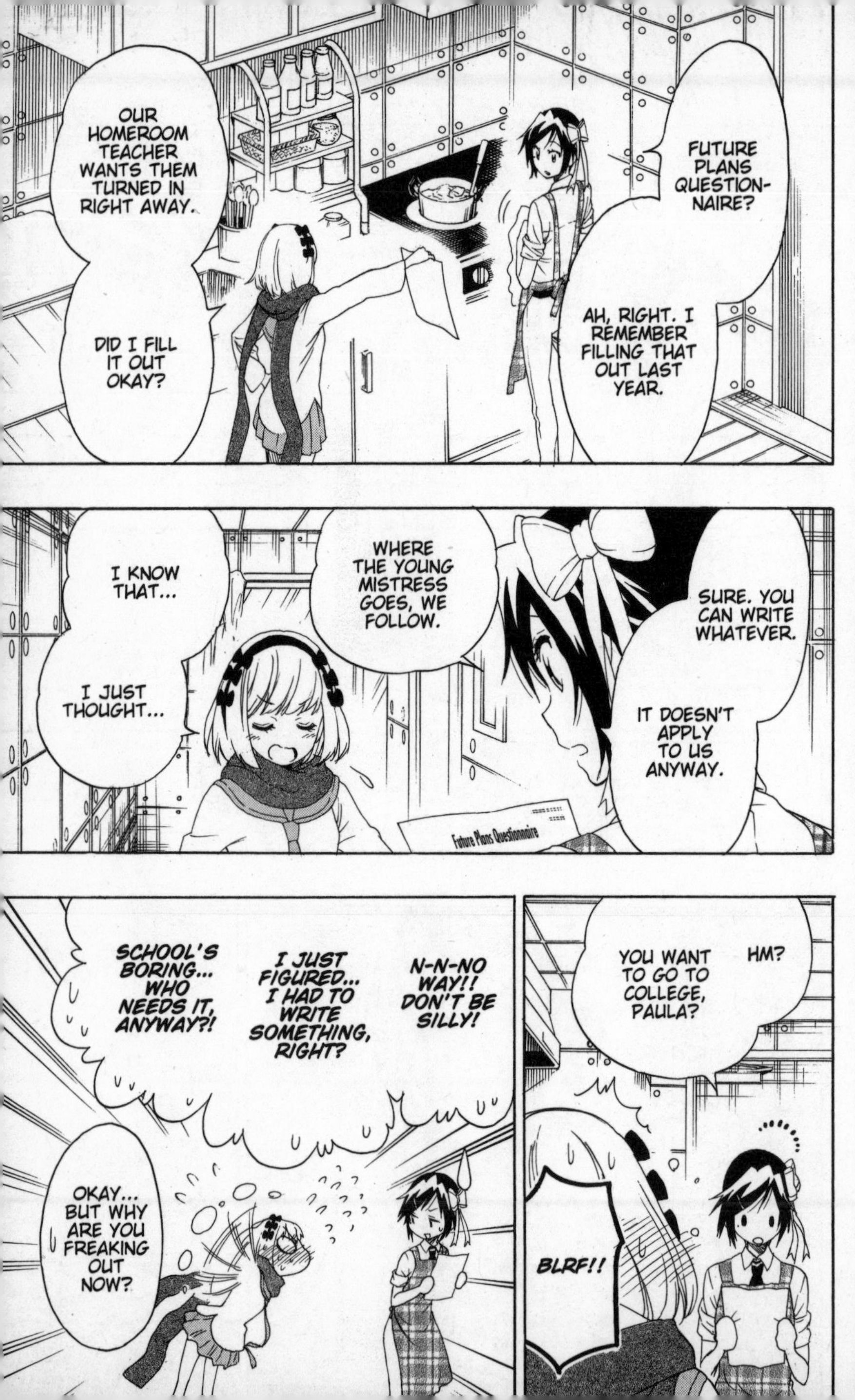
FUTURE PLANS QUESTIONNAIRE?
OUR HOMEROOM TEACHER WANTS THEM TURNED IN RIGHT AWAY.
AH, RIGHT. I REMEMBER FILLING THAT OUT LAST YEAR.
DID I FILL IT OUT OKAY?
SURE. YOU CAN WRITE WHATEVER.
IT DOESN'T APPLY TO US ANYWAY.
WHERE THE YOUNG MISTRESS GOES, WE FOLLOW.
I KNOW THAT...
I JUST THOUGHT...
Future Plans Questionnaire
HM?
YOU WANT TO GO TO COLLEGE, PAULA?
BLRF!!
N-N-NO WAY!! DON'T BE SILLY!
I JUST FIGURED... I HAD TO WRITE SOMETHING, RIGHT?
SCHOOL'S BORING... WHO NEEDS IT, ANYWAY?!
OKAY... BUT WHY ARE YOU FREAKING OUT NOW?

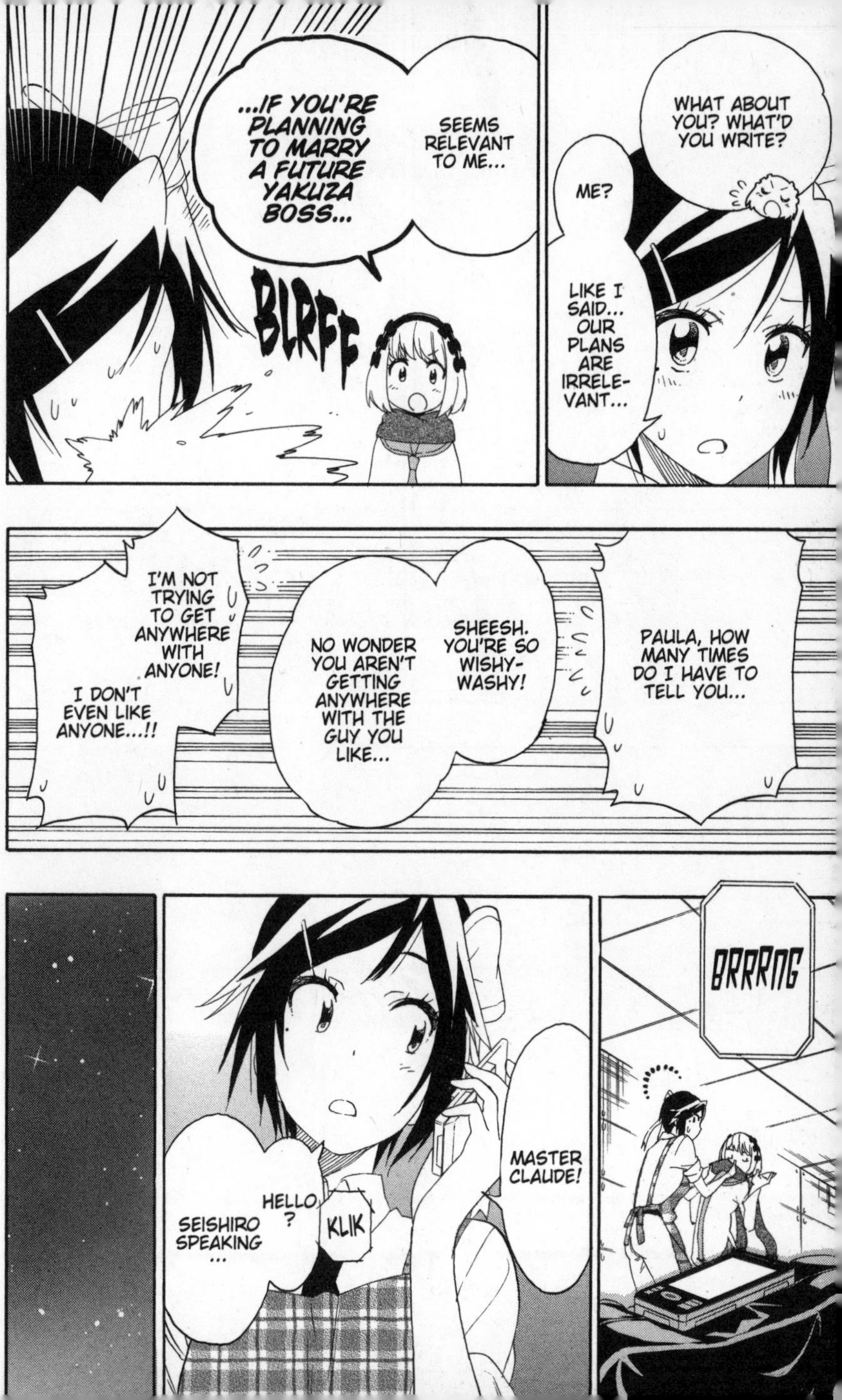
WHAT ABOUT YOU? WHAT'D YOU WRITE?
ME?
LIKE I SAID... OUR PLANS ARE IRRELEVANT...
SEEMS RELEVANT TO ME...
...IF YOU'RE PLANNING TO MARRY A FUTURE YAKUZA BOSS...
BLRFF
PAULA, HOW MANY TIMES DO I HAVE TO TELL YOU...
SHEESH. YOU'RE SO WISHY-WASHY!
NO WONDER YOU AREN'T GETTING ANYWHERE WITH THE GUY YOU LIKE...
I'M NOT TRYING TO GET ANYWHERE WITH ANYONE!
I DON'T EVEN LIKE ANYONE...!!
BRRRNG
MASTER CLAUDE!
KLIK
HELLO?
SEISHIRO SPEAKING...

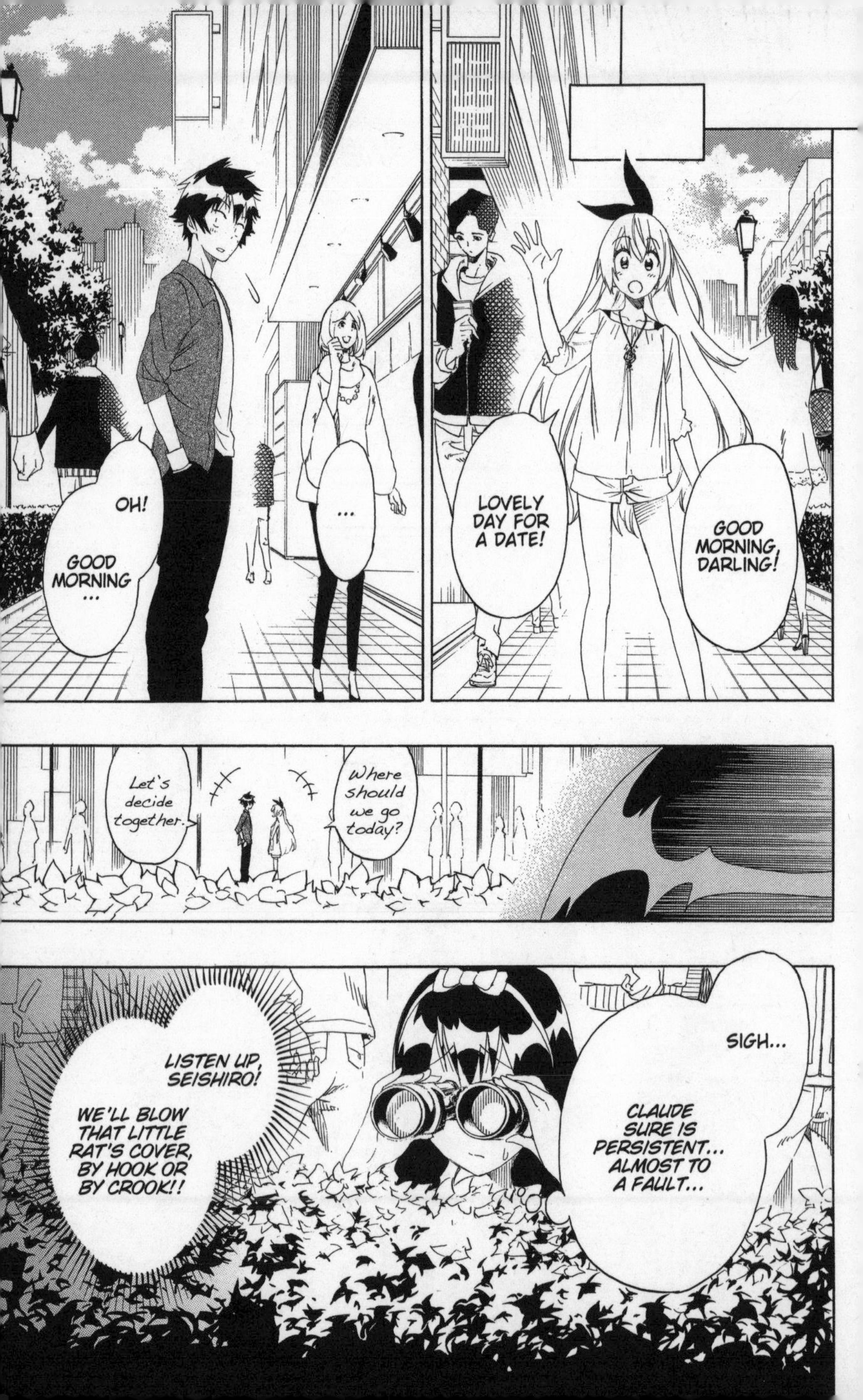
GOOD MORNING, DARLING!
LOVELY DAY FOR A DATE!
...
OH!
GOOD MORNING...
Where should we go today?
Let's decide together.
SIGH...
CLAUDE SURE IS PERSISTENT... ALMOST TO A FAULT...
LISTEN UP, SEISHIRO!
WE'LL BLOW THAT LITTLE RAT'S COVER, BY HOOK OR BY CROOK!!

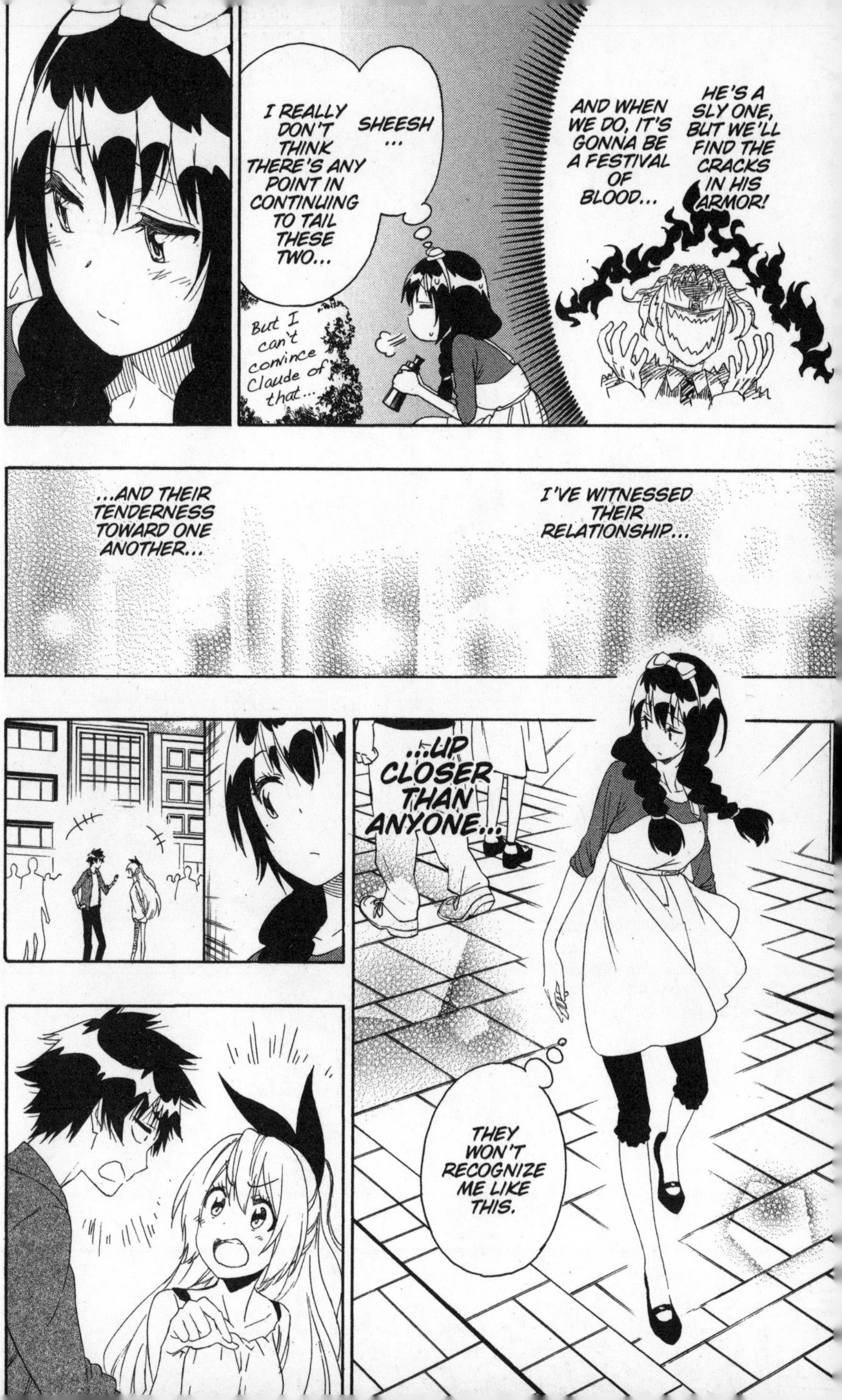
HE'S A SLY ONE, BUT WE'LL FIND THE CRACKS IN HIS ARMOR!
AND WHEN WE DO, IT'S GONNA BE A FESTIVAL OF BLOOD...
SHEESH...
I REALLY DON'T THINK THERE'S ANY POINT IN CONTINUING TO TAIL THESE TWO...
But I can't convince Claude of that...
I'VE WITNESSED THEIR RELATIONSHIP...
...AND THEIR TENDERNESS TOWARD ONE ANOTHER...
...UP CLOSER THAN ANYONE...
THEY WON'T RECOGNIZE ME LIKE THIS.

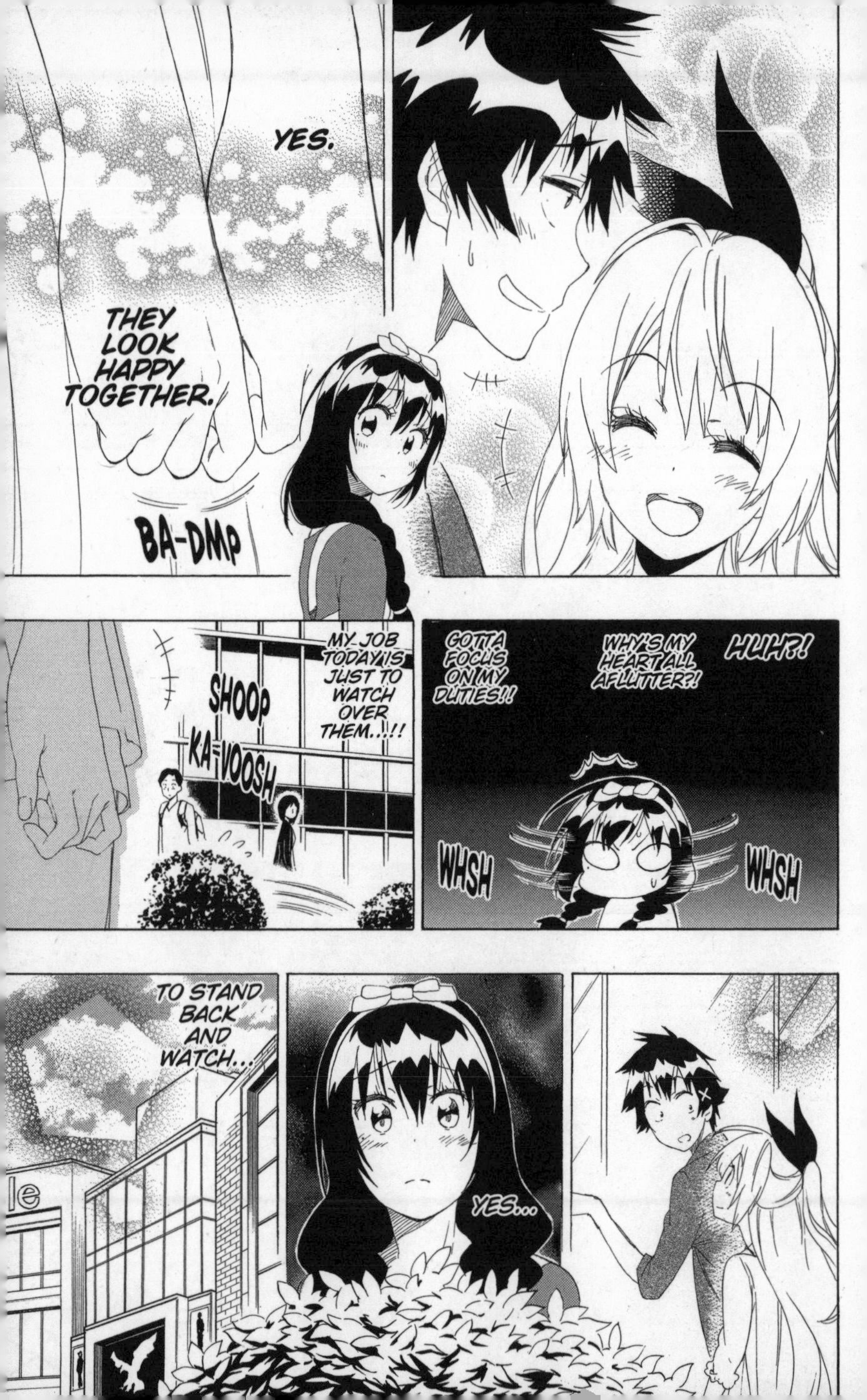
YES.
THEY LOOK HAPPY TOGETHER.
BA-DMP
HUH?!
WHY'S MY HEART ALL AFLUTTER?!
GOTTA FOCUS ON MY DUTIES!!
WHSH
WHSH
MY JOB TODAY IS JUST TO WATCH OVER THEM...!!!
SHOOP
KA-VOOSH
YES...
TO STAND BACK AND WATCH...

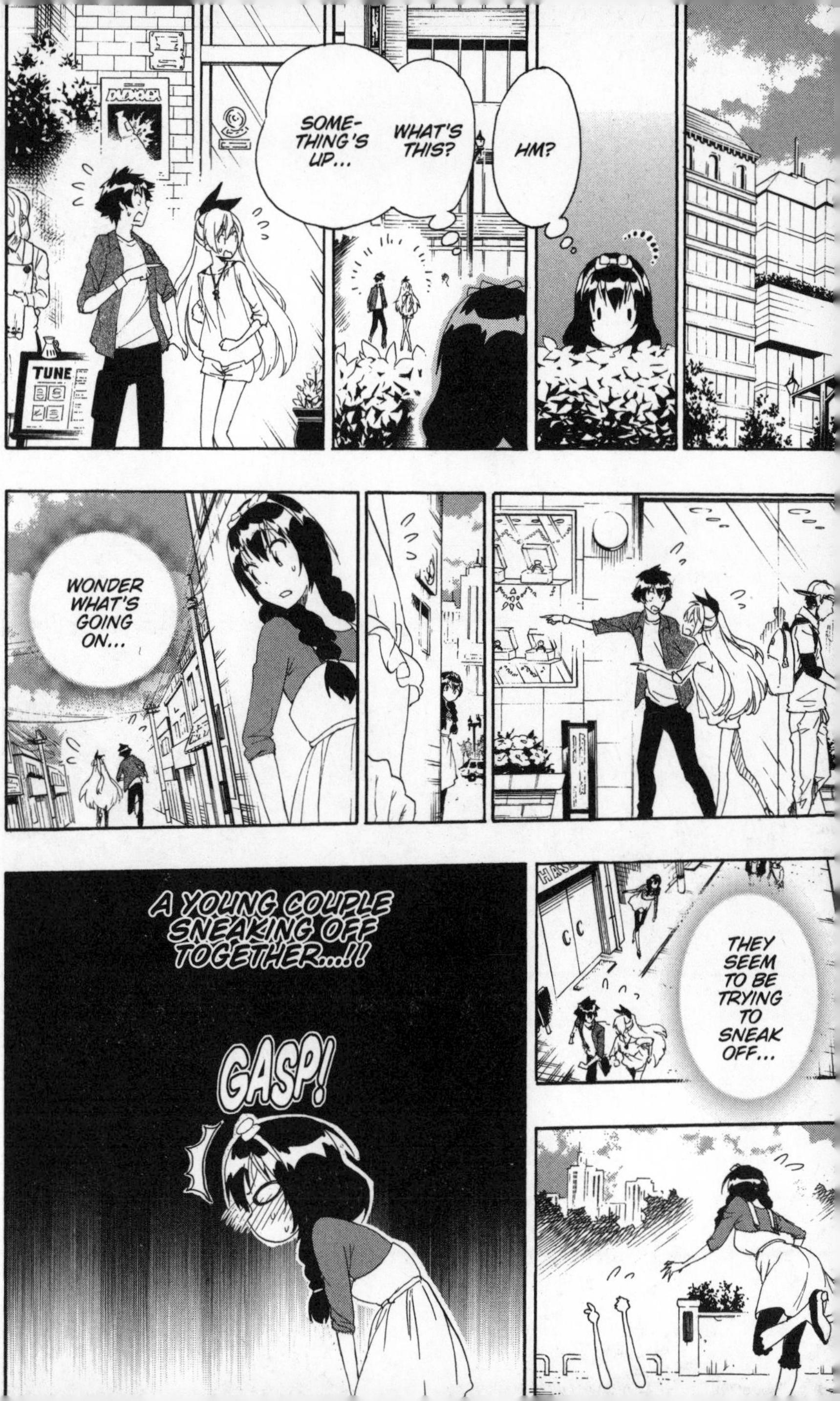
HM?
WHAT'S THIS?
SOME-THING'S UP...
TUNE
WONDER WHAT'S GOING ON...
THEY SEEM TO BE TRYING TO SNEAK OFF...
A YOUNG COUPLE SNEAKING OFF TOGETHER...!!
GASP!

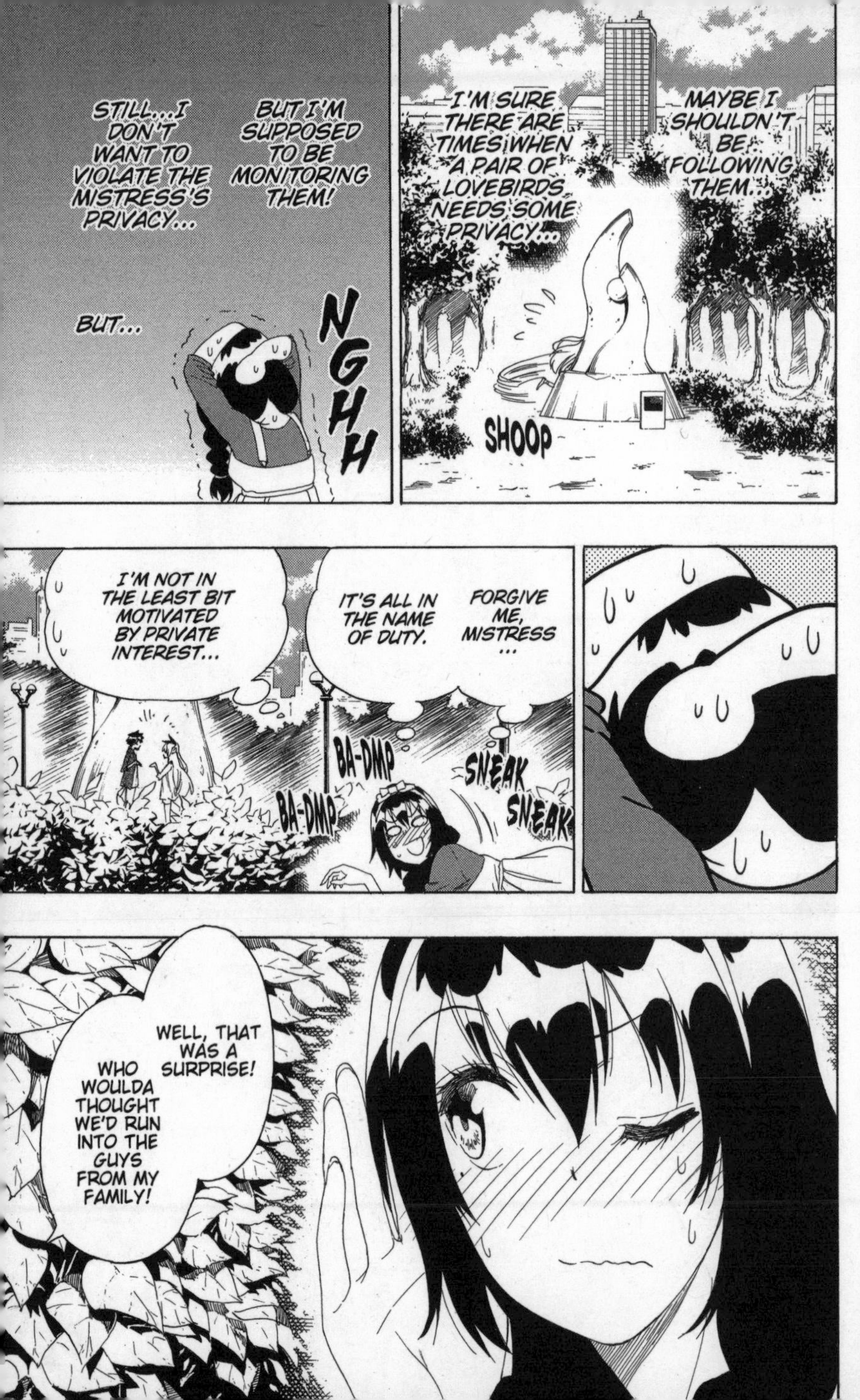
MAYBE I SHOULDN'T BE FOLLOWING THEM...
I'M SURE THERE ARE TIMES WHEN A PAIR OF LOVEBIRDS NEEDS SOME PRIVACY...
SHOOP
BUT I'M SUPPOSED TO BE MONITORING THEM!
STILL...I DON'T WANT TO VIOLATE THE MISTRESS'S PRIVACY...
BUT...
NGHH
FORGIVE ME, MISTRESS ...
IT'S ALL IN THE NAME OF DUTY.
I'M NOT IN THE LEAST BIT MOTIVATED BY PRIVATE INTEREST...
SNEAK SNEAK
BA-DMP BA-DMP
WELL, THAT WAS A SURPRISE! WHO WOULDA THOUGHT WE'D RUN INTO THE GUYS FROM MY FAMILY!

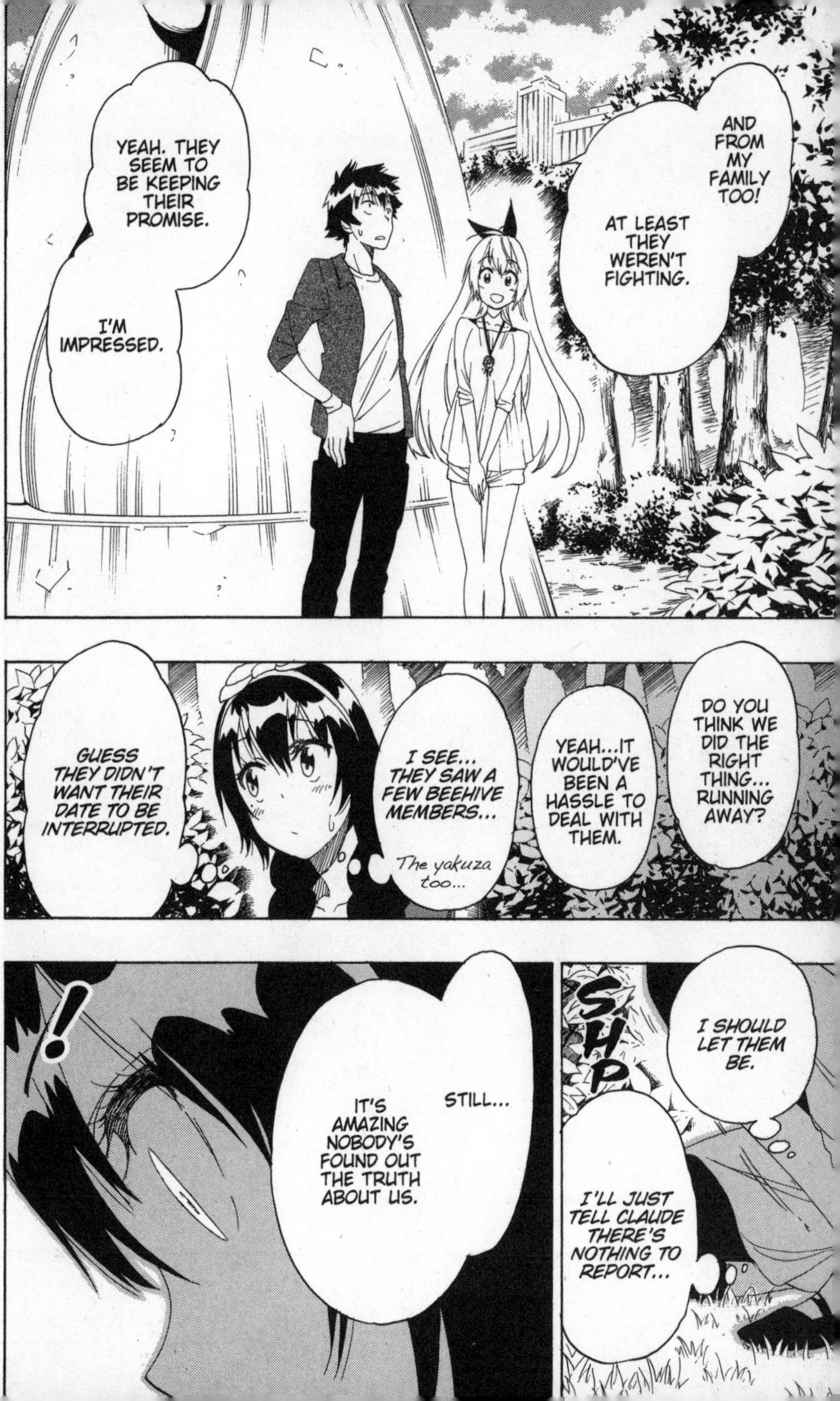
AND FROM MY FAMILY TOO!
AT LEAST THEY WEREN'T FIGHTING.
YEAH. THEY SEEM TO BE KEEPING THEIR PROMISE.
I'M IMPRESSED.
DO YOU THINK WE DID THE RIGHT THING... RUNNING AWAY?
YEAH...IT WOULD'VE BEEN A HASSLE TO DEAL WITH THEM.
I SEE... THEY SAW A FEW BEEHIVE MEMBERS...
The yakuza too...
GUESS THEY DIDN'T WANT THEIR DATE TO BE INTERRUPTED.
SHP
I SHOULD LET THEM BE.
I'LL JUST TELL CLAUDE THERE'S NOTHING TO REPORT...
!
STILL...
IT'S AMAZING NOBODY'S FOUND OUT THE TRUTH ABOUT US.

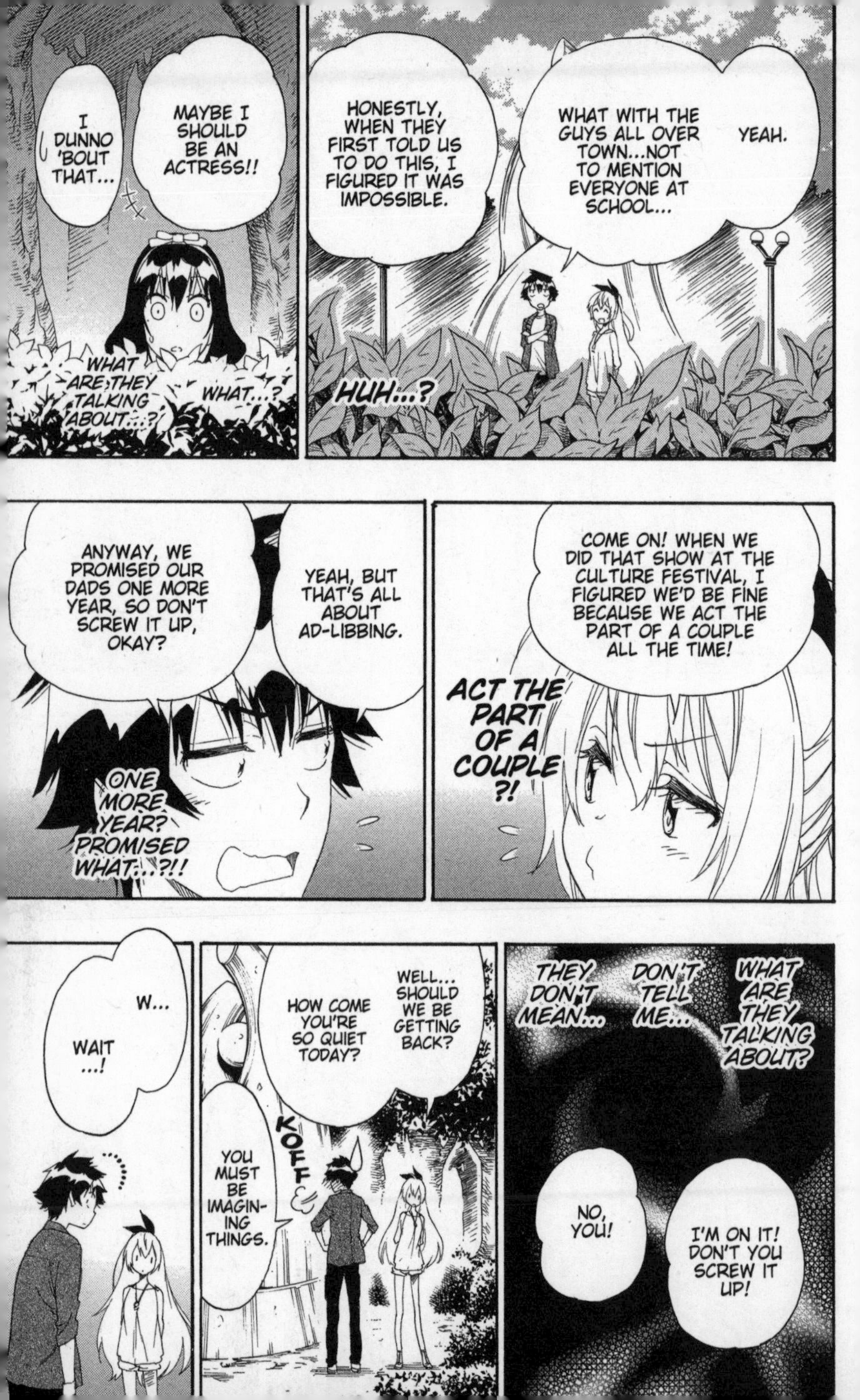
YEAH.
WHAT WITH THE GUYS ALL OVER TOWN...NOT TO MENTION EVERYONE AT SCHOOL...
HONESTLY, WHEN THEY FIRST TOLD US TO DO THIS, I FIGURED IT WAS IMPOSSIBLE.
HUH...?
MAYBE I SHOULD BE AN ACTRESS!!
I DUNNO 'BOUT THAT...
WHAT...?
WHAT ARE THEY TALKING ABOUT...?
COME ON! WHEN WE DID THAT SHOW AT THE CULTURE FESTIVAL, I FIGURED WE'D BE FINE BECAUSE WE ACT THE PART OF A COUPLE ALL THE TIME!
ACT THE PART OF A COUPLE ?!
YEAH, BUT THAT'S ALL ABOUT AD-LIBBING.
ANYWAY, WE PROMISED OUR DADS ONE MORE YEAR, SO DON'T SCREW IT UP, OKAY?
ONE MORE YEAR? PROMISED WHAT...?!!
WHAT ARE THEY TALKING ABOUT?
DON'T TELL ME...
THEY DON'T MEAN...
I'M ON IT! DON'T YOU SCREW IT UP!
NO, YOU!
WELL... SHOULD WE BE GETTING BACK?
HOW COME YOU'RE SO QUIET TODAY?
KOFF
YOU MUST BE IMAGINING THINGS.
W...
WAIT ...!

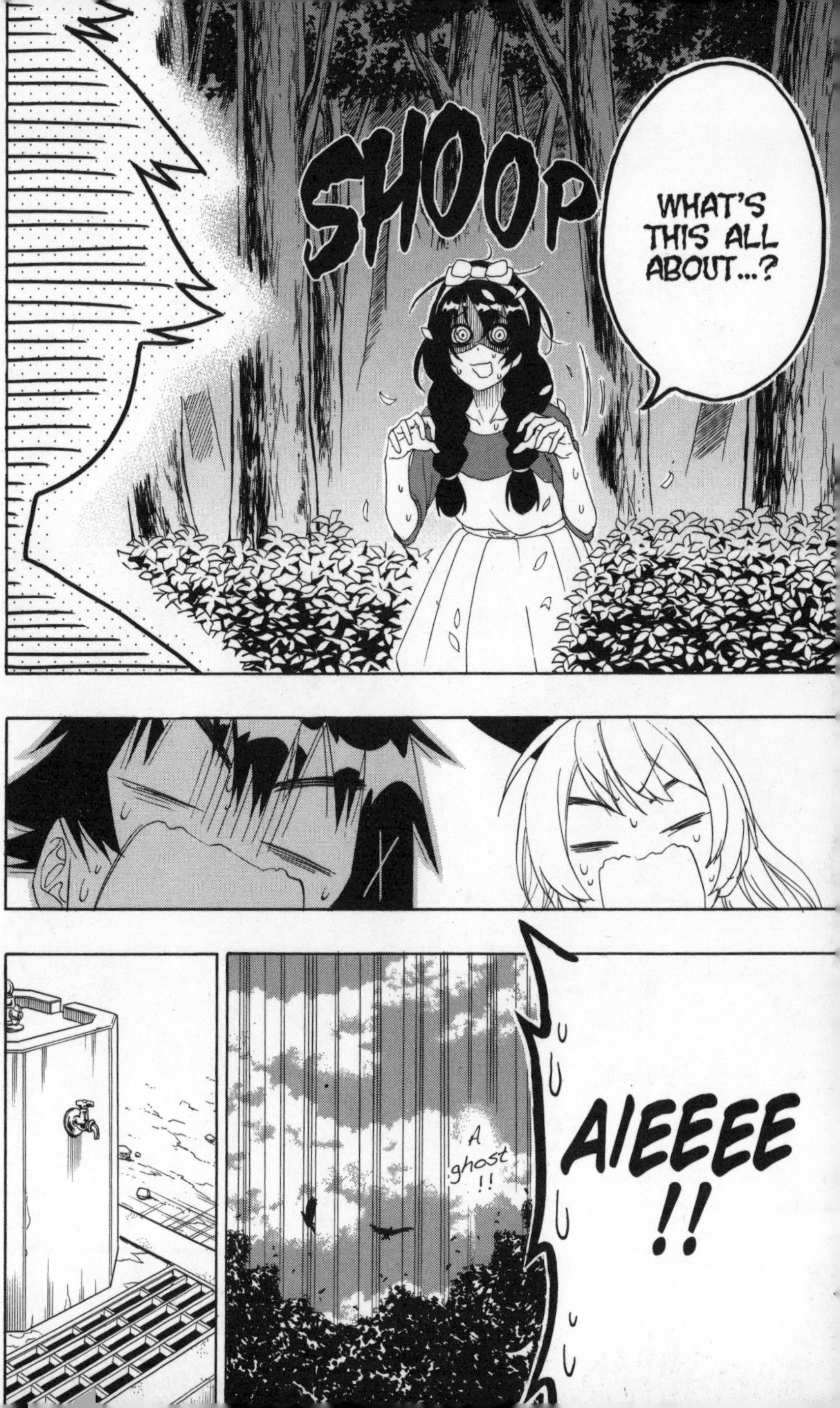
WHAT'S THIS ALL ABOUT...?
SHOOP
AIEEEE !!
A ghost !!

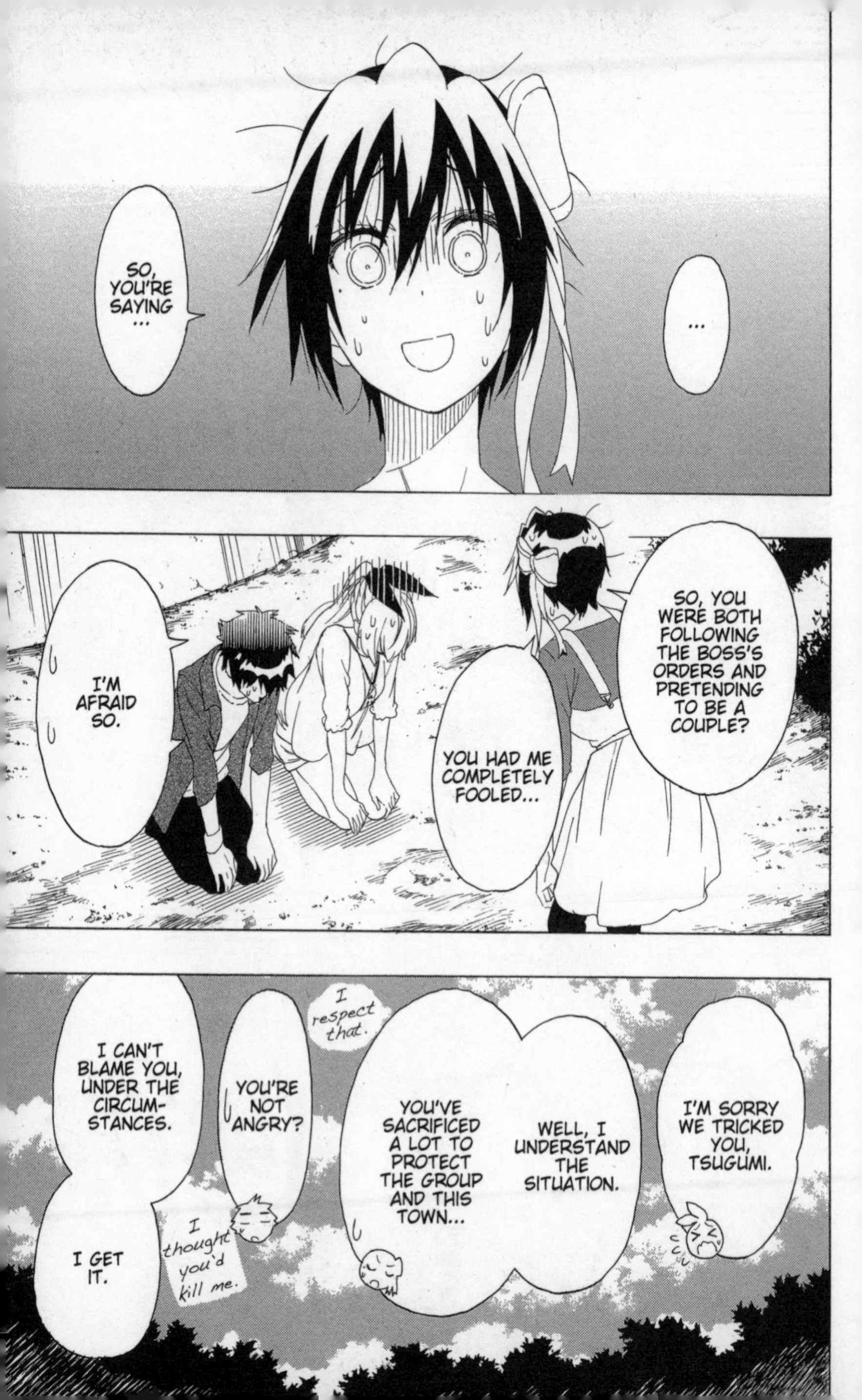
...
SO, YOU'RE SAYING ...
SO, YOU WERE BOTH FOLLOWING THE BOSS'S ORDERS AND PRETENDING TO BE A COUPLE?
YOU HAD ME COMPLETELY FOOLED...
I'M AFRAID SO.
I'M SORRY WE TRICKED YOU, TSUGUMI.
WELL, I UNDERSTAND THE SITUATION.
YOU'VE SACRIFICED A LOT TO PROTECT THE GROUP AND THIS TOWN...
I respect that.
YOU'RE NOT ANGRY?
I thought you'd kill me.
I CAN'T BLAME YOU, UNDER THE CIRCUMSTANCES.
I GET IT.

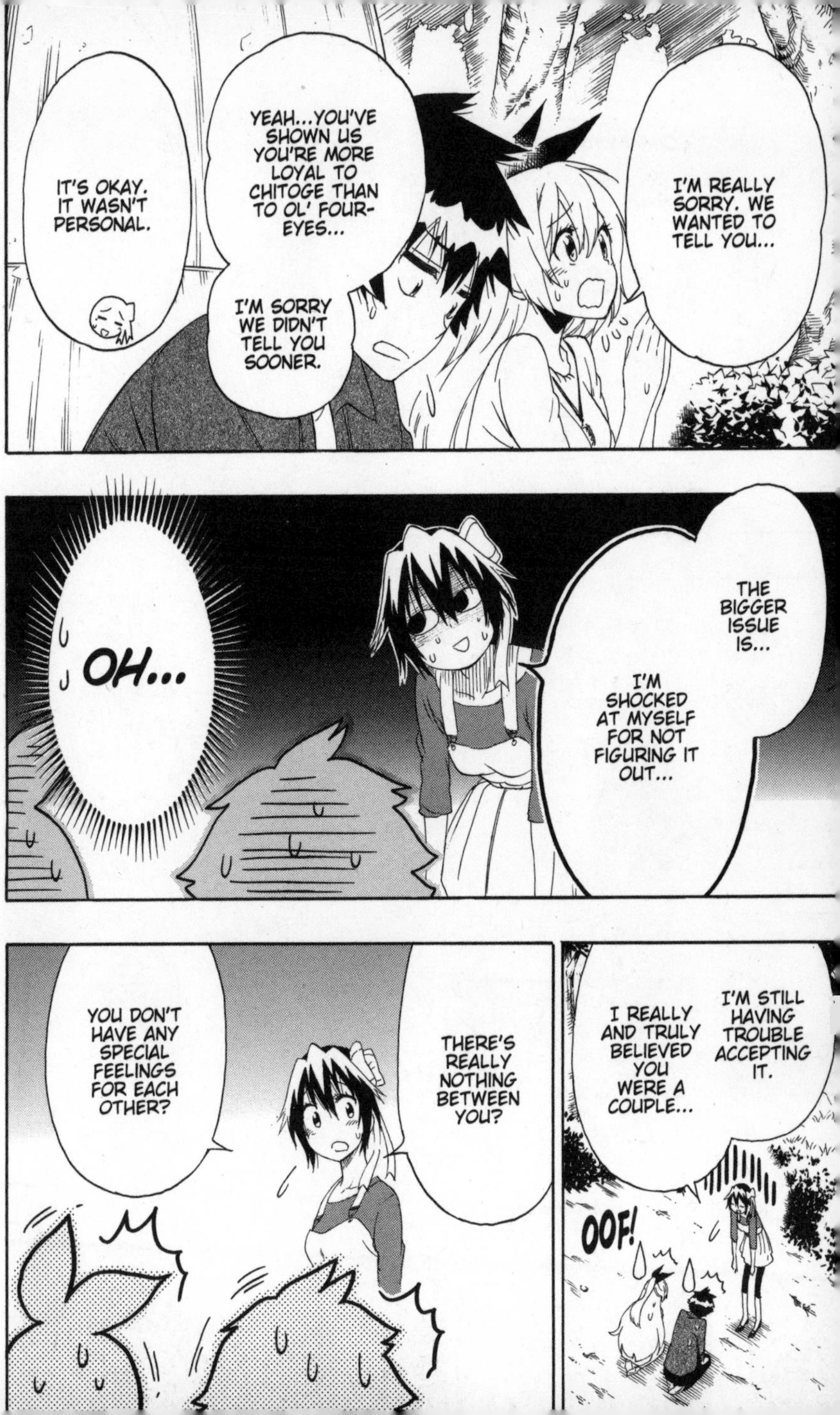
I'M REALLY SORRY. WE WANTED TO TELL YOU...
YEAH...YOU'VE SHOWN US YOU'RE MORE LOYAL TO CHITOGE THAN TO OL' FOUR-EYES...
I'M SORRY WE DIDN'T TELL YOU SOONER.
IT'S OKAY. IT WASN'T PERSONAL.
THE BIGGER ISSUE IS...
I'M SHOCKED AT MYSELF FOR NOT FIGURING IT OUT...
OH...
I'M STILL HAVING TROUBLE ACCEPTING IT.
I REALLY AND TRULY BELIEVED YOU WERE A COUPLE...
OOF!
THERE'S REALLY NOTHING BETWEEN YOU?
YOU DON'T HAVE ANY SPECIAL FEELINGS FOR EACH OTHER?

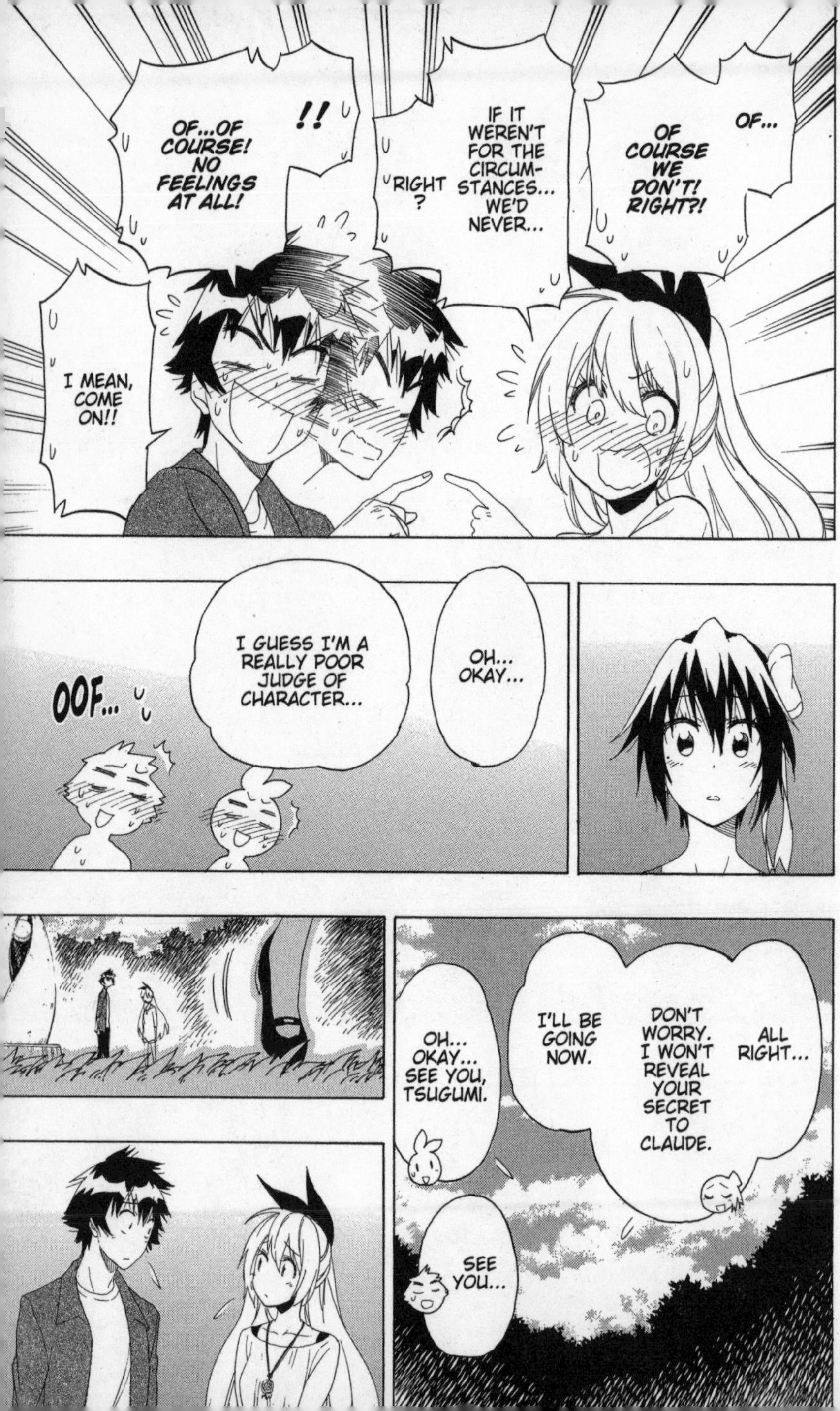
OF...
OF COURSE WE DON'T! RIGHT?!
IF IT WEREN'T FOR THE CIRCUMSTANCES... WE'D NEVER...
RIGHT?
!!
OF...OF COURSE! NO FEELINGS AT ALL!
I MEAN, COME ON!!
OH... OKAY...
I GUESS I'M A REALLY POOR JUDGE OF CHARACTER...
OOF...
ALL RIGHT...
DON'T WORRY. I WON'T REVEAL YOUR SECRET TO CLAUDE.
I'LL BE GOING NOW.
OH... OKAY... SEE YOU, TSUGUMI.
SEE YOU...

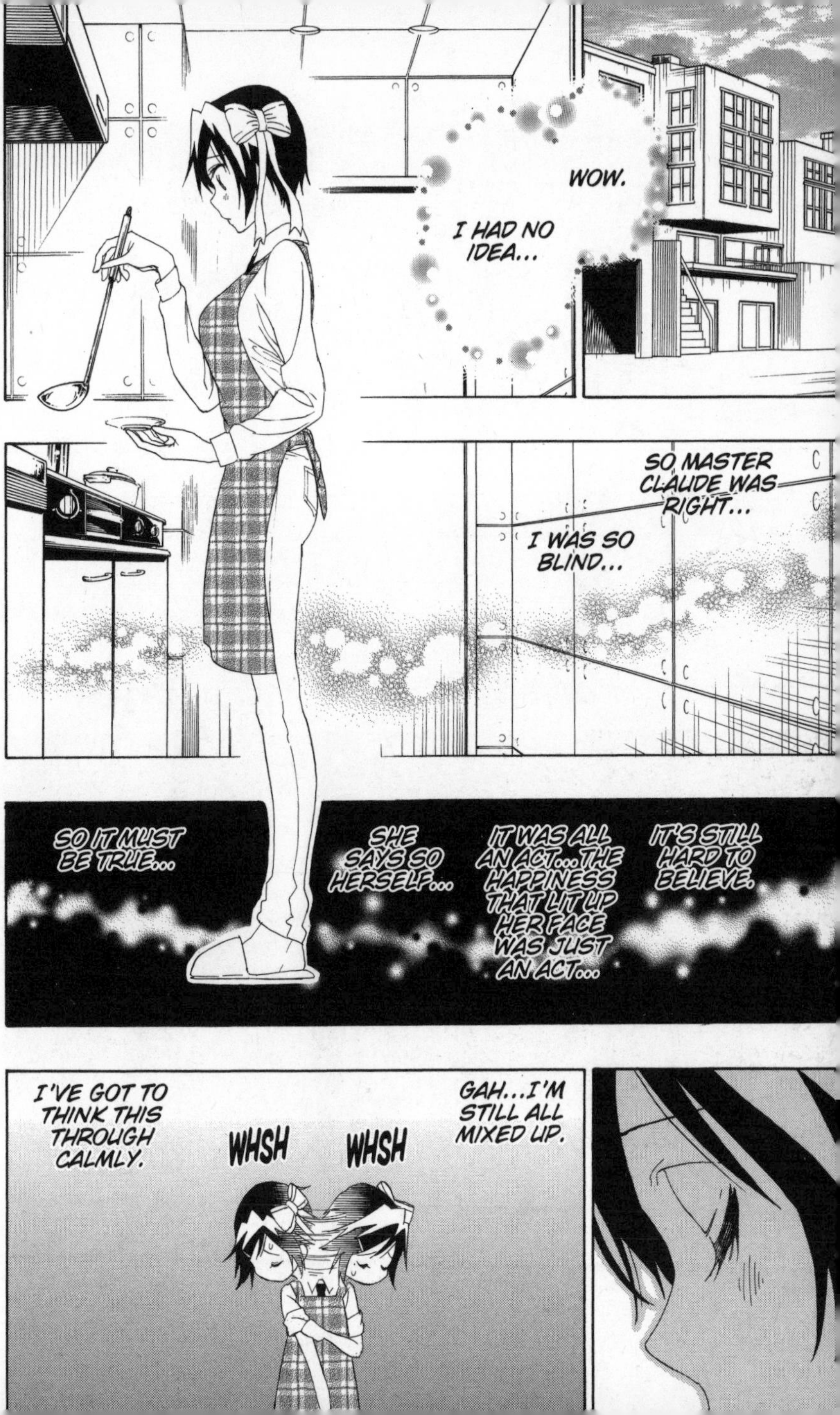
WOW.
I HAD NO IDEA...
SO MASTER CLAUDE WAS RIGHT...
I WAS SO BLIND...
IT'S STILL HARD TO BELIEVE.
IT WAS ALL AN ACT... THE HAPPINESS THAT LIT UP HER FACE WAS JUST AN ACT...
SHE SAYS SO HERSELF...
SO IT MUST BE TRUE...
GAH...I'M STILL ALL MIXED UP.
WHSH
WHSH
I'VE GOT TO THINK THIS THROUGH CALMLY.

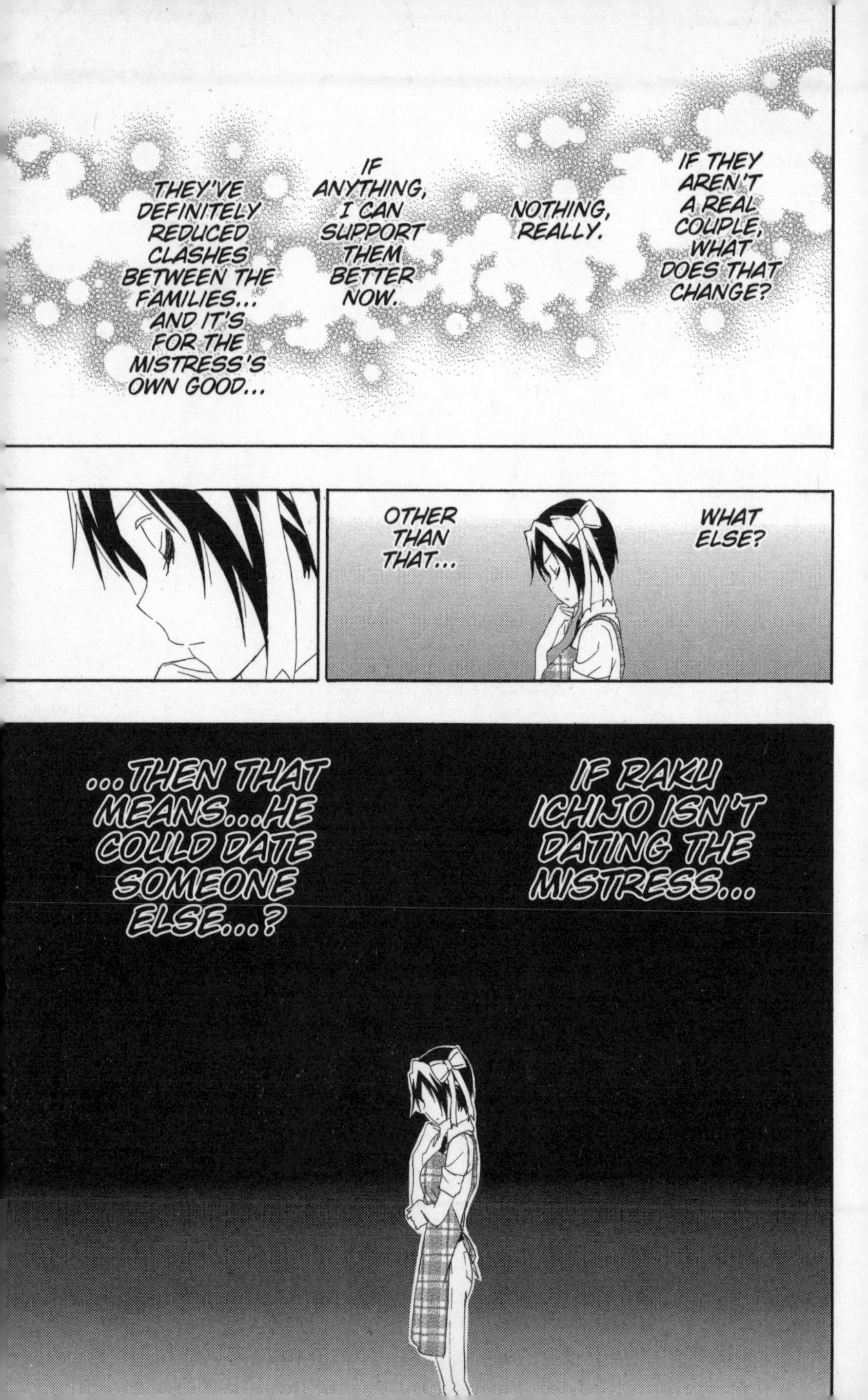
IF THEY AREN'T A REAL COUPLE, WHAT DOES THAT CHANGE?
NOTHING, REALLY.
IF ANYTHING, I CAN SUPPORT THEM BETTER NOW.
THEY'VE DEFINITELY REDUCED CLASHES BETWEEN THE FAMILIES... AND IT'S FOR THE MISTRESS'S OWN GOOD...
WHAT ELSE?
OTHER THAN THAT...
IF RAKU ICHIJO ISN'T DATING THE MISTRESS...
...THEN THAT MEANS...HE COULD DATE SOMEONE ELSE...?

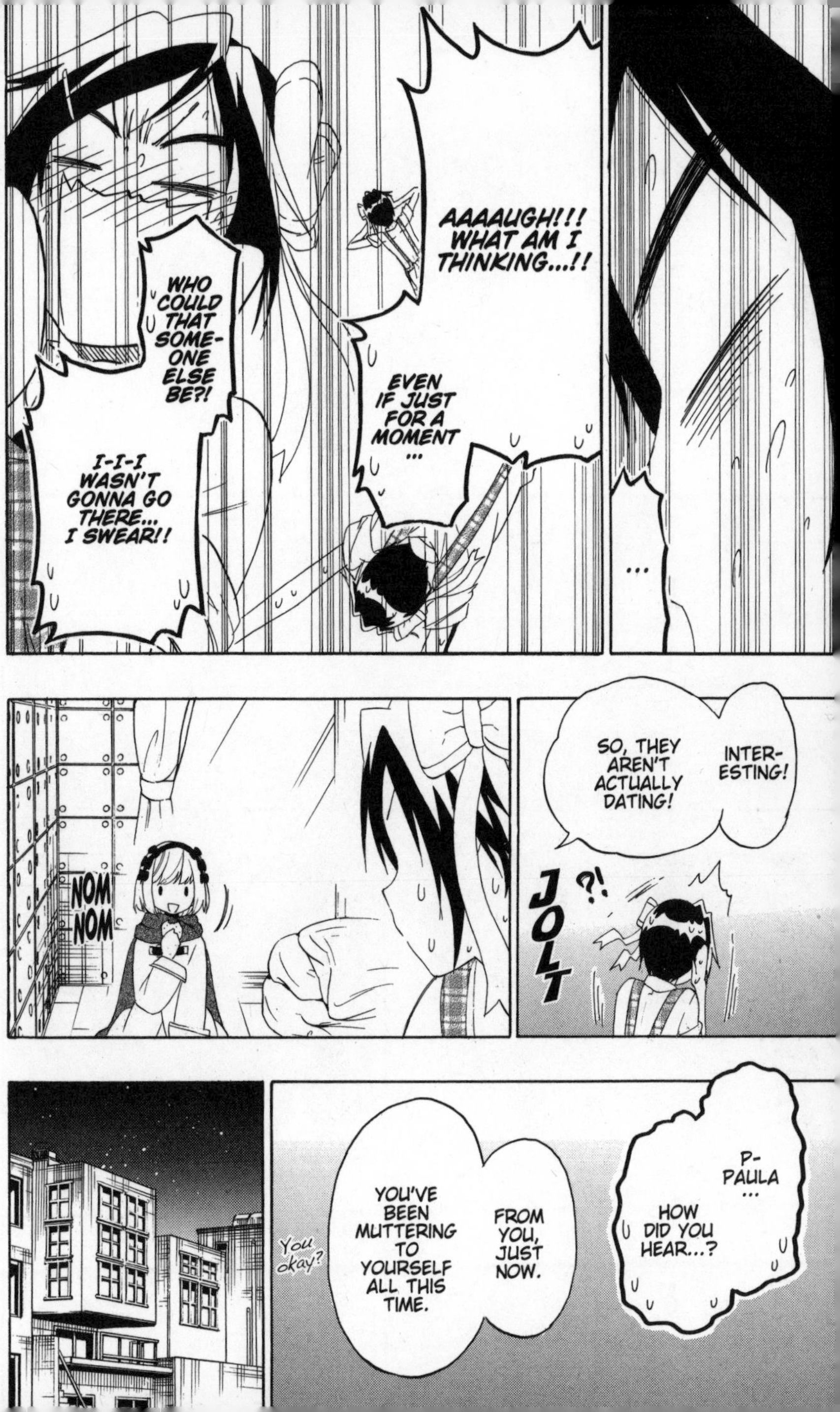
...
AAAAUGH!!! WHAT AM I THINKING...!!
EVEN IF JUST FOR A MOMENT...
WHO COULD THAT SOMEONE ELSE BE?!
I-I-I WASN'T GONNA GO THERE... I SWEAR!!
INTERESTING!
SO, THEY AREN'T ACTUALLY DATING!
JOLT
?!
NOM NOM
P-PAULA...
HOW DID YOU HEAR...?
FROM YOU, JUST NOW.
YOU'VE BEEN MUTTERING TO YOURSELF ALL THIS TIME.
You okay?

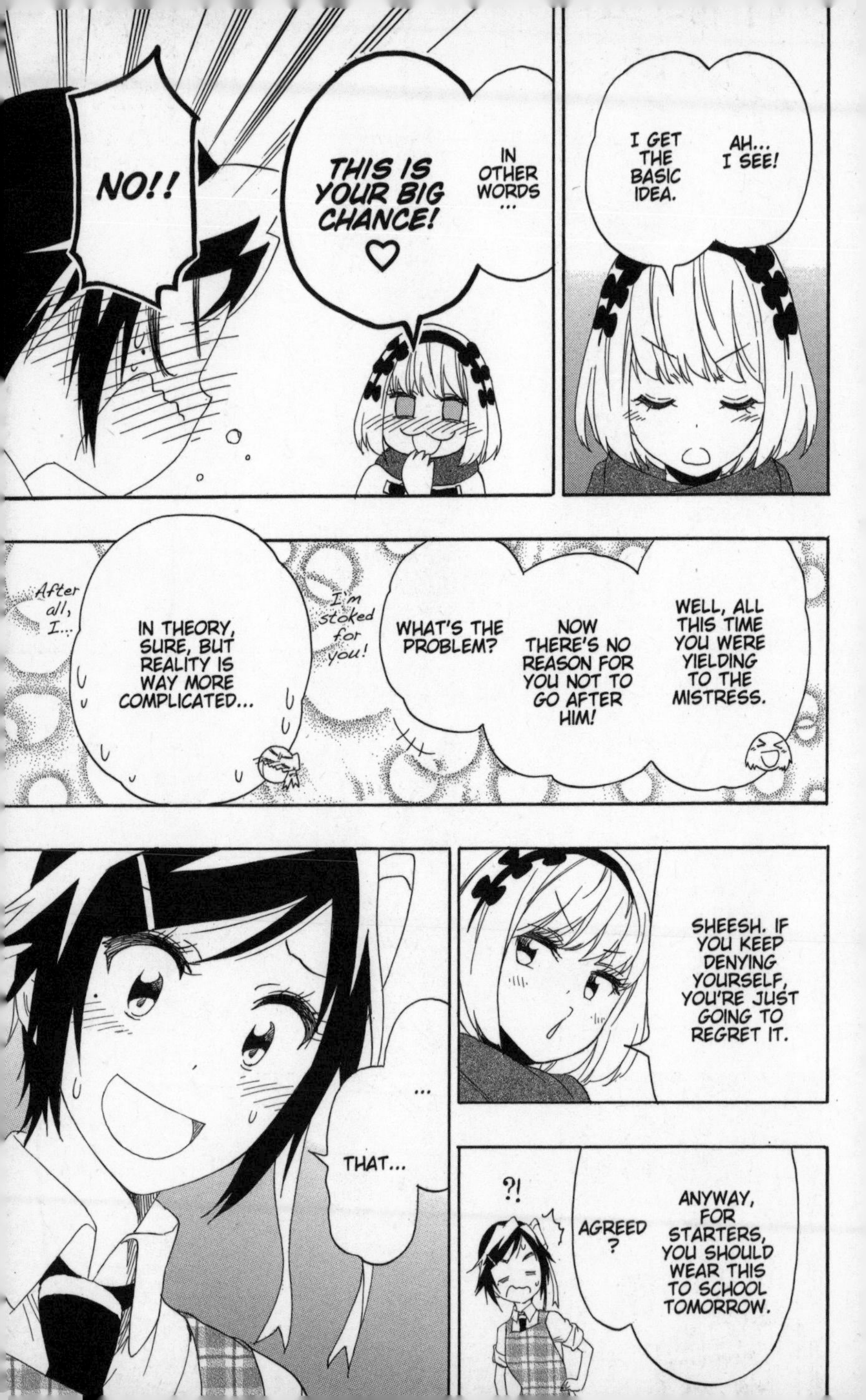
AH... I SEE!
I GET THE BASIC IDEA.
IN OTHER WORDS...
THIS IS YOUR BIG CHANCE! ♡
NO!!
WELL, ALL THIS TIME YOU WERE YIELDING TO THE MISTRESS.
NOW THERE'S NO REASON FOR YOU NOT TO GO AFTER HIM!
WHAT'S THE PROBLEM?
I'm stoked for you!
IN THEORY, SURE, BUT REALITY IS WAY MORE COMPLICATED...
After all, I...
SHEESH. IF YOU KEEP DENYING YOURSELF, YOU'RE JUST GOING TO REGRET IT.
ANYWAY, FOR STARTERS, YOU SHOULD WEAR THIS TO SCHOOL TOMORROW.
AGREED?
?!
...
THAT...

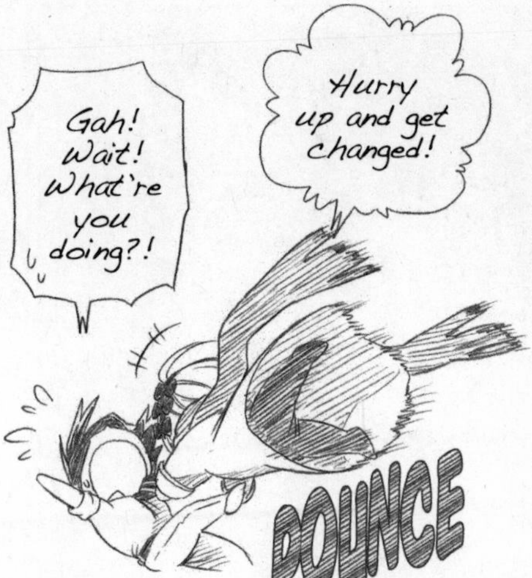
Hurry up and get changed!
Gah! Wait! What're you doing?!
POUNCE

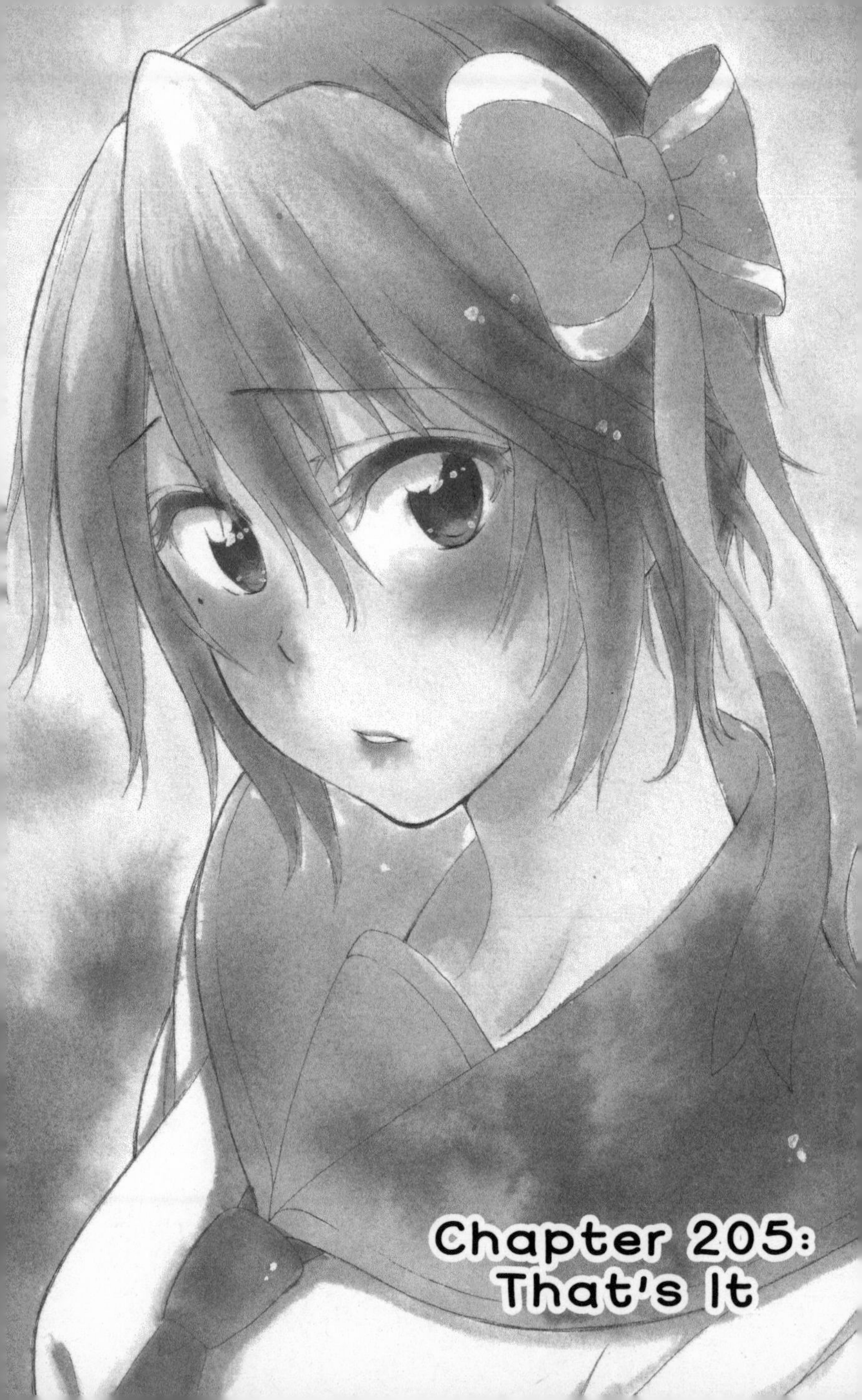
Chapter 205:
That's It

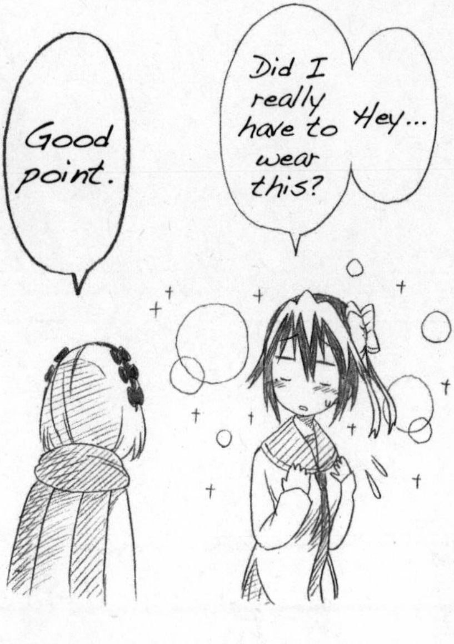
Hey...
Did I really have to wear this?
Good point.

The day before

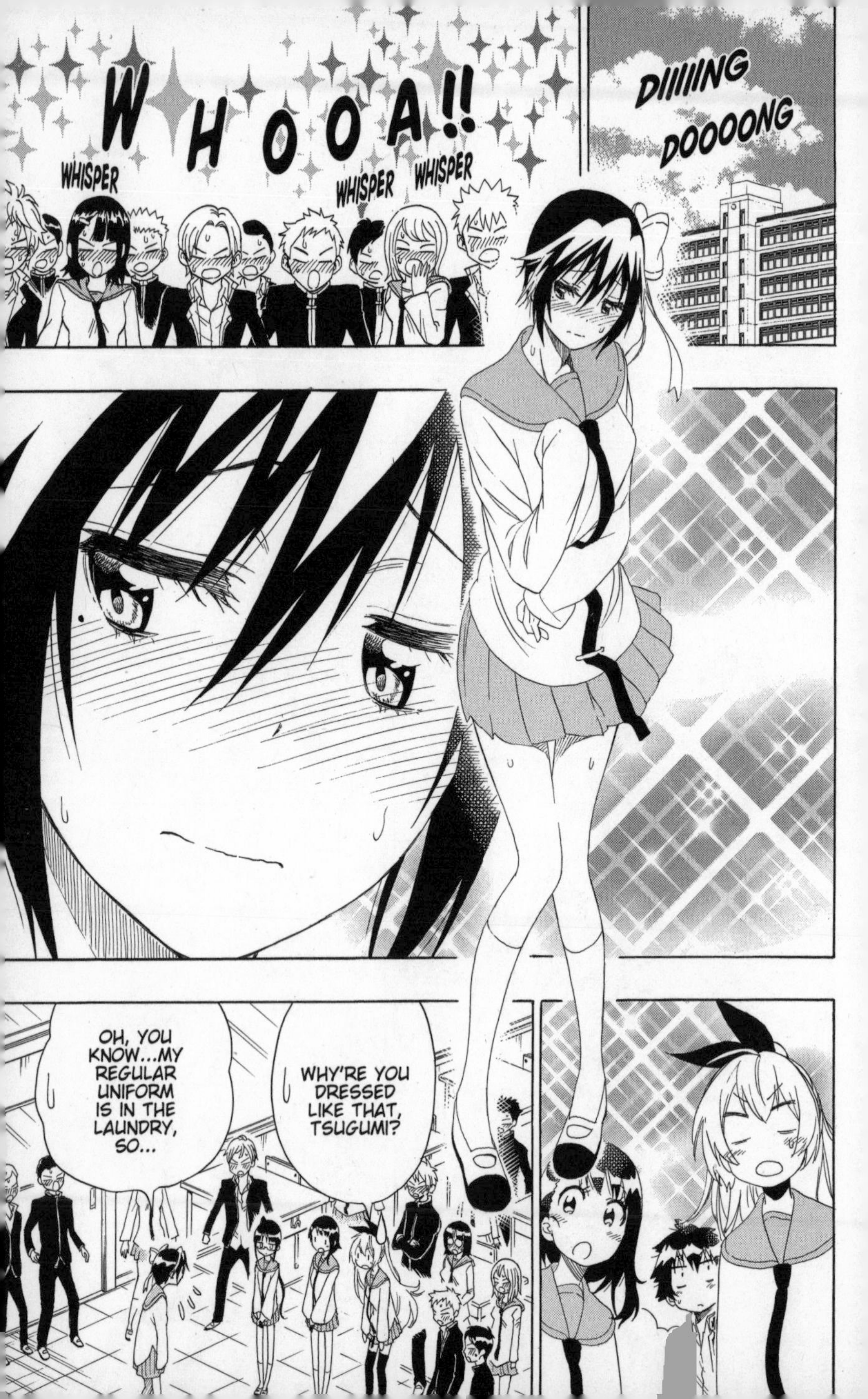
DIIIIING
DOOOONG
WHOOA!!
WHISPER
WHISPER
WHISPER
WHY'RE YOU DRESSED LIKE THAT, TSUGUMI?
OH, YOU KNOW...MY REGULAR UNIFORM IS IN THE LAUNDRY, SO...

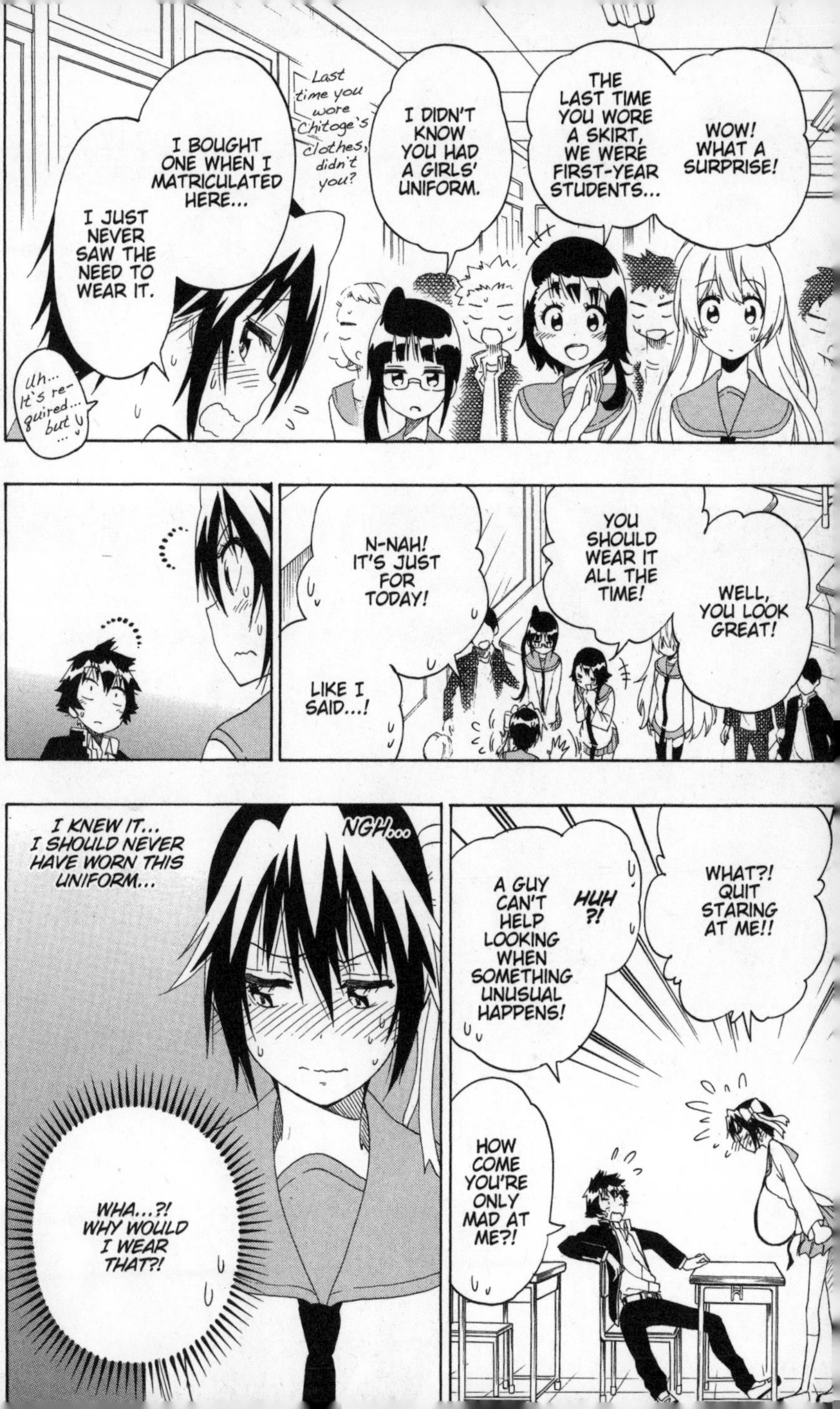
WOW! WHAT A SURPRISE!
THE LAST TIME YOU WORE A SKIRT, WE WERE FIRST-YEAR STUDENTS...
I DIDN'T KNOW YOU HAD A GIRLS' UNIFORM.
Last time you wore Chitoge's clothes, didn't you?
I BOUGHT ONE WHEN I MATRICULATED HERE...
I JUST NEVER SAW THE NEED TO WEAR IT.
Uh... It's re-quired... but...
WELL, YOU LOOK GREAT!
YOU SHOULD WEAR IT ALL THE TIME!
N-NAH! IT'S JUST FOR TODAY!
LIKE I SAID...!
WHAT?! QUIT STARING AT ME!!
HUH ?!
A GUY CAN'T HELP LOOKING WHEN SOMETHING UNUSUAL HAPPENS!
HOW COME YOU'RE ONLY MAD AT ME?!
NGHooo
I KNEW IT... I SHOULD NEVER HAVE WORN THIS UNIFORM...
WHA...?! WHY WOULD I WEAR THAT?!

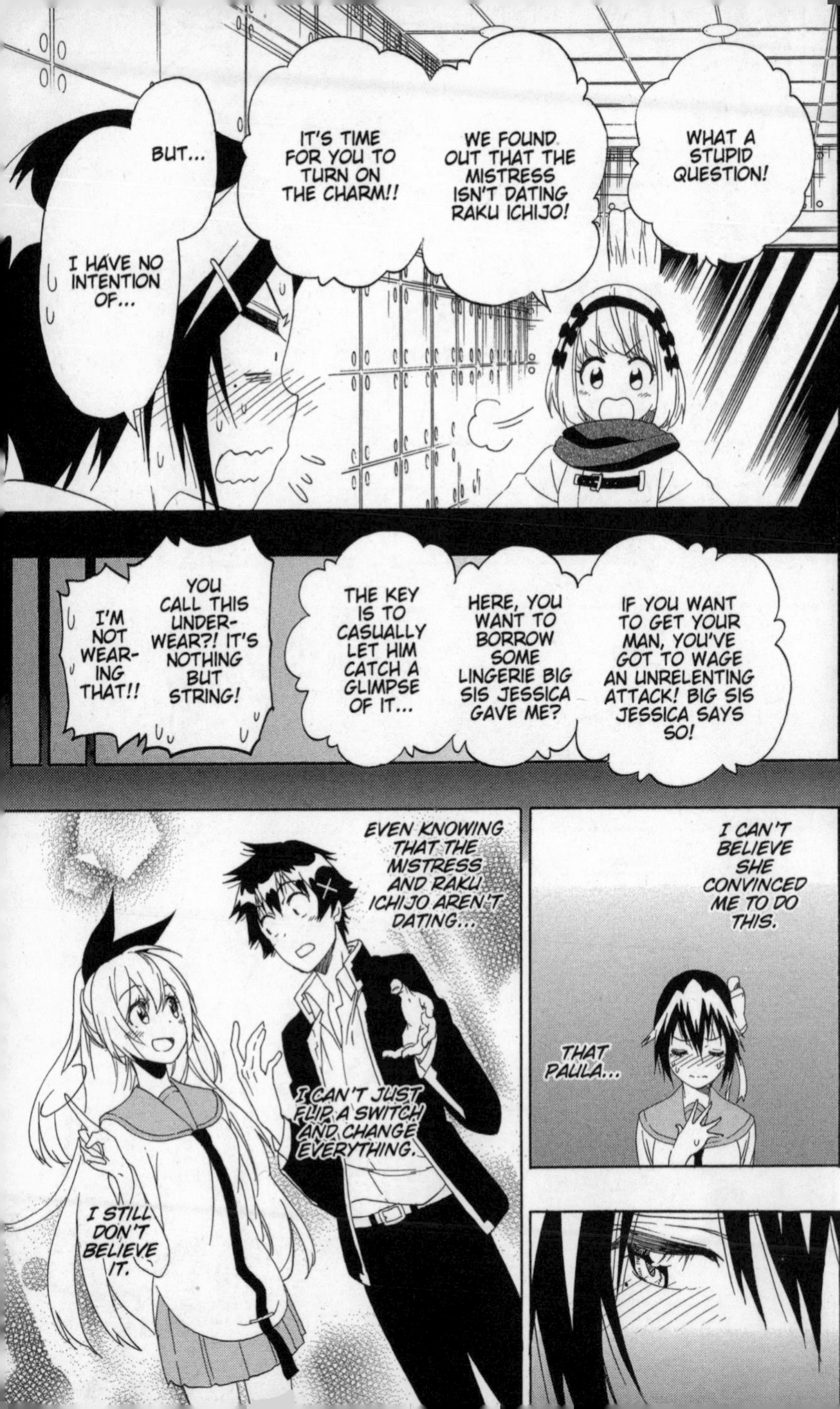
WHAT A STUPID QUESTION!
WE FOUND OUT THAT THE MISTRESS ISN'T DATING RAKU ICHIJO!
IT'S TIME FOR YOU TO TURN ON THE CHARM!!
BUT...
I HAVE NO INTENTION OF...
IF YOU WANT TO GET YOUR MAN, YOU'VE GOT TO WAGE AN UNRELENTING ATTACK! BIG SIS JESSICA SAYS SO!
HERE, YOU WANT TO BORROW SOME LINGERIE BIG SIS JESSICA GAVE ME?
THE KEY IS TO CASUALLY LET HIM CATCH A GLIMPSE OF IT...
YOU CALL THIS UNDER-WEAR?! IT'S NOTHING BUT STRING!
I'M NOT WEAR-ING THAT!!
I CAN'T BELIEVE SHE CONVINCED ME TO DO THIS.
THAT PAULA...
EVEN KNOWING THAT THE MISTRESS AND RAKU ICHIJO AREN'T DATING...
I CAN'T JUST FLIP A SWITCH AND CHANGE EVERYTHING.
I STILL DON'T BELIEVE IT.

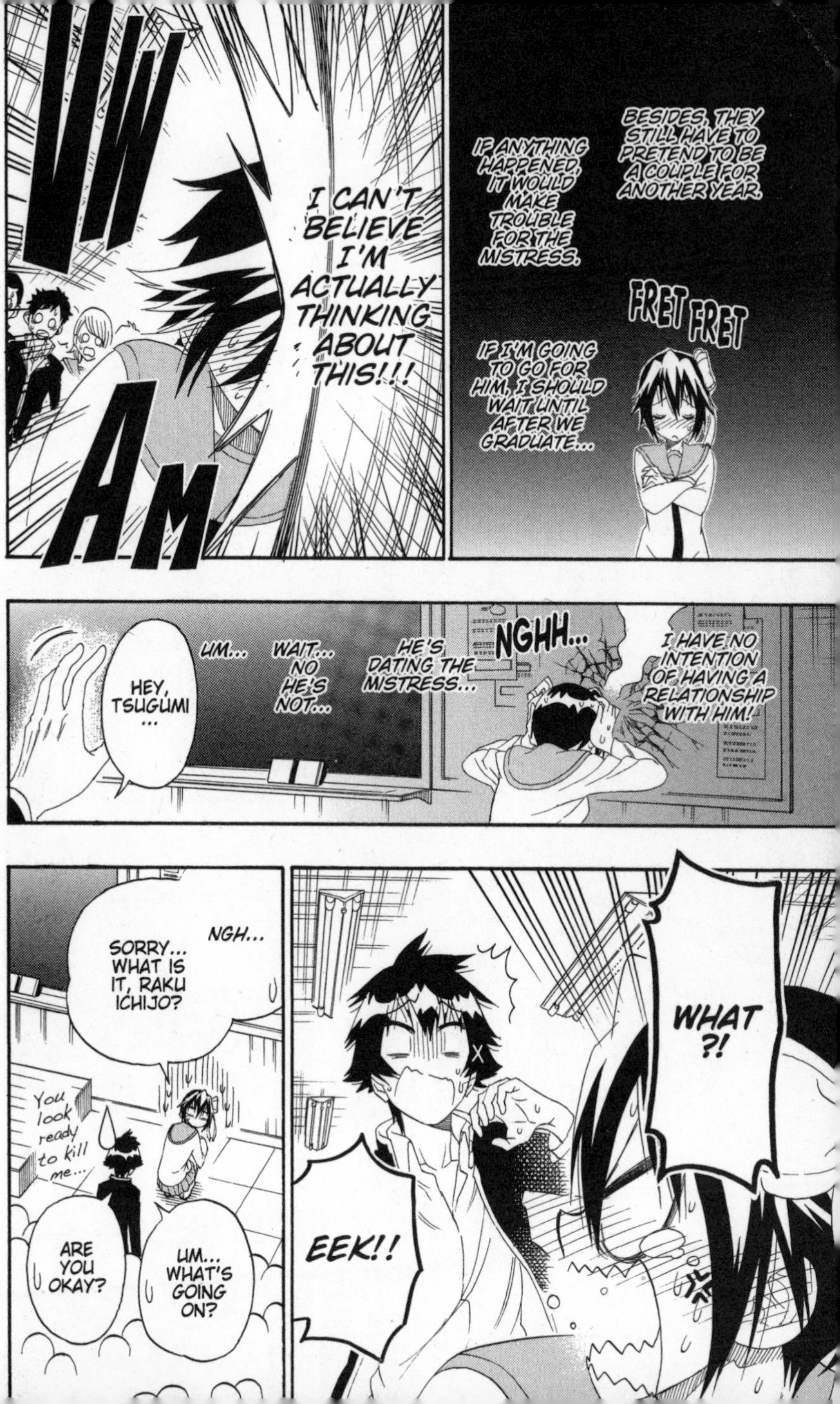
BESIDES, THEY STILL HAVE TO PRETEND TO BE A COUPLE FOR ANOTHER YEAR.
IF ANYTHING HAPPENED, IT WOULD MAKE TROUBLE FOR THE MISTRESS.
FRET FRET
IF I'M GOING TO GO FOR HIM, I SHOULD WAIT UNTIL AFTER WE GRADUATE...
I CAN'T BELIEVE I'M ACTUALLY THINKING ABOUT THIS!!!
I HAVE NO INTENTION OF HAVING A RELATIONSHIP WITH HIM!
NGHH...
HE'S DATING THE MISTRESS...
WAIT... NO HE'S NOT...
UM...
HEY, TSUGUMI...
WHAT ?!
EEK!!
NGH...
SORRY... WHAT IS IT, RAKU ICHIJO?
You look ready to kill me...
UM... WHAT'S GOING ON?
ARE YOU OKAY?

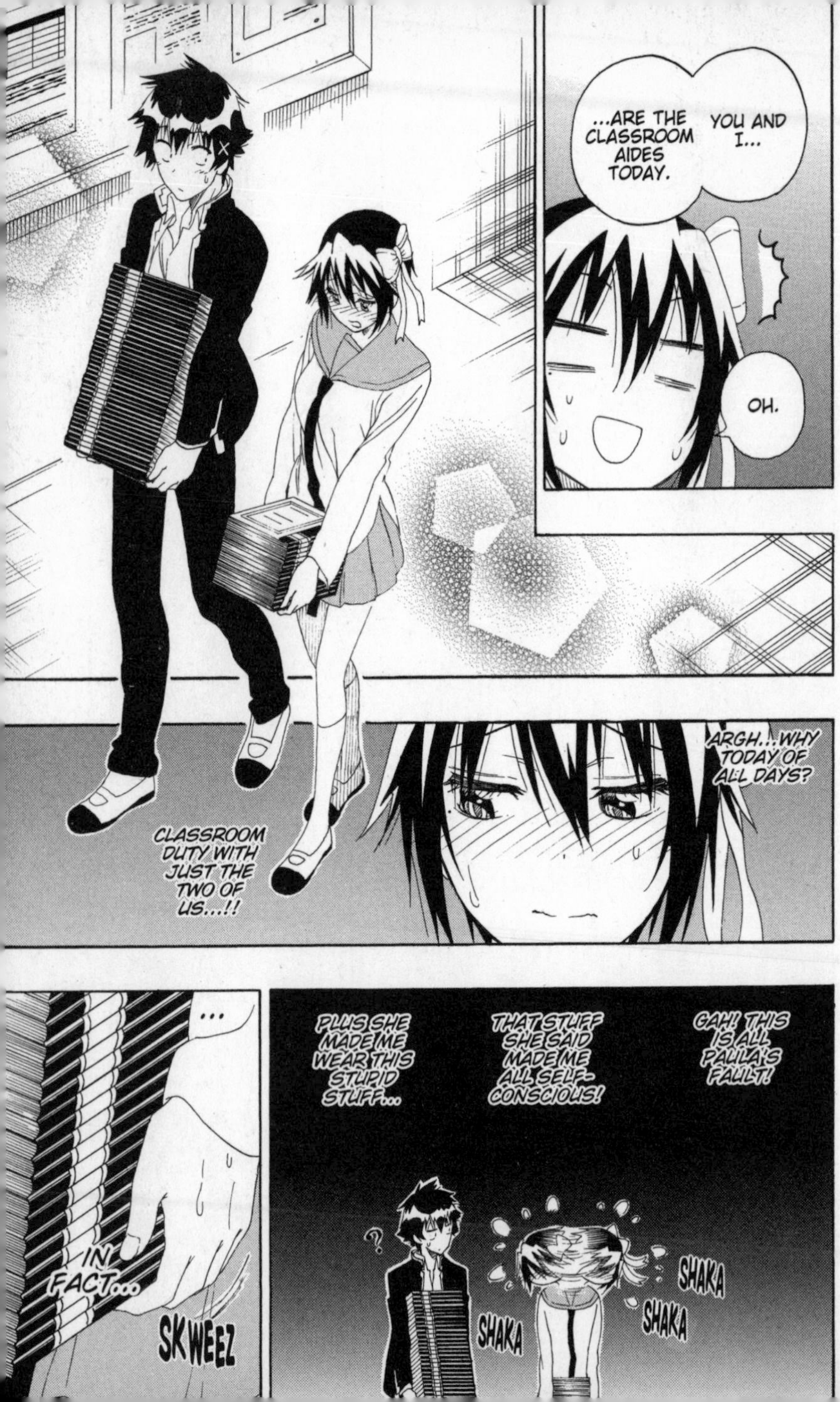
YOU AND I...
...ARE THE CLASSROOM AIDES TODAY.
OH.
ARGH...WHY TODAY OF ALL DAYS?
CLASSROOM DUTY WITH JUST THE TWO OF US...!!
GAH! THIS IS ALL PAULA'S FAULT!
THAT STUFF SHE SAID MADE ME ALL SELF-CONSCIOUS!
PLUS SHE MADE ME WEAR THIS STUPID STUFF...
?
SHAKA
SHAKA
SHAKA
...
IN FACT...
SKWEEZ

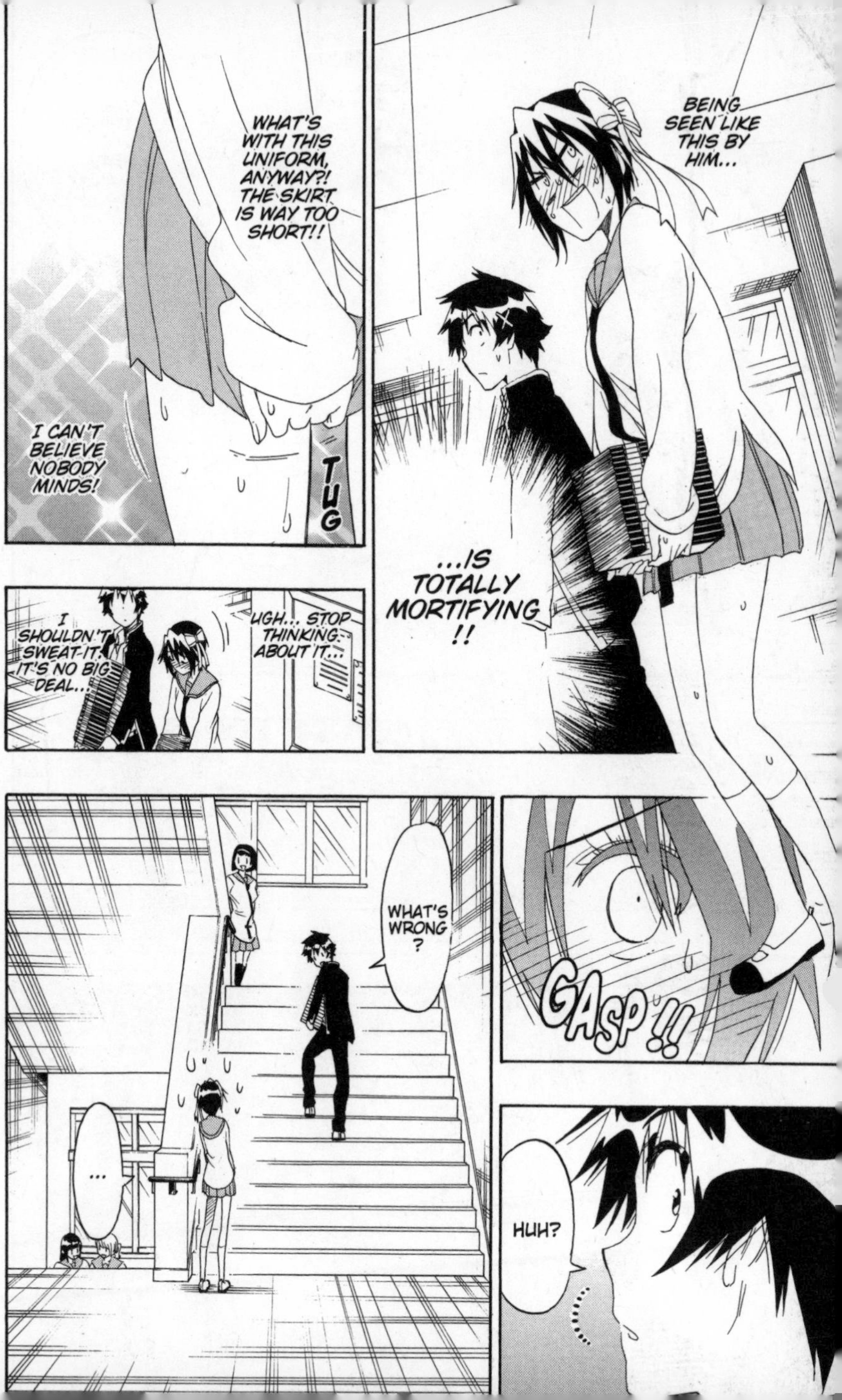

BEING SEEN LIKE THIS BY HIM...
...IS TOTALLY MORTIFYING!!
WHAT'S WITH THIS UNIFORM, ANYWAY?! THE SKIRT IS WAY TOO SHORT!!
TUG
I CAN'T BELIEVE NOBODY MINDS!
UGH... STOP THINKING ABOUT IT...
I SHOULDN'T SWEAT IT. IT'S NO BIG DEAL...
GASP!!
HUH?
WHAT'S WRONG?
...

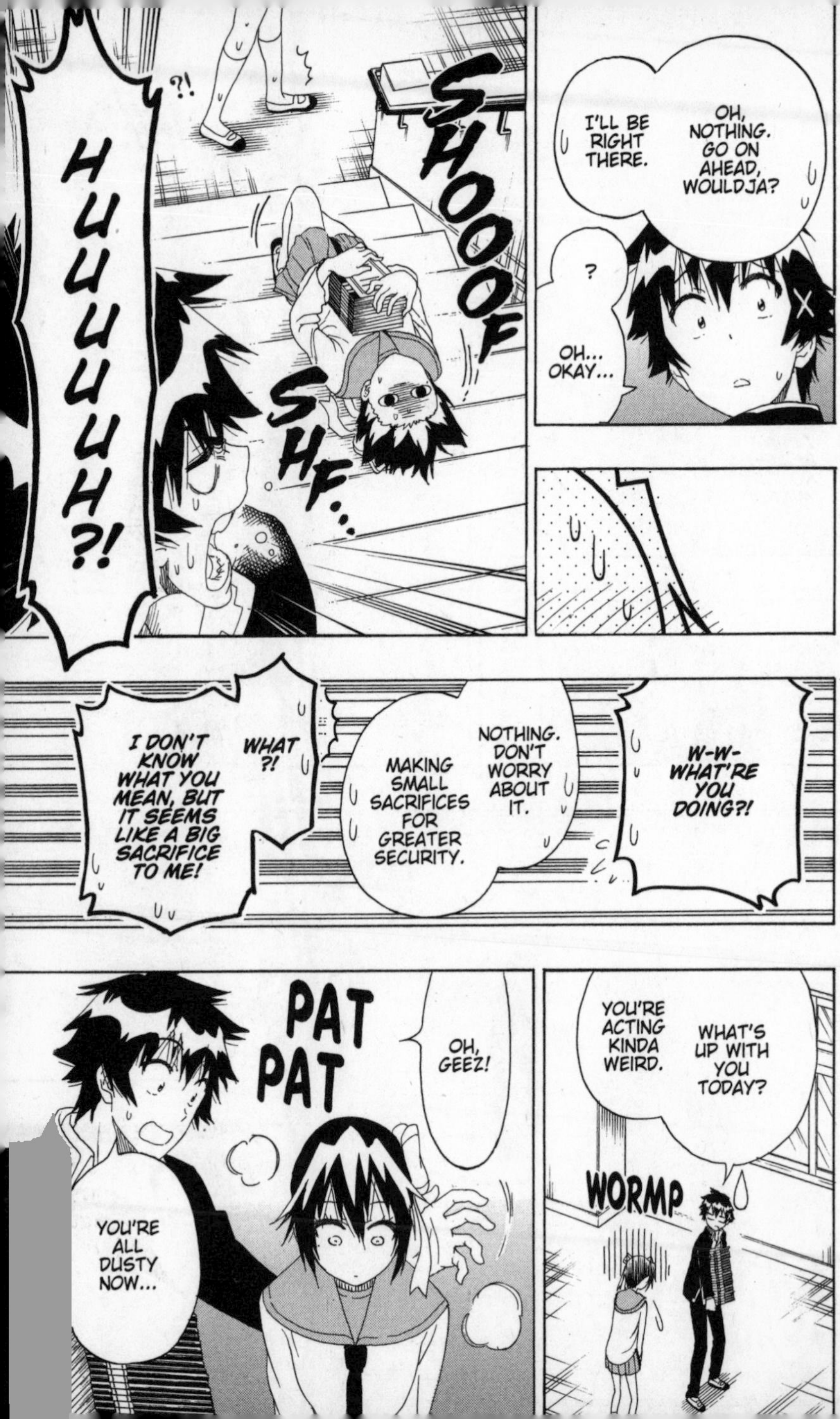
OH, NOTHING. GO ON AHEAD, WOULDJA?
I'LL BE RIGHT THERE.
?
OH... OKAY...
SHOOOF
SHF...
?!
HUUUUUH?!
W-W-WHAT'RE YOU DOING?!
NOTHING. DON'T WORRY ABOUT IT.
MAKING SMALL SACRIFICES FOR GREATER SECURITY.
WHAT?!
I DON'T KNOW WHAT YOU MEAN, BUT IT SEEMS LIKE A BIG SACRIFICE TO ME!
WHAT'S UP WITH YOU TODAY?
YOU'RE ACTING KINDA WEIRD.
WORMP
OH, GEEZ!
PAT PAT
YOU'RE ALL DUSTY NOW...

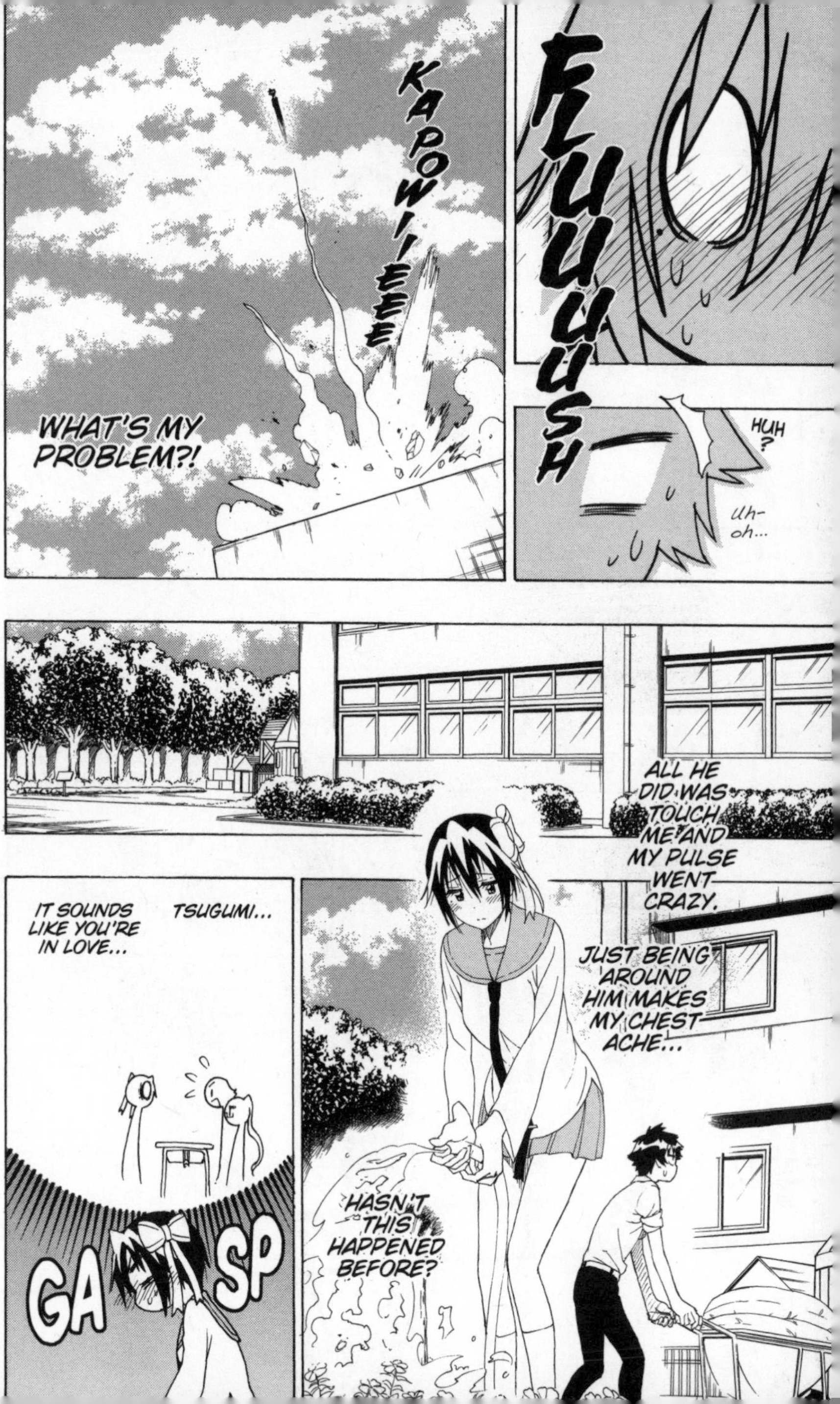
FLUUUUSH
HUH?
Uh-oh...
KAPOWIIEEE
WHAT'S MY PROBLEM?!
ALL HE DID WAS TOUCH ME AND MY PULSE WENT CRAZY.
JUST BEING AROUND HIM MAKES MY CHEST ACHE...
HASN'T THIS HAPPENED BEFORE?
TSUGUMI...
IT SOUNDS LIKE YOU'RE IN LOVE...
GASP

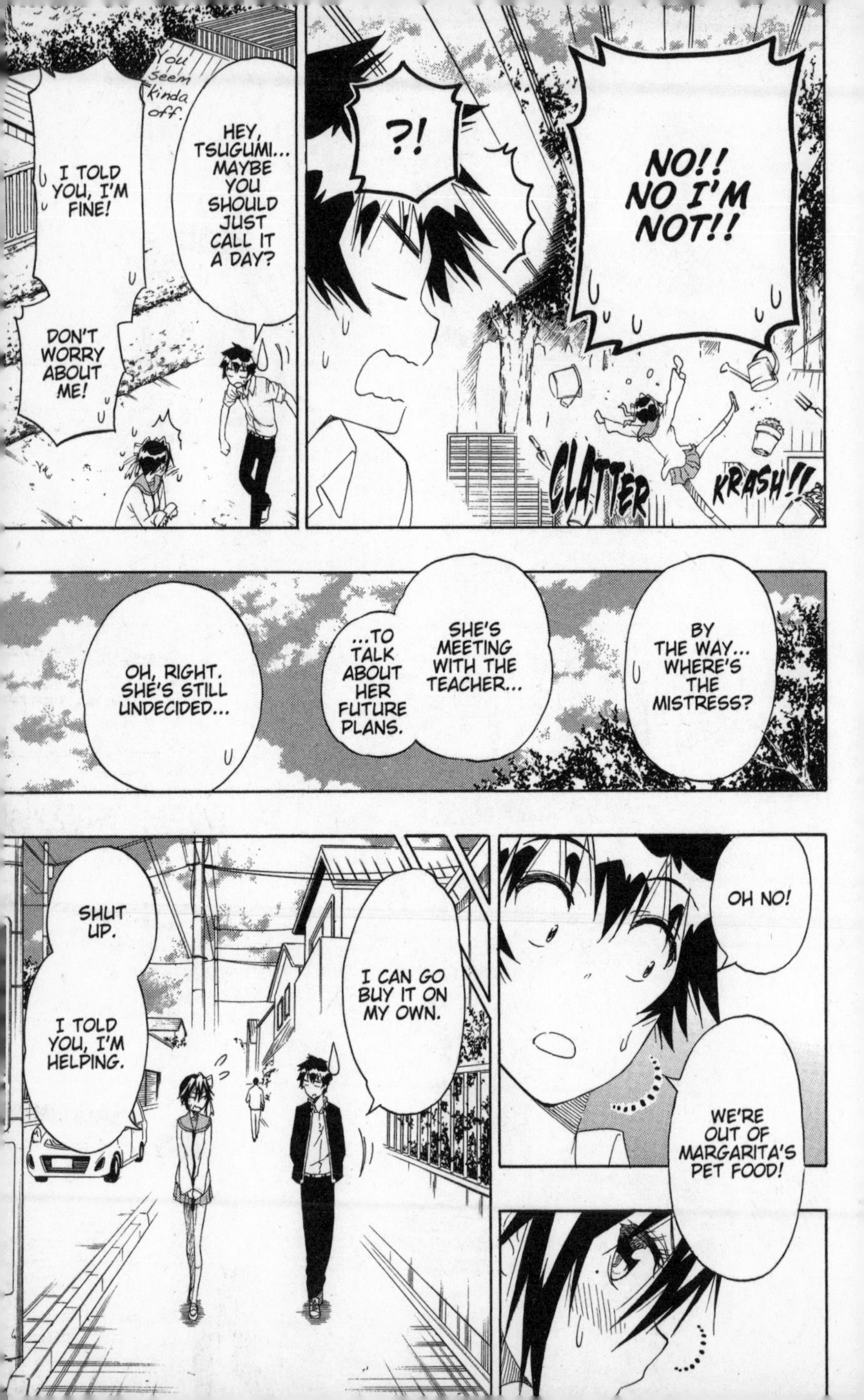
?!
NO!! NO I'M NOT!!
KRASH!!
CLATTER
You seem kinda off.
HEY, TSUGUMI... MAYBE YOU SHOULD JUST CALL IT A DAY?
I TOLD YOU, I'M FINE!
DON'T WORRY ABOUT ME!
BY THE WAY... WHERE'S THE MISTRESS?
SHE'S MEETING WITH THE TEACHER...
...TO TALK ABOUT HER FUTURE PLANS.
OH, RIGHT. SHE'S STILL UNDECIDED...
OH NO!
WE'RE OUT OF MARGARITA'S PET FOOD!
I CAN GO BUY IT ON MY OWN.
SHUT UP.
I TOLD YOU, I'M HELPING.

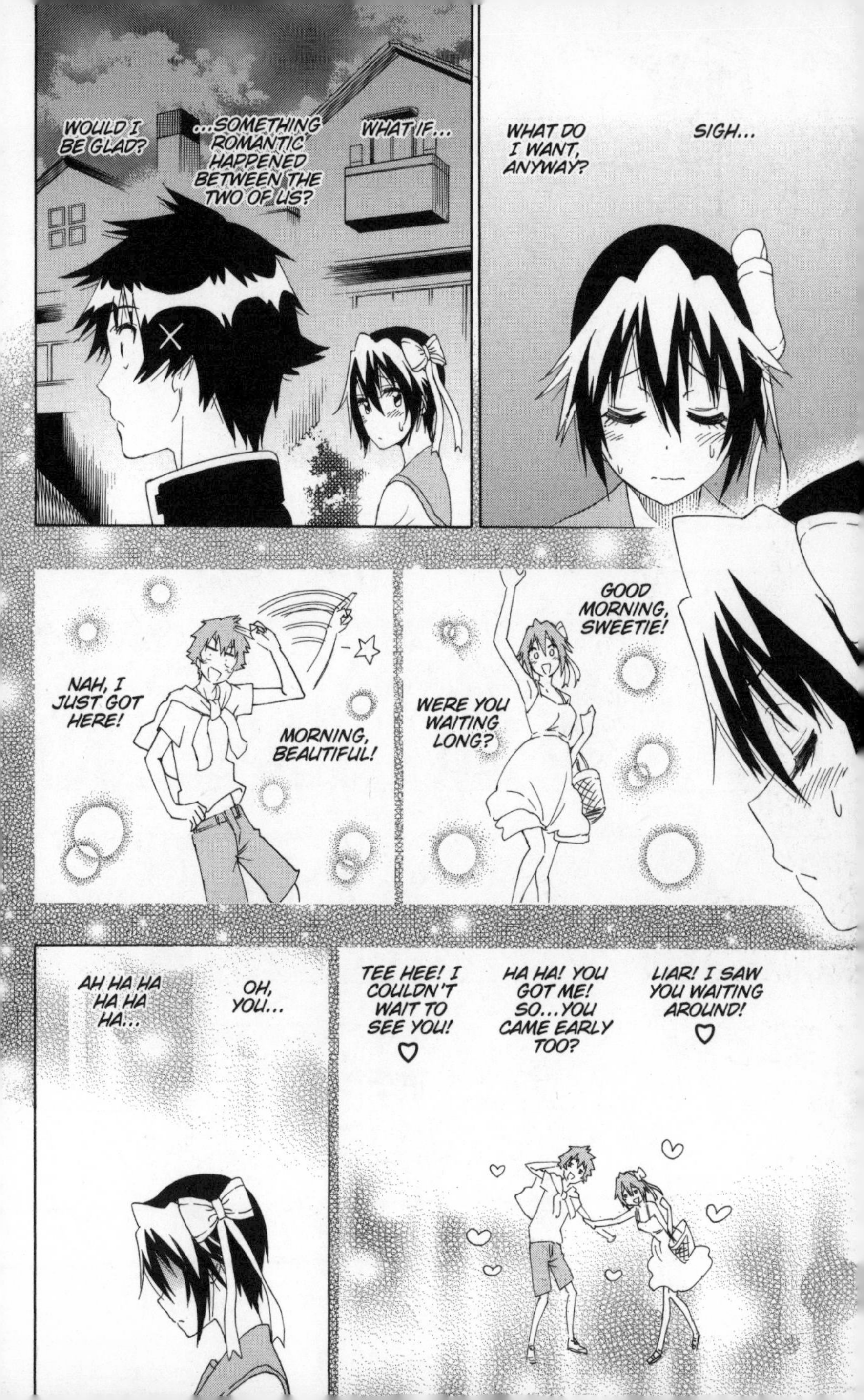
SIGH...
WHAT DO I WANT, ANYWAY?
WHAT IF...
...SOMETHING ROMANTIC HAPPENED BETWEEN THE TWO OF US?
WOULD I BE GLAD?
GOOD MORNING, SWEETIE!
WERE YOU WAITING LONG?
MORNING, BEAUTIFUL!
NAH, I JUST GOT HERE!
LIAR! I SAW YOU WAITING AROUND! ♡
HA HA! YOU GOT ME! SO...YOU CAME EARLY TOO?
TEE HEE! I COULDN'T WAIT TO SEE YOU! ♡
OH, YOU...
AH HA HA HA HA HA...

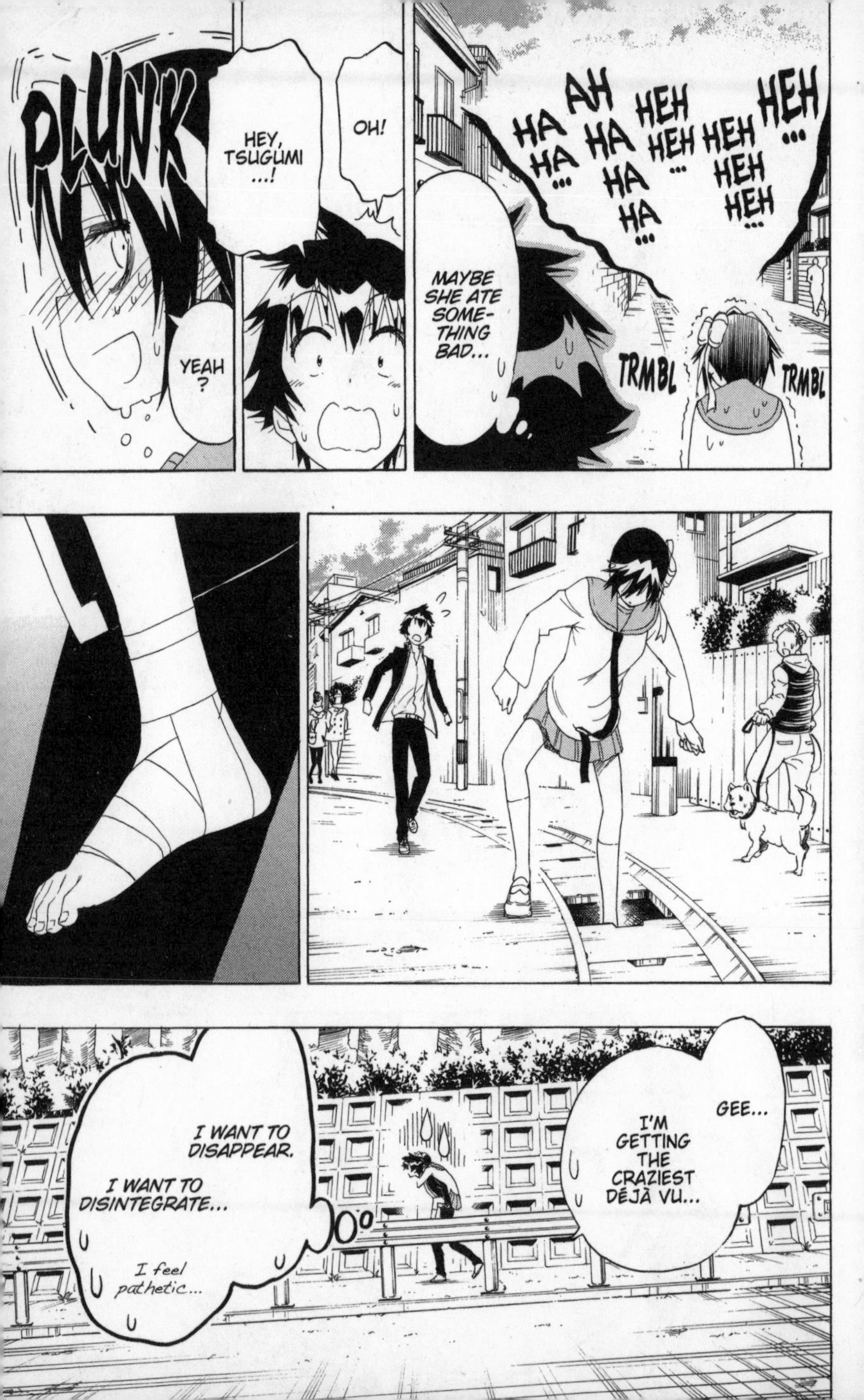

HA HA HA...
AH HA HA HA HA...
HEH HEH HEH...
HEH HEH HEH HEH...
HEH...
TRMBL
TRMBL
MAYBE SHE ATE SOMETHING BAD...
OH!
HEY, TSUGUMI...!
PLUNK
YEAH?
GEE...
I'M GETTING THE CRAZIEST DÉJÀ VU...
I WANT TO DISAPPEAR.
I WANT TO DISINTEGRATE...
I feel pathetic...

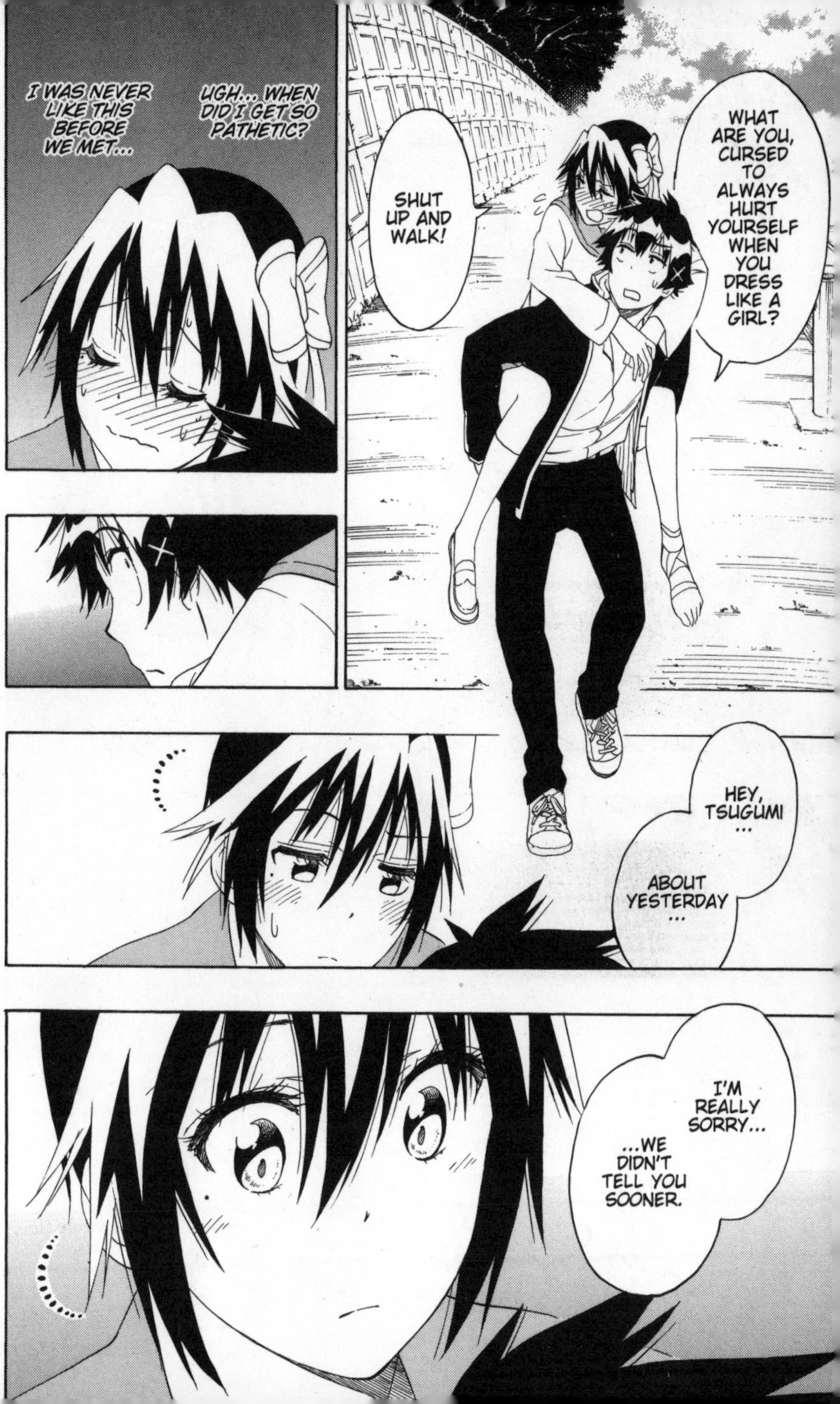
WHAT ARE YOU, CURSED TO ALWAYS HURT YOURSELF WHEN YOU DRESS LIKE A GIRL?
SHUT UP AND WALK!
UGH... WHEN DID I GET SO PATHETIC?
I WAS NEVER LIKE THIS BEFORE WE MET...
HEY, TSUGUMI...
ABOUT YESTERDAY...
I'M REALLY SORRY...
...WE DIDN'T TELL YOU SOONER.

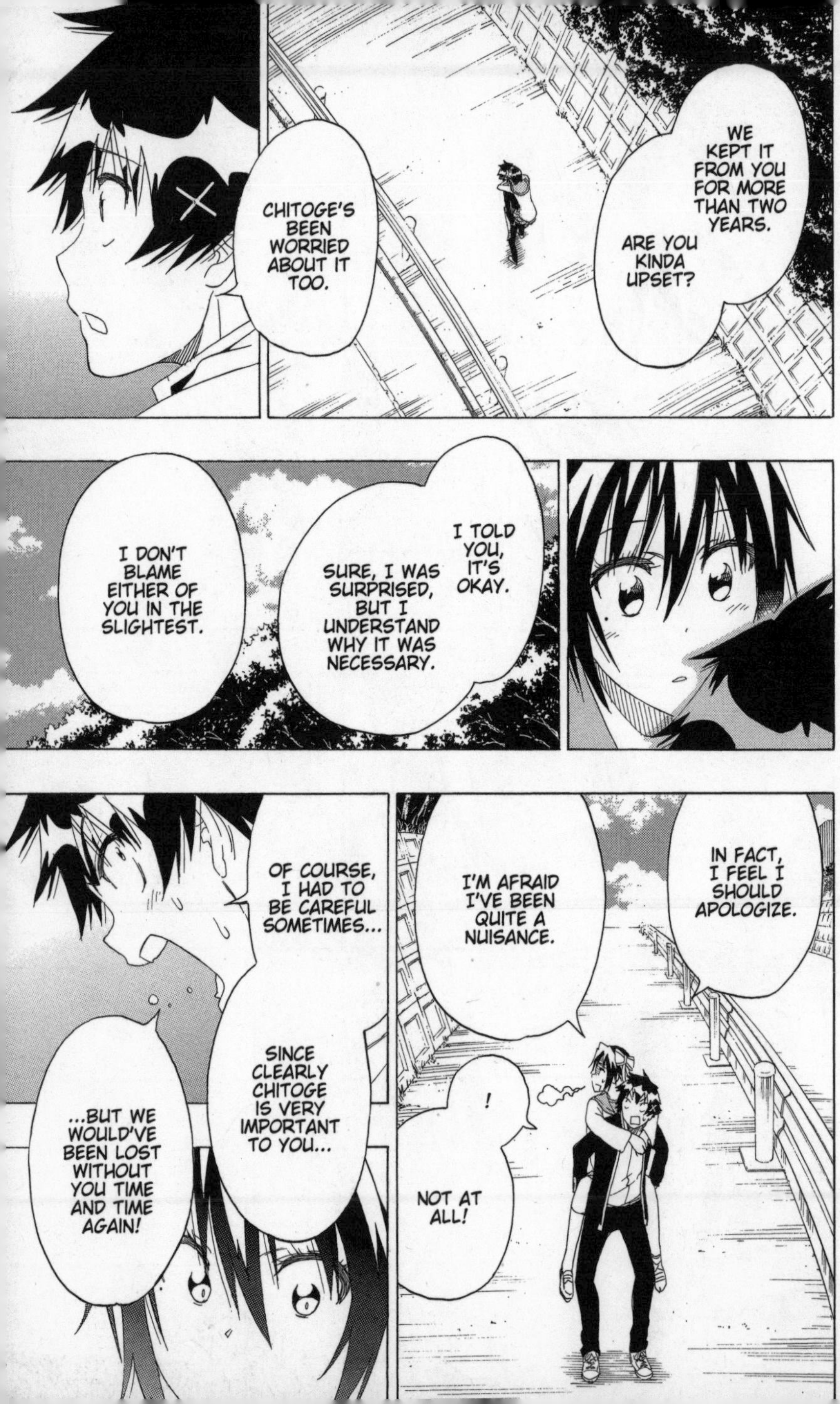
WE KEPT IT FROM YOU FOR MORE THAN TWO YEARS.
ARE YOU KINDA UPSET?
CHITOGE'S BEEN WORRIED ABOUT IT TOO.
I TOLD YOU, IT'S OKAY.
SURE, I WAS SURPRISED, BUT I UNDERSTAND WHY IT WAS NECESSARY.
I DON'T BLAME EITHER OF YOU IN THE SLIGHTEST.
IN FACT, I FEEL I SHOULD APOLOGIZE.
I'M AFRAID I'VE BEEN QUITE A NUISANCE.
!
NOT AT ALL!
OF COURSE, I HAD TO BE CAREFUL SOMETIMES...
SINCE CLEARLY CHITOGE IS VERY IMPORTANT TO YOU...
...BUT WE WOULD'VE BEEN LOST WITHOUT YOU TIME AND TIME AGAIN!

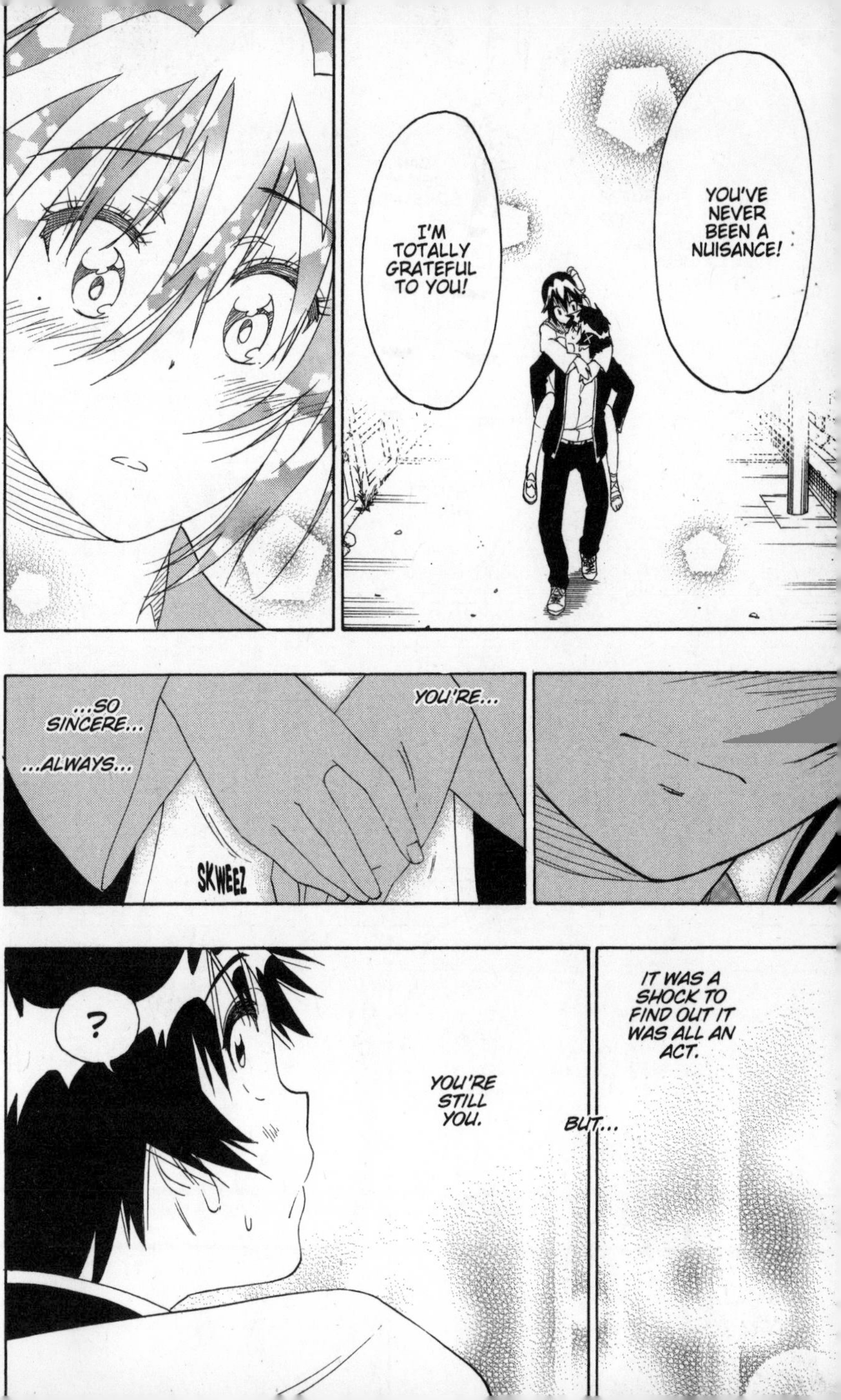

YOU'VE NEVER BEEN A NUISANCE!
I'M TOTALLY GRATEFUL TO YOU!
YOU'RE...
...SO SINCERE...
...ALWAYS...
SKWEEZ
IT WAS A SHOCK TO FIND OUT IT WAS ALL AN ACT.
BUT...
YOU'RE STILL YOU.
?

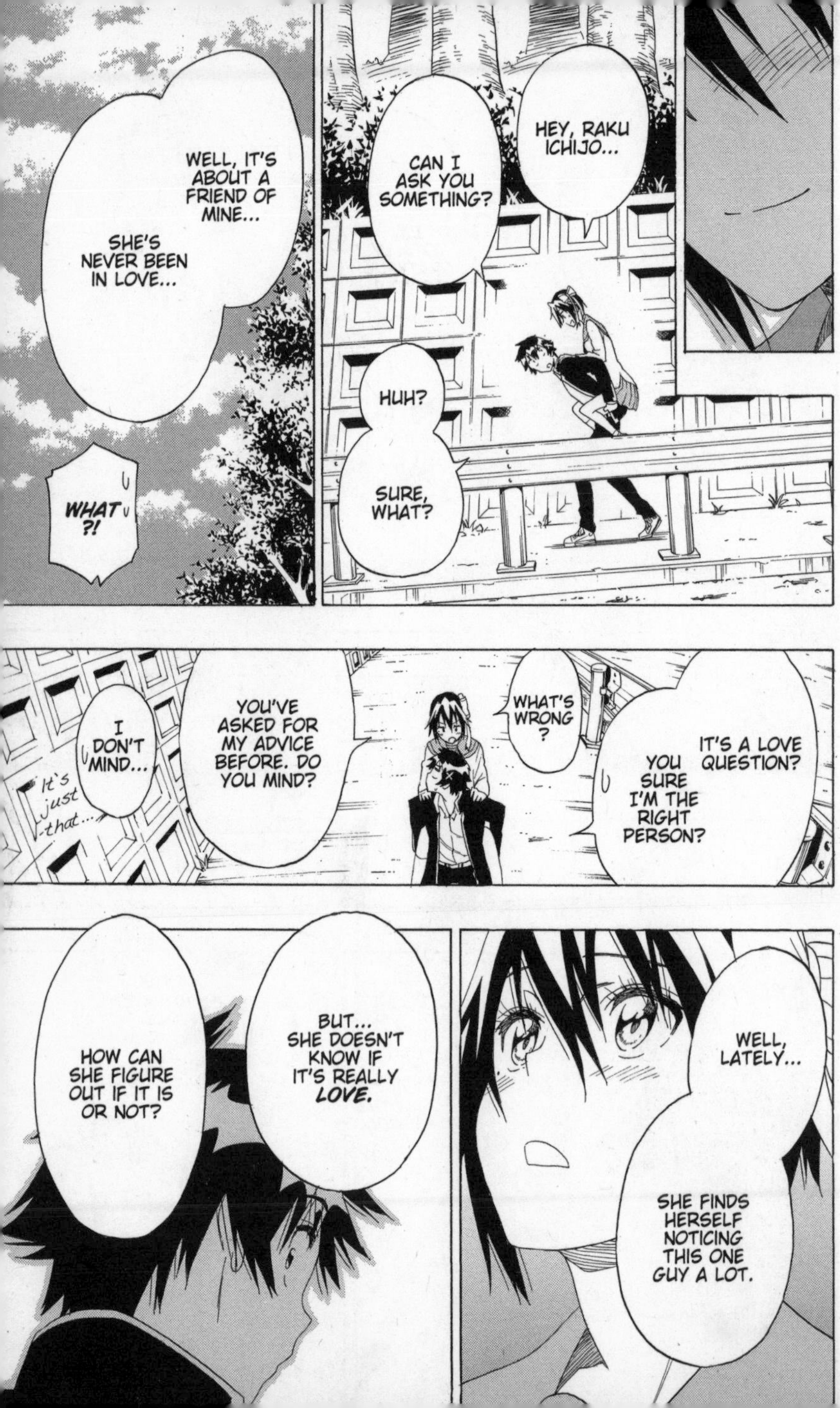
HEY, RAKU ICHIJO...
CAN I ASK YOU SOMETHING?
HUH? SURE, WHAT?
WELL, IT'S ABOUT A FRIEND OF MINE... SHE'S NEVER BEEN IN LOVE...
WHAT?!
IT'S A LOVE QUESTION? YOU SURE I'M THE RIGHT PERSON?
WHAT'S WRONG?
YOU'VE ASKED FOR MY ADVICE BEFORE. DO YOU MIND?
I DON'T MIND...
It's just that...
WELL, LATELY... SHE FINDS HERSELF NOTICING THIS ONE GUY A LOT.
BUT... SHE DOESN'T KNOW IF IT'S REALLY LOVE.
HOW CAN SHE FIGURE OUT IF IT IS OR NOT?

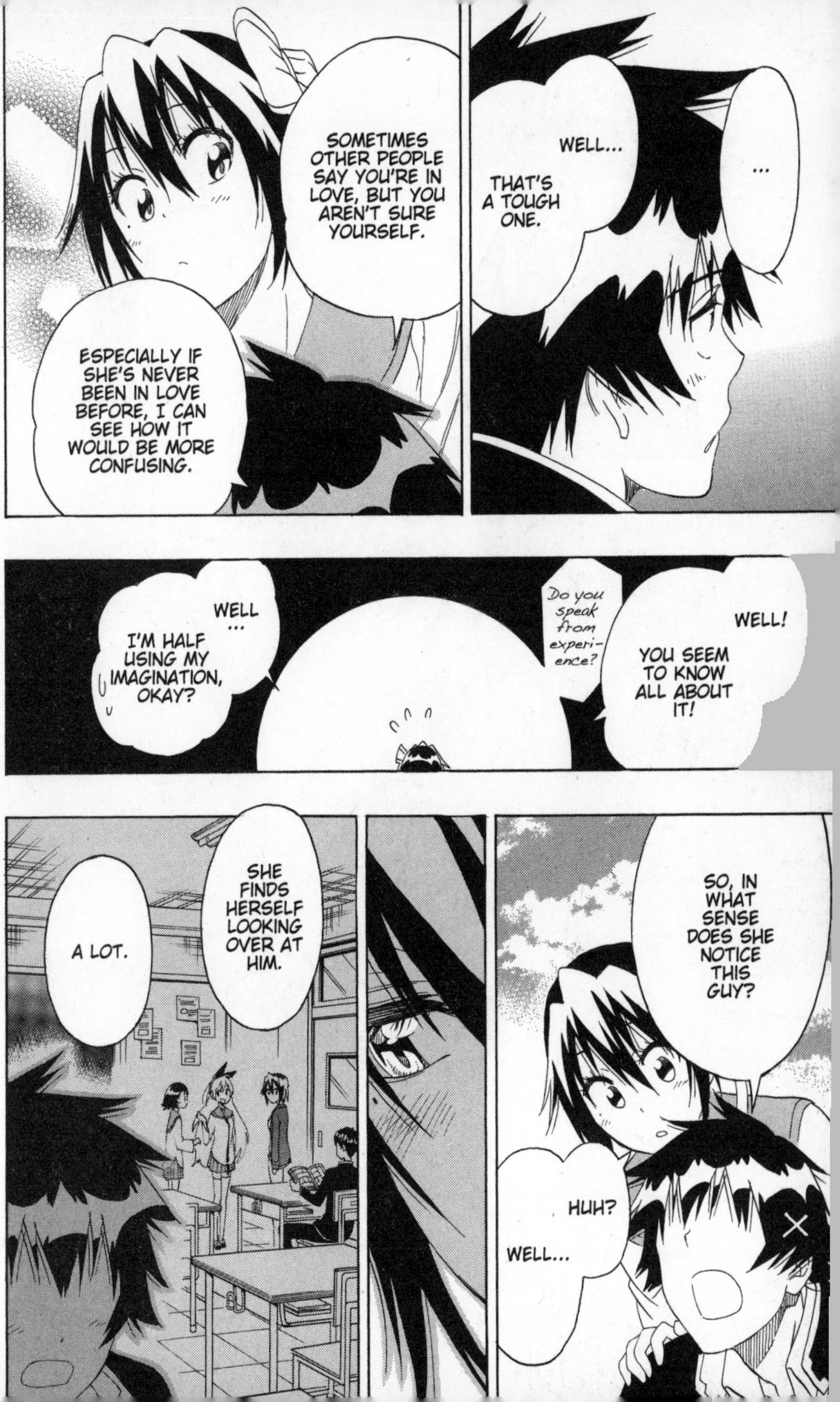
...
WELL... THAT'S A TOUGH ONE.
SOMETIMES OTHER PEOPLE SAY YOU'RE IN LOVE, BUT YOU AREN'T SURE YOURSELF.
ESPECIALLY IF SHE'S NEVER BEEN IN LOVE BEFORE, I CAN SEE HOW IT WOULD BE MORE CONFUSING.
WELL! YOU SEEM TO KNOW ALL ABOUT IT!
Do you speak from experi-ence?
WELL ... I'M HALF USING MY IMAGINATION, OKAY?
SO, IN WHAT SENSE DOES SHE NOTICE THIS GUY?
HUH? WELL...
SHE FINDS HERSELF LOOKING OVER AT HIM.
A LOT.

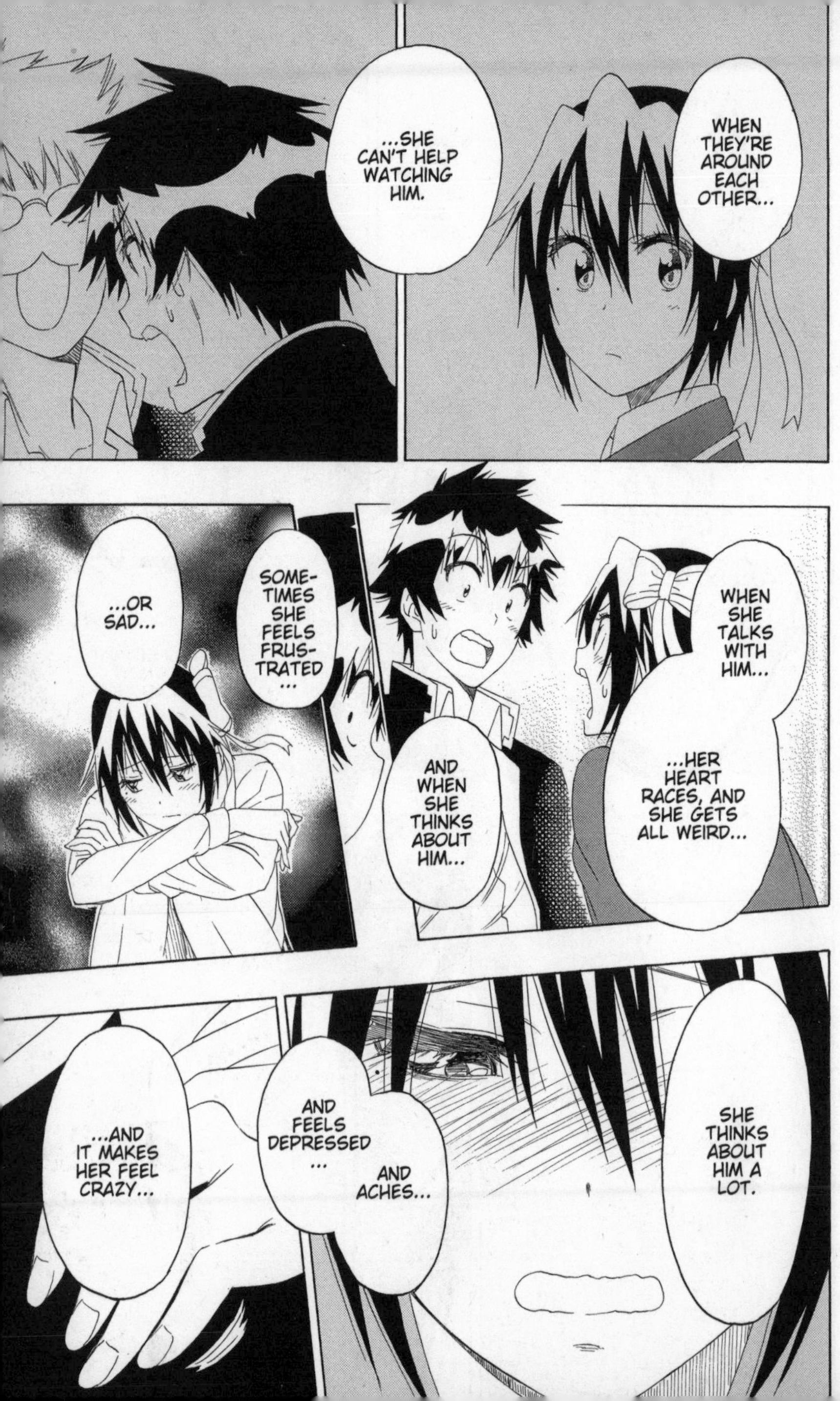
WHEN THEY'RE AROUND EACH OTHER...
...SHE CAN'T HELP WATCHING HIM.
WHEN SHE TALKS WITH HIM...
...HER HEART RACES, AND SHE GETS ALL WEIRD...
AND WHEN SHE THINKS ABOUT HIM...
SOME-TIMES SHE FEELS FRUS-TRATED...
...OR SAD...
SHE THINKS ABOUT HIM A LOT.
AND FEELS DEPRESSED... AND ACHES...
...AND IT MAKES HER FEEL CRAZY...

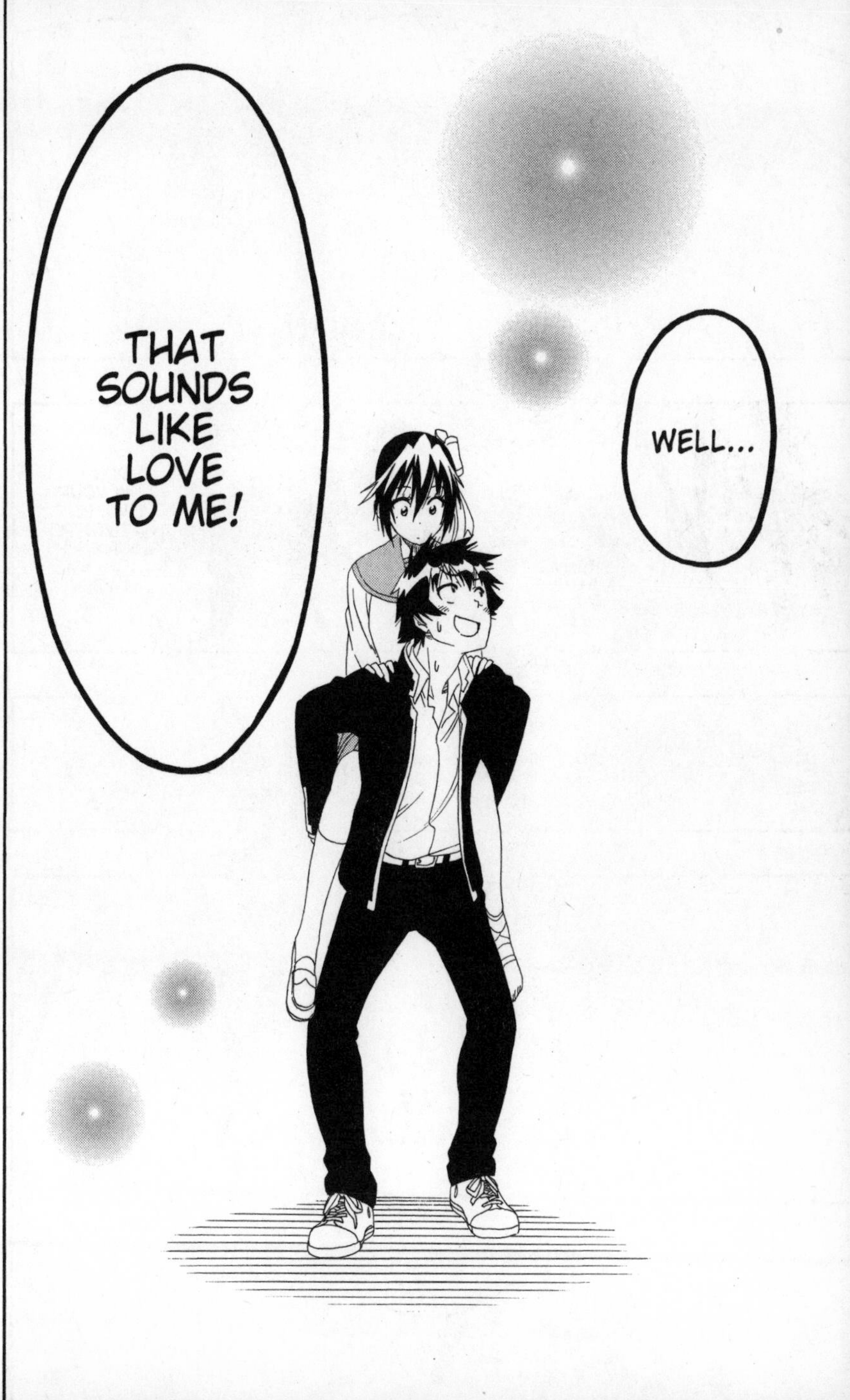
WELL...
THAT SOUNDS LIKE LOVE TO ME!

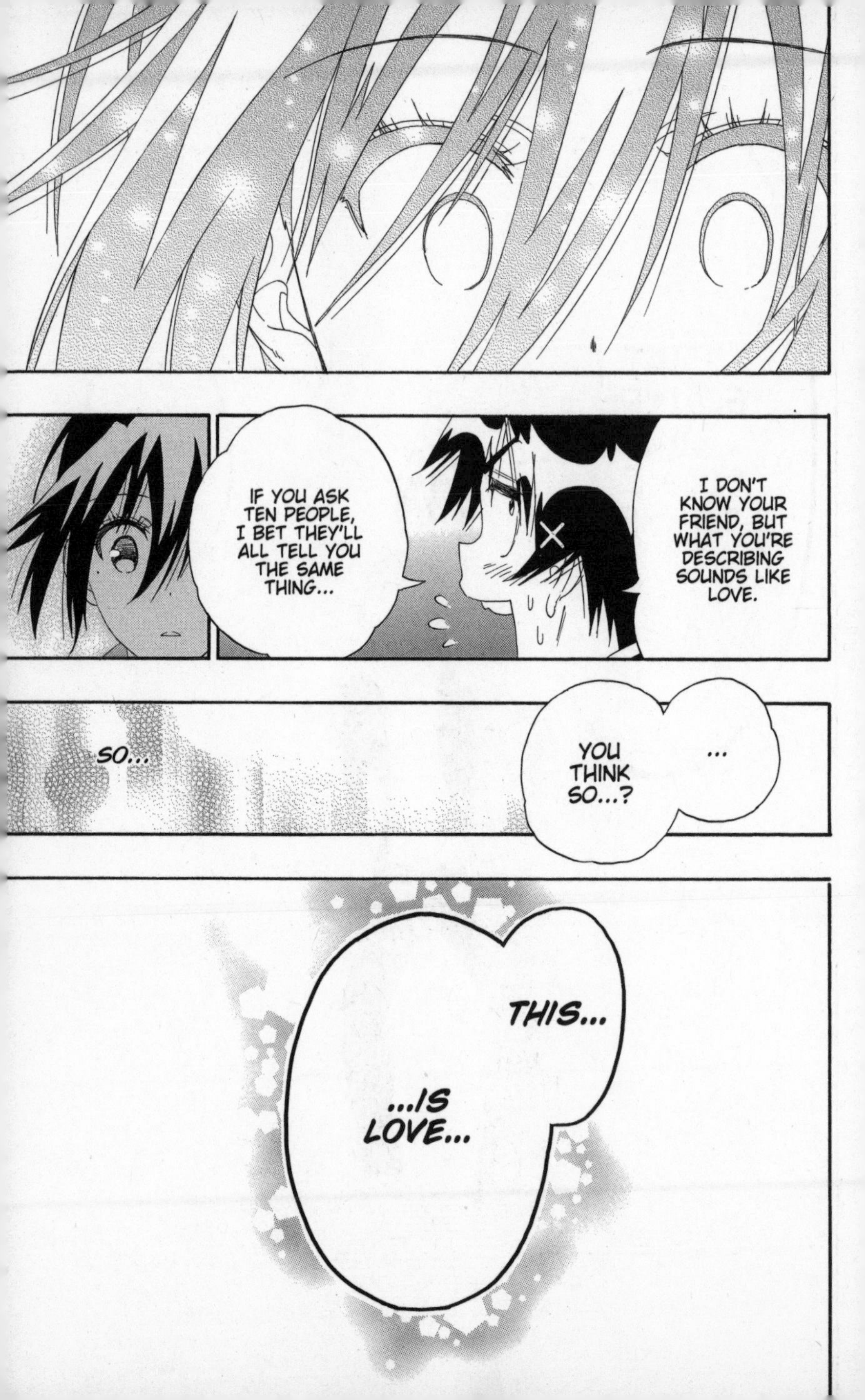
I DON'T KNOW YOUR FRIEND, BUT WHAT YOU'RE DESCRIBING SOUNDS LIKE LOVE.
IF YOU ASK TEN PEOPLE, I BET THEY'LL ALL TELL YOU THE SAME THING...
...
YOU THINK SO...?
SO...
THIS...
...IS LOVE...

Chapter 206: One Day

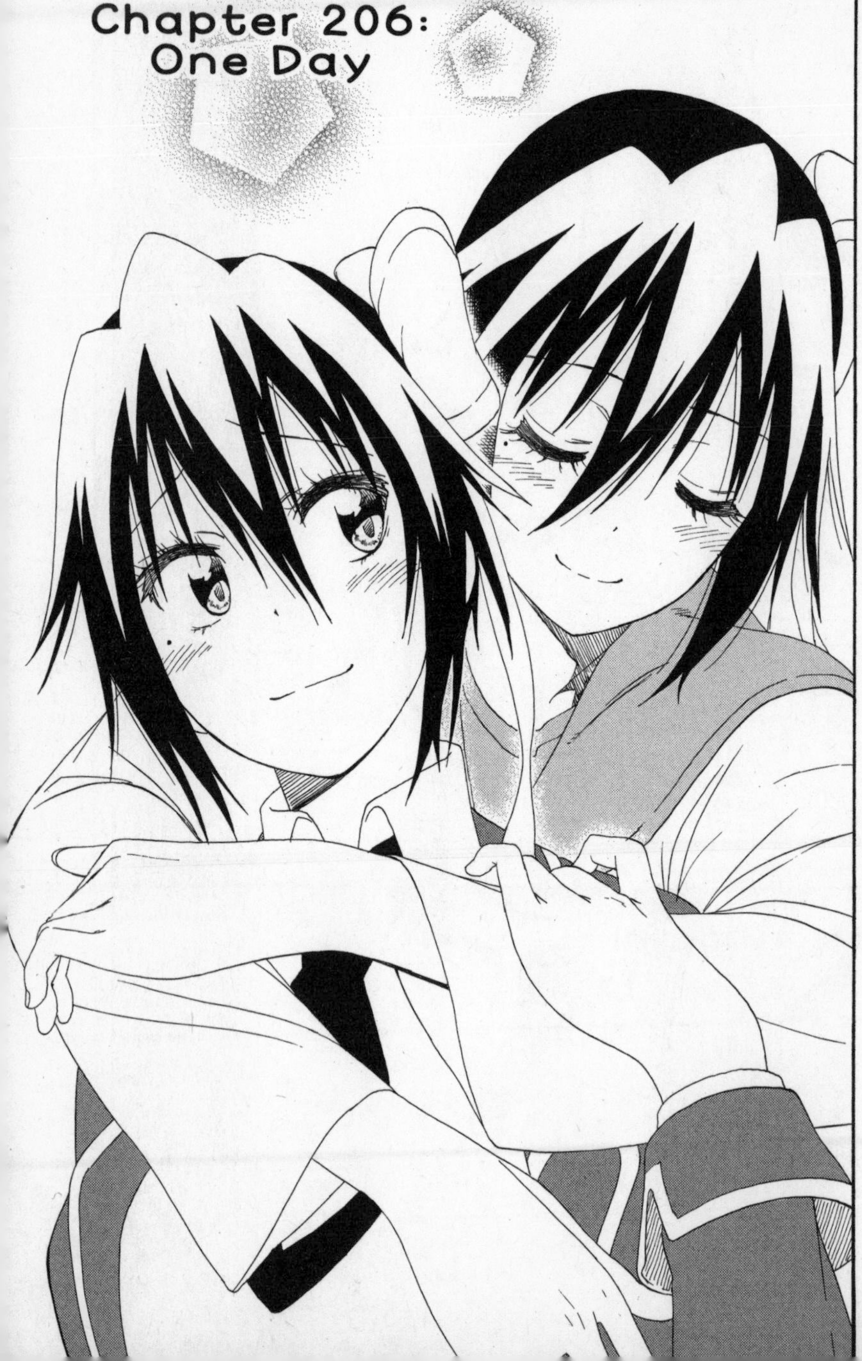

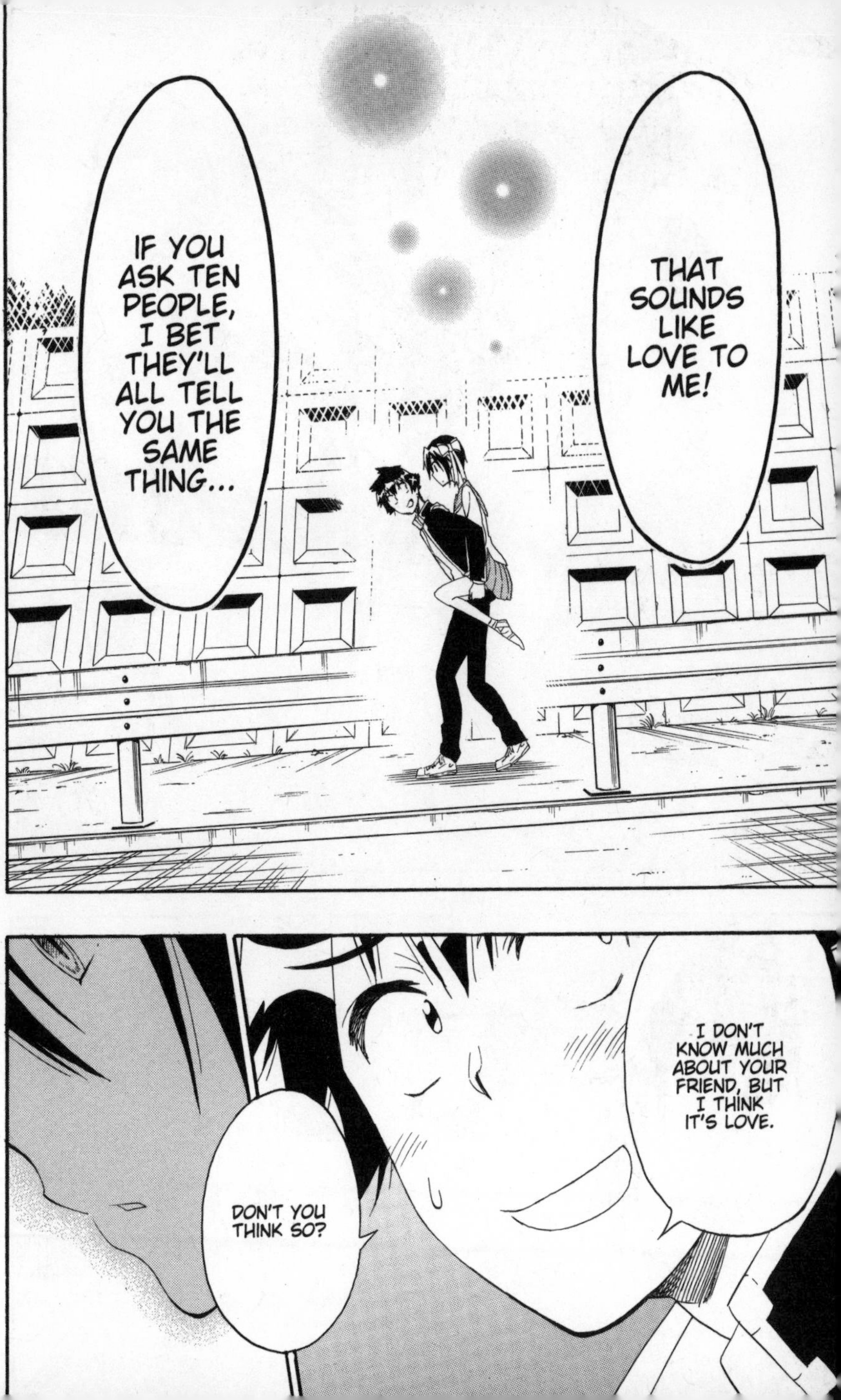
THAT SOUNDS LIKE LOVE TO ME!
IF YOU ASK TEN PEOPLE, I BET THEY'LL ALL TELL YOU THE SAME THING...
I DON'T KNOW MUCH ABOUT YOUR FRIEND, BUT I THINK IT'S LOVE.
DON'T YOU THINK SO?

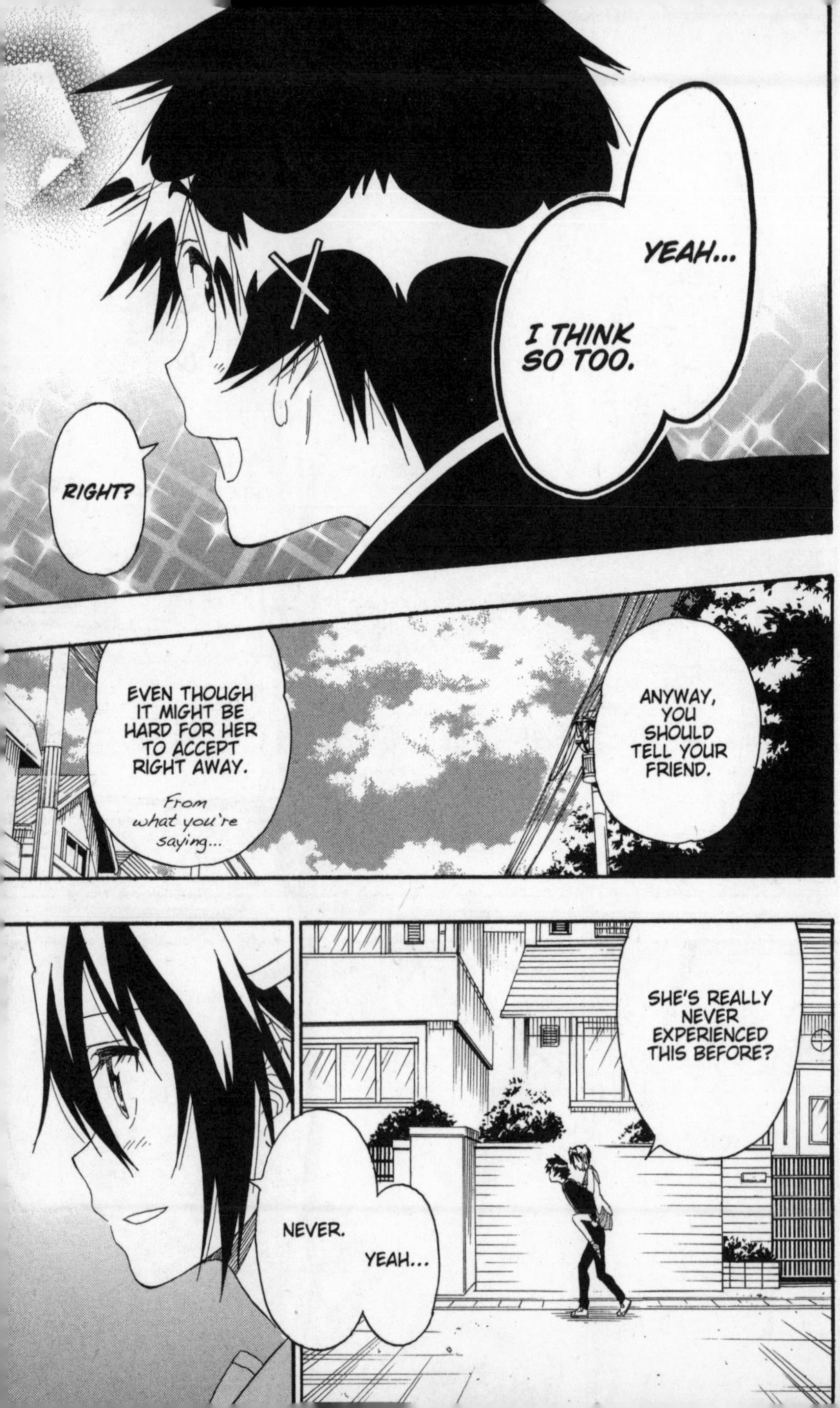
YEAH... I THINK SO TOO.
RIGHT?
ANYWAY, YOU SHOULD TELL YOUR FRIEND.
EVEN THOUGH IT MIGHT BE HARD FOR HER TO ACCEPT RIGHT AWAY.
From what you're saying...
SHE'S REALLY NEVER EXPERIENCED THIS BEFORE?
NEVER.
YEAH...

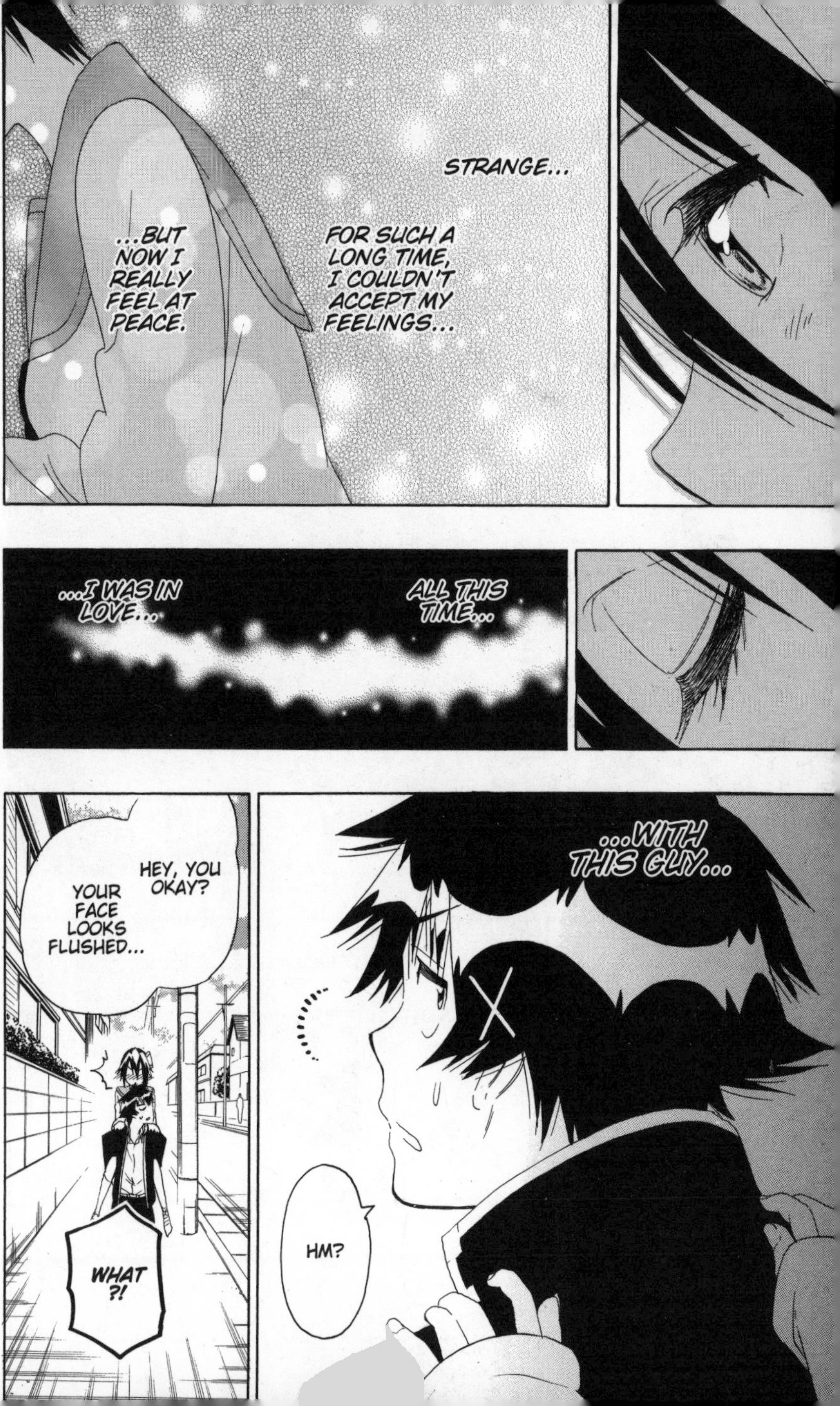
STRANGE...
FOR SUCH A LONG TIME, I COULDN'T ACCEPT MY FEELINGS...
...BUT NOW I REALLY FEEL AT PEACE.
ALL THIS TIME...
...I WAS IN LOVE...
...WITH THIS GUY...
HM?
HEY, YOU OKAY?
YOUR FACE LOOKS FLUSHED...
WHAT ?!

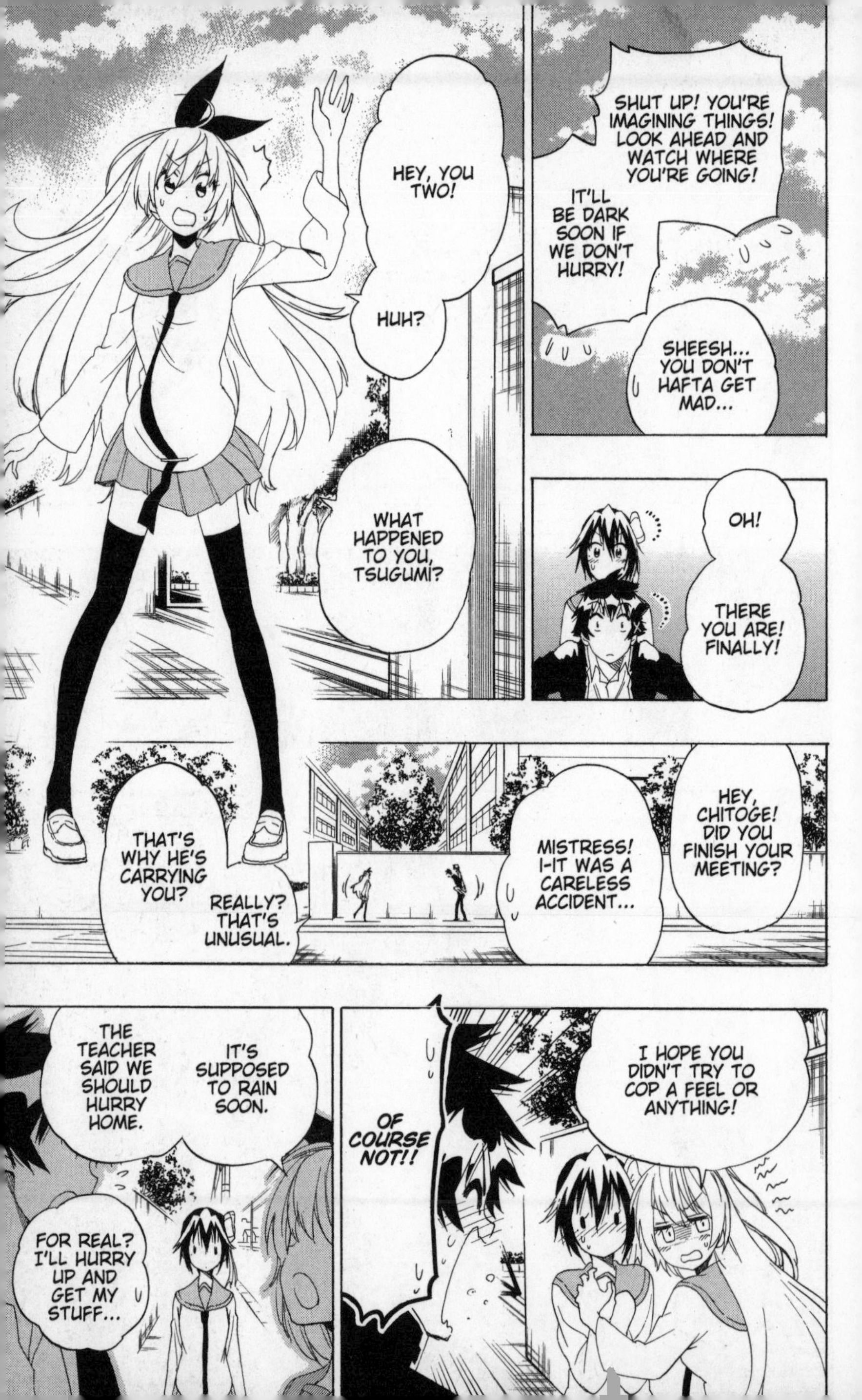
SHUT UP! YOU'RE IMAGINING THINGS! LOOK AHEAD AND WATCH WHERE YOU'RE GOING!
IT'LL BE DARK SOON IF WE DON'T HURRY!
SHEESH... YOU DON'T HAFTA GET MAD...
OH!
THERE YOU ARE! FINALLY!
HEY, YOU TWO!
HUH?
WHAT HAPPENED TO YOU, TSUGUMI?
HEY, CHITOGE! DID YOU FINISH YOUR MEETING?
MISTRESS! I-IT WAS A CARELESS ACCIDENT...
REALLY? THAT'S UNUSUAL.
THAT'S WHY HE'S CARRYING YOU?
I HOPE YOU DIDN'T TRY TO COP A FEEL OR ANYTHING!
OF COURSE NOT!!
IT'S SUPPOSED TO RAIN SOON.
THE TEACHER SAID WE SHOULD HURRY HOME.
FOR REAL? I'LL HURRY UP AND GET MY STUFF...

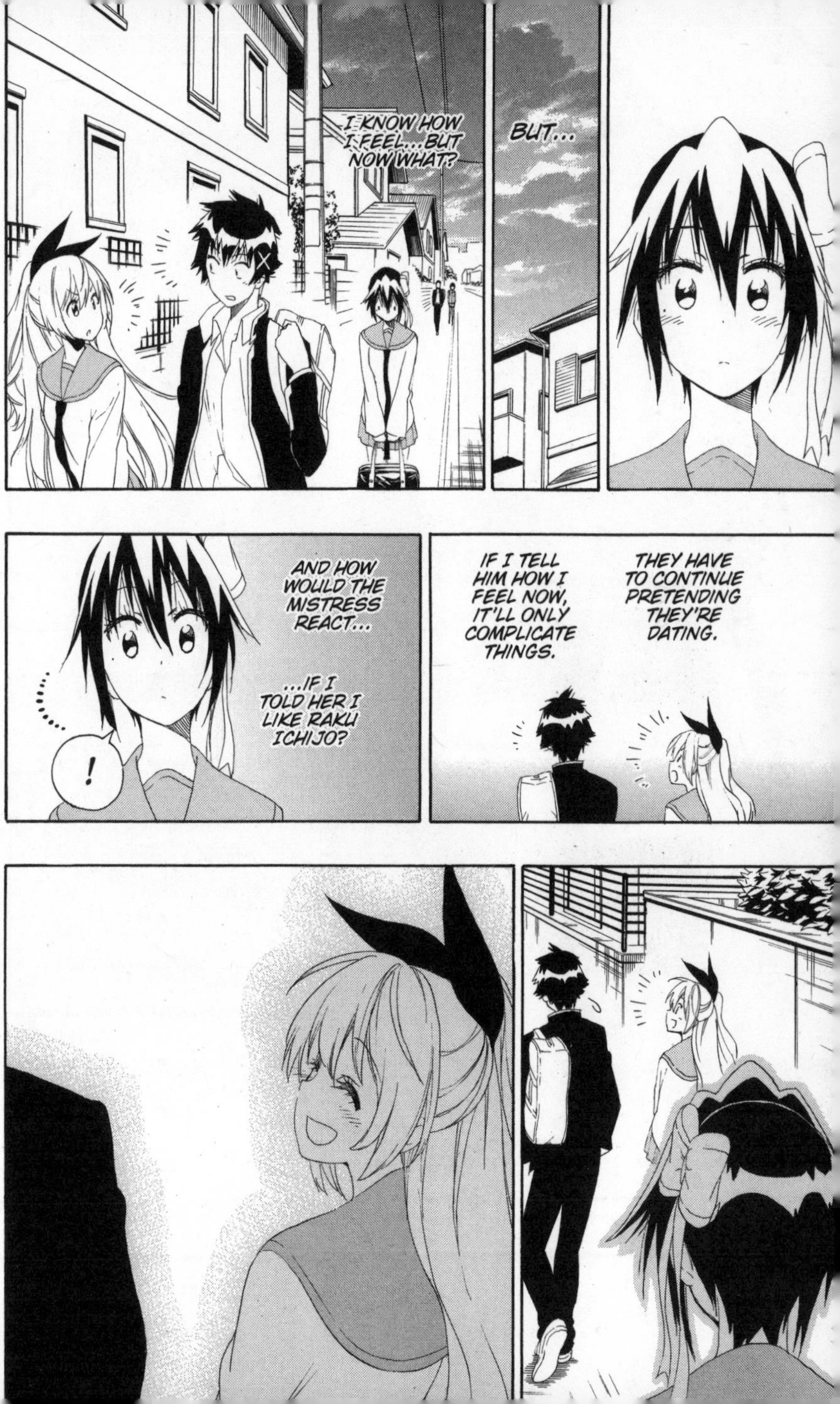
BUT...
I KNOW HOW I FEEL... BUT NOW WHAT?
THEY HAVE TO CONTINUE PRETENDING THEY'RE DATING.
IF I TELL HIM HOW I FEEL NOW, IT'LL ONLY COMPLICATE THINGS.
AND HOW WOULD THE MISTRESS REACT...
...IF I TOLD HER I LIKE RAKU ICHIJO?
......
!

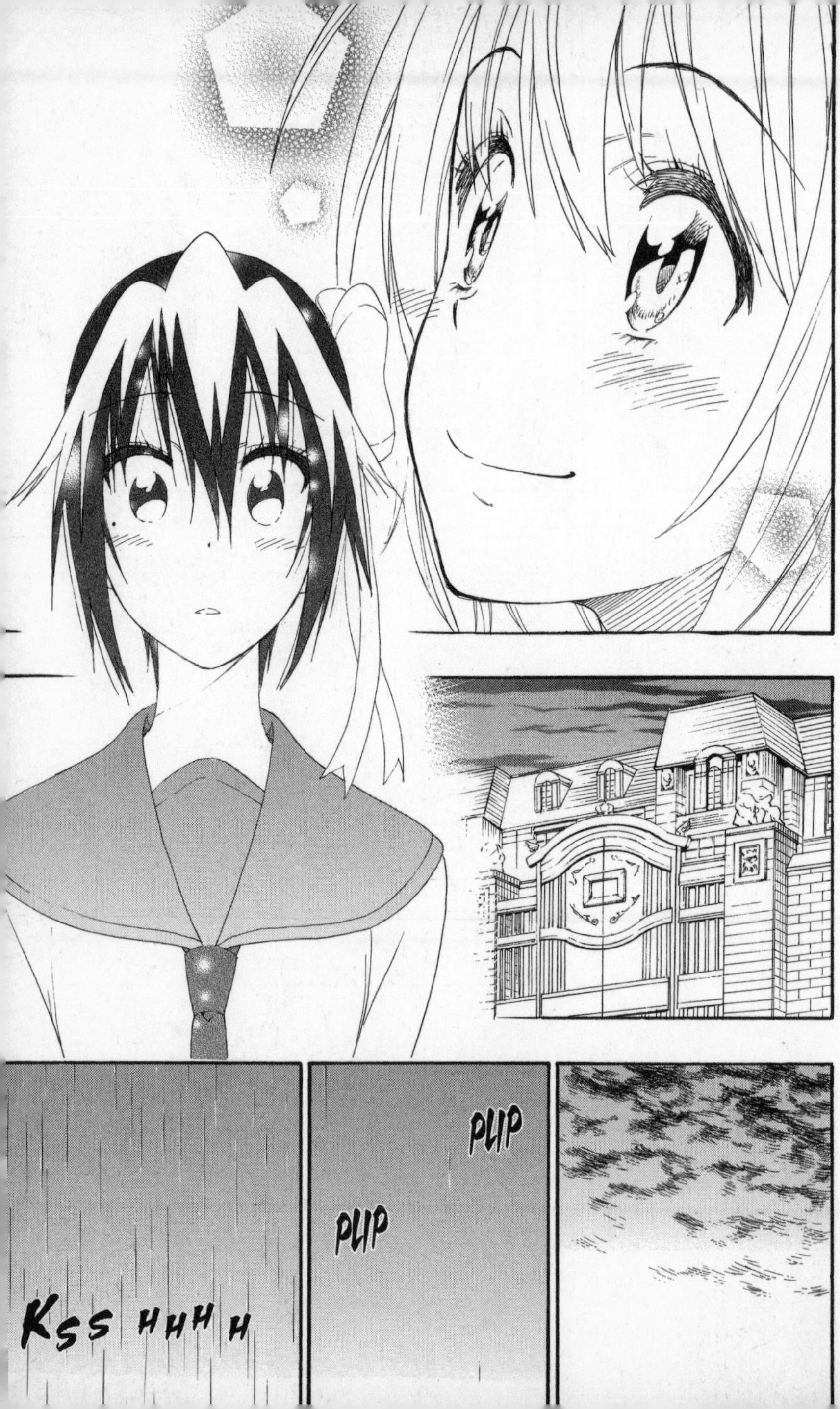
PLIP
PLIP
KSS HHHH

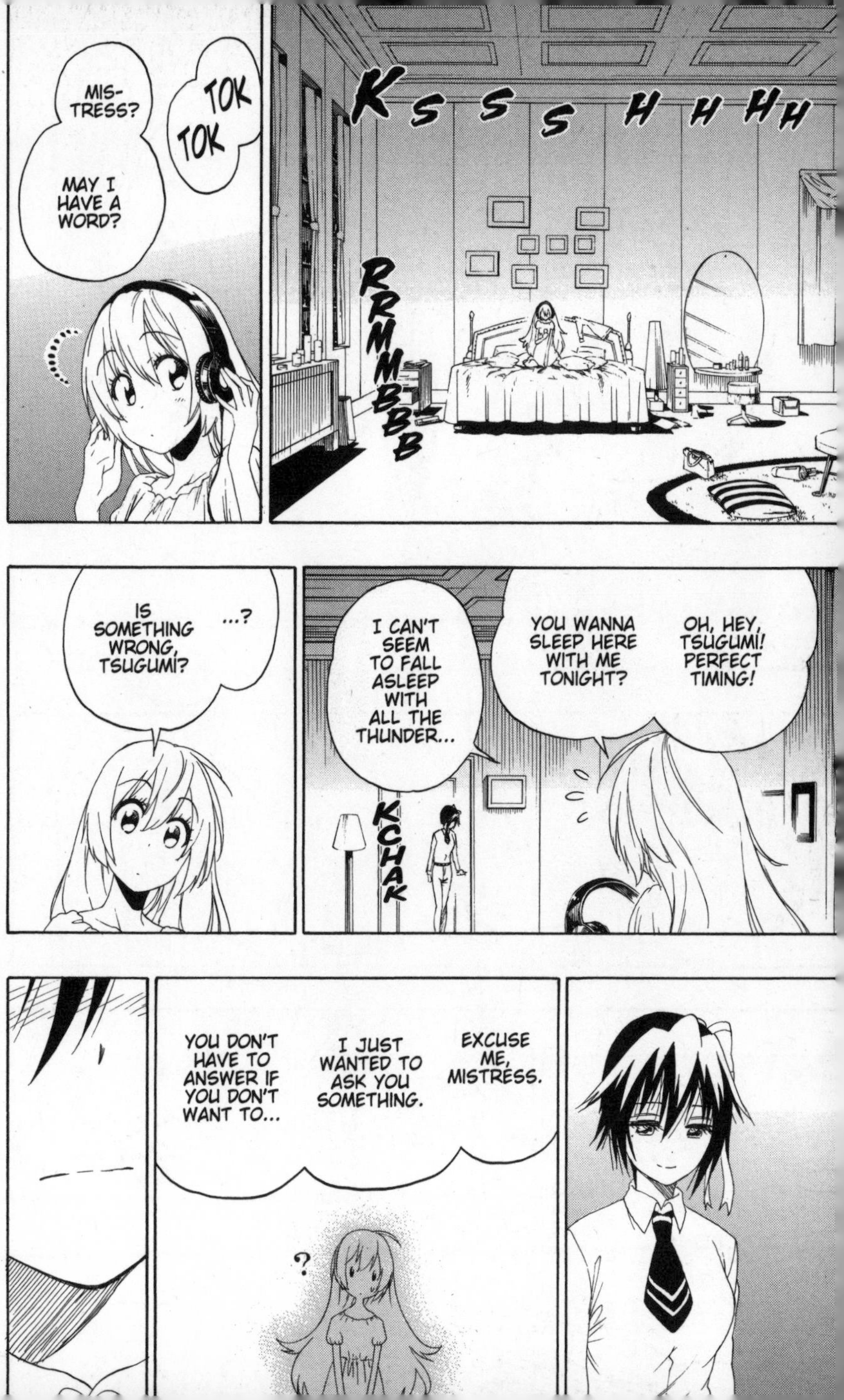
KSSSHHHH
RRMMBBB
TOK TOK
MIS-TRESS?
MAY I HAVE A WORD?
OH, HEY, TSUGUMI! PERFECT TIMING!
YOU WANNA SLEEP HERE WITH ME TONIGHT?
I CAN'T SEEM TO FALL ASLEEP WITH ALL THE THUNDER...
KCHAK
...?
IS SOMETHING WRONG, TSUGUMI?
EXCUSE ME, MISTRESS.
I JUST WANTED TO ASK YOU SOMETHING.
YOU DON'T HAVE TO ANSWER IF YOU DON'T WANT TO...
?

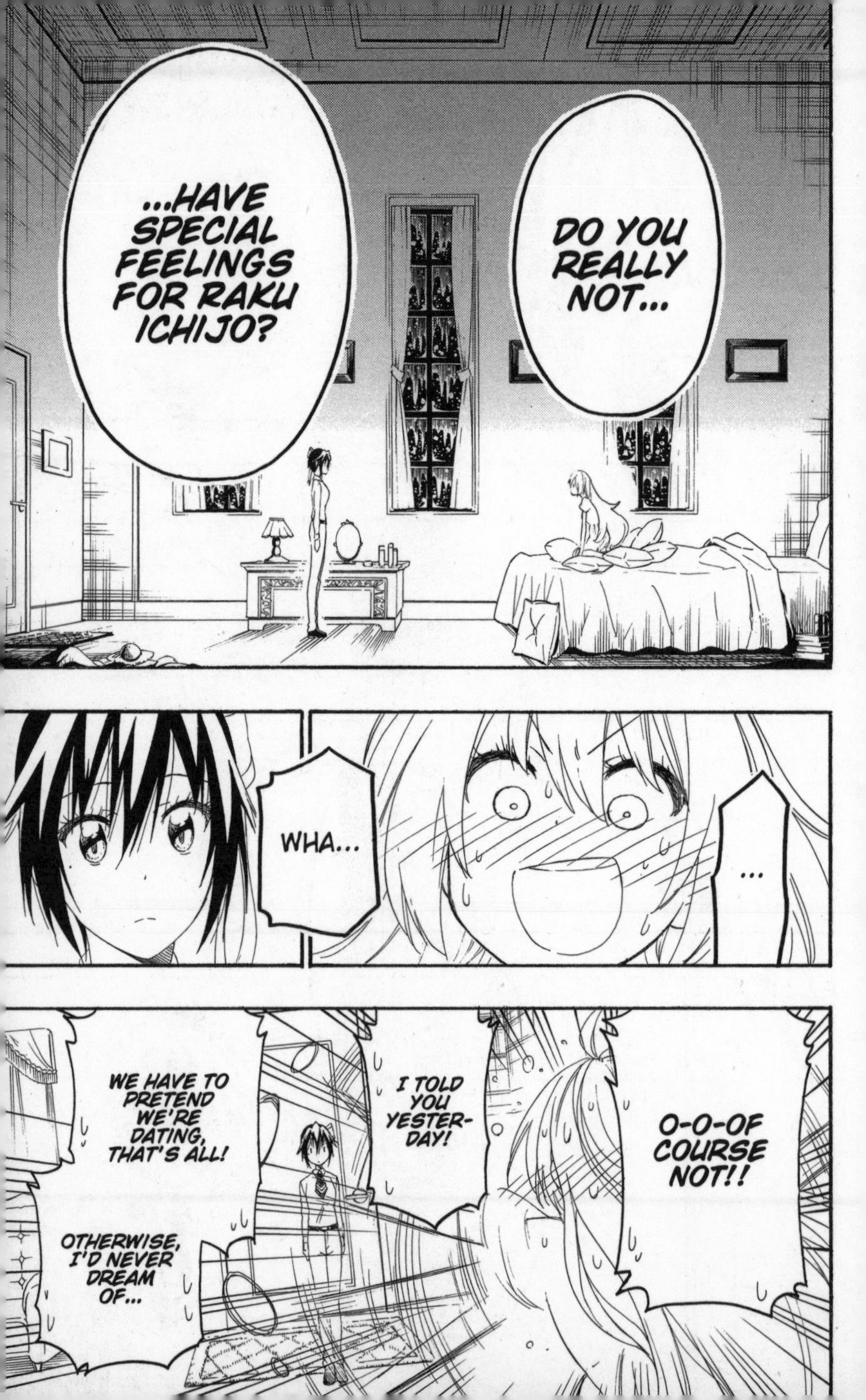
DO YOU REALLY NOT...
...HAVE SPECIAL FEELINGS FOR RAKU ICHIJO?
...
WHA...
O-O-OF COURSE NOT!!
I TOLD YOU YESTER-DAY!
WE HAVE TO PRETEND WE'RE DATING, THAT'S ALL!
OTHERWISE, I'D NEVER DREAM OF...

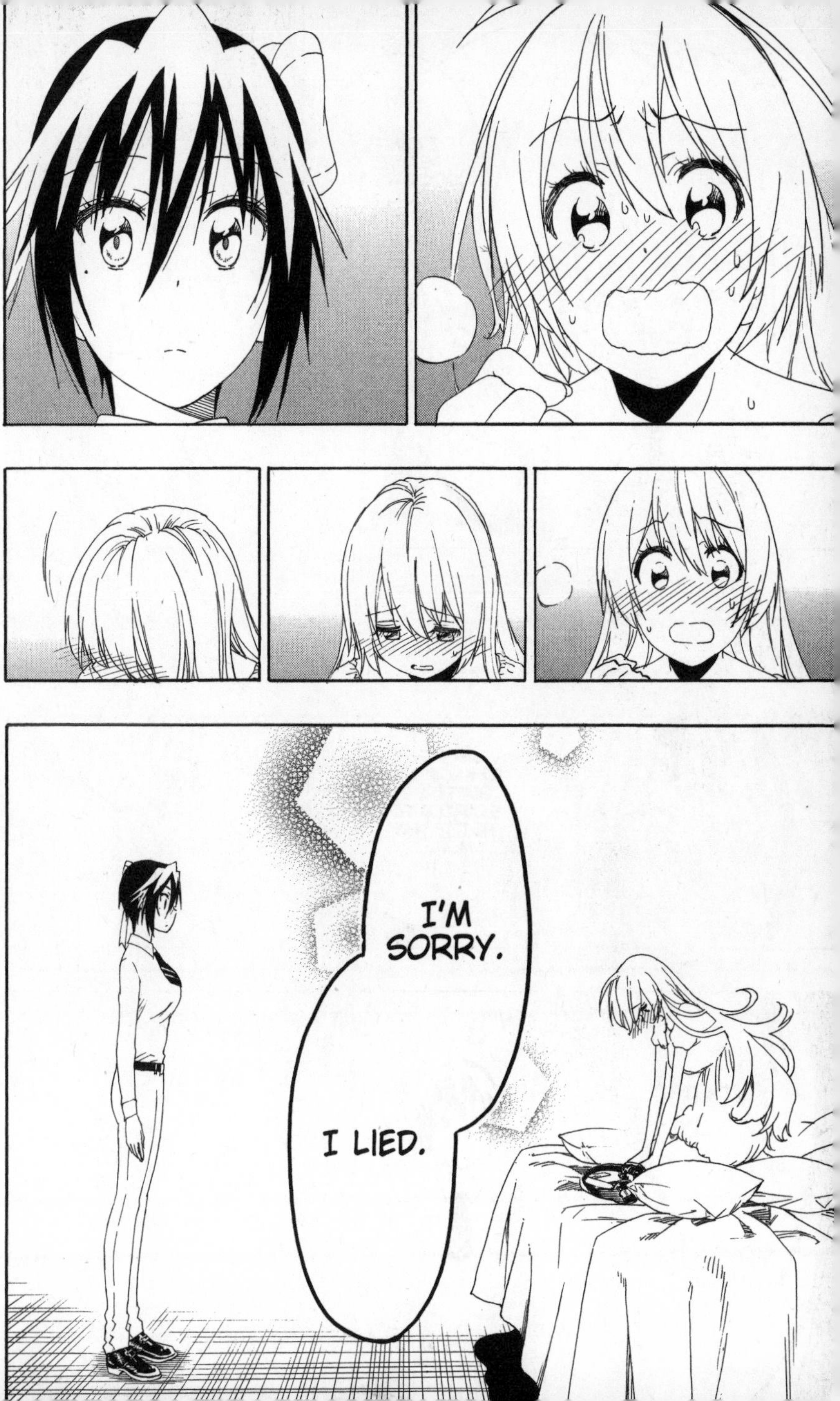
I'M SORRY.
I LIED.

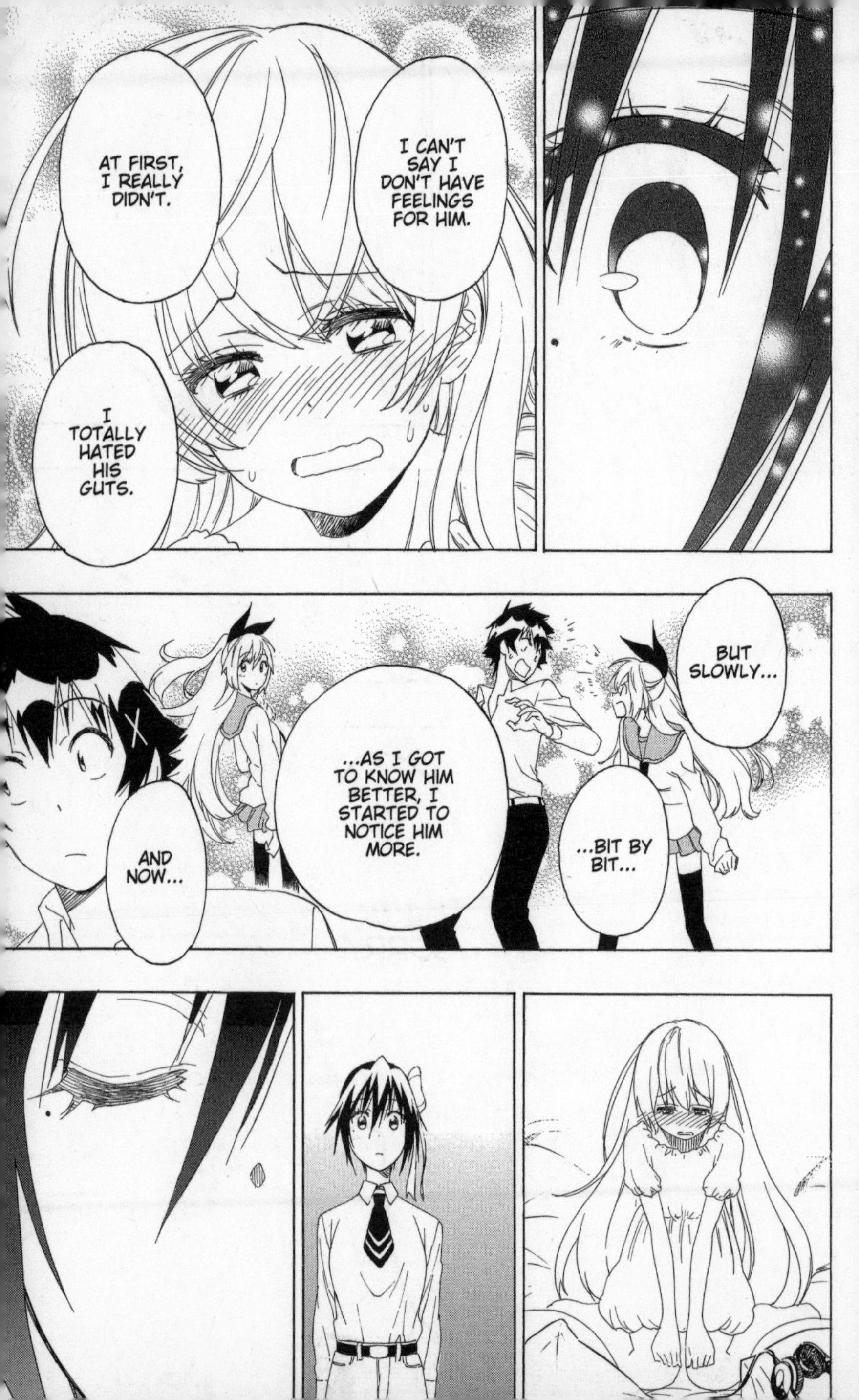
I CAN'T SAY I DON'T HAVE FEELINGS FOR HIM.
AT FIRST, I REALLY DIDN'T.
I TOTALLY HATED HIS GUTS.
BUT SLOWLY...
...BIT BY BIT...
...AS I GOT TO KNOW HIM BETTER, I STARTED TO NOTICE HIM MORE.
AND NOW...

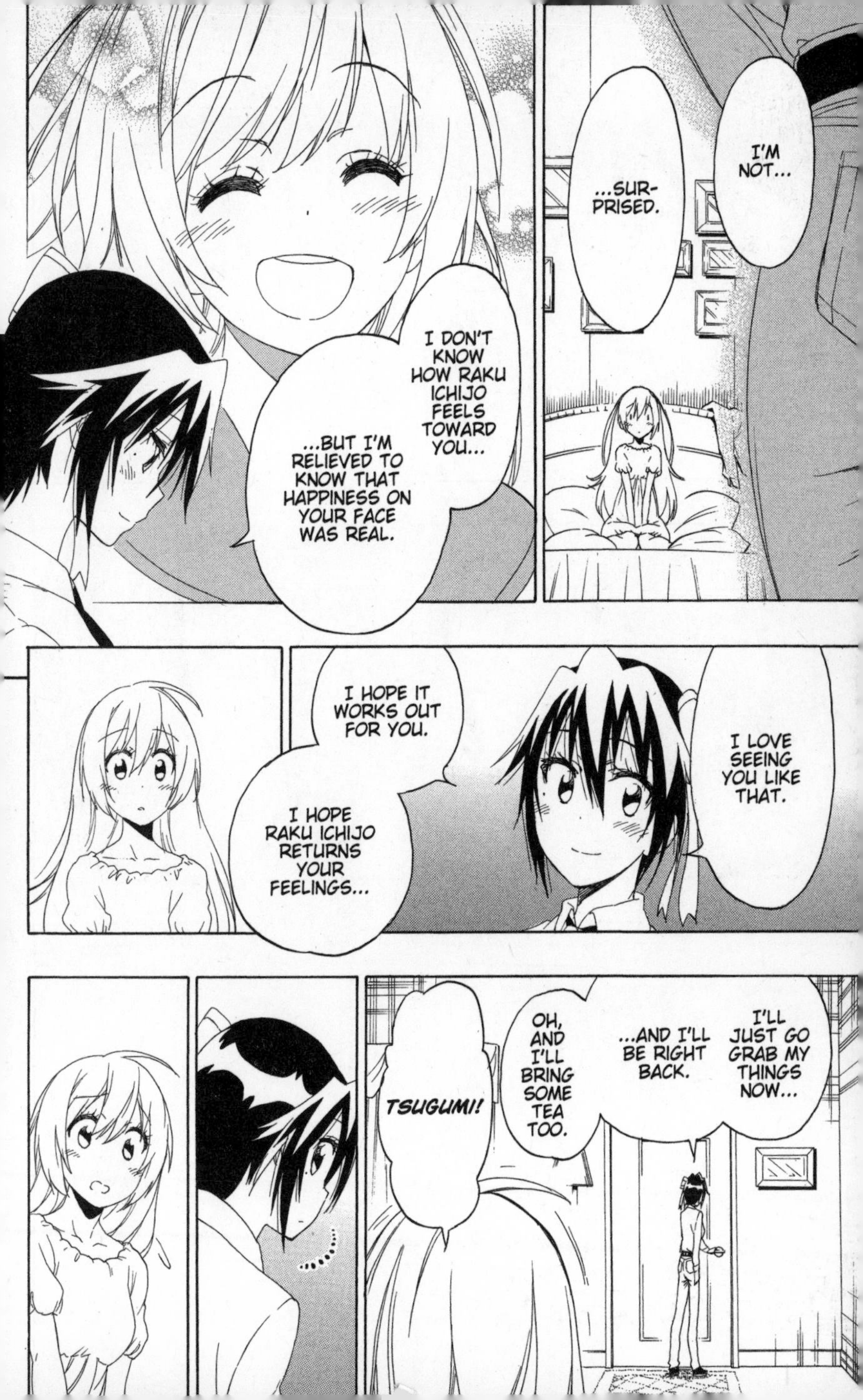
I'M NOT...
...SURPRISED.
I DON'T KNOW HOW RAKU ICHIJO FEELS TOWARD YOU...
...BUT I'M RELIEVED TO KNOW THAT HAPPINESS ON YOUR FACE WAS REAL.
I LOVE SEEING YOU LIKE THAT.
I HOPE IT WORKS OUT FOR YOU.
I HOPE RAKU ICHIJO RETURNS YOUR FEELINGS...
I'LL JUST GO GRAB MY THINGS NOW...
...AND I'LL BE RIGHT BACK.
OH, AND I'LL BRING SOME TEA TOO.
TSUGUMI!

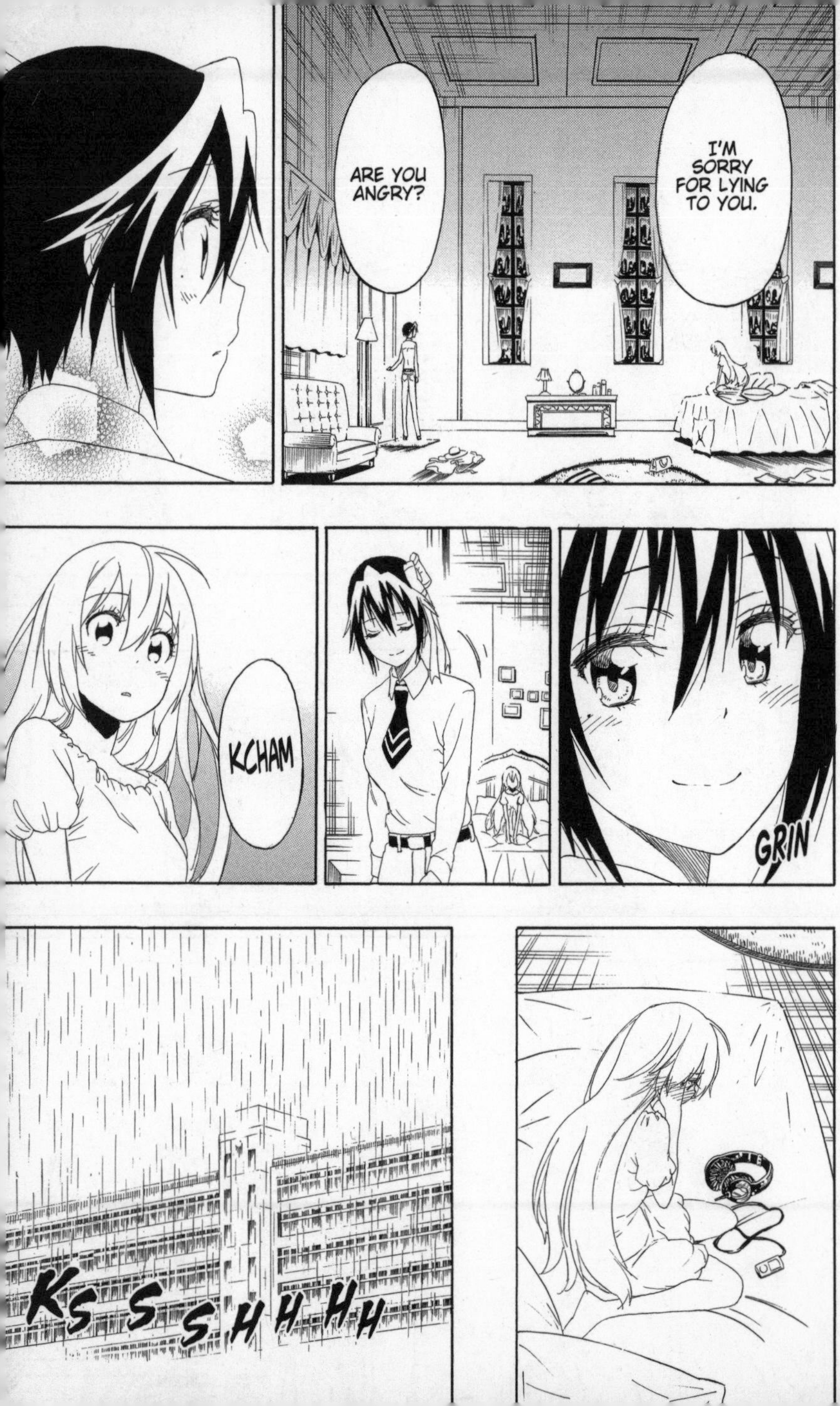
I'M SORRY FOR LYING TO YOU.
ARE YOU ANGRY?
GRIN
KCHAM
KSSSHHHH

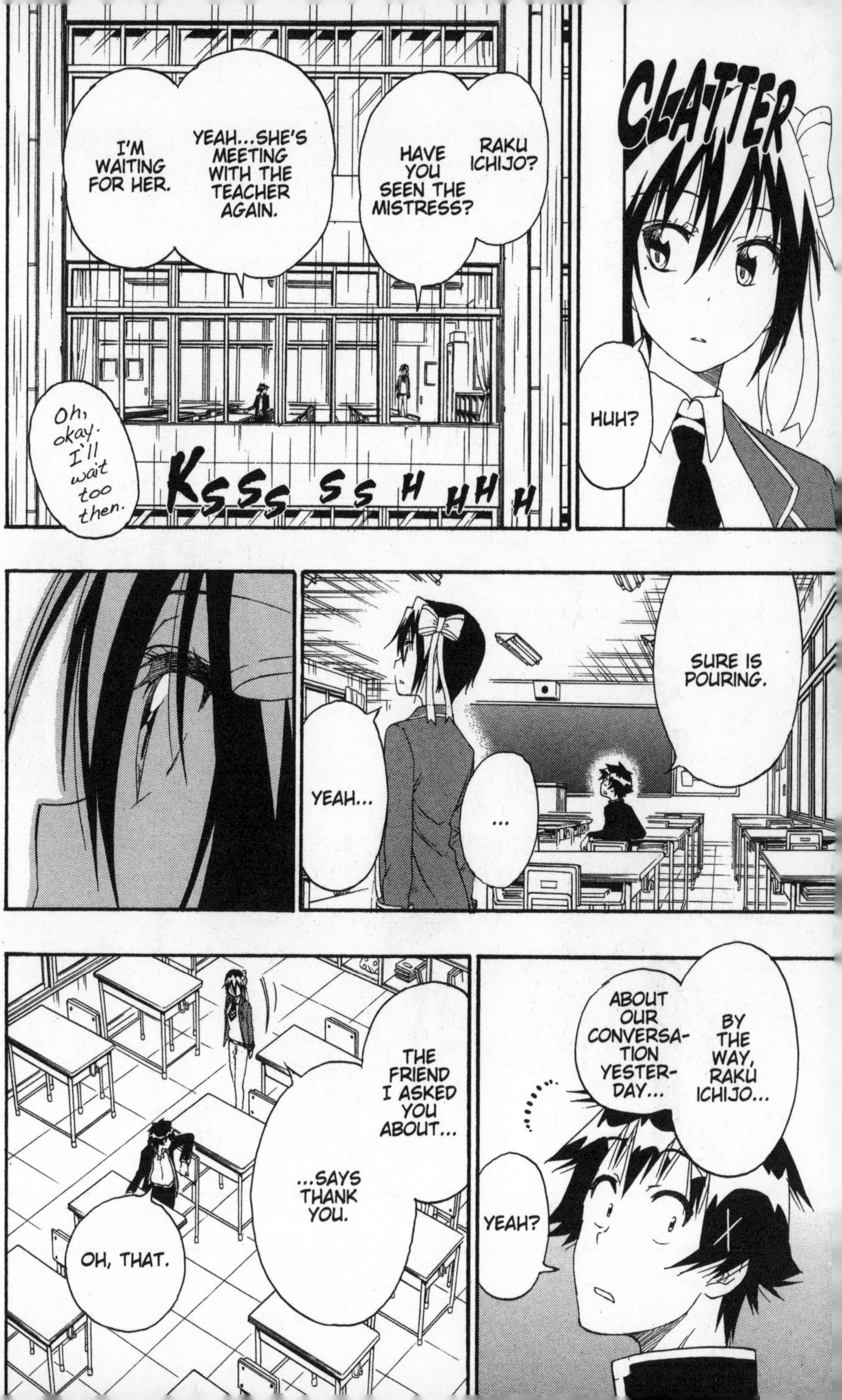
CLATTER
HUH?
RAKU ICHIJO? HAVE YOU SEEN THE MISTRESS?
YEAH...SHE'S MEETING WITH THE TEACHER AGAIN.
I'M WAITING FOR HER.
Oh, okay. I'll wait too then.
KSSSSSHHHHH
SURE IS POURING.
...
YEAH...
BY THE WAY, RAKU ICHIJO...
ABOUT OUR CONVERSATION YESTERDAY...
...
YEAH?
THE FRIEND I ASKED YOU ABOUT...
...SAYS THANK YOU.
OH, THAT.

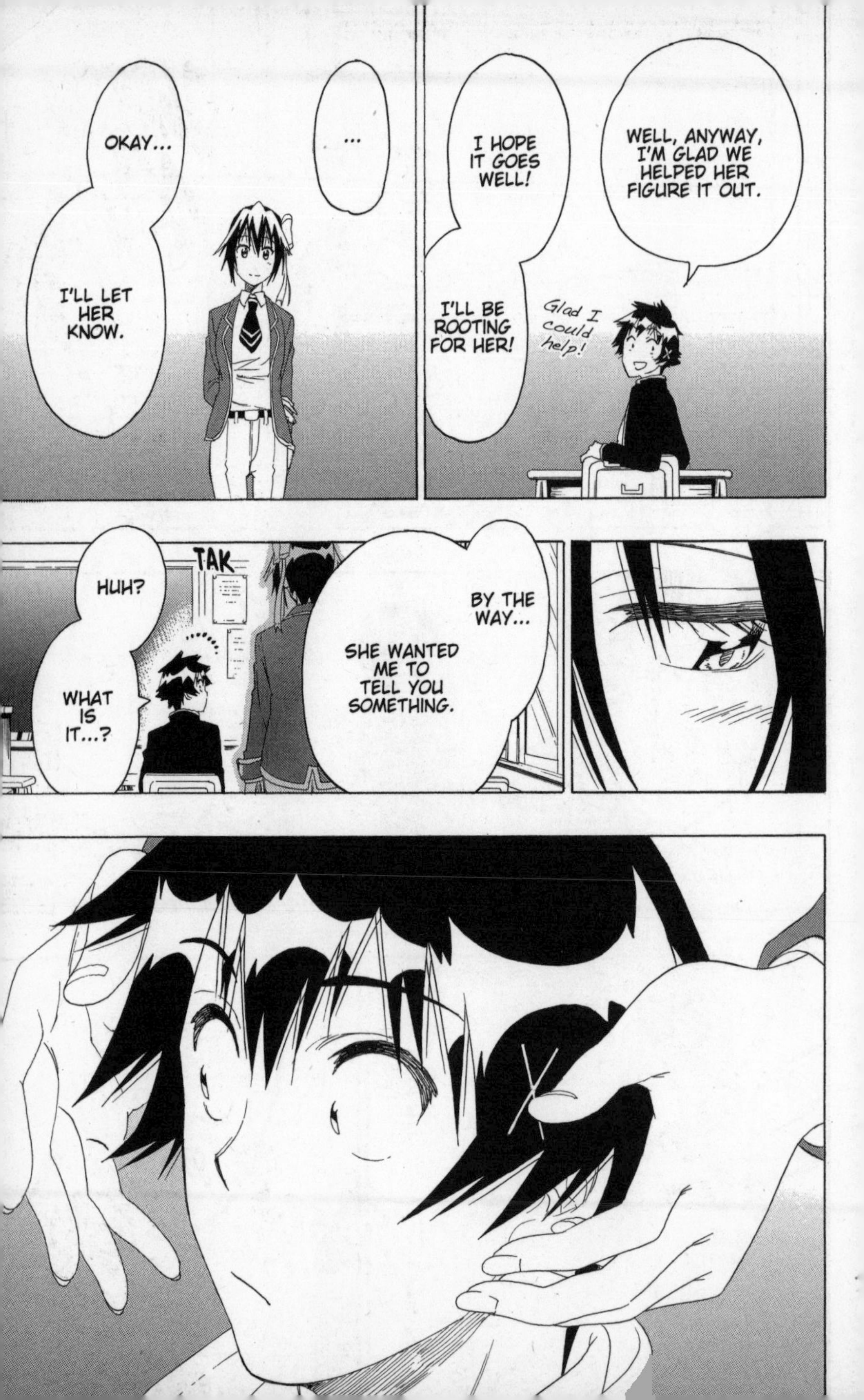
WELL, ANYWAY, I'M GLAD WE HELPED HER FIGURE IT OUT.
Glad I could help!
I HOPE IT GOES WELL!
I'LL BE ROOTING FOR HER!
...
OKAY...
I'LL LET HER KNOW.
BY THE WAY...
SHE WANTED ME TO TELL YOU SOMETHING.
TAK
HUH?
WHAT IS IT...?

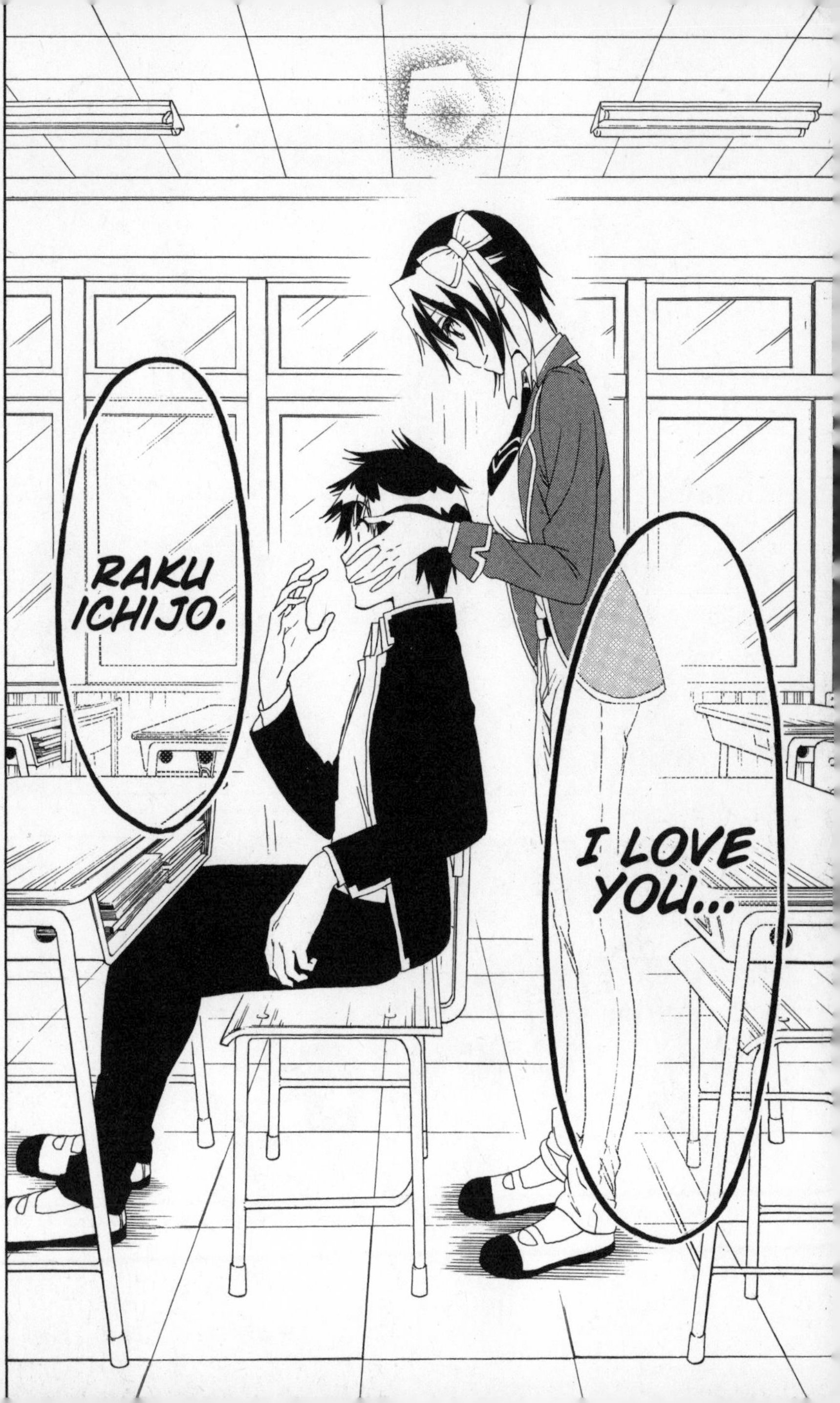
RAKU ICHIJO.
I LOVE YOU...

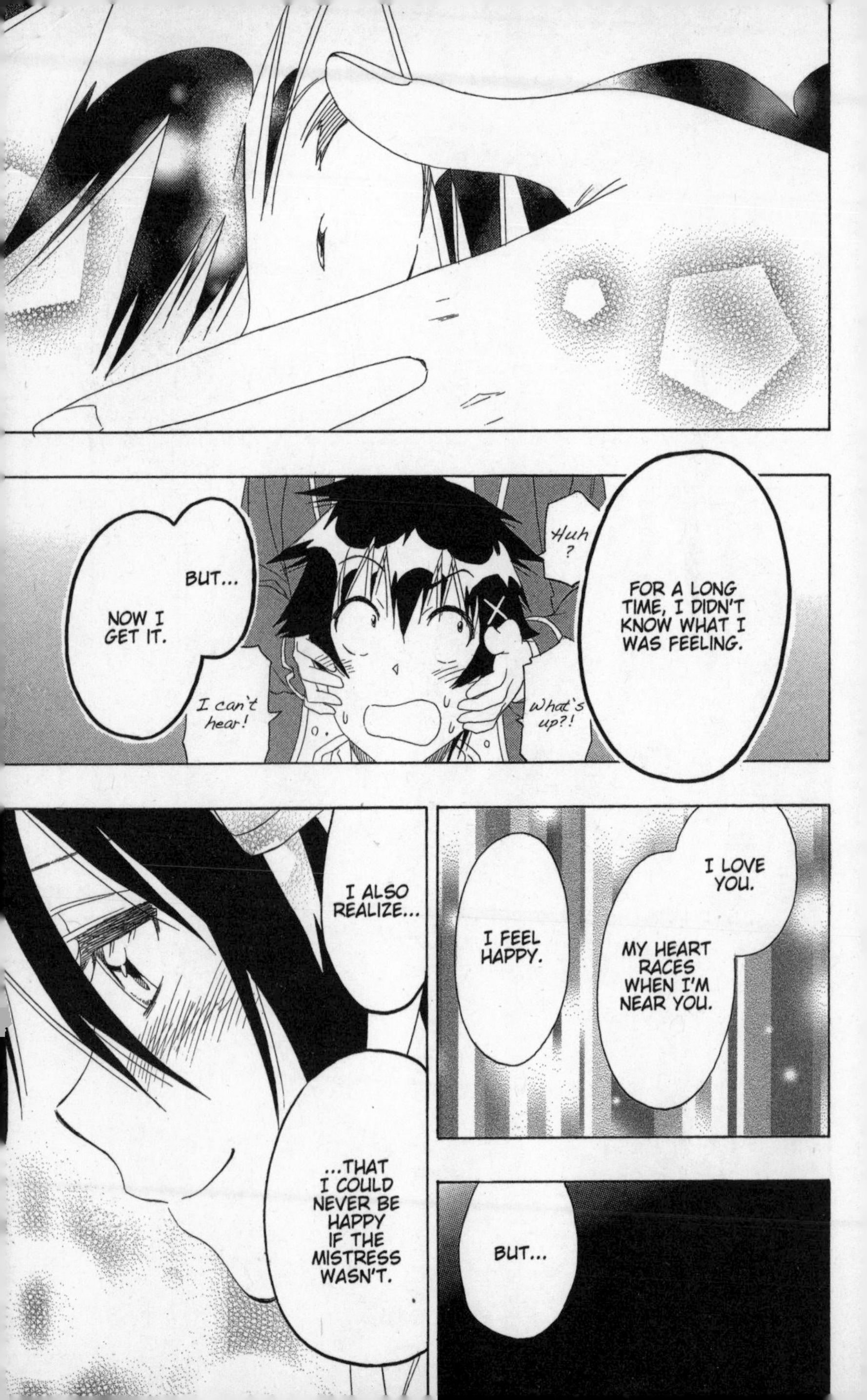
FOR A LONG TIME, I DIDN'T KNOW WHAT I WAS FEELING.
Huh ?
What's up?!
BUT...
NOW I GET IT.
I can't hear!
I LOVE YOU.
MY HEART RACES WHEN I'M NEAR YOU.
I FEEL HAPPY.
BUT...
I ALSO REALIZE...
...THAT I COULD NEVER BE HAPPY IF THE MISTRESS WASN'T.

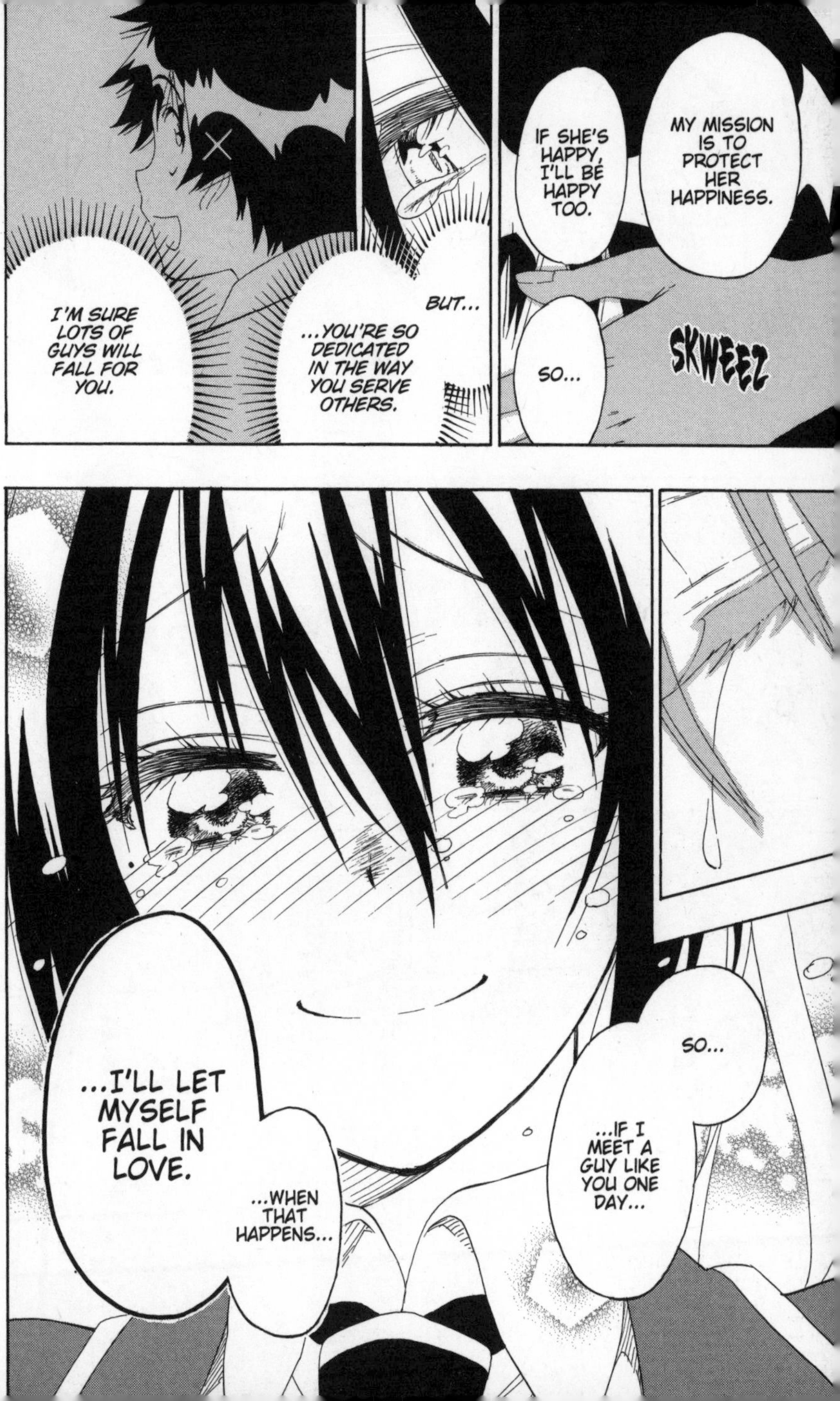
MY MISSION IS TO PROTECT HER HAPPINESS.
IF SHE'S HAPPY, I'LL BE HAPPY TOO.
SO...
SKWEEZ
BUT...
...YOU'RE SO DEDICATED IN THE WAY YOU SERVE OTHERS.
I'M SURE LOTS OF GUYS WILL FALL FOR YOU.
SO...
...IF I MEET A GUY LIKE YOU ONE DAY...
...WHEN THAT HAPPENS...
...I'LL LET MYSELF FALL IN LOVE.

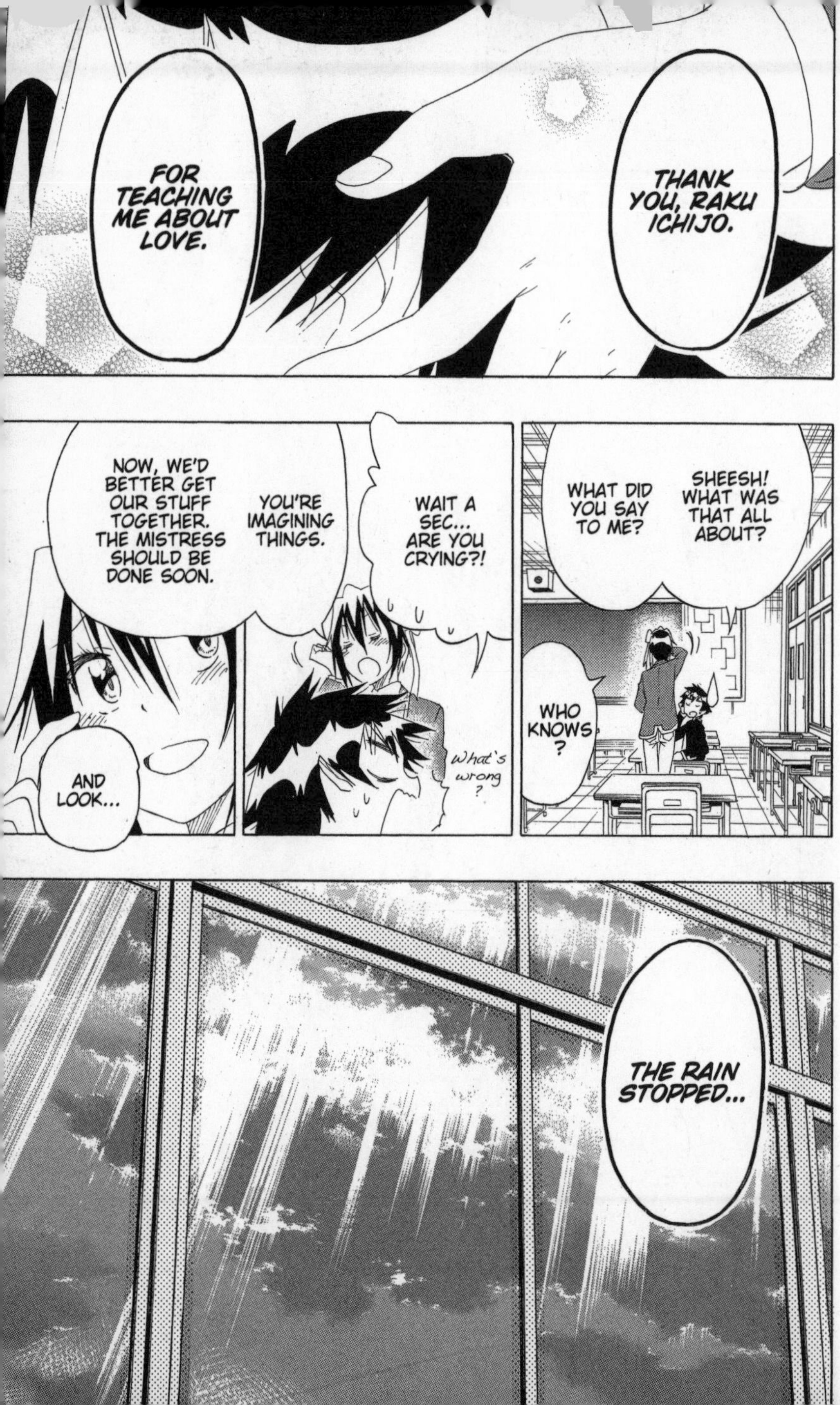
THANK YOU, RAKU ICHIJO.
FOR TEACHING ME ABOUT LOVE.
SHEESH! WHAT WAS THAT ALL ABOUT?
WHAT DID YOU SAY TO ME?
WHO KNOWS?
WAIT A SEC... ARE YOU CRYING?!
YOU'RE IMAGINING THINGS.
What's wrong?
NOW, WE'D BETTER GET OUR STUFF TOGETHER. THE MISTRESS SHOULD BE DONE SOON.
AND LOOK...
THE RAIN STOPPED...

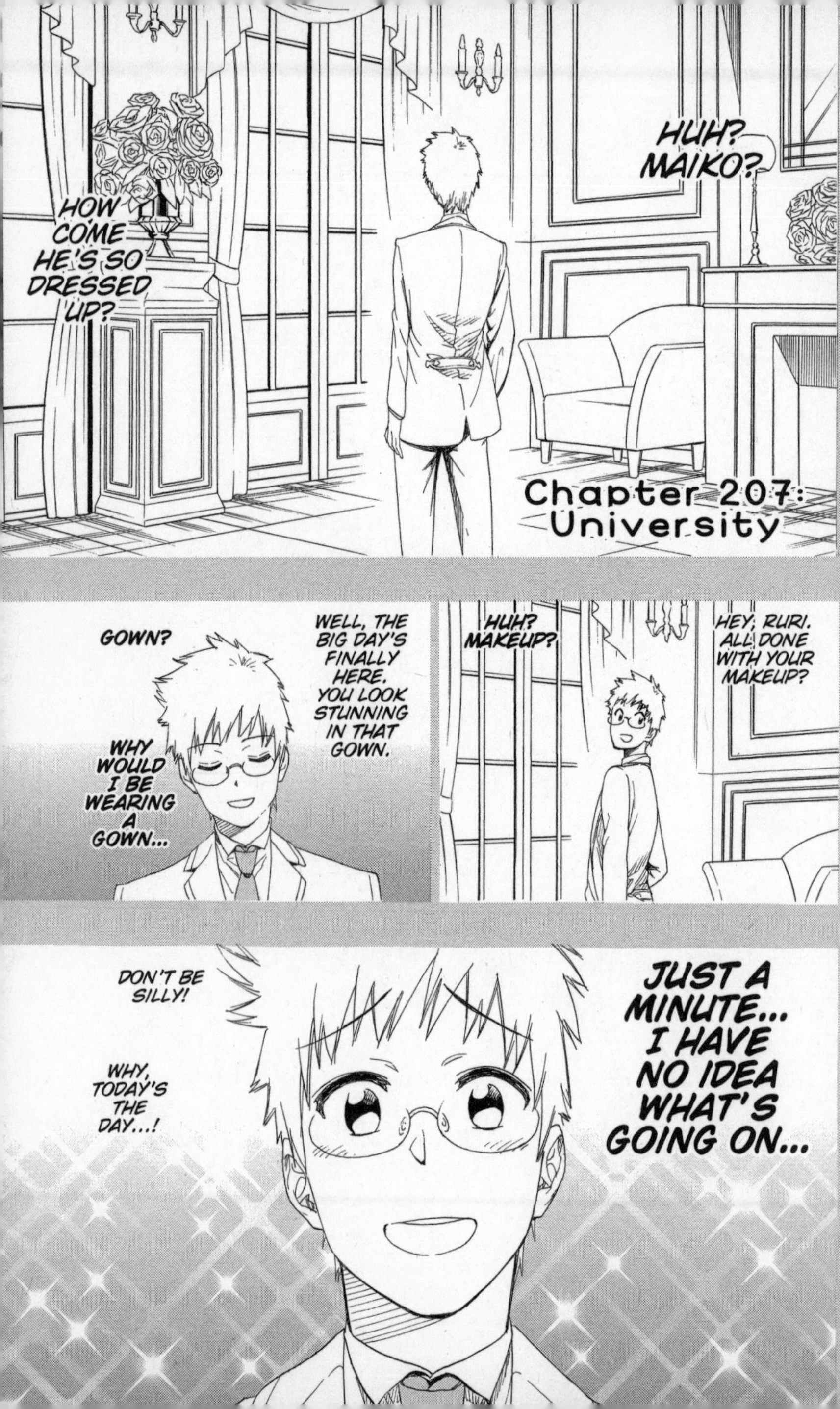
HUH? MAIKO?
HOW COME HE'S SO DRESSED UP?
Chapter 207: University
HEY, RURI. ALL DONE WITH YOUR MAKEUP?
HUH? MAKEUP?
WELL, THE BIG DAY'S FINALLY HERE. YOU LOOK STUNNING IN THAT GOWN.
GOWN?
WHY WOULD I BE WEARING A GOWN...
JUST A MINUTE... I HAVE NO IDEA WHAT'S GOING ON...
DON'T BE SILLY!
WHY, TODAY'S THE DAY...!

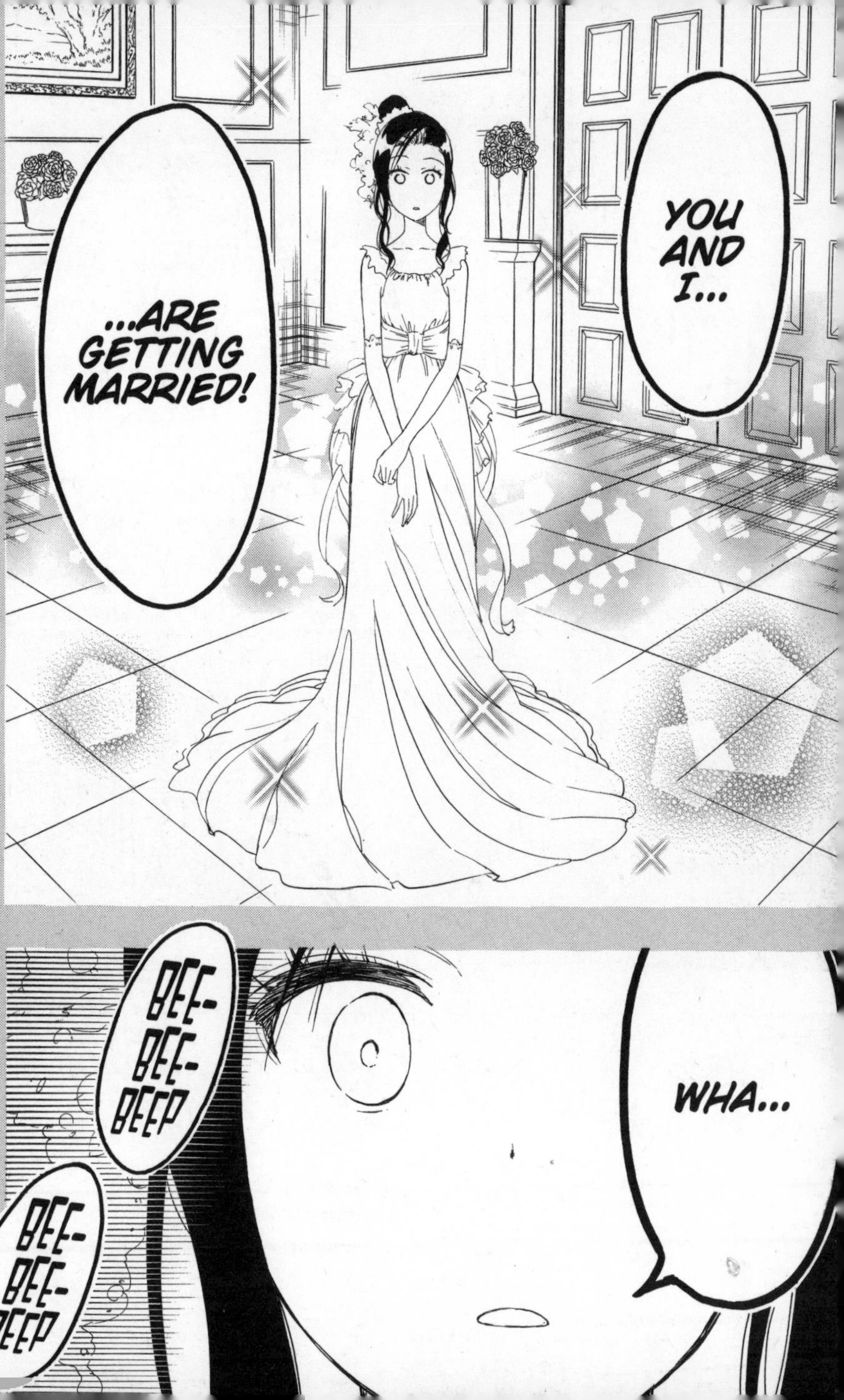
YOU AND I...
...ARE GETTING MARRIED!
WHA...
BEE-BEE-BEEP
BEE-BEE-BEEP

BEE-BEE-BEEP

BEE-BEE-BEEP

BEE-BEE-BEEP

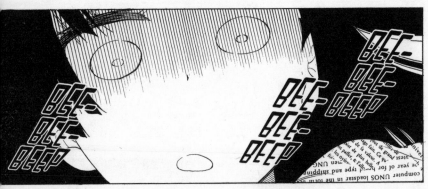

BEE-BEE-BEEP

BEE-BEE-BEEP

TIIIIING TOOOOONG

DIIIIING DOOOOONG

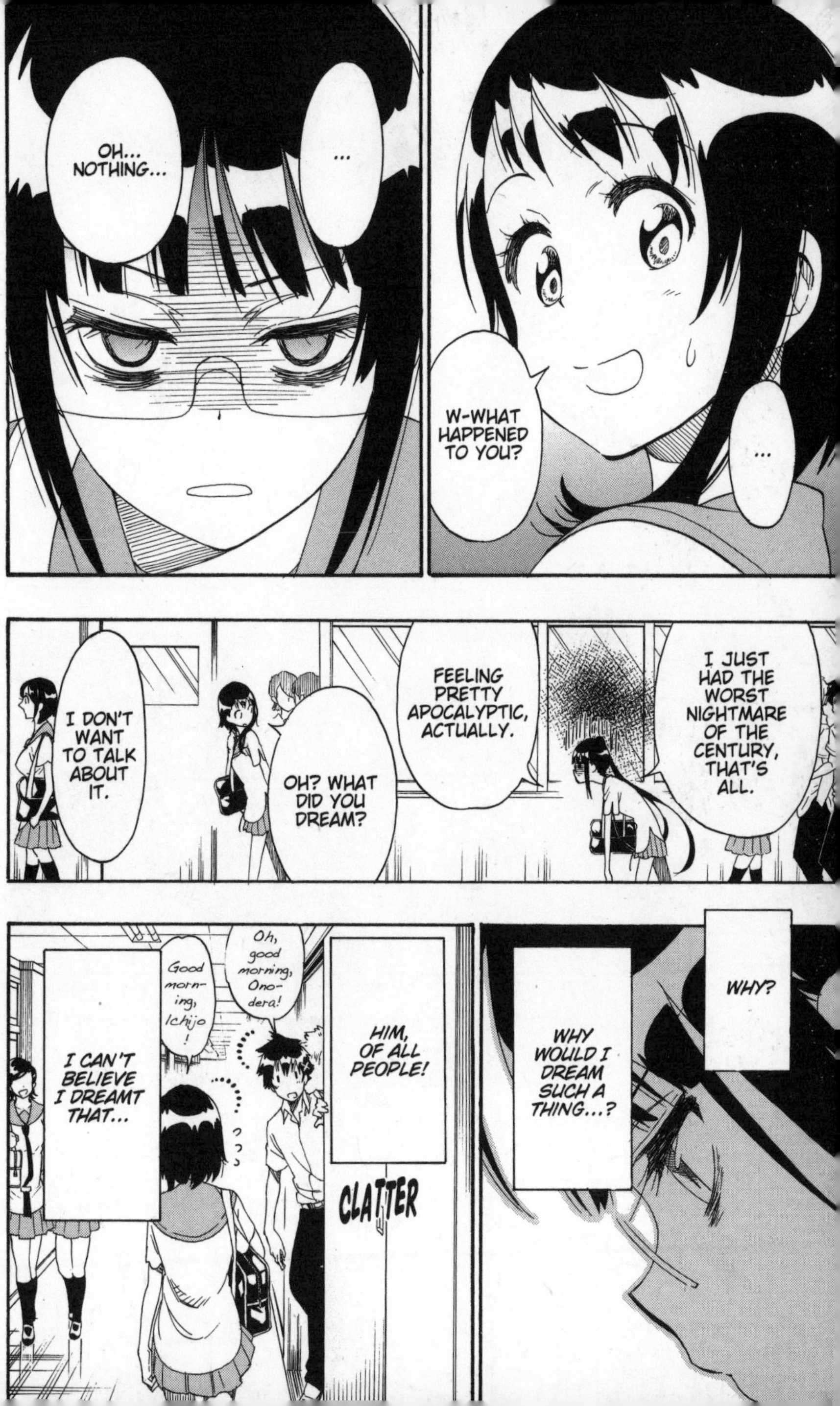
...
W-WHAT HAPPENED TO YOU?
...
OH... NOTHING...
I JUST HAD THE WORST NIGHTMARE OF THE CENTURY, THAT'S ALL.
FEELING PRETTY APOCALYPTIC, ACTUALLY.
OH? WHAT DID YOU DREAM?
I DON'T WANT TO TALK ABOUT IT.
WHY?
WHY WOULD I DREAM SUCH A THING...?
HIM, OF ALL PEOPLE!
CLATTER
Oh, good morning, Onodera!
Good morning, Ichijo!
I CAN'T BELIEVE I DREAMT THAT...

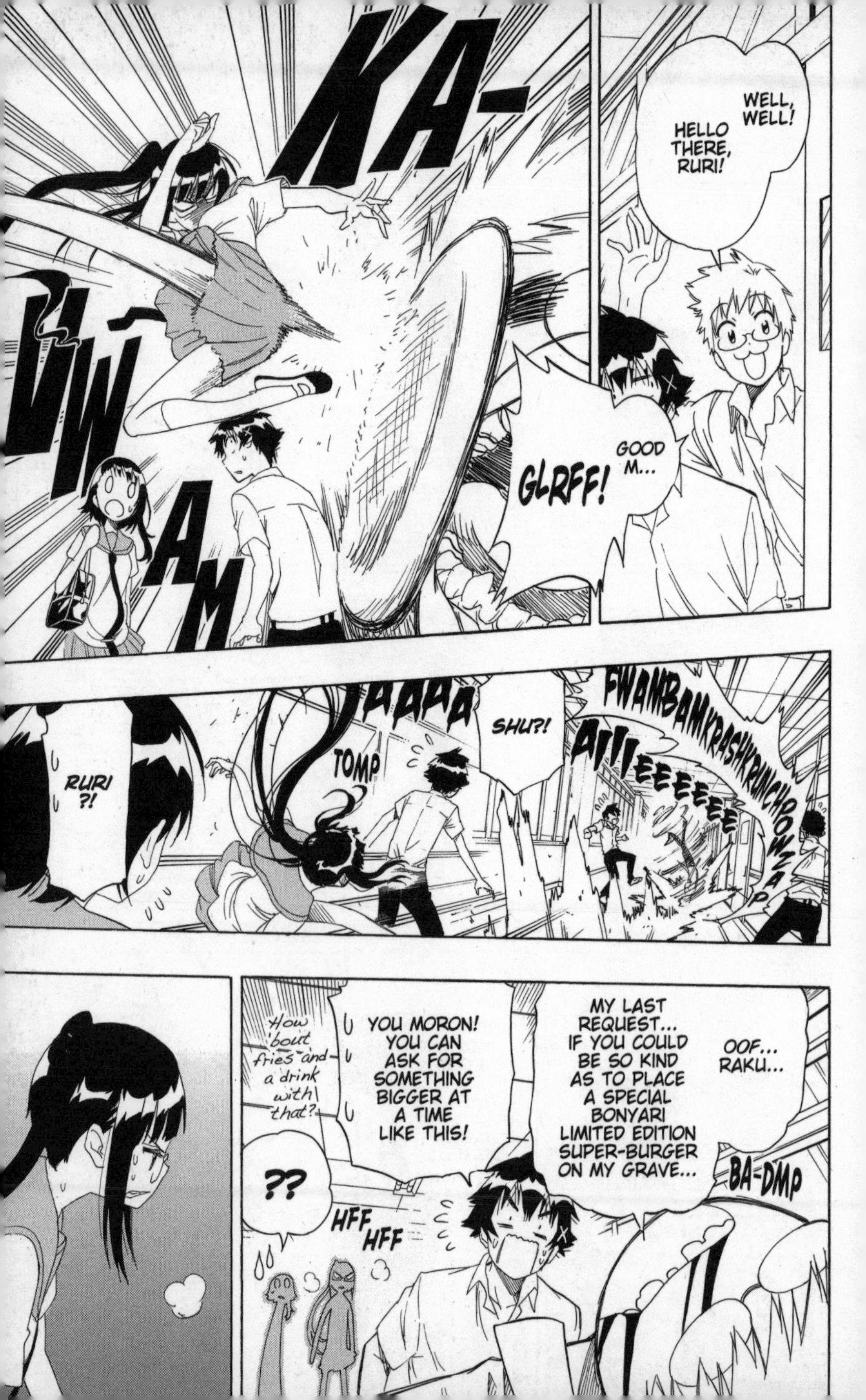
WELL, WELL!
HELLO THERE, RURI!
KA-
GOOD M...
GLRFF!
FWAMBAMKRASHKRUNCHPOWZAP
AIIIEEEEEEE
SHU?!
TOMP
RURI ?!
OOF... RAKU...
BA-DMP
MY LAST REQUEST... IF YOU COULD BE SO KIND AS TO PLACE A SPECIAL BONYARI LIMITED EDITION SUPER-BURGER ON MY GRAVE...
YOU MORON! YOU CAN ASK FOR SOMETHING BIGGER AT A TIME LIKE THIS!
How 'bout fries and a drink with that?
??
HFF HFF

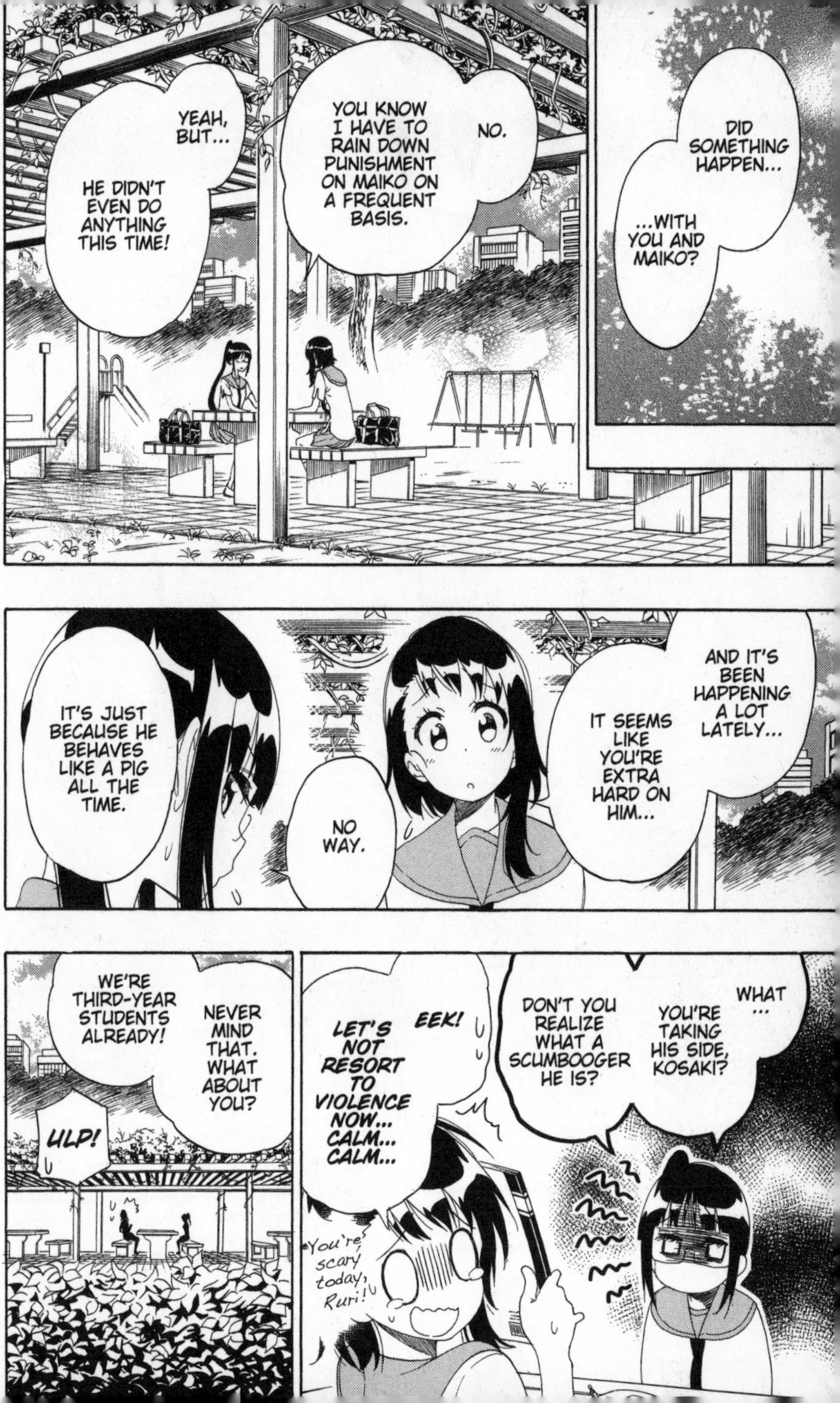
DID SOMETHING HAPPEN...
...WITH YOU AND MAIKO?
NO.
YOU KNOW I HAVE TO RAIN DOWN PUNISHMENT ON MAIKO ON A FREQUENT BASIS.
YEAH, BUT...
HE DIDN'T EVEN DO ANYTHING THIS TIME!
AND IT'S BEEN HAPPENING A LOT LATELY...
IT SEEMS LIKE YOU'RE EXTRA HARD ON HIM...
NO WAY.
IT'S JUST BECAUSE HE BEHAVES LIKE A PIG ALL THE TIME.
WHAT...
YOU'RE TAKING HIS SIDE, KOSAKI?
DON'T YOU REALIZE WHAT A SCUMBOOGER HE IS?
EEK!
LET'S NOT RESORT TO VIOLENCE NOW... CALM... CALM...
You're scary today, Ruri!
NEVER MIND THAT. WHAT ABOUT YOU?
WE'RE THIRD-YEAR STUDENTS ALREADY!
ULP!

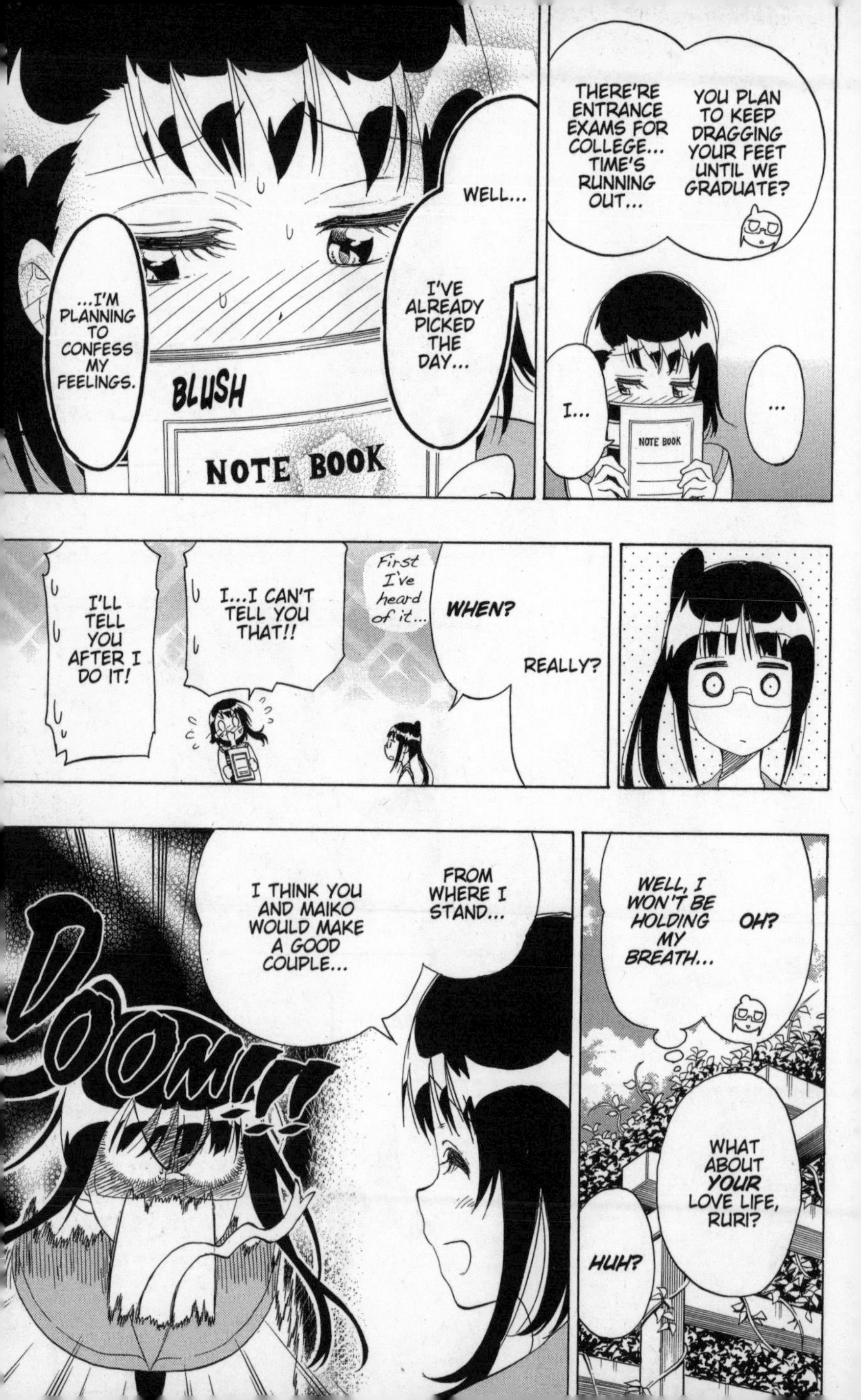
YOU PLAN TO KEEP DRAGGING YOUR FEET UNTIL WE GRADUATE?
THERE'RE ENTRANCE EXAMS FOR COLLEGE... TIME'S RUNNING OUT...
...
I...
NOTE BOOK
WELL...
I'VE ALREADY PICKED THE DAY...
...I'M PLANNING TO CONFESS MY FEELINGS.
BLUSH
NOTE BOOK
REALLY?
WHEN?
First I've heard of it...
I...I CAN'T TELL YOU THAT!!
I'LL TELL YOU AFTER I DO IT!
OH?
WELL, I WON'T BE HOLDING MY BREATH...
WHAT ABOUT YOUR LOVE LIFE, RURI?
HUH?
FROM WHERE I STAND...
I THINK YOU AND MAIKO WOULD MAKE A GOOD COUPLE...
DOOM!!

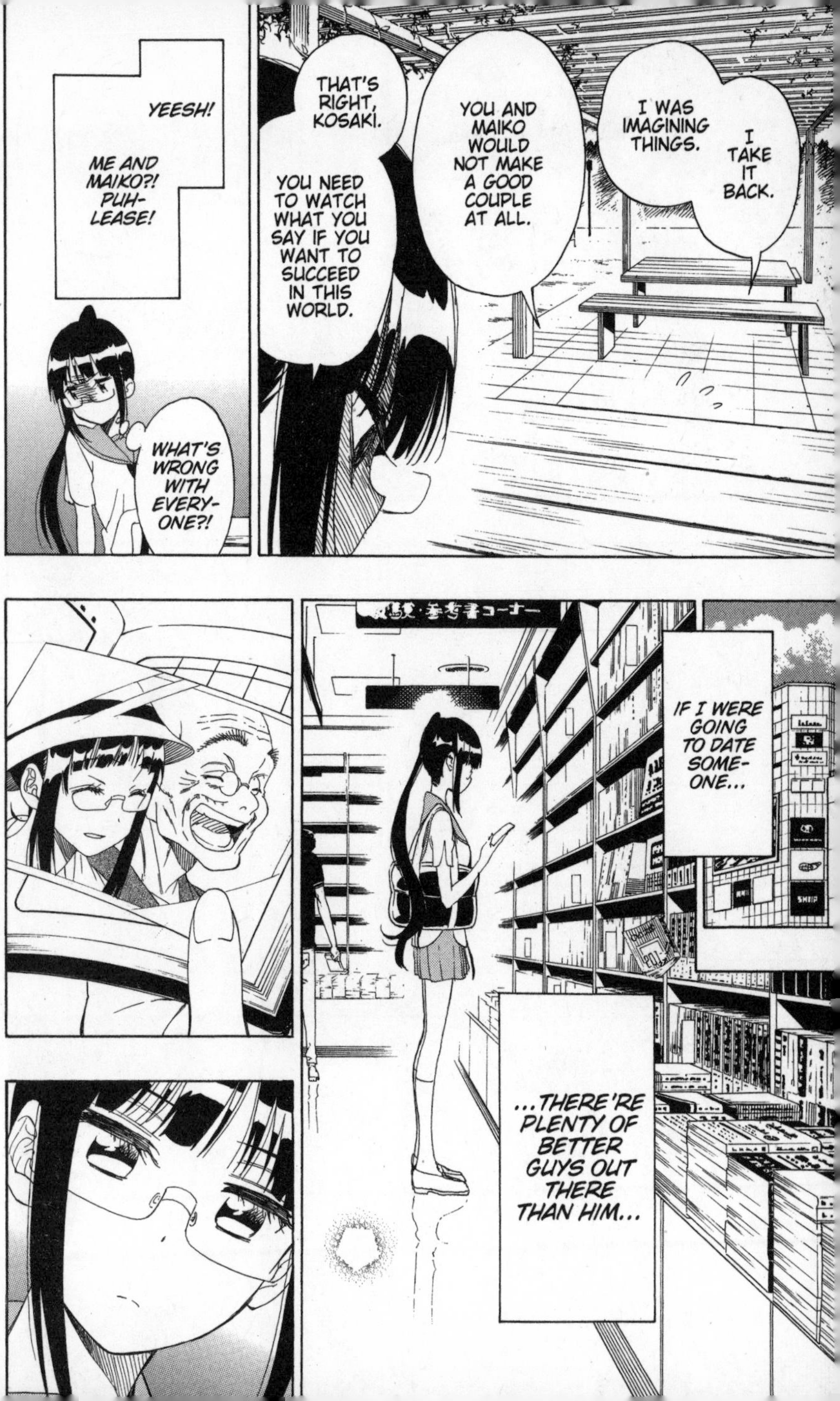
I TAKE IT BACK.
I WAS IMAGINING THINGS.
YOU AND MAIKO WOULD NOT MAKE A GOOD COUPLE AT ALL.
THAT'S RIGHT, KOSAKI.
YOU NEED TO WATCH WHAT YOU SAY IF YOU WANT TO SUCCEED IN THIS WORLD.
YEESH!
ME AND MAIKO?! PUH-LEASE!
WHAT'S WRONG WITH EVERY-ONE?!
IF I WERE GOING TO DATE SOME-ONE...
...THERE'RE PLENTY OF BETTER GUYS OUT THERE THAN HIM...

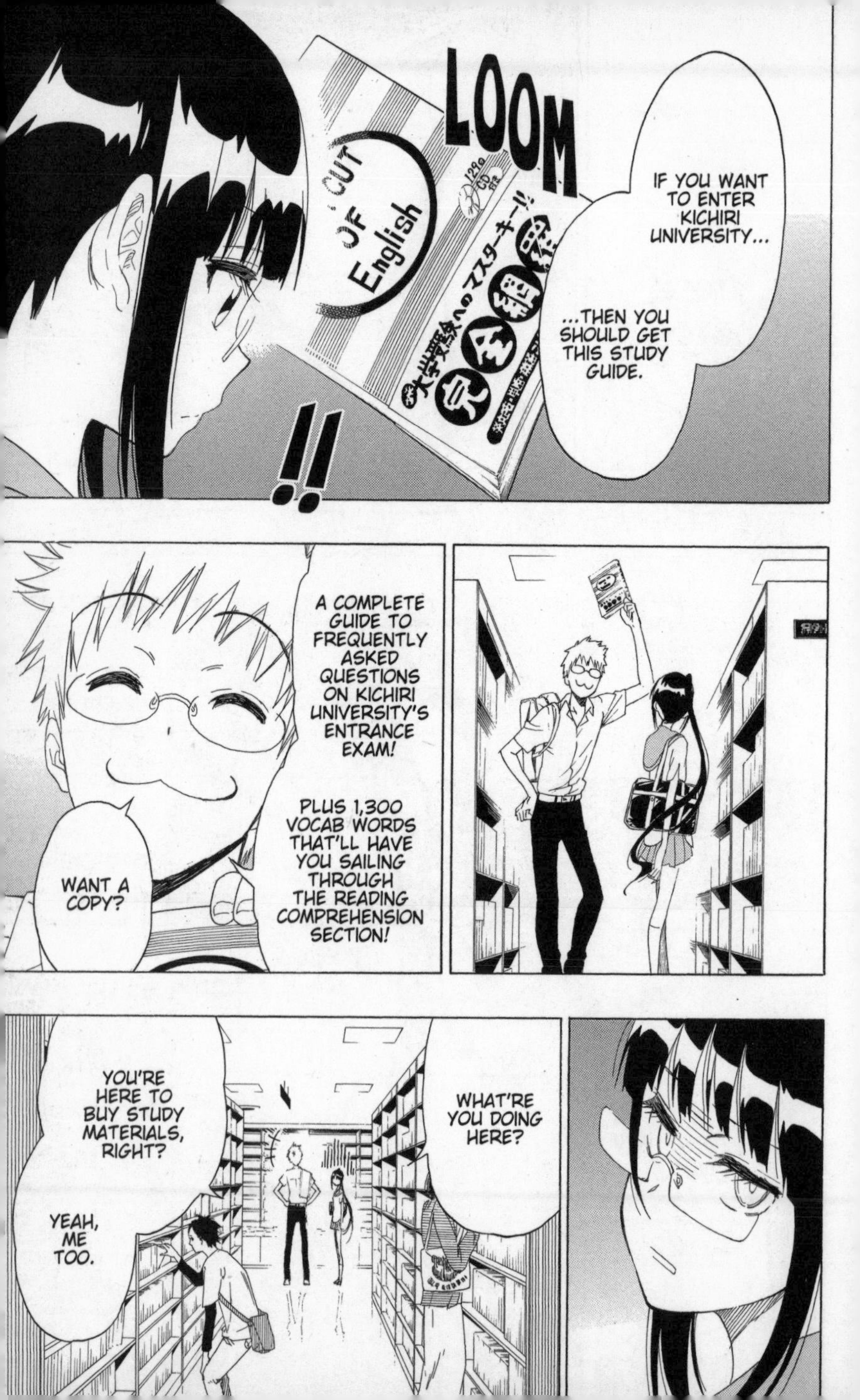
LOOM
CUT OF English
IF YOU WANT TO ENTER KICHIRI UNIVERSITY...
...THEN YOU SHOULD GET THIS STUDY GUIDE.
!!
A COMPLETE GUIDE TO FREQUENTLY ASKED QUESTIONS ON KICHIRI UNIVERSITY'S ENTRANCE EXAM!
PLUS 1,300 VOCAB WORDS THAT'LL HAVE YOU SAILING THROUGH THE READING COMPREHENSION SECTION!
WANT A COPY?
WHAT'RE YOU DOING HERE?
YOU'RE HERE TO BUY STUDY MATERIALS, RIGHT?
YEAH, ME TOO.

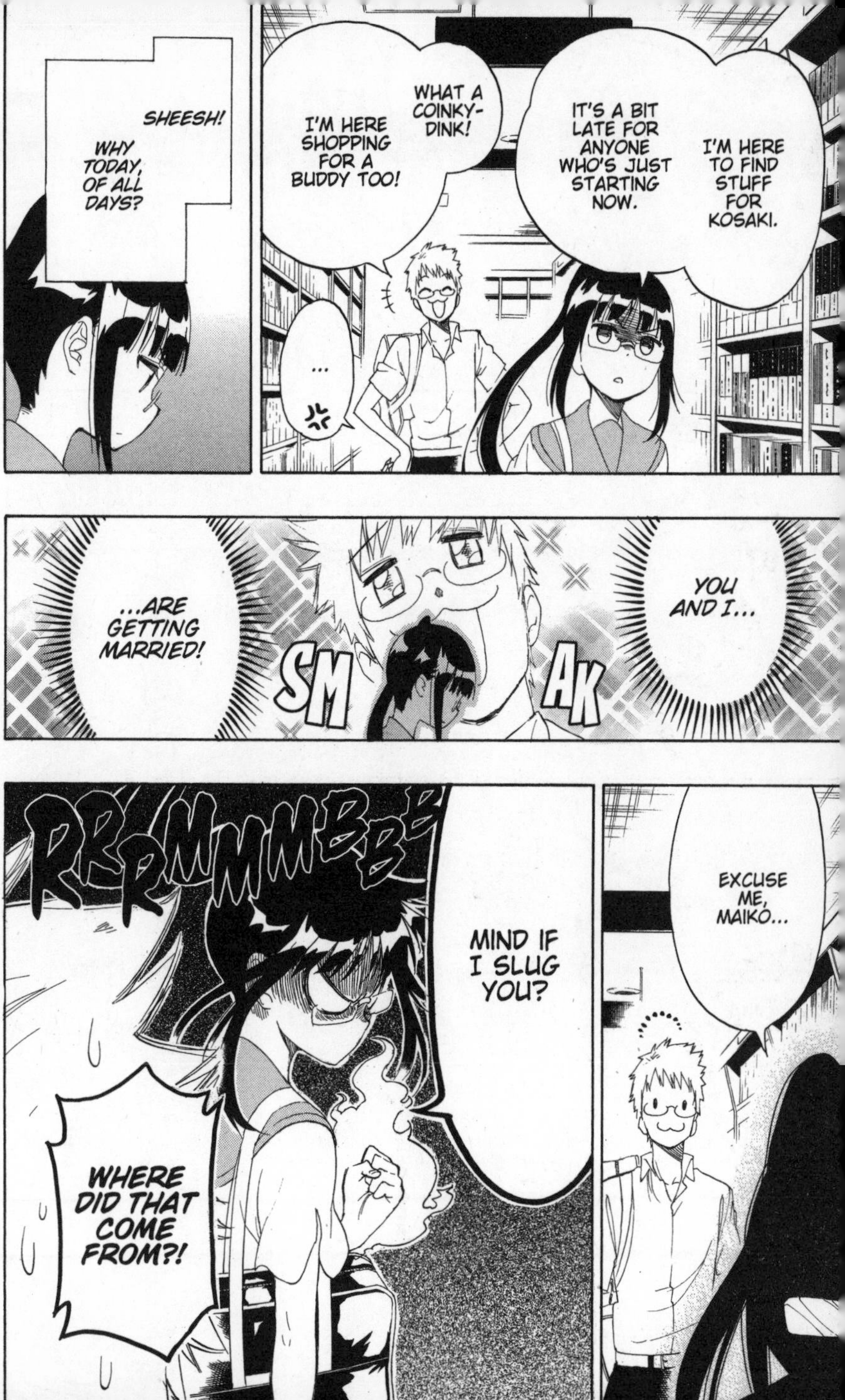
I'M HERE TO FIND STUFF FOR KOSAKI.
IT'S A BIT LATE FOR ANYONE WHO'S JUST STARTING NOW.
WHAT A COINKY-DINK!
I'M HERE SHOPPING FOR A BUDDY TOO!
...
SHEESH!
WHY TODAY, OF ALL DAYS?
YOU AND I...
SMAK
...ARE GETTING MARRIED!
EXCUSE ME, MAIKO...
MIND IF I SLUG YOU?
DRRMMMMBBB
WHERE DID THAT COME FROM?!

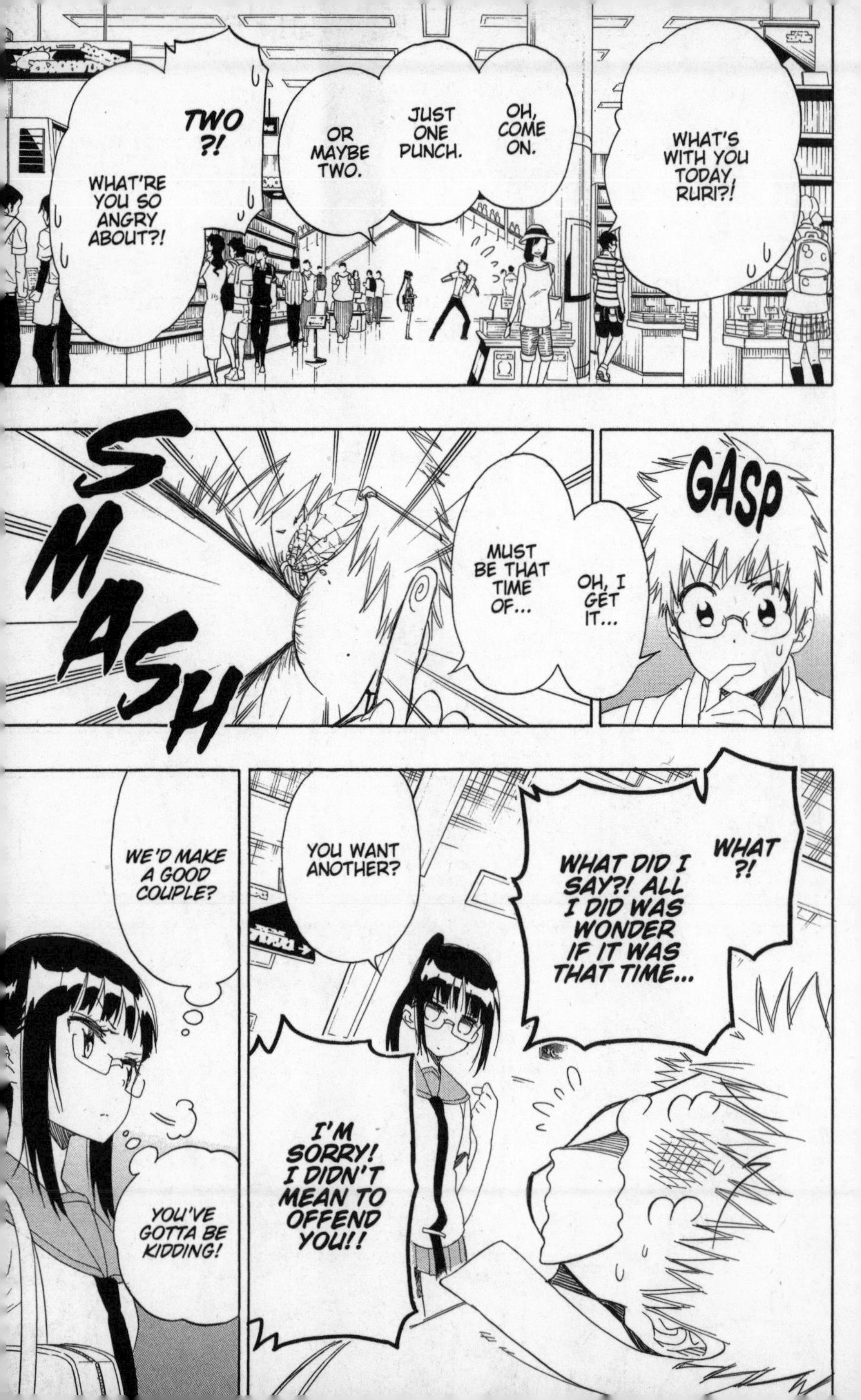
WHAT'S WITH YOU TODAY, RURI?!
OH, COME ON.
JUST ONE PUNCH.
OR MAYBE TWO.
TWO?!
WHAT'RE YOU SO ANGRY ABOUT?!
GASP
OH, I GET IT...
MUST BE THAT TIME OF...
SMASH
WHAT?!
WHAT DID I SAY?! ALL I DID WAS WONDER IF IT WAS THAT TIME...
YOU WANT ANOTHER?
I'M SORRY! I DIDN'T MEAN TO OFFEND YOU!!
WE'D MAKE A GOOD COUPLE?
YOU'VE GOTTA BE KIDDING!

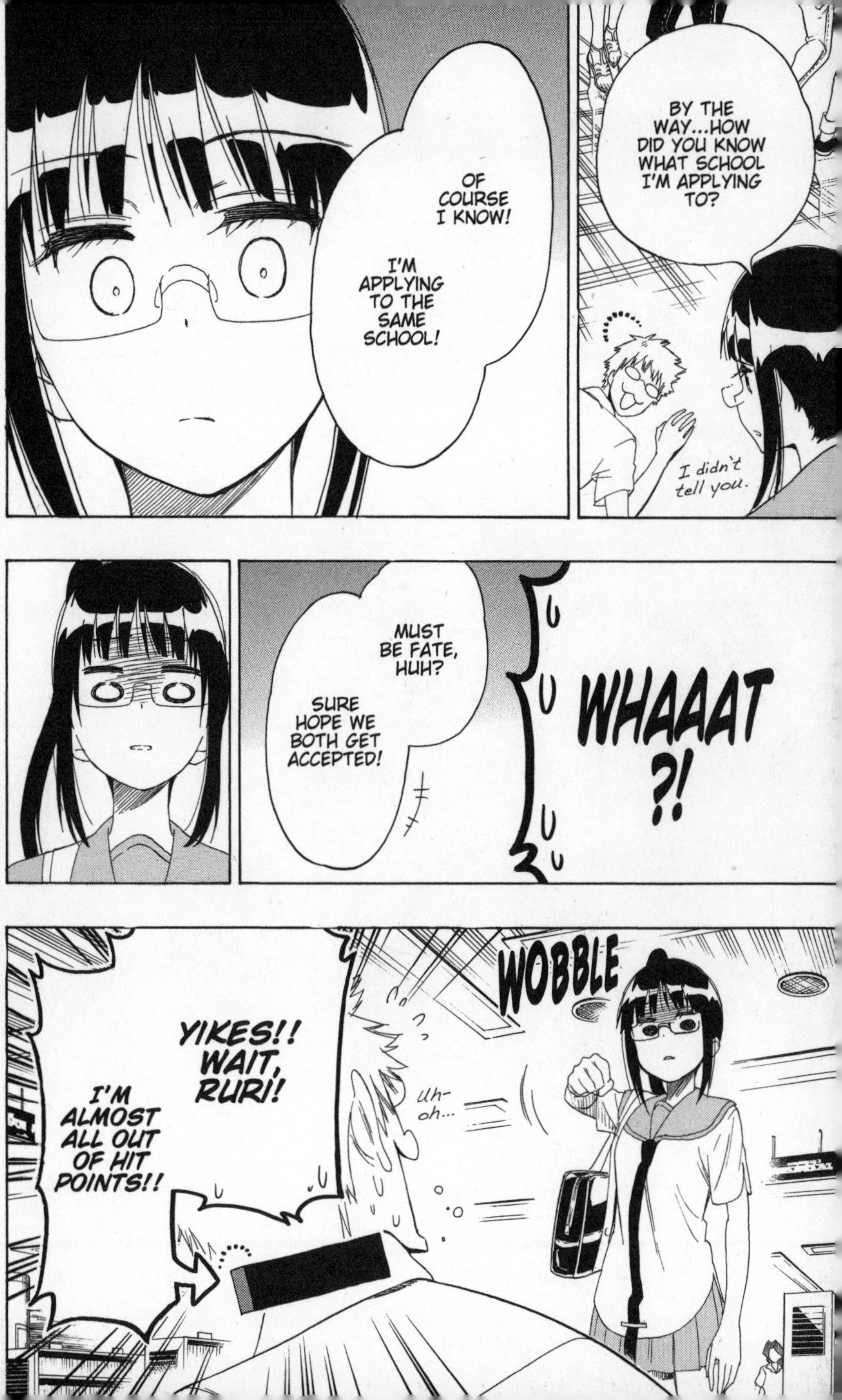
BY THE WAY...HOW DID YOU KNOW WHAT SCHOOL I'M APPLYING TO?
I didn't tell you.
OF COURSE I KNOW!
I'M APPLYING TO THE SAME SCHOOL!
MUST BE FATE, HUH?
SURE HOPE WE BOTH GET ACCEPTED!
WHAAAT ?!
WOBBLE
Uh-oh...
YIKES!! WAIT, RURI!
I'M ALMOST ALL OUT OF HIT POINTS!!

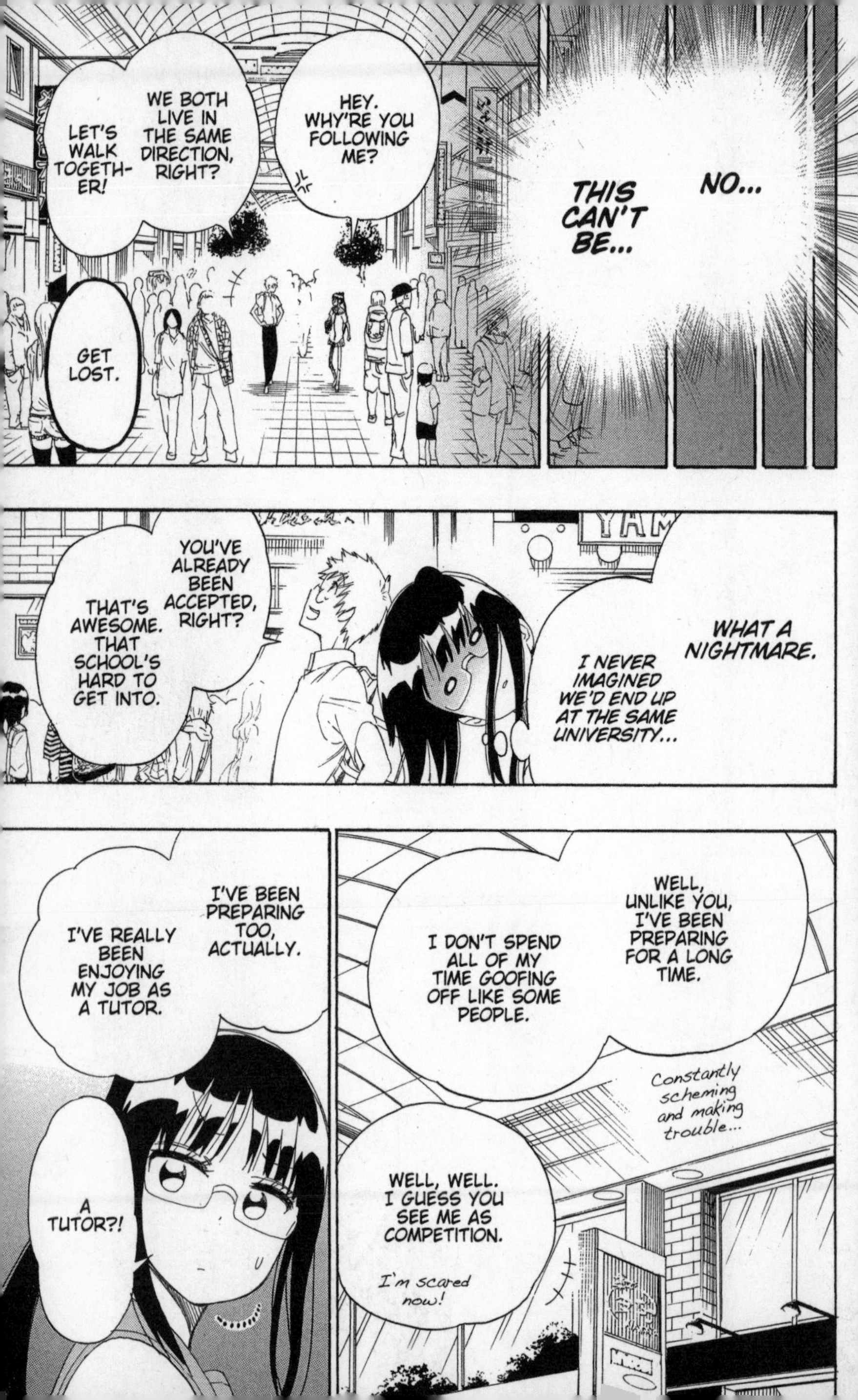
NO...
THIS CAN'T BE...
HEY. WHY'RE YOU FOLLOWING ME?
WE BOTH LIVE IN THE SAME DIRECTION, RIGHT?
LET'S WALK TOGETHER!
GET LOST.
WHAT A NIGHTMARE.
I NEVER IMAGINED WE'D END UP AT THE SAME UNIVERSITY...
YOU'VE ALREADY BEEN ACCEPTED, RIGHT?
THAT'S AWESOME. THAT SCHOOL'S HARD TO GET INTO.
WELL, UNLIKE YOU, I'VE BEEN PREPARING FOR A LONG TIME.
I DON'T SPEND ALL OF MY TIME GOOFING OFF LIKE SOME PEOPLE.
Constantly scheming and making trouble...
WELL, WELL. I GUESS YOU SEE ME AS COMPETITION.
I'm scared now!
I'VE BEEN PREPARING TOO, ACTUALLY.
I'VE REALLY BEEN ENJOYING MY JOB AS A TUTOR.
A TUTOR?!

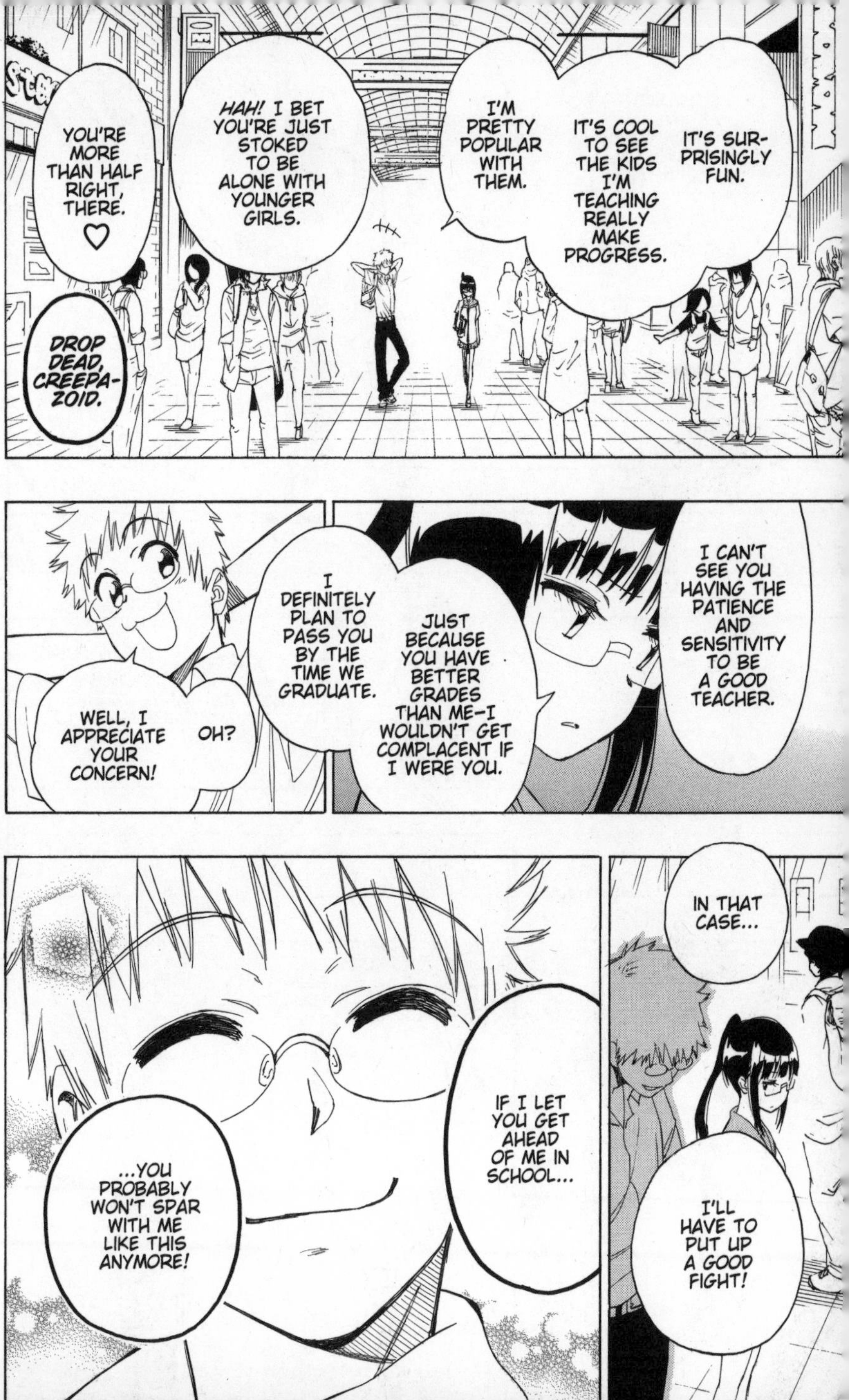

IT'S SURPRISINGLY FUN.
IT'S COOL TO SEE THE KIDS I'M TEACHING REALLY MAKE PROGRESS.
I'M PRETTY POPULAR WITH THEM.
HAH! I BET YOU'RE JUST STOKED TO BE ALONE WITH YOUNGER GIRLS.
YOU'RE MORE THAN HALF RIGHT, THERE. ♡
DROP DEAD, CREEPAZOID.
I CAN'T SEE YOU HAVING THE PATIENCE AND SENSITIVITY TO BE A GOOD TEACHER.
JUST BECAUSE YOU HAVE BETTER GRADES THAN ME—I WOULDN'T GET COMPLACENT IF I WERE YOU.
I DEFINITELY PLAN TO PASS YOU BY THE TIME WE GRADUATE.
OH?
WELL, I APPRECIATE YOUR CONCERN!
IN THAT CASE...
I'LL HAVE TO PUT UP A GOOD FIGHT!
IF I LET YOU GET AHEAD OF ME IN SCHOOL...
...YOU PROBABLY WON'T SPAR WITH ME LIKE THIS ANYMORE!

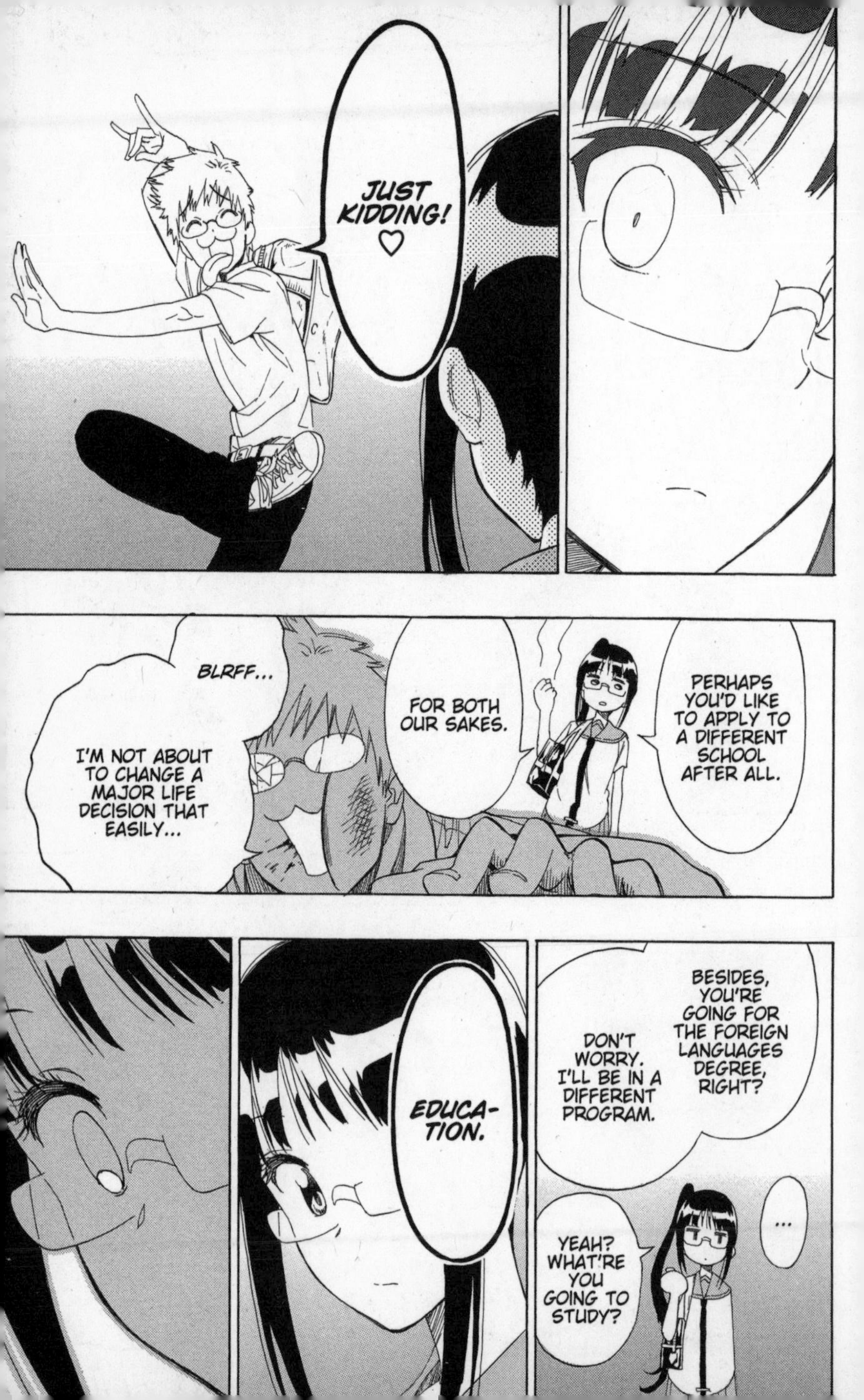
JUST KIDDING! ♡
PERHAPS YOU'D LIKE TO APPLY TO A DIFFERENT SCHOOL AFTER ALL.
FOR BOTH OUR SAKES.
BLRFF...
I'M NOT ABOUT TO CHANGE A MAJOR LIFE DECISION THAT EASILY...
BESIDES, YOU'RE GOING FOR THE FOREIGN LANGUAGES DEGREE, RIGHT?
DON'T WORRY. I'LL BE IN A DIFFERENT PROGRAM.
...
YEAH? WHAT'RE YOU GOING TO STUDY?
EDUCATION.

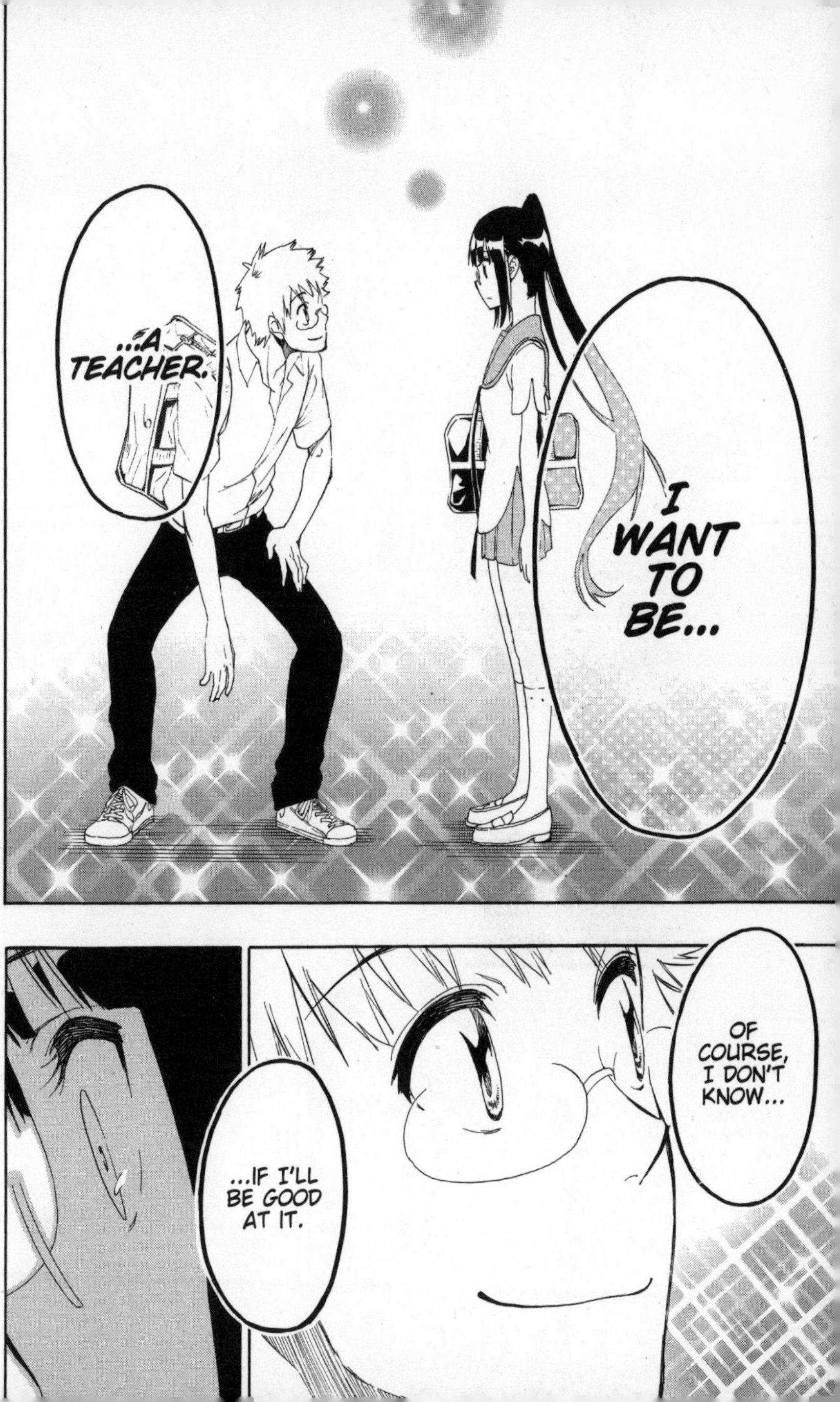
I WANT TO BE...
...A TEACHER.
OF COURSE, I DON'T KNOW...
...IF I'LL BE GOOD AT IT.

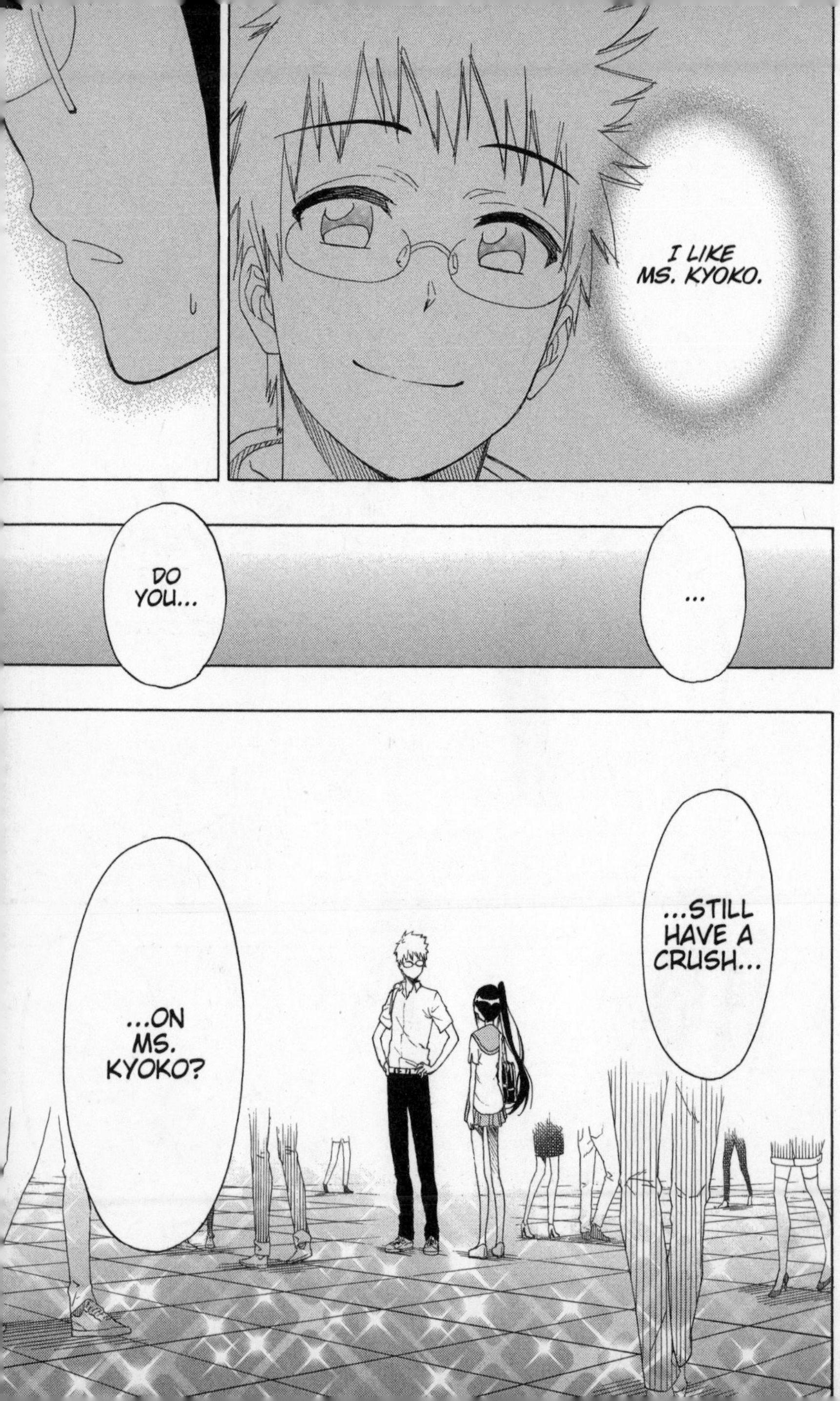
I LIKE MS. KYOKO.
...
DO YOU...
...STILL HAVE A CRUSH...
...ON MS. KYOKO?

WHAT?!

WHY DID I ASK THAT?!

GASP

...I'M THE SLIGHTEST BIT INTERESTED...

IT'S NOT AS IF...

BAM

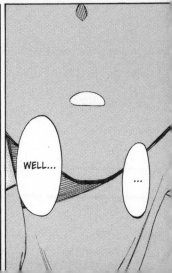

WELL...

...

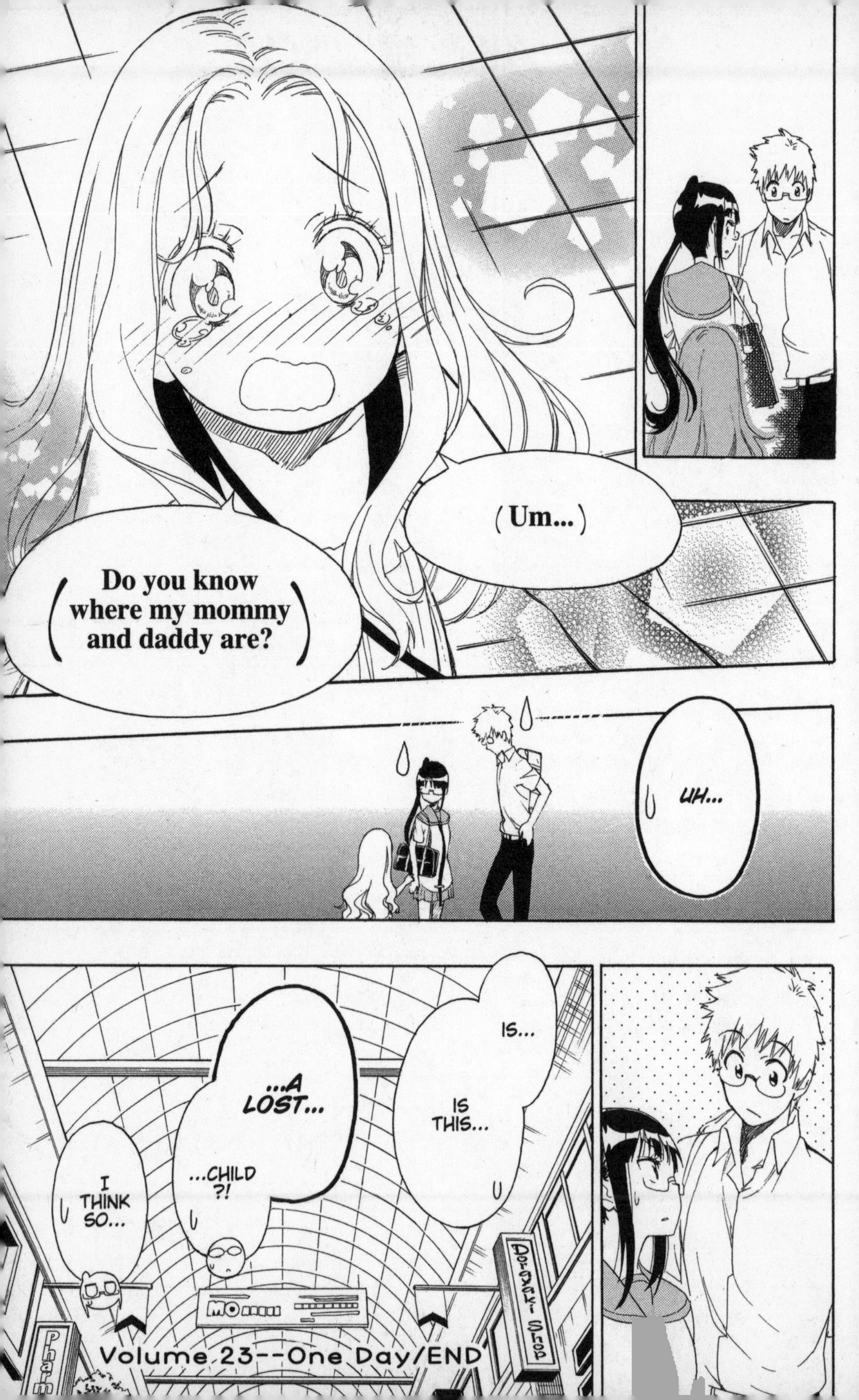
(Um...)
(Do you know where my mommy and daddy are?)
UH...
IS...
IS THIS...
...A LOST...
...CHILD?!
I THINK SO...
Dorayaki Shop
Pharm
Volume 23--One Day/END

BONUS COMIC: NEIGHBORS

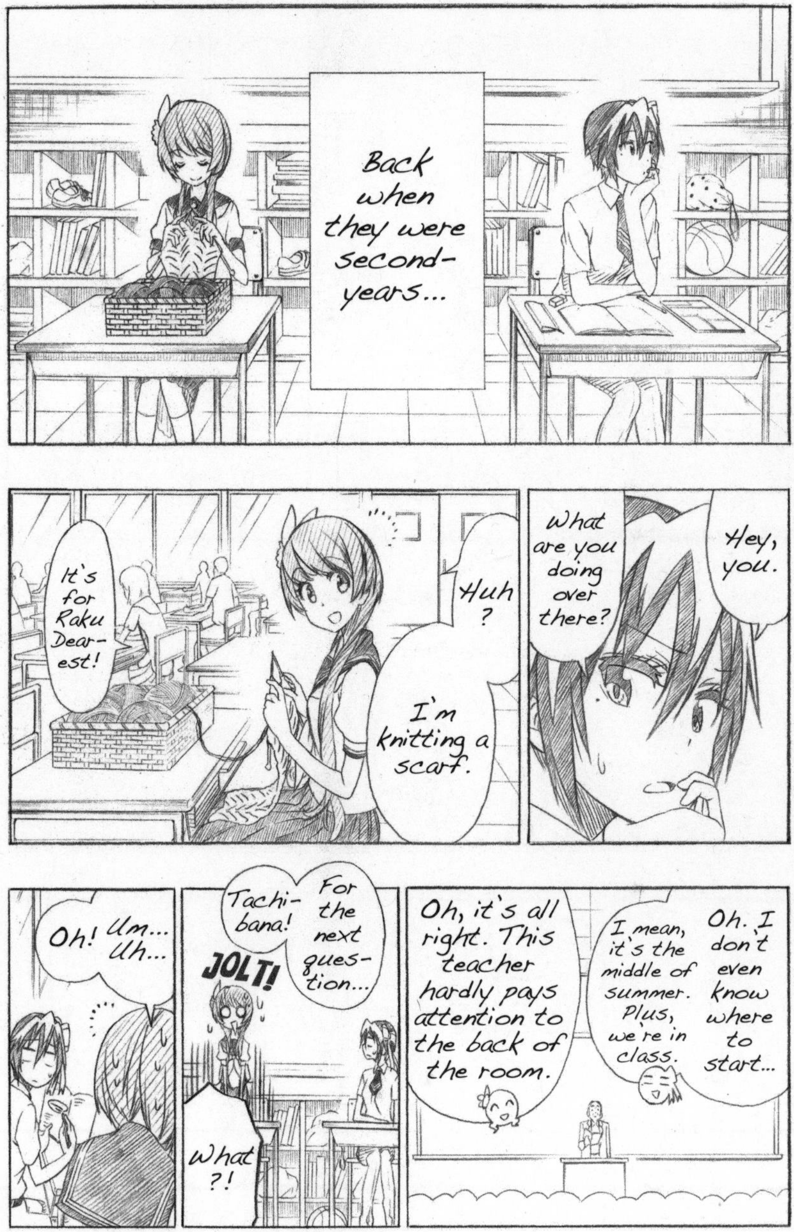
Back when they were second-years...
Hey, you.
What are you doing over there?
Huh?
I'm knitting a scarf.
It's for Raku Dearest!
Oh. I don't even know where to start...
I mean, it's the middle of summer. Plus, we're in class.
Oh, it's all right. This teacher hardly pays attention to the back of the room.
For the next question...
Tachibana!
JOLT!
What?!
Um... Uh...
Oh!

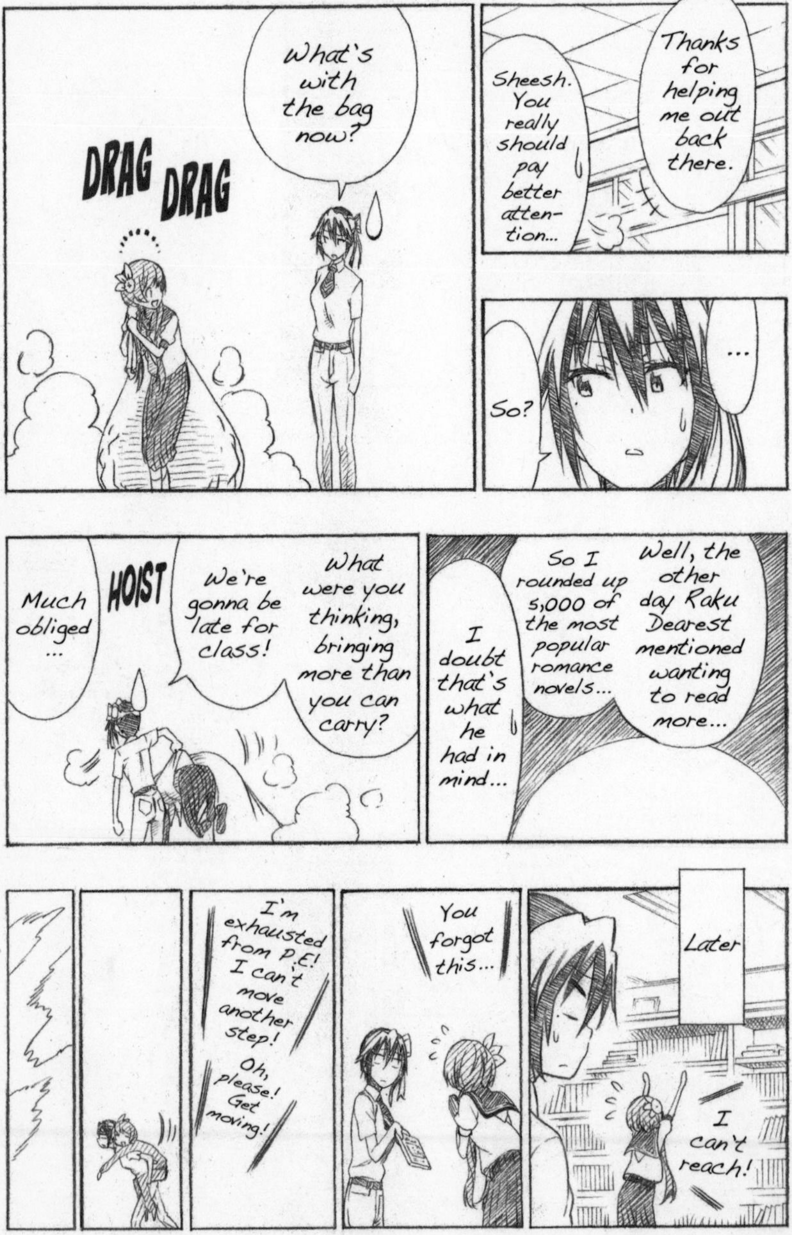

Thanks for helping me out back there.
Sheesh. You really should pay better attention...
...
So?
What's with the bag now?
DRAG DRAG
Well, the other day Raku Dearest mentioned wanting to read more...
So I rounded up 5,000 of the most popular romance novels...
I doubt that's what he had in mind...
What were you thinking, bringing more than you can carry?
We're gonna be late for class!
HOIST
Much obliged...
Later
I can't reach!
You forgot this...
I'm exhausted from P.E.! I can't move another step!
Oh, please! Get moving!

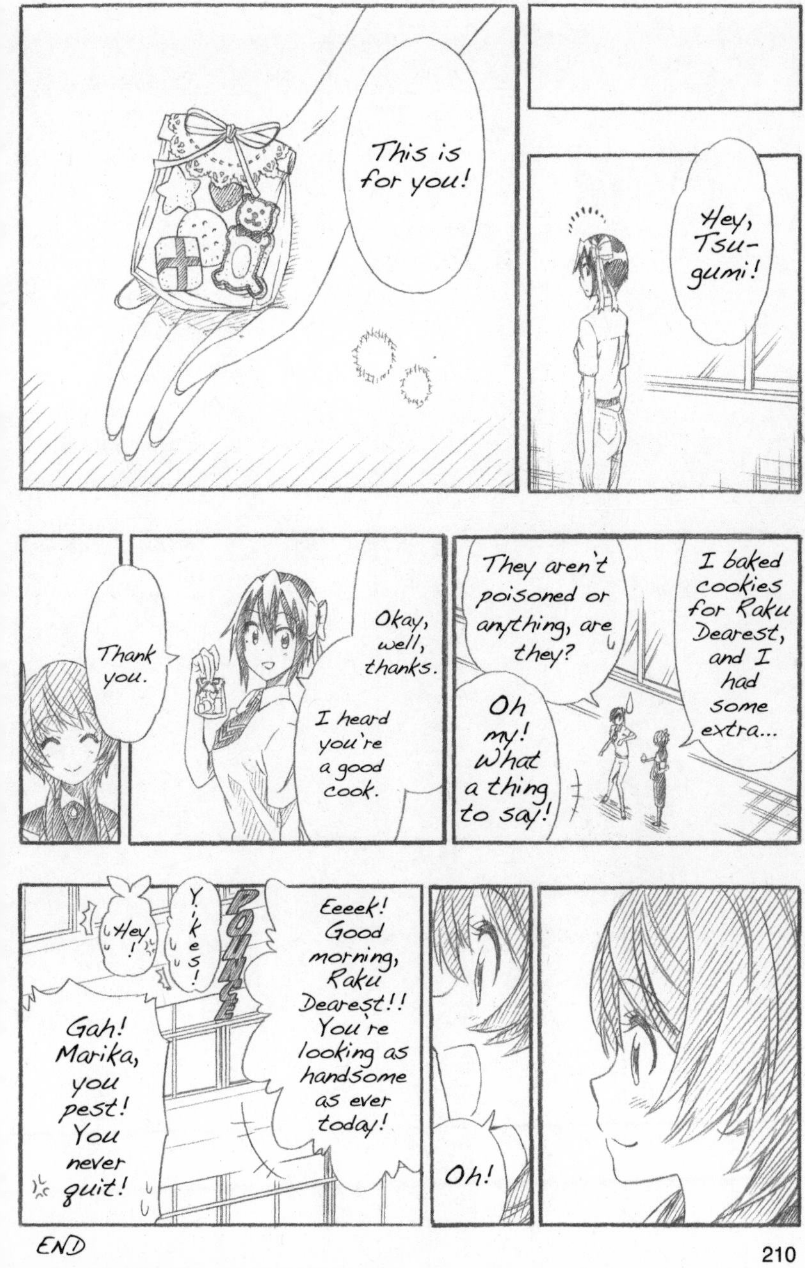
Hey, Tsugumi!
This is for you!
I baked cookies for Raku Dearest, and I had some extra...
They aren't poisoned or anything, are they?
Oh my! What a thing to say!
Okay, well, thanks.
I heard you're a good cook.
Thank you.
Oh!
Eeeek! Good morning, Raku Dearest!! You're looking as handsome as ever today!
POUNCE
Yikes!
Hey!
Gah! Marika, you pest! You never quit!

END

NISEKOI

False Love

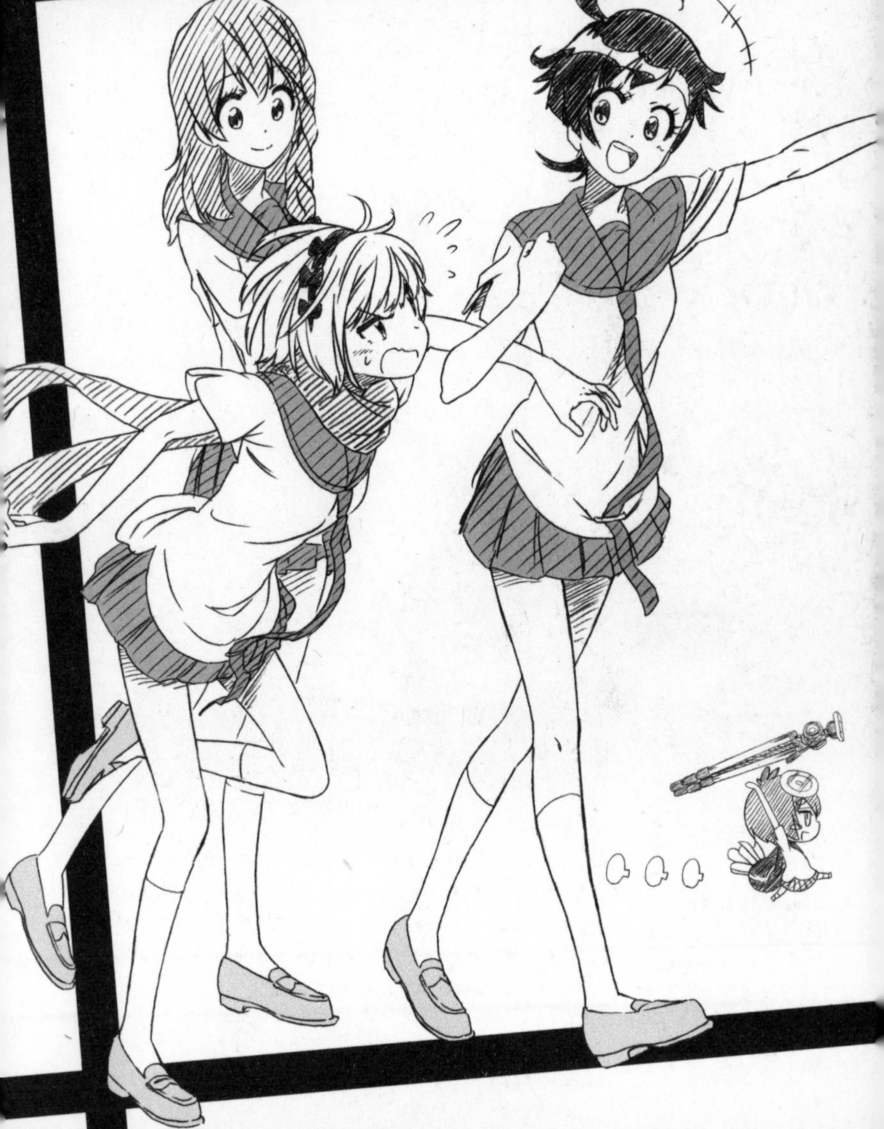

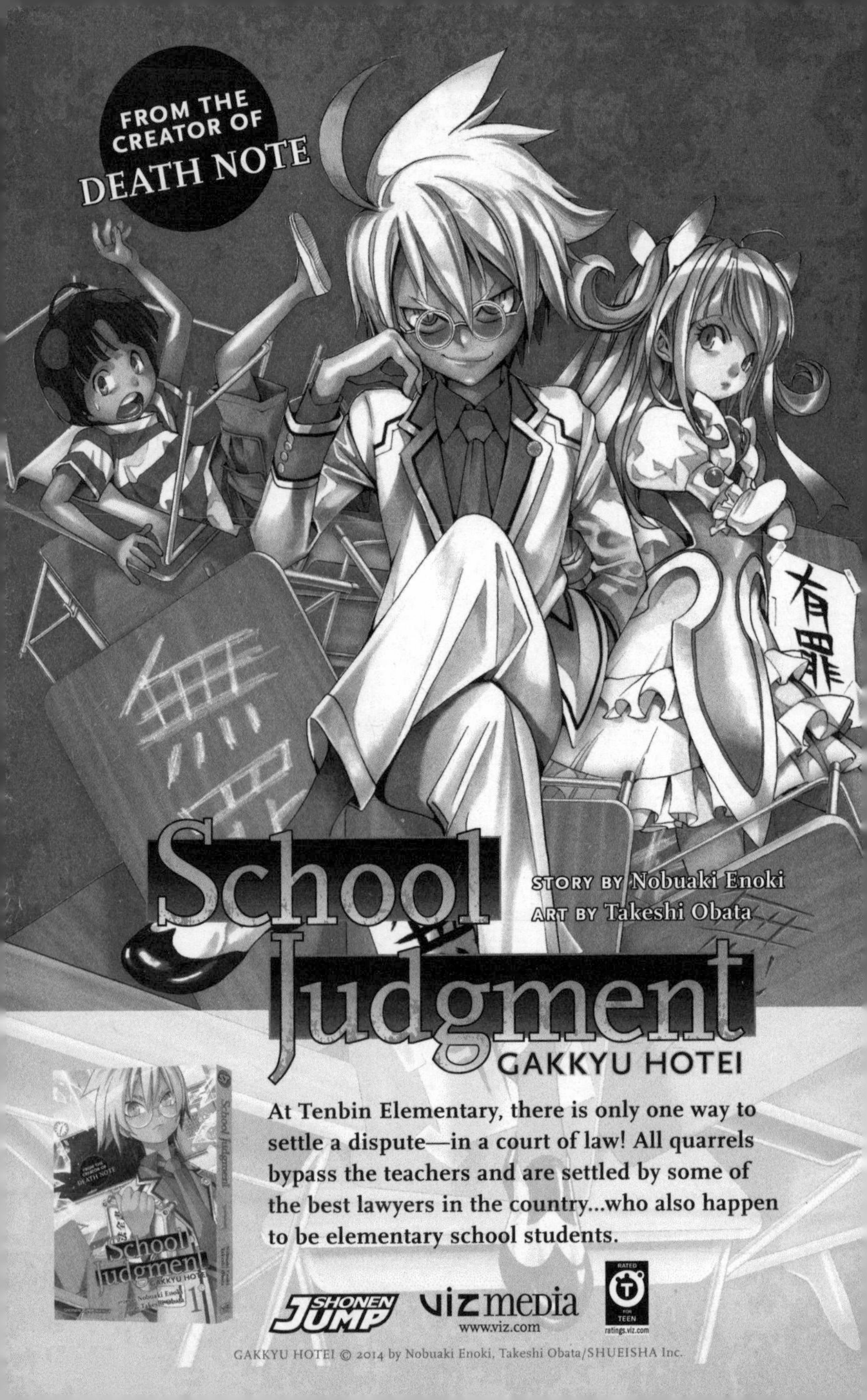
FROM THE CREATOR OF DEATH NOTE
School Judgment
GAKKYU HOTEI
STORY BY Nobuaki Enoki
ART BY Takeshi Obata
At Tenbin Elementary, there is only one way to settle a dispute—in a court of law! All quarrels bypass the teachers and are settled by some of the best lawyers in the country...who also happen to be elementary school students.
SHONEN JUMP
VIZ media
www.viz.com
RATED T FOR TEEN
ratings.viz.com
GAKKYU HOTEI © 2014 by Nobuaki Enoki, Takeshi Obata/SHUEISHA Inc.

Black ✦ Clover

STORY & ART BY YŪKI TABATA

Asta is a young boy who dreams of becoming the greatest mage in the kingdom. Only one problem—he can't use any magic! Luckily for Asta, he receives the incredibly rare five-leaf clover grimoire that gives him the power of anti-magic. Can someone who can't use magic really become the Wizard King? One thing's for sure—Asta will never give up!

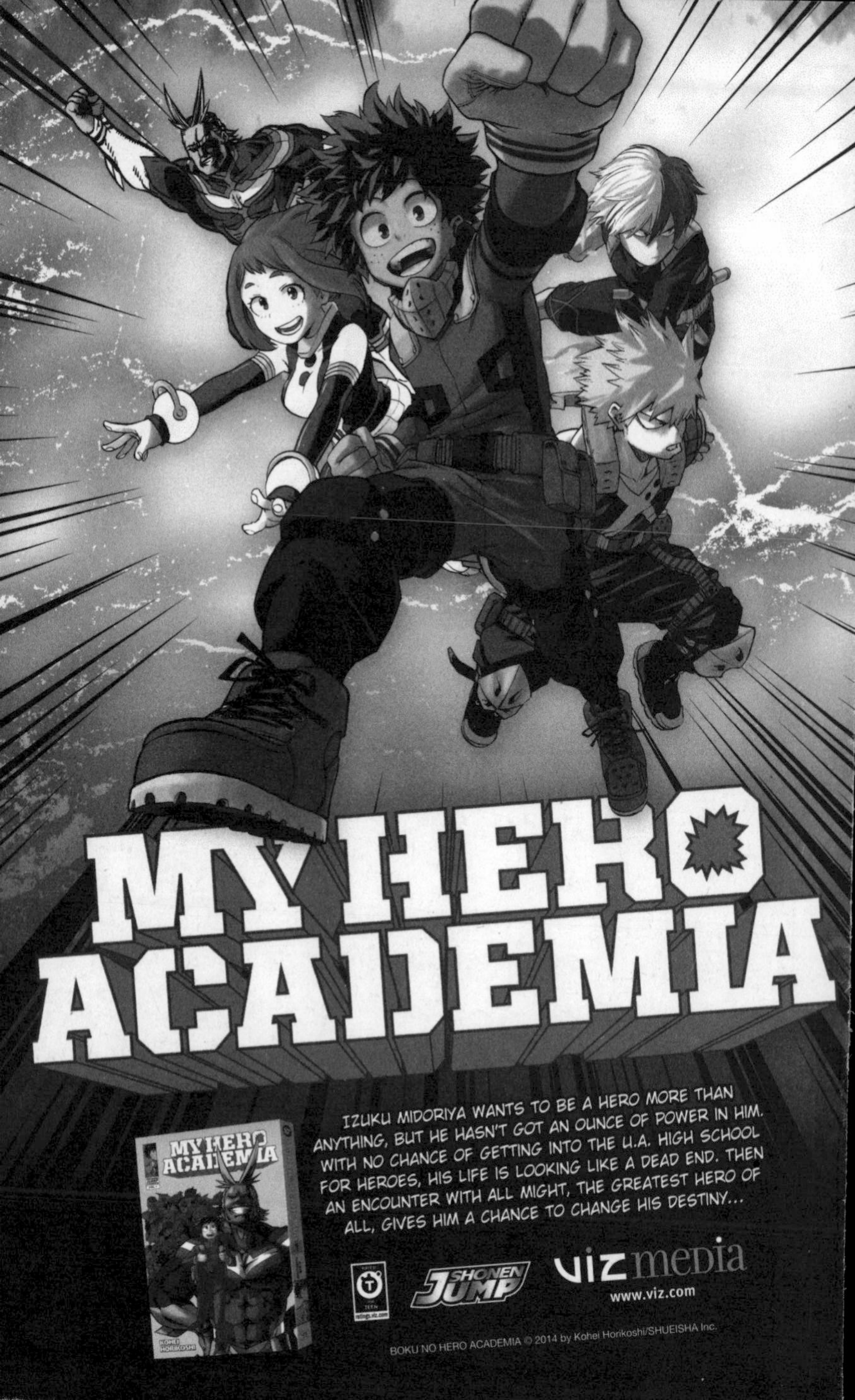
MY HERO ACADEMIA
IZUKU MIDORIYA WANTS TO BE A HERO MORE THAN ANYTHING, BUT HE HASN'T GOT AN OUNCE OF POWER IN HIM. WITH NO CHANCE OF GETTING INTO THE U.A. HIGH SCHOOL FOR HEROES, HIS LIFE IS LOOKING LIKE A DEAD END. THEN AN ENCOUNTER WITH ALL MIGHT, THE GREATEST HERO OF ALL, GIVES HIM A CHANCE TO CHANGE HIS DESTINY...
MY HERO ACADEMIA
Kohei Horikoshi
TEEN
ratings.viz.com
SHONEN JUMP
VIZ media
www.viz.com
BOKU NO HERO ACADEMIA © 2014 by Kohei Horikoshi/SHUEISHA Inc.

You're Reading the WRONG WAY!

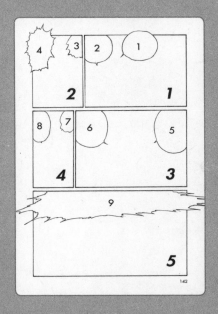

NISEKOI reads from right to left, starting in the upper-right corner. Japanese is read from right to left, meaning that action, ___ed effects, and ___ reve___